Rude Girls
Women in 2 Tone and One Step Beyond

Rude Girls

Women in 2 Tone and One Step Beyond

HEATHER AUGUSTYN

Foreword by Dunia Best

Sally Brown Publishing

Library of Congress Cataloguing-In-Publication Data
Augustyn, Heather, 1972-
Rude Girls: Women in 2 Tone and One Step Beyond / Heather Augustyn ; with foreword
by Dunia Best, used by permission.
Includes bibliographical references and index.

Cover image: Sarah-Jane Owen, photographed by Toni Tye, used by permission.
Cover design: Sha'Quiel Smith
Foreword: Dunia Best
Sally Brown Publishing logo: Hunt Emerson

For Ron, Sid, and Frank

Other books by Heather Augustyn

Ska: An Oral History, McFarland
Don Drummond: The Genius and Tragedy of the World's Greatest Trombonist, McFarland
Ska: The Rhythm of Liberation, Rowman & Littlefield
Songbirds: Pioneering Women in Jamaican Music, Half Pint Press
Alpha Boys' School: Cradle of Jamaican Music, Half Pint Press
Operation Jump Up: Jamaica's Campaign for a National Sound, Half Pint Press
Women in Jamaican Music, McFarland

Table of Contents

Acknowledgements

I am profoundly grateful to the following people who have helped me in the writing of this book.

To my family:
Ron, Sid, and Frank for supporting me, listening to me, and allowing me to indulge in my fangirl hobby. My mom and dad for giving me my love of music and taking me to concerts in the family van—all three days of the Joshua Tree Tour at age 13 made a big impact! Charlie, Liz, Eleanor, Alice, and Hugo, for conversations and analysis, and laughs. And for taking me to my first ska concert, the Toasters—thanks Charlie! I love you all so much. Aunt Rose, Uncle Lou, and Jesse, for your support and love.

To my fellow skamrades:
Darren Reggae who combed through his massive archives and passed along obscure knowledge, and even a few pieces of vinyl—I am thankful for your help and friendship, my fellow region rat. Chuck Wren for your wisdom, innovation, and expertise, your honesty, support, and friendship. Joanna Wallace for allowing me to dive into your rabbit hole with you. You shared your passion and your research and we shall find her one day! Thank you, my friend. Kevin Feinberg, thank you for taking time to read and edit my work, and for giving me the breadcrumbs to find voices long unheard. Your detailed expertise and guidance all through this project is invaluable and I thank you for this gift. Marc Wasserman, I am grateful to have your support as a colleague and friend. Thank you for reading my work before it saw the light of day. Your expert eye is a gift. Respect. Dunia Best for writing the foreword to this book. I am deeply honored.

To the women of this book and beyond:
Pauline Black, Juliet De Valero Wills, Sarah-Jane Owen, Stella Barker, Penny Leyton, Judy Parsons, Jennie McKeown Margot Olavarria, Kathy Valentine, Molly and Polly Jackson, June Miles-Kingston, Caroline Lavelle, Ingrid Schroeder, Annie Whitehead, Nicky Holland, Holly Beth Vincent, Helen O'Hara, Jane Bayley, Valerie Webb, Adele Carden, Tammy Dixon, Jenny Jones, Sara Raybould, Jane Perry Crockford, Ramona Carlier, Melissa Ritter, Anouchka Grose, Jackie Betterton, Angela Duignan, Germaine Dolan, Barbara Gaskin, Bunny Newth, Denyze Alleyne-Johnson, Julie Liggett, Serena Parsons, Dill Hammond, Verona Davis, Amanda Fen, Gilly Johns, Sara McGuinness, Paula Richards, Denise Butler, Lesley Beach, Debbie Evans, Clare Kenny, Margo Sagov, Clare Hirst, Caroline McCookweir, Kay Charlton, Jan Hewison, Amanda Duncan, Annabella Lwin, Lu Hersey.

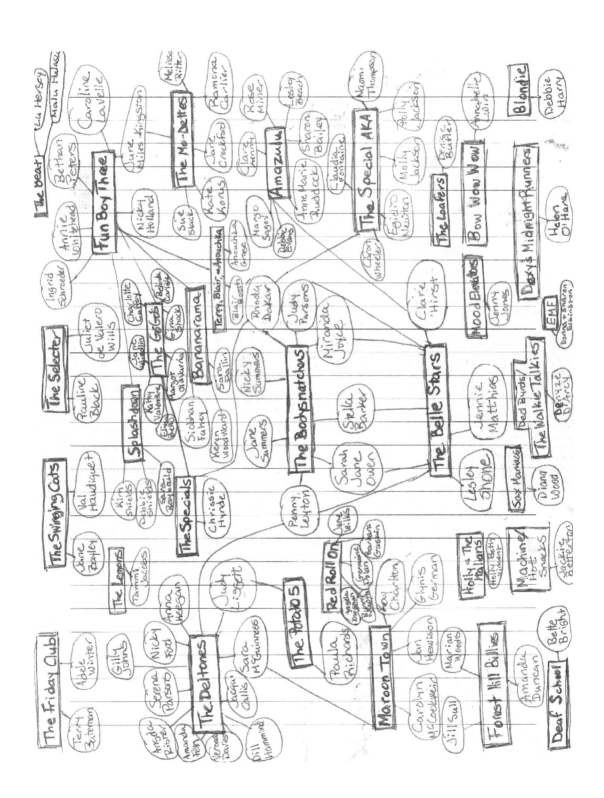

10

Foreword
By Dunia Best

Those first seven plaintive guitar notes followed by the hard lilt of Pauline Black's lyric "Celebrate the Bullet!" pretty much sealed it all for me. I danced to the sweet skanking beats of the Specials, swooned at the romantic notions of the Beat, but it was this woman's heart, soaring past those minor intonations, which hooked me into what I later found out was called "Two Tone".

Her ability to find the groove in those words, while ridiculing destruction, worked the same way Rhoda Dakar got us in "the Boiler." You're just walking along, a groove in your headphones, when the tears start, then the screams—the blood-curdling, gut-wrenching screams—while the band plays on. The same way Deborah Harry brought my Bronx youth to the world by introducing Fab Five Freddie to kids who grew up in the projects of London and Paris, linking us forever, while simultaneously recalling the sweet harmonies of sixties Jamaica.

For a nerdy kid with Caribbean family, growing up in the benign neglect of '80's New York, these sounds of escape pointed me toward a future tribe of creative misfits. It's a tribe that includes people from all over the world, fighting for cultural equality and an end to police brutality for everyone. It's a tribe that wears locks and braids and colors in their hair, a tribe that makes its own rules about fashion. It's a tribe that welcomes differences in all aspects of life.

I was born to native New Yorkers into a culture of music and activism. My parents were members of a theater company called Theater Black that performed around New York City. My brothers and I were raised with a strong emphasis on our identity as Americans of African and Caribbean descent. We attended Dance Africa, Harlem Week and other cultural festivals around New York. We saw Alvin Ailey and the Dance Theater of Harlem. We sat backstage as my mother rehearsed with the group Women of the Calabash and my father worked the cameras on the set of "Good Morning, America." Every year, during Kwanzaa they played an album called *Alkebu-Lan* by James Mtume. We listened to Miles, Coltrane, Pharoah, Stevie, Ella, Chaka, Diana, Lambert Hendricks and Ross, Labelle, Parliament and Funkadelic. I took classes in modern, West African and Caribbean dance with my mother. My brothers and I were made aware that there was nothing stopping us from being whatever we wanted to be. But what did I want to be?

I attended the Dalton School in Manhattan on a partial academic scholarship that was awarded to kids from certain New York neighborhoods. In this environment, surrounded by the children of wealthy entertainers and captains of Industry, I was thrust into my first big cultural shift. Suddenly my world included the sounds of punk and new wave. I was introduced to MTV, which brought a lot of English music and style to the USA. I was thrust into a world of houndstooth and checkerboard and suits, with cool hats and combat boots. I imitated my new three minute heroes and learned a Northern English accent. With it came a new mainstream love for Caribbean rhythms. Boy George popularized a modified Rasta style that I quickly adopted, recognizing a kinship with an English musical movement of which I had no direct knowledge. My best friend Kathy and I declared the 8th of every month "Boy George Day," and wore our freak flags all the way out. Kathy and I recognized pretty quickly that our culture was closer to Culture Club than it was to the Dalton School.

When I was a teen, my family moved out of a New York City succumbing to the crack epidemic to Maplewood, NJ, where I attended Columbia High School and was introduced to my second big culture shock. I took my English-to-New-York punky new wave music fandom with me and felt wholly uncomfortable in Suburbia. Swaying and skanking to the upbeats and unity messages coming out of England, I found myself landing in the hardscrabble, downbeat world of Bruce Springsteen and Bon Jovi. Despite its physical proximity to my original hometown, I felt like I had been dropped in the middle of a wasteland. In this desert, I found an oasis in my friend and fellow serious new wave fan, Sheli. We dug in our boot heels, began wearing fedoras and dressing like my favorite icons, in button down shirts, in black and white with purple accents (I was also a crazy Prince fan).

Searching for my own identity while navigating my parents' world and the world of school and peers led me to college at NYU, where I finally found out the music I had been skirting around all these years was called "ska." My new friends, local ska band the Slackers gave me a concentrated lesson. Just formed, they were striving to put their own stamp on what had been known as "Two Tone." My best friend Gail shared my deep and abiding love for this music through the band Fishbone and their song called "Lyin' Ass Bitch," sung by Lisa Grant, who was not a member of the band. When it was time for me to start my own band, Agent 99, Gail was my partner in crime. We listened to all the women ska singers, but especially Pauline Black and Rhoda Dakar.

By nature, I am a seriously judgmental person, something I likely learned as a member of a family of performers. But starting Agent 99 taught me about building community, something I had begun to learn as a member of the Slackers. When UK ska began it was closely allied with punk, and it was punk that taught me about different kinds of proficiency, different skills that can be brought to the stage. When I worked at Shakespeare & Co. Bookstore on lower Broadway, I became borderline obsessed with punk feminists like Kathy Acker and bell hooks. Learning about performing artists like Annie Sprinkle and photographers like Cindy Sherman, I suspected I was part of that continuum. My suspicions were confirmed when I was tapped to perform in the Fierce Pussy Fest in Tompkins Square Park, perhaps one of the first Riot Grrrl festivals. We performed with women bands for women and men from the Lower East Side and beyond. Annie Sprinkle herself was in the audience, dancing. It was pretty miraculous, watching our community swirl together from all walks of life, just wanting openness and freedom.

The next morning, the Riot Grrrls held a meeting, which they filmed, introducing themselves to the New York counter-cultural community. At the time, being the New York peace punk that I am, I could not see the point in creating a category for us. It wasn't the only time I rejected labels (a belief I sing about in "Little Rude Riding Hood," a personal favorite of my own compositions.) While I respected their hustle, I did not want to be a hypocrite and submit my own hard-won identity to joining any kind of grouping. Perhaps it was my loss….

Alas, those technicolor days of Tompkins soon faded to grey, washed out by a rising tide of addiction and homelessness, slid away, accompanied by a new neighborhood sound we called "Crack Rocksteady:" a crazy, anarchistic, punk sound that reflected many of the players' drug of choice. The tide rose and swept away with it Agent 99's bass player, Alec Baillie. My new music partner, bassist and spouse-to-be, Aram, and I needed a new focus. Through a mutual friend, we met keyboardist Todd Nocera and began a band we would call Brave New Girl, adding jazz and soul grooves to Agent 99's ska and reggae elements. Though I was unfamiliar with scenes other than ska and punk, I did know that ska fans tend to be generous and open-minded. Still Anglophiles, our sound echoed the relaxed, danceable jazz of Sade and Lisa Stansfield, following the path laid down by Fun Boy 3 and General Public.

We met Ari Up, lead singer of the Slits, at a show with the Slackers at Wetlands. She was also going through a transformation, having just returned to the United States from Belize and Jamaica. It was an instant hit, our friendship. We talked and talked, met up again and talked some more. We recognized kinship immediately. Through her I met Slits bassie Tessa Pollitt and singer Hollie Cook, still a young teen at the time and just beginning to perform with the Slits. Watching them work, I could see Ari pushing hard at the limitations of their fame, set on putting the prototypical She-Punks back on the map as a punky reggae force. Our spirited discussions about the role of music and culture in politics ran into the wee hours. She was the only person who could get us to watch the television show, "American Idol." We were scholars of culture together.

After Ari's body succumbed to the ravages of cancer, Aram and I wanted to celebrate her life with a small concert. It was then that a friend Ari had been trying to hook us up with for years, Vivien Goldman, contacted us and connected us to the rest of Ari's world. From beyond, at last Ari united her friends for a common goal. We could not hold a small concert. It had to be big. And it had to be a celebration of women. All the Slits came. All of the Slits's friends came. All of Ari's friends came. We put together a show for the ages. It was a miraculous happening of punk and post-punk heroes from near and far. There, I would meet Neneh Cherry, Bruce Smith, Jeni and Paul Cook and many more of the British members of Ari's tribe, the people who built the world I had admired since watching videos on the UHF channels in the Bronx as a child. My friends from the ska and punk scenes of New York like Tamar-Kali, Honeychild Coleman, King Django and the Bandroidz slotted into Ari's original crew like missing pieces in a global music jigsaw, finally finding some completion onstage at the Music Hall of Williamsburg, for our lost *sistr'en*.

The sweet new soul sounds of Brave New Girl became reacquainted with our kinky dub reggae and ska origins when we created Dubistry in Los Angeles with guitar player Matt Urbania. Dubistry tore at the roots of its forebears and pieced together a music that drew from jungle and drum 'n' bass as well as all our old band's beloved grooves. With my brother, Ahmed, on drums, we employed the skills of a DJ and a percussionist. It was brand new, but Dubistry pointed us back toward the ska scene, toward Two Tone, toward old, familiar territory. The scene vibrated with energy and enthusiasm. Each encounter became an adventure. We met an early version of the band the Aggrolites and Jason Lawless, a young promoter and Star Wars fanatic. For Lawless, we recorded an acoustic version of our song "Roll Away" over a weekend at Matt's house. Channeling the spontaneity of ska, Matt and Aram switched bass and guitar as we used cardboard boxes, handclaps and spoons as percussion to make a "yard" version—and it is still one of our most popular songs.

Ska, the music that liberated and uplifted me (and introduced me to my life partner) has recently resurfaced as the sound of dance, fun and unity in countries all over the world. The resurgence of ska has brought together rudies speaking every language. This renaissance has itself birthed a miraculous supergroup that I'm lucky to be a part of called Rude Girl Revue, an all-female ska orchestra with 11 touring members and guests from everywhere on the planet. The brainchild of guitarist/songwriter Kristin Forbes, saxophonist/singer Jenny Whiskey and podcaster Tara Kish of Checkered Cast, Rude Girl Revue was first presented to the world on stage at Virginia's Supernova Ska Festival in 2021.

With a renewed sense of feminism in our society, interest in the role of women in music and in ska music in particular has grown to an all-time high. From Joanna Wallace's biography of Brigitte Bond, the woman who inspired the English Beat's logo, to new music by woman-fronted bands like the Skints, Stop the Presses, the Scotch Bonnets, Hub City Stompers and the Sklutts to supergroups like Sweet Girls of Ska from Latin America to singers like Hollie Cook and Caz Gardiner—and even me! We continue to take inspiration from our Two Tone sisters who began dancing and singing for equality and respect in a changing world. Pauline Black has even received an OBE (Officer of the British Empire) from King Charles III. I guess we know who *his* favorite ska band is.

Dunia Best (center) with Rhoda Dakar (left) and Jenny Whiskey (right) after Rude Girl Revue's performance at the Specialized Festival in London in 2022

Introduction

I began work on this book some nine months before the pandemic. I thought it would be a relatively small project—after all, as I was told by Rhoda Dakar, "If you are concentrating on 2 Tone, there was only me, Pauline and Juliet, the Selecter's manager."[1] Though I knew that wasn't true—there was Rhoda's own group, for one, the Bodysnatchers, and women in 2 Tone bands like the Friday Club and the Swinging Cats, I still recognized the reality of Rhoda's comment—women in this era of ska were rare. They were relegated to novelty status. They were unequal in the very movement that prioritized equality and unity. If that movement applied to race, why did it not apply to gender? Author, historian, and musician Marc Wasserman stated in his podcast, "One of the first times I had the opportunity to talk to Pauline Black of the Selecter, she noted that 2 Tone wasn't just supposed to be about addressing racism, but also sexism. On the latter, the all-male bands that made up the 2 Tone movement missed opportunities to address the challenges facing women and women of color in particular in England in the late 70s and early 80s."[2] Truer words about 2 Tone have rarely been spoken. How strange for bands of five, six, seven men, even though they are black and white, to sing about unity and never have it dawn on them that there weren't any women in their new era.

Because women signed to the 2 Tone label were rare, I thought I would cast my net a little wider, hence the "one step beyond" part of my title. In doing this, I ended up discovering there were many women who were empowered by punk and reggae to play ska. This is not to say that there was anything even close to parity, but the realization that there were dozens and dozens of women who touched 2 Tone in some way—performing in bands, playing as session musicians, singing backup or even in the spotlight—was exciting. I knew this project was now becoming much larger than I had anticipated, and as a result, much more important.

Recognizing that there were women who were part of this movement, beyond the one or two in front, is crucial to both proper historical record, and for representation. The women whose stories are told here in this book show that access was demanded then, so that it can be realized now. Marian Wright Edelman, founder and president emeritus of the Children's Defense Fund observed, "It's hard to be what you can't see."[3] Young girls see women on the stage and see that playing the drums in a band is possible. Black women see a black woman on stage and see that leading a band with white men is possible. Everyone hears lyrics written by women and understand that the female perspective is possible. This book is about

---

[1] Facebook Messenger, 31 May 2020.

[2] Wasserman, Marco. "2 Tone Legacy—Easy Life." Ska Boom: An American Ska & Reggae Podcast. 26 May 2022. podcasts.apple.com/us/podcast/2-tone-legacy-easy-life/id1530868357?i=1000564028481. Accessed 13 Jan. 2023.

[3] Edelman, Marian Wright. "It's Hard to Be What You Can't See." Children's Defense Fund. 21 Aug. 2015. childrensdefense.org/child-watch-columns/health/2015/its-hard-to-be-what-you-cant-see. Accessed 13 Jan 2023.

representation to inspire the next musician, the next songwriter, the next music connoisseur.

Being female in a male space is tough. No denying that. I can relate. As a female writer in the largely male space of music, and especially in Jamaican music and ska, I have encountered my share of sexism and misogyny. Buy me a beer and I'll tell you about it sometime. But hearing these women talk about their experiences in music during the '70s and '80s didn't feel discouraging or infuriating. These stories made me feel energized. They made me laugh and cheer. Because despite the conditions, created by forces complex and systemic, women are strong. Women are powerful. Writing this book, especially during the pandemic, felt really really good, and I hope it feels good to read, no matter who you are.

A few notes about my approach with this book, because there are bound to be some questions. I wrote about all-female bands, as well as bands with females. These bands are not strictly 2 Tone, nor are they strictly ska. However, they are all related to 2 Tone and ska during this era in the UK, as detailed in each chapter. Sometimes this link might be stronger than others, but I felt the fans of one band might be fans of another. If that isn't the case, then perhaps the stories stand by themselves. There might be some questions about why a particular band was included and not another, and I hope that I make that argument in the chapter, but ultimately it was the editorial decision of this writer.

The women whose stories follow here are certainly trailblazers. If there are ska "waves," then certainly there are waves created from the ripples of these women, by stepping on stage, by stepping into the studio. Their impact is exponential. These are our sisters, and we stand on their shoulders. Women are part of the ska community and therefore, part of the conversation. The following women share how they have been inspired by women in 2 Tone, and one step beyond:

"Pauline Black has always been an icon for me. Her style, her talent, and her personality in general. She is gracious to fans and always makes time for them. But my most beloved women in the end were the girls I shared the stage with in local bands, and the girls I saw on the dancefloor. And many of them I still talk to today. One of the beautiful things about the ska scene is that it's pretty small. So if you're in a band and you play a lot locally, chances are you will have a chance to interact with your ska idols at some point in time. When I did meet her, it was the end of the night after a long performance. I was the LAST fan to approach her. And honestly I probably said something like, 'I carried a watermelon,' or something because I was just grateful that she took the time to meet everyone. If I could redo that moment, I'd say, 'Thanks for kicking so much ass for all these years. You have no idea how much it means to women like me.'" **–Jenny Whiskey, New Jersey**

"The presence of women in ska music was a model for what could be possible. From my first 2-Tone single, the Selecter's 'Three Minute Hero,' to falling in love with Phyllis Dillon – hunting down her music pre-internet boom and getting to meet her and watch her perform, to the history of all-women ska bands before me—2-Tone group the Bodysnatchers and 1990s L.A. band the Shantees, I felt like women were central to ska music and I could be too. I looked up to Queen P of Ocean 11 when their band was active and have continued to look up through all her collaborations with Jamaican artists. I joined an all-girl ska group called the Cover-Ups in the late 1990s, and later an all-girl boss reggae band called Tight Spot. When I began collecting records, there weren't many women selectors locally, but a role model from the Northern Soul scene (Nancy Yahiro) demonstrated how women can be serious collectors and selectors. I was lucky to have close mentors and positive role models and try to model those behaviors myself and uplift other women." –**Nina Cole, Bay Area, California**

"Ska has allowed me to make friends with so many cool people at shows. It's helped me build confidence, and it's exposed me to so much diversity and openness. Seeing women bands like the Interrupters and Bad Cop Bad Cop (especially in a mostly male community), it's shown me how to combine more masculinity with femininity in my clothing choices. If I could meet Pauline Black, I would want to thank her for being herself and showing that intersectionalism is the key to the future." –**Autumn Gooding, Chicago**

"To this day, I still have yet to hear a satisfactory explanation as to why we see proportionally few women in ska music, especially musicians. Which makes Millie Small, Patsy Todd, Pauline Black, Doreen Shaffer, Rhoda Dakar even more remarkable. Of all of them, Pauline Black resonates with me the most; she was perhaps the first female member of a band that didn't promote or highlight her gender, as most bands do. The Selecter might have been the first band I saw that took her gender out of the performance, because it was irrelevant. She wore a suit, dammit! Pauline commanded her time onstage and was pleasantly intimidating in a way that blew me away. I was starry-eyed and completely impressed by her. Though my career path was completely unrelated (I'm a pastry chef), like so many professional sectors, women have had to push harder for just a few steps forward. Definitely have had to summon my 'inner' Pauline Black to power through some situations, and I'd love to thank her for that someday." –**Annie Clemmons, Washington, DC**

"The ska subculture and its values are a huge part of my identity and everyday life from the day I went to my first show. The ethics of equality and inclusion set the true north for my moral compass. The subcultural style has directed my overall aesthetic. The community has been my everything. It has given me my chosen family, inspired my art, a good excuse to travel, lifelong friendships, and has guided me to my partner. The music itself has led me on a journey of exploring music from around the globe from different time periods that I likely would not have dug into if it weren't for my interest in ska and all the genres that influenced ska. It is hard to imagine my life without the influence of ska and the ska culture since it seeps into nearly every single aspect of my life every single day." –**Joanna Wallace, Minneapolis**

"I've become a really big fan in the last 10 years or so with the advent of Spotify & Bandcamp. I like 90% of ska, which means I have found something I can listen to and almost always like, which never happened with any other genre. As a result, I've gotten interested in many groups, current and past. I go to see almost any ska band that comes to town and have met a group of other ska fans who do the same and I have become friends with quite a few of them. I can go to a show by myself and almost always run into someone (usually multiple people) that I know." –**Joan Engebretson, Chicago**

"The impact was amazing. Ska makes me feel stronger and focus. Big inspiration everyday." –**PaoLis Ska, BuenosAires, Argentina**

"In my country, Fiorella Cava (in the past Sergio Cava) the leader of JAS, may be the first trans in ska history in Latin America. The generation of 80s grew up listening the song 'Ya no quiero mas ska.' Now many women are new in many countries, maybe in Latin America, Betania López from Chile. And in the actual story of ska Doreen Shaffer and Pauline Black." –**Milagros Paredes, Lima Perú**

"The 2 Tone unity, inclusion, family—it was the first time I felt complete. I am Puerto Rican and multiracial but it always seems like I don't fit in on either side of my family. Yet to be different and to stand up for what I believe in through lyrics and in song was not only embraced in the ska community but it was a commonality we all shared. My thoughts were lifted up, and together we could all change the world one song at a time. I was driven and supported in the process. We [her band, the Miggedys] were young but we were able to connect with other ska bands from all over and each and every one became friends and even better, family. We encouraged each other, we supported each other, and then my mom died. The Miggedys wrapped their arms around me and when we did our CD, the entire ska community became that much more important to me—an outlet, and a purpose." –**Tricia Lynn Gonzalez-Johnson, New York**

"The Bodysnatchers, like all the women in the 2 Tone movement, inspired me just by making space for girls within the boy's club of ska. There are so many men in ska bands, so a band like the Bodysnatchers makes it much easier for people to comprehend and accept women singing and playing this music. Because of the paths they carved, bands like Rude Girl Revue have been more readily accepted within the scene. Pauline Black's androgynous, sharp yet feminine way of dressing literally created classic Rude Girl style. She taught us tough girls who wanted to look good how to dress!" –**Kristin Forbes, Baltimore, Maryland**

Let's all continue the conversation on how women in ska helped to form and support the community we call family—black, white, men, women—true unity.

Author Heather Augustyn (above) and members of Rude Girl Review (below) at the Supernova International Ska Festival 2021

The Beat Girl

Brigitte Bond/Brigitte Saint John

2 Tone, and all ska music ever since, has been associated with Walt Jabsco—the sharp-dressed rude boy illustrated by Jerry Dammers as a logo for his new label. Dammers based his illustration on Peter Tosh as photographed on the cover of the Wailing Wailers album.[4] But the counterpart to Walt, one designed by illustrator Hunt Emerson, was the Beat Girl. She became associated with the Beat, hence her name, and their label, Go Feet. She too was based on a real person. Hunt had seen a photo in the *Melody Maker* on May 19, 1979, and used it as inspiration for his art. The photo depicts a young Prince Buster having just arrived at the airport, greeted by a beautiful woman who dances with him, bending her legs, swaying to the music, caught in the energy of the moment. The photo was one of many taken by photographer George Stroud that day, February 25, 1964. Prince Buster had come to promote ska and his own music at the May Fair Hotel in London that winter, but in doing so, he was also promoting his female companion. A decade and a half later, that photo of the young girl dancing reappeared in the press and inspired Emerson's illustration used by the Beat on all of their promotional material, thereby becoming an icon, like Walt, and a symbol for ska itself.

Hunt Emerson tells the story of the origin of his work, and the creation of the Beat Girl, which was purely a chance encounter of seeing this photo and being in that proverbial right place at the right time. "I was born in 1952 in the northeast of England, and I always drew, since I was a toddler. I did a couple of years at art college in Newcastle on Tyne, a general foundation course, and then moved south to Birmingham to do a degree course in painting. I lasted a year before I dropped out. I was hopeless as a student. I was a very naïve 21-year-old kid, and what I wanted to be was a hippie. As part of hippie life, I came across the underground comix from San Francisco, New York, and London that were part of the 1968 cultural revolution. They were funny, crazy, rude and subversive, and I loved them! They started me on a career as a cartoonist that, somehow, I have managed to sustain to this day. I have a very recognisable style, and my cartoons are reckoned to be funny," he says.[5]

Emerson crossed paths with the members of the Beat during their earliest performances. "Around 1978, I was living in Handsworth, Birmingham, where I live still. I had a couple of friends who were acting as agents under the name of 20/21 Music (B20 and B21 are Handsworth's postal districts), in a fairly low-key way for a local reggae band. There was music everywhere in Birmingham then, with lots of pub gigs and lots of post-punk, new romantic bands around. I remember another mate saying, 'You've got to hear this! This is the next big music,' and he played the Specials

---

[4] Augustyn, Heather. *Ska: An Oral History*. McFarland, 2010, p. 91.
[5] Emerson, Hunt. All quotations, unless otherwise noted, from interview with the author, 18 Jul. 2022.

first record, 'Gangsters,' an early pressing. He was right. He also became the Beat's manager. So, a young band, a four piece, came into 20/21 Music and asked if they could do something for them. They were, of course, the Beat. I saw one of their earliest gigs, and they were playing this ska and punk music. And Ranking Roger joined them unannounced to toast. They were great! Soon after that, Saxa joined them, and they were off! They got a one-off single deal with 2 Tone for 'Tears of a Clown,' and they went on tour with the 2 Tone circus, and suddenly they needed some graphics—a band logo, and they wanted some sort of figure to go with the Specials' Walt Jabsco. I was the only person in the vicinity who knew how to hold a pencil, so I was asked to do something," Emerson recalls.

The charge given to Emerson was, according to Dave Wakeling, to create a female image to curb male aggression. Wakeling describes the logic, "Skinhead dances in the '70's were run by the skinhead girls, dancing in circles around their handbags, whilst the boys tried to pick up the courage to ask for a dance! Shy and on best behaviour, the skinhead boys acted quite differently from at the football games. But while doing our first two tone shows, I was shocked that there were so many skinheads seeking bovver. So, I suggested we had a female logo to temper the 2 Tone man! Within a few weeks of the Beat Girl's appearance, our crowds were sporting quite a few Beat Girls, in costume, and the skinhead boys were behaving nicely, wearing their smarter clothing instead of their fighting gear, and we ended up with a lot less fights than some of the other bands. Although we knew nothing about Brigitte Bond, the Melody Maker photo was a perfect start. We wanted an accessible logo, that anyone could relate to, regardless of colour or ethnicity. Also, we gave her no name for the same reason, just the Beat Girl, from the '60's Adam Faith movie."[6]

Emerson continues his memory of the creation, "My cartoon work, 'what I do,' is very cartoony. The first thing that the Beat established was that they didn't want my cartoons. They were looking for a slightly retro style, with slightly clumsy lines. So, I had to start working in a different way. I don't remember specific conversations, but the idea of feminising things a bit was in the air. What Dave says about aggression at the gigs was a big thing then, and dominated discussions. The usual teenage argy-bargy was starting to become more politicised and nasty. The Beat took a very firm stand about their politics and what we now call 'diversity,' and, as they didn't happen to have a woman in the band, they wanted a girl-figure that looked cool but was tough and self-knowing, as part of their image. So, we were looking for a teenage, rock-n-roll type graphic of a girl. That photo came up, of Prince Buster dancing with Brigitte Bond, in *Melody Maker*. It was possibly me that found it, as I worked for *Melody Maker* too, but the music papers would be around the office, so somebody spotted it. Interest was expressed in the image, so I went away and worked up the Beat Girl. It had to be black and white, simple, able to be adapted to all sorts of uses—posters, t-shirts, buttons, etc. At the same time, I designed the band logo—

6 Wakeling, Dave. Email correspondence with the author, 25 Jan. 2023.

the Beat with the 'B' as a musical note. That was Dave's idea. That logo is clunky and ugly, and I love it! Incidentally, we never called her anything but the Beat Girl."

Emerson describes the process of using the iconic Prince Buster and Brigitte Bond photo for his work. "I cut the photo out of *Melody Maker*, drew a pencil grid over it, and started tracing and enlarging and adapting. That's why we've never had access to a clean version of the photo until now. The Beat Girl is devilishly difficult to draw! Just tracing her from the photo results in an unbalanced figure, so I had to do a lot of work to get her right. It's all to do with balance and sway. Today it would all be made easier with a computer, but then I was juggling photocopies and trace-offs, and there never was a definitive drawing of the Beat Girl. So, the logo and the Beat Girl were plastered all over Britain for an exciting season while the band raced around on tour and started making records. They wanted a refreshed image to start this phase of their career, and to separate them from the 2 Tone thing. So I had to do a redesigned Beat Girl, along with all the livery for Go-Feet Records, and the first album sleeve, *I Just Can't Stop It!* that is still one of my best designs ever. I also did the second album, which is the worst. I hated it then and I hate it now. But there was a lot of pressure!"

According to *Record Collector* magazine, the Beat Girl received extra publicity when it appeared in a video—though not one by the Beat. It states, "The Beat Girl reached a global audience when Sting wore a Beat T-shirt in the Police's 'Don't Stand So Close to Me' video."[7] Since then, with or without the help of Sting, the Beat Girl has gone global. When asked what he thinks of that fact that his drawing is ubiquitous with ska fans today, appearing everywhere over the decades from scooters to tattoos, Emerson says he is honored. "I loved having her and the logo on everything from tacky plastic pins to big gig posters, all sorts of buttons, jacket patches, hats, and the bootleg t-shirts, with their odd re-workings of Beat/Specials/Madness artwork! I loved all that mix. It has become a tribal thing, ska and 2 Tone, with its own tribal signs and markings. I just love that my designs are part of that, and have become, in a way, anonymous."

Emerson says that he still runs into the image from time to time in the most unlikely places. "There are a couple of stories. One day I saw a Lambretta scooter in our local mall. It was beautiful, all in black, with the 2 Tone and Beat graphics in white. I got chatting with the guy; he was a fan from 20 years back, and although he believed me, he was surprised that anyone designed the Beat Girl. He thought it was done by some sort of machine. Then around 1991 I was in Paris. At a café with a friend, we noticed some school kids with the Beat graphics drawn in ball point on their folders. My friend, a Frenchman, leaned over and had a quiet word with one of them. "Do you see that guy over there? Etcetera." The kid looked at me, looked at his drawings, looked at me, then curled his lip and said, 'Fuck off,' in French. He didn't believe it!"

---

[7] "The Beat." *Record Collector*. 11 Jul 2018. recordcollectormag.com/articles/beat. Accessed 20 Jul. 2022.

It is without argument that the Beat Girl is iconic, known the world over. So too, it appears, was the real Beat Girl, in many ways. Her name was Brigitte Bond, and according to the *Daily Mirror*, when she and Prince Buster posed for their photo at the airport on February 25, 1964, it was the first time the two had met. "The 'King and Queen of Blue Beat' met for the first time yesterday. This picture was taken a few minutes after the 'King'—26-year-old Jamaican Prince Buster—stepped off the plane at London Airport from Paris. The 'Queen,' 19-year-old Brigitte Bond, and a crowd of Mods, were there to greet him. Prince Buster, in regulation Mod uniform of narrow-brimmed trilby and shirt with a 'Dr. Kildare' collar, is here for television and a month's concert tour. He said, 'I sing West Indian blues. My record 'Wash, Wash,' is No. 1 in the Jamaican charts. It will take this country by storm. We will outst the Beatles. They are good boys and have harmony, but they need my rhythm.' Brigitte has made several records, including 'Blue Beat Baby.'"[8]

Both Prince Buster and Brigitte Bond were artists on the Blue Beat label which was founded by Emil Shallit in 1949 in England. Brigitte Bond & the Blue Beats recorded "Blue Beat Baby" with the flip side "Oh Yeah Baby." It is not clear exactly when this record came out, but given the year of release, 1964, and the newspaper accounts of the record having been released during the time of Prince Buster's visit, it would be logical that Shallit released the single sometime in either January or February of 1964.

Brigitte Bond's first performance in England, according to newspaper archives, was in early February 1964 when she appeared with a band called the Contrasts at Southall Community Center in Middlesex where she was advertised as a "Beautiful, shapely French Rock Singer."[9] The following month, in March 1964, she performed with Eddie Langdon and the Cracksmen at a venue called the Top Twenty Club which was located in the Bridgwater Town Hall. This venue was only open for six years but it was host to such legends as The Who, The Small Faces, and Van Morrison.[10] According to a blog devoted to the Top Twenty Club, Eddie Langdon was billed as the "new singing star from London's 2 I's Coffee Bar" on the advertisement and the band "appear along with the delightful Brigitte Bond."[11] Brigitte appeared regularly at the 2 I's Coffee Bar in Soho which displayed a poster of her performances in the window. The venue was small and contained room for only about 20 people. The 2 I's Coffee Bar in London's Soho district was a launch pad for many young stars including Tommy Steele, Mickie Most, and a number of skiffle bands.

In April 1964, Brigitte performed at the Marquee as the "Blue Beat Baby," according to the advertisement in the *Record Mirror* which ran a glamorous photo of

[8] "The King and Queen of Blue Beat meet." *Daily Mirror*, 26 Feb. 1964 p. 26.
[9] *West Middlesex Gazette*, 1 Feb 1964, p. 13.
[10] "Do You Remember the Top Twenty?" *Bridgwater Mercury*. 14 Sept. 2010. bridgwatermercury.co.uk/news/8389671.do-you-remember-the-top-twenty. Accessed 25 Jul. 2022.
[11] toptwentyclub.co.uk/the-artists-1964. Accessed 25 Jul. 2022.

Brigitte, arms raised, hands in her hair.[12] In May 1964 she appeared on the cover of a magazine called *Tit-Bits*, a weekly British magazine founded in 1881 that began the genre of popular journalism. The cover exclaimed, "Brigitte Bond: She has a built-in licence to thrill." The article read, "Brigitte Bond, self-styled Queen of the Blue Beat in Britain, has plenty in common with her namesakes, Brigitte Bardot and James Bond. Like Bardot and 007, Brigitte has a licence to thrill. She thrilled me when I saw her in a Soho coffee bar—and not just by her stunning looks. Her accent fascinated me when she told me about herself. Said the smouldering mam'selle: 'My mozzair ees in textiles. Beeg beezness in Marseilles, much money. Beeg house, everysing. Me, I do not want. Money, yes. Beezness, no. So I come away.' In search of pop-singing fame, 19-year-old Brigitte came straight to London's Two I's coffee bar, where manager Tom Littlewood has steered many a vocalist to fame. Brigitte latched on to the West Indian blue beat sound and soon won a recording contract for Blue Beat Baby and Oh Yeah, Baby. 'Ees a marvellous noise,' she said as we played the disc. 'I just have to move wiz eet.' And how she moves!"[13]

Brigitte Bond was launching her own career, attracting the spotlight of the stage and the eye of admirers. One of these admirers was a British noble and the two were quickly engaged to marry. The connection came through her manager, Tom Littlewood. An article ran on their engagement in the *Evening Standard* on May 21, 1964 with the headline, "I'll be Lady Waller in 4 months says Brigitte." The article stated, "Brigitte Bond perched on a coffee bar stool in Soho today and announced: 'In four months I will be Lady Waller.' Dark-eyed Brigitte, aged 20, plans to marry 46-year-old Sir John Waller, the seventh baronet. Today she talked of her fortnight's courtship and her plans after marriage. 'It may seem strange to some people, but he proposed when we met only two weeks ago. He had bought a record of mine and saw my photograph outside the Two I's coffee bar. One day he rang up and invited me to lunch at the Stork Room. During lunch he asked me to marry him and I said "Yes." Since then we have been seeing a lot of each other. Last night he came to the coffee bar where I sometimes sing and told me he had bought a ring. He will be giving it to me on Friday.' Brigitte said she had already met some of Sir John's relatives and was being introduced to his friends. The age difference, Brigitte contended, didn't really apply. 'He's a wonderful man: so terribly polite and well mannered. He has the spirit of a 20-year-old and likes my music.'"

The article continued, "Sir John was a little more cautious about his wedding plans. Speaking from his flat in Kensington, he said: 'We have only met a few times and you can certainly say that marriage has been discussed. We are gradually getting to know each other. One has to be careful. This isn't like buying a new pair of shoes. Wives are permanent.' Commenting on a report that Sir John will get £250,000 from a trust when he has a son aged 10, Brigitte said: 'Money just doesn't come into it. I earn £120 a week net and will be doing so for the next 10 years. I know Sir John—he

---

[12] *Record Mirror*, 28 Mar. 1964.
[13] Hunn, David. "Mam'Selle Bond has a licence to thrill." *Tit-Bits*. 9 May 1964, p. 13.

calls me "the flower of his life"—has a lot of money, but I do well enough.' She added: 'But we will have a baby. I have, of course, warned him that it could be a girl.' Brigitte, who is French-Maltese, has written to her mother of her wedding plans. She hopes the wedding will coincide with the launching of her latest record—I'm a Big Girl Now. Mr. Tom Littlewood, Brigitte's manager, has known Sir John for about six years. 'He's very interested in Brigitte's singing and I wasn't a bit surprised when I heard him talking about his proposal,' he said."[14] It is not known what happened with the recording mentioned in this account nor why it was never released, though one can speculate.

Sir John Waller was 7th Baronet, meaning he was descended from a knighted relative. He was a published poet and in 1974 won the Keats Prize. After serving in the Middle East with the Royal Army Service Corps in the 1940s, Waller became a member of the Ministry of Information.[15] Waller's estate contained a provision that he could not inherit money in his trust fund until his wife bore a son, as he explained in a Sydney, Australian newspaper. The article with the title, "Women Must Be Insane: Rush to Marry Baronet," ran two years before he met Brigitte. "'Really it doesn't matter who I marry,'" he stated in the article, "But then he listed three qualifications for his wife: She must be young. 'At my age I'm interested in young girls and I suppose I could marry one without a penny.' She must have £50,000 sterling as a dowry and preferably a flat in Paris. She must be interested in literature. 'She mustn't keep asking me, 'who wrote that,' when I quote poetry to her.' She must be Roman Catholic 'so that she can't divorce me.' Sir John explained that he had inherited a £200,000 sterling trust fund from his cousin, Lady Viola Waller, under which he receives £7,000 a year. The only condition on which he can receive the trust fund capital is if he marries and his son reaches 10 years of age. … He also has unusual ideas on children. 'A daughter would be no good—she'd only be a damned expense,' he said. 'I'd like to have five sons as pets. You can train children whereas animals are difficult.'"[16]

Given Waller's position and, for lack of a better word, perspective, it should come as no surprise then that he was evidently enraged when he discovered that Brigitte Bond did not meet his requirements for a wife. Likely evidence of his rage came in the form of press after the engagement was called off in June 1964. Articles on her ran in Fremont, Ohio; Alliance, Nebraska; Staunton, Virginia; Princeton, Indiana; Circleville, Ohio; Cannonsburg, Pennsylvania; Beckley, West Virginia; Bedford, Indiana; Madera, California; Kane, Pennsylvania; and Linton, Indiana. All ran the same photo of Brigitte, all proclaimed the same headline: "Where Boys Were." Brigitte Bond was born a boy. The headline spoofed the Connie Francis song of three years earlier, but such an overt public outing was anything but funny. The clip beneath her photo read, "Brigitte Bond, 22, is going back to a singing career instead of becoming a bride in London. Her engagement to Sir John Waller was broken when

[14] "I'll be Lady Waller in 4 months says Brigitte." *Evening Standard*. 21 May 1964, p. 11.
[15] salamanderoasis.org/poets/w/waller-john. Accessed 25 Jul. 2022.
[16] "Women Must Be Insane: Rush to Marry Baronet." *Sydney Morning Herald*. 4 Nov. 1962, p. 19.

he learned they couldn't have children, as she had led him to believe she could. Brigitte underwent a sex change operation to become the girl she is."[17] One can only imagine how the news was received, or why it was printed in the first place, in rural locations throughout the United States. One can also only imagine the pain caused to Brigitte who now had no control over her professional career and personal life, outed so publicly. As a side note, Sir John Waller, who was by all accounts an alcoholic, ended up marrying a much-younger Anne Mileham in 1974. An article ran the day after their wedding with the headline, "Baronet Bride Missing After Night's Club Crawl," and he stated, "I mislaid her last night. I can't remember where it was I last saw her. You know what it's like when you've had a few drinks."[18] Lady Waller gave birth to a baby girl in 1975, as newspapers reported. "Oh Baby You Cost a Mint," ran the headline in the *Daily Mirror*. "Sir John Waller drank a toast yesterday to the baby who cost him a £100,000 fortune," stated the article.[19] The couple later divorced with no male heir. Lady Waller filed for bankruptcy in 1990.[20]

What opportunities were there for a transgender woman in 1964 London? For Brigitte, who obviously dreamt of being a star of stage and screen, she continued to seek the spotlight, especially in the press. An article in the *Stampa Sera*, a newspaper based in Torino, Italy, ran a story in late June about one of Brigitte's adventures. The article details the topless fashion trend in Germany and includes the account in London. The translation reads, "In London, the singer Brigitte Bond appeared last night in the Hilton hotel nightclub wearing an evening dress that left her chest completely uncovered but no one showed to notice. The singer stayed in the club for about an hour. Brigitte, who was born in Malta to a French father and Maltese mother, reported that she bought the dress in a London department store last Friday. 'I had a great desire to put it on and my friends suggested that I go to the Hilton for a drink. I thought it was the opportunity I was looking for. Once I got there, I felt really comfortable. It was a wonderful experience.'"[21]

No longer represented by Tom Littlewood, Brigitte sought the help of another advocate, though this one, the Arthur Lowe Agency, promoted her "new singing cabaret act," billing her as "the controversial Sex Change girl with the velvet singing voice" in a newspaper advertisement that August.[22] The cabarets were a welcoming outlet for Brigitte's talent. In August she performed at the Cavendish Club, promoted now as the "Controversial Singing and Dancing Star."[23] That same month she left for a tour of Africa, performing at cabarets in Mombasa and Nairobi in Kenya, and Salisbury, now called Harare, in Zimbabwe. The brief announcement of this tour in the newspaper called her "Blue Beat Bond" and also called her "controversial."[24]

[17] "Where Boys Were." *Madera Tribune*. 10 Jun. 1964, p. 2.
[18] "Baronet Bride Missing After Night's Club Crawl." *Evening Chronicle*, 4 Apr. 1974, p. 12.
[19] "Oh Baby You Cost a Mint." *Daily Mirror*, 8 Sept. 1975, p. 3.
[20] *The London Gazette*, 20 June 1990, p. 10846.
[21] "La moda del topless Conquista la Germania." *Stampa Sera*. 30 June 1964, p. 3.
[22] *The Stage*, 13 Aug. 1964, p. 5.
[23] *Evening Chronicle*, 12 Aug. 1964, p. 2.
[24] *The Stage and Television Today*, 30 Jul. 1964.

In addition to cabarets, Brigitte also performed in strip clubs. In November of that same year, her performance was told with the newspaper headline, "Tales of Strip Dancers Bared in London Court." The story, which ran in Albuquerque, New Mexico after having appeared via the UPI wire, detailed an undercover cop's account of seeing strippers at The Pelican Club in Soho. The article read, "On another occasion, the officer testified, a dancer introduced as 'The Fabulous Brigitte Bond' danced nude before about 70 men then lay across the laps of three club members while the rest of the audience yelled, 'More.'"[25]

The following year, in early April 1965, Brigitte returned to Britain to perform at La Dolce Vita in Newcastle. One article called her "Busy Brigitte" and said she had returned "after a highly successful tour of South Africa and Rhodesia."[26] In another, she was billed as "Sensational Sizzling Brigitte Bond" for a week-long cabaret performance with Jimmy Wheeler.[27] After her successful performance at this venue, she secured a residency for two months at the La Dolce Vita in Madrid, Spain. According to newspapers, after her residency there, she planned to "make a return visit to South Africa."[28] She was talent for the Bailey Organisation which comprised a "night-club empire" including the La Dolce Vita clubs, the Cavendish Club where she had performed, as well as a network of about a dozen other clubs in England.[29]

Brigitte began her residency in Madrid at the La Dolce Vita club in July 1965, but before that she appeared at one other club called the Luss-May. An article announcing her appearances stated in the title, via translation, "Brigitte Bond, Formerly A Soldier of the British Empire and Now Famous 'Star' from English Music." There is no other mention of her involvement in the military, but the rest of the article states, "He has arrived in the capital of Spain to perform at the Luss-May. Brigitte Bond, today's beautiful and statuesque English 'star,' is an analogous case. I go to the also famous Coccinelle, who performed in Madrid about two years ago. The Miss Brigitte—twenty-three years old—after completing military service, like a gentleman, now he travels with a passport feminine, turned into an important attraction of international 'music-halls.' Brigitte Bond has arrived in Madrid to make her debut in a brilliant nightclub."[30] By the end of June, however, she was entertaining at La Dolce Vita in Madrid and advertisements declared she was an "incomparable vedette," "internacional," and "diferente a todas," or different from everything.[31] She left La Dolce Vita at the beginning of August 1965, but then took a residency in November of that year at the York Club in Madrid.[32] She continued to perform here through January of 1966. As a note, since this term will continue to appear, a vedette

[25] "Tales of Strip Dancers Bared in London Court." *Albuquerque Journal*. 15 Nov. 1964, p. 58.
[26] *The Stage*, 8 Apr. 1965.
[27] *Evening Chronicle*, 7 Apr. 1965.
[28] *The Stage and Television Today*, 15 July 1965, p. 3.
[29] Morton, David. "Newcastle's La Dolce Vita nightclub and the Swinging 60s on Tyneside." 6 Feb. 1968. chroniclelive.co.uk/news/history/newcastles-la-dolce-vita-nightclub-14251443. Accessed 25 Jul. 2022.
[30] *ABC*, 30 June 1965, p.82.
[31] *ABC*, 8 July 1965, p. 81.
[32] *ABC*, 10 Nov. 1965, p. 113.

is a performer in the cabaret, typically headlining shows where she danced, sang, and entertained the crowd with burlesque. A supervedette is a star in this category.

In mid-1966, however, accounts have Brigitte changing her name—from Brigitte Bond to Brigitte St. John, sometimes spelled out as Brigitte Saint John. She reappeared in London where she engaged in a rather ambitious and courageous protest of a visit by American evangelist Billy Graham who came to Soho to preach about "sin" and sell his religion. Whether she changed her name to reinvent herself in Britain post-Waller, or because the James Bond moniker was no longer as desirable, or she just wanted a new name, it is not clear. What is clear is that Brigitte still attracted cameras everywhere she went, and she knew she could grab them from Graham. She was incredibly successful in her endeavor, even garnering an article in *Time Magazine*. The article, accompanied by a photo of Brigitte, tells what happened when Graham, according to his press release, "is not going to Soho to condemn, but to show his concern for all people." This is when Brigitte became involved. The article continues, "… the evangelist had planned an hour's walk through Soho, but a mob of 2,000 zealots swarmed all over him just across the way from the Old Compton Street Cinema (current attraction: Orgy at Lil's Place). A stripper named Brigitte St. John screamed: 'Billy, what do you think of my mini-skirt?' and flung herself onto his car. As the reverend rode out of the bedlam, an aide was murmuring, 'We're lucky to get away with our lives.'"[33] The event and a photo of Brigitte, smiling with policemen grabbing her by the arm and around her neck, ran in numerous newspapers throughout the United States, including one on the front page in Charlotte, North Carolina with the headline, "Billy is Popular in Soho."[34] Another in Dayton, Ohio stated, "Strip Joint Tour Halted: Fuss in Soho Sends Graham Back to Arena," and said, "A blonde stripper named Brigitte St. John jumped on top of his car and had to be taken down by police," followed by the statement from a seemingly-deaf Graham, "I was moved that so many people in Soho would be interested."[35] Much of the other press was also deaf, not including any mention of Brigitte's interruption at all and instead painting the event as smooth and laudable with such headlines as "Graham Socks the Devil in London."[36]

The *Sunday Mirror*, however, featured a full-page cover photo of Brigitte St. John and a story of her account. The article titled "Sin and Miniskirts—by the girl on Billy Graham's car," states, "The strip girl who perched on evangelist Dr. Billy Graham's car in Soho said yesterday: 'Mini-skirts are NOT sinful. It is all in the mind.' The girl, blonde, brown-eyed Brigitte St. John, was trying to protest to Dr. Graham about his views that mini-skirts are 'sinful.' But she found herself on the roof of his car, cheered on by 2,000 men. Dr. Graham had planned an hour-long preaching tour of Soho on Friday night. It ended after five minutes when police dispersed the crowd—and Brigitte. In Soho yesterday, Maltese-born Brigitte, 21, said: 'I think Dr.

---

[33] *Time*, 24 June 1966, p. 48.
[34] "Billy Is Popular in Soho." *Charlotte Observer*. 19 Jun. 1966, p. 1.
[35] "Fuss in Soho Sends Graham Back to Arena." *Dayton Daily News*, 19 June 1965, p. 2.
[36] *Daily News*, New York. 19 Jun 1965, p. 18.

Graham is doing a wonderful job. I would love to see him working but I just haven't had the time. But I felt really angry when I read that he said short skirts bring sin. They don't bring sin, and I wanted very much to tell him this. But it was impossible to get near him because of the crowd. Suddenly I found myself on top of his car. See this skirt I'm wearing now?' said Brigitte. 'It is only six inches above my knees. That is not sinful either. It is just fashionable. Mind you, if they go any higher than ten inches the girls might as well wear nothing at all. They might just as well flaunt their bodies openly and that would be nasty,' said Brigitte. 'People will say stripping in front of men is sinful. It is not. It is artistry, especially if it is done properly.' Dr. Graham says he intends to visit a basement coffee bar in Soho this week. If he does, Brigitte will be waiting. She said, 'I will put on a MINI-MINI-skirt and see what he thinks of that. He may not like it but the boys will—they appreciate fashions.'"[37]

Brigitte was certainly protesting, but she was also promoting herself, which she continued to do in provocative ways. In 1967, an article in the *Diario de Burgos* newspaper detailed some of the publicity methods that celebrities, like Marilyn Monroe and Jayne Mansfield, engaged in to promote themselves. One of the local celebrities mentioned in this article was none other than Brigitte. Translated from Spanish to English, the author states, "Publicity eccentricity is the one that a few days ago offered us the explosive Brigitte St. John in the middle of the Gran Via, allowing herself to be photographed in a long skirt between two taxis, in the middle of the road, and with a huge cluster of onlookers gawking around her. She is looking for a position in the cinema, and she does not stop taking advantage of the circumstance of making herself known, by whatever method."[38] Brigitte's "publicity eccentricity" was much more than that, however. It was an act of defiance and protest, as she had already displayed in London with Billy Graham, and in this case against the totalitarian Francoist government, as will be discussed further on.

Another account of this event was found in a recollection of an architect from Madrid who witnessed Brigitte's stunt. Translated from Spanish, the description reads, "The man who also stopped traffic called himself Brigitte and she wasn't an urban guard, she was supervedette. Her stage name was Brigitte St. Jones [sic] and advertised herself as 'the famous star who was considered a man for 11 years…' And if, friends of the cause, she had every right to call herself whatever she wanted. … The French woman sat on the terrace of Manila in Callao. After a while, he would get up on his heels—OOOOOOOH—grab his puppy and cross the Gran Via—ZAS, ZAS, ZAS—DRY BRAKE! He sat on the other side of the avenue, on the terrace of Nebraska and after a while, ZAS, ZAS, again to cut traffic."[39]

If her intention, as the first account says, was to find a role in film, Brigitte did, in fact, secure that position she sought in cinema—three of them. In 1967 she appeared as a "dancer" in the movie *Herostratus*. This film was Dame Helen Mirren's

[37] "Sin and Mini Skirts." *Sunday Mirror*. 19 Jun 1965, p. 1.
[38] "El Afan de la Publicidad: Metodos…Logica…Consecuencias." *Diario de Burgos*, 20 Sept. 1976, p. 3.
[39] From generoful.blogspot.com/2009/07/arquitectura-urbanismo-y-monumentos.html?m=1. Accessed 20 Jul. 2022.

first screen performance and was directed by Don Levy. It was the inspiration for Stanley Kubrick's *A Clockwork Orange*, but Levy's film was largely unsuccessful with audiences. The film's plot tells "the story of Max, a young poet who proposes to a marketing firm that they turn into a mass media spectacle his suicide by jumping off a tall building, a final performance that he conceives as a sacrificial act of protest against modern society," according to the British Film Institute.[40] Brigitte's appearance as a dancer involves the deeper meaning of the film. "As Levy was at pains to point out, though, the basic plot of the film is just the surface of a deeper narrative, a complex interconnected web of images and sounds designed to trigger emotional reflexes in the viewer's subconscious. Images of postwar urban decay and juxtapositions of burlesque stripteases with carcasses hanging in an abattoir frequently recur."[41] Brigitte was one of those performing a burlesque striptease.

The following year, Brigitte also appeared as a dancer in the film *1001 Nights* which was titled in Spanish, *La esclava del paraíso*. The film was made in Madrid and directed by José María Elorrieta. According to imdb, "Omar and his friend, Ali, returning to Moorish Granada after several years in the Middle East, discover that an evil usurper is now in power. With the help of a female genie, Omar sets about restoring freedom and justice."[42] Brigitte is billed as a dancer, though she does not actually dance in the film. She is a member of a group of women who perform for Omar and Ali. She then seduces one of them but is interrupted. Clad in a costume no doubt inspired by I Dream of Jeannie, Brigitte's character has a few short lines, all spoken in Spanish. That same year she also performed in Lisbon, Portugal at the Maria Vittoria Theater, so she likely continued to tour as her schedule permitted.[43]

In 1969, Brigitte appeared in *The Girl of the Nile*, also titled *La muchacha del Nilo* and also known as *The Emerald of Artatama*. She appeared as the character, "Brigitte St. Shons." This 81-minute film was also directed by José María Elorrieta. In this film, "An odd assortment of treasure hunters ventures out into the Egyptian desert and find a 'lost' tomb only to start fighting over the spoils."[44] Brigitte was a member of one of these treasure hunting groups and she is featured in a number of scenes with a few small speaking parts.

In 1970, Brigitte took up some modeling, although it was for a rather amateurish nudie magazine called *Spick* which was published in London. The very same photos displayed in *Spick* also ran in two years later in the same publication. But most of Brigitte's live performances in the mid to late 1960s and early 1970s center around Madrid, which seems to have been her most constant home post-London. She had an agent in Barcelona as indicated on her headshots from 1970. Additionally, she did secure residencies in other countries from time to time, including one in Italy in May 1972 at the Teatro Alcione where she was billed as a vedette, appearing with

---

[40] screenonline.org.uk/film/id/797491/synopsis.html. Accessed 25 Jul 2022.

[41] Ibid.

[42] imdb.com/title/tt0062940. Accessed 25 Jul 2022.

[43] *Diario de Lisboa*. 2 Oct. 1968, p. 4.

[44] imdb.com/title/tt0062001/?ref_=tt_mv_desc. Accessed 24 Jul 2022.

Nathalie and Remo, also vedettes. She was also billed here as a supervedette, headlining the other performers. Brigitte performed frequently with Coccinelle, the first person in France to undergo gender confirmation surgery.

Coccinelle traveled to Casablanca in 1958 for the surgery which was pioneered by Dr. Georges Burou, a gynecologist, at his Clinic du Parc. "Dr Burou rectified the mistake nature had made and I became a real woman, on the inside as well as the outside." After the operation, the doctor just said, 'Bonjour, Mademoiselle,' and I knew it had been a success," she said.[45] George Burou was sought by hundreds of individuals who came to him for help. "They are nearly always people who spent all their lives yearning to be women," said Burou in a rare interview in 1974.[46] It is not clear if Brigitte ever met Dr. Burou but it is definitely possible, considering the time period and the fact that those around her had been to Dr. Burou, including April Ashley, the first woman in the UK to have sex confirmation surgery, Capucine, Amanda Lear, Bambi (Marie-Pierre Pruvot), and Coccinelle. But Dr. Burou did not follow up with his patients by design, so any records of his have largely been lost to time. "I think most of them want to forget they ever had to undergo such an operation," he said.[47]

Coccinelle appeared in numerous films and had her own revue, Cherchez la Femme. Prior to her surgery, Coccinelle had performed in Paris at Madame Arthur and Carrousel de Paris and afterward she continued to perform at these clubs along with numerous others all over the world. It was at one of these clubs in Madrid that Coccinelle and Brigitte appeared on bills together, the Gay Club in Madrid which opened its doors in 1974. Coccinelle and Brigitte were most definitely influenced by the same icon, Brigitte Bardot, as they both declare in interviews. Brigitte's affinity for the actress can be found in her choice of name. All three of these women—Brigitte Bond, Brigitte Bardot, and Coccinelle—were blond bombshells who attracted the press everywhere they went. But for Brigitte Bond and Coccinelle, their performances, unlike those of Brigitte Bardot, were dangerous. In fact, their performances could get them killed.

Madrid, Spain was a deadly place during the reign of dictator Francisco Franco. Franco was homophobic and he led a brutal regime of torture and persecution. He and his followers "considered homosexuals a threat to their ideal of a 'macho' Spanish male. 'Any effeminate or introvert who insults the movement will be killed like a dog,' General Quepio del Llano, Franco's favourite broadcaster, once threatened."[48] In 1970, the Franco regime enacted La Ley de Peligrosidad y Rehabilitacion Social, or the Law of Social Danger and Rehabilitation. This law "included a list of punishments against gay and transgender people including

[45] Rickman, Catherine. "What You Should Know About Coccinelle, France's First Trans Celebrity." 24 Jun 2021. frenchly.us/what-you-should-know-about-coccinelle-frances-first-trans-celebrity. Accessed 25 Jul 2022.
[46] "Sex Surgeon Gives Rare Interview." New Jersey Evening Times. 19 May 1974.
Transascity.org/files/news/1974_05_19_Trenton_New_Jersey_Evening-Times.jpg. Accessed 20 Jul. 2022.
[47] Ibid.
[48] Tremlett, Giles. "Gays persecuted by Franco lose criminal status at last." The Guardian. 13 Dec. 2001. theguardian.com/world/2001/dec/13/gayrights.gilestremlett. Accessed 25 Jul 2022.

confinement to asylums and banishment from their hometowns. … These homophobic laws saw many people sent to 'colonies,' a softer term for concentration camps for gay people. … Thousands of people experienced these camps, suffering hunger, torture and hard labour. More than 5,000 people—in particular transgender people and gay men—were imprisoned and accused of 'scandalous public behaviour' (escándalo público), labelled a danger to society. The ruling powers designed the camps to correct their behaviour and their 'deviency.' … Many different scientific disciplines joined forces to develop a legal medical treatment to eradicate homosexuality, and electro-shock and aversion therapy was born."[49]

For performers like Coccinelle and Brigitte, appearing at the Gay Club was risky during the era of these sadistic laws. The venue was located on the ground floor of the Hotel Nacional on Paseo del Prado. Here the audience of 500 people could regularly enjoy cabaret and burlesque shows, though a level of protection activated by the box office ensured the safety of the performers. A red light in the dressing room alerted the vedettes if authorities were present. When this happened, performers "put on another type of show, more adapted to the morality of the moment."[50]

One performer, Paco Espana, recalls an interaction with Brigitte, whom he refers to as "the trans Brigitte Saint John a supervedette." Espana states, "Then an Italian debuted who said that she was a woman, and that her name was Brigitte St. John. She was half crazy… hysterical, she was classic hysteria. She said that she was a woman and there was no one to take her out of here. We knew he was a boy. She walked around the room in a robe…one day I was at the bar with a rhinestone bracelet, dressed as a boy because they wouldn't let us dress as women. And Brigitte goes and tells me, 'Aren't you embarrassed to wear a diamond bracelet?' And I told her, 'Are you no longer ashamed that being a vedette you walk around the room, full as she is, with a robe and house slippers?' At this moment she disappeared from my side and after a while she appeared with a wonderful dress and scandalous shoes and she told me, 'Do you like it better like this?' and I replied, 'Well, it's better like this.'"[51]

Novelist and journalist Arturo Perez-Reverte recalls seeing Brigitte at Gay Club when he visited. He writes, "The club was called Gay Club and it was very close to the Pueblo newspaper where I, in my early twenties, had just made my debut as a reporter. Often, when closing the edition, a few geeks with little desire to sleep … would go there to have drinks. … At that time the Gay Club show was called Loco Loco Cabaret and it featured the transsexuals Brigitte Saint John and Coccinelle, Victor Campanini, David Vilches and the tranformist Patrick-you-owe-me-a-kiss, among others."[52]

[49] Pira, Luca Gaetano, "Outlawed queers: A cultural history of the Spanish Pink Triangles." *Archer Magazine*, 13 Jul 2018. archermagazine.com.au/2018/07/outlawed-queers-spanish-pink-triangles. Accessed 24 Jul 2022.
[50] Radio Madrid, cadenaser.com/emisora/2020/02/23/radio_madrid/1582467992_454382.html. Accessed 25 Jul. 2022.
[51] Antonielli, Carla. carlaantonelli-com.translate.goog/. Accessed 25 Jul 2022.
[52] Reverte, Perez. 27 Feb 2012. perezreverte.com/articulo/patentes-corso/667/guerra-para-mi-cuerpo. Accessed 25 Jul 2022.

Brigitte also performed in Palma in Mallorca, Spain, as one article from 1975 states. "The vedettes were in charge of making way for the strippers. From 1975, several nightclubs in the archipelago added to their advertisements to tell this new format of the show. So, they hired a set of professionals previously engaged in the most daring scenarios of the main European capitals, such as Justin Queen (Sa majeste, la femme!) and Brigitte St. John, who arrived in Palma in 1975. They came with a contract of two and a half weeks, but their success on the stages was so clamorous that they ended up begging for their stay of nearly four months."[53] Brigitte performed at a nightclub called Jartan's on Dameto Street.[54]

The last accounts of Brigitte St. John appear in spring of 1976. She performed at the Rialto Teatro in Barcelona throughout March, then was in a small city called Lleida at Club Scarlet throughout April. It was here that a reporter interviewed her and after that, no other mention of her is found. The article, which featured a small photo of her, is translated with the headline, "Self-defines as 'girl-showman; inside the music hall show.'" The rough translation reads, "If we really had to make a critique of the performance, with which she delighted the audience on the day of her debut at Club Scarlet Party Hall, Brigitte Saint-John, I think it would be quite difficult for us, as we were not used to seeing anything in this category, so colorful. Brigitte is Italian from Malta; her real name is Giovanna, and what is certain about her performance is that she has many 'boards' on her feet, which is the same as a long time on stage. He greets us in his dressing room, full of suits and scattered stools. We grabbed one, sat down and asked: How long in the entertainment world Brigitte? 'From the age of 16.' What is your strength? 'I'm a girl-singer-showman, inside the music hall.' I understand that by singing you do well (I laugh). 'Look, I have records recorded in my country, in Italy.' Is Brigitte the woman who speaks it half in Italian, half in Spanish. He explains that he has visited every continent, that he has performed in Las Vegas, USA. The only countries he has not performed in have been the communists, at the same time he explains to us, that they do not allow such shows there. How long have you been in Spain? Have you ever been to Lleida? 'I was in Spain before I got married. I have now spent two months between Barcelona, Madrid, and the Costa Brava. With regard to your second question, I will tell you that this is the first time I have come to Lleida.' And what do you think? 'I'm sorry but I can't answer because I don't know yet, I just arrived.' How many numbers can you present to the public? 'Many. I usually change more numbers each year. The ones I present at Scarlet are now two.' The first of these is entitled 'Las Vegas,' in which he sings the theme 'Fever.' The second of these, entitled 'Paris 1900.' Like the previous number it is an American-style show. Brigitte, who's preparing you? the numbers? 'Gino Landi prepares them for me, he is

[53] Canyelles, Tomeau. "Sexualitat I doble moral a les illes Balears (1960-1975)." 4 Jun 2017. revistes.ub.edu/index.php/cercles/article/download/cercles2017.20.1005/22624/45742. Accessed 24 Jul 2022.
[54] Riera, Joan. "El dictador, y su representante, contra los músicos." *Diario de Mallorca*. 30 Jul 2020. diariodemallorca.es/cultura/2020/07/30/dictador-representante-musicos-9031305.html. Accessed 25 Jul 2022.

the same one who makes them for Rafaella Carrá.' What staff have you worked with? 'For example with Don Lurió, in Las Vegas.' Besides where your family lives, where would you choose to live? 'Italy.' ... and then? 'Spain, for its sun, its sea, its people, its everything.' City, or country you have the worst memory of? 'Cairo (Egypt) is a very beautiful city. Dirty.' And the most beautiful? 'Rhodesia, East Africa, Cape Town.' How long will you keep going? 'Up to the age of forty, there are still ten left.' And then what do you plan to do? 'I have my house in Campagna (Italy), with land that I plan to cultivate with my husband, plant trees, plants ... see and live the life of the countryside.' How would you define yourself? 'People tell me I'm very nervous, but nice; good and with character, easygoing.' What are your hobbies Brigitte? 'Cooking, reading makes my husband angry, (laughs, her husband just entered the dressing room), I'm also a great lover of art, I love to visit monuments.' Finally we ask Brigitte, what do you think of love? 'It is the most wonderful thing in the world, if you really want it and without self-interest.' The performance is waiting for you, you have to put on make-up, change, in short, get ready to go on stage. Down there are a hundred people waiting for you in the smoke of the cigarettes and a whisky on the rocks. Good luck and success."[55]

What happened to Brigitte Bond/Brigitte St. John after that is a mystery. Could she have been imprisoned, sent to a penal colony, even killed at the hands of the Franco regime which still wielded its power? It had only been months since Franco died when this last article ran and the transition to a new government took time. Transition to a new society, would not come for many decades beyond this, if ever. One reporter writes, "After the Franco's death in 1975, an informal political agreement called the Pacto del Olvido, or Pact of Forgetting, made it a national taboo to acknowledge fascist war crimes. Two years later, the Spanish legislature passed a law preventing those crimes from being investigated and tried in court. ... The exact number of dead is unknown, but historian Paul Preston puts the number of men and women executed during the war at approximately 200,000. Fascists killed another 20,000 supporters of the Republic after the war ended; tens of thousands more died in prisons and concentration camps, including Nazi concentration camps. Franco himself was known to sign sheaves of death warrants after lunch. It wasn't until 2007, with the Law of Historical Memory, that victims' families began to see meaningful reparations: monetary aid, mass grave exhumations, the removal of fascist symbols and monuments."[56] If Brigitte was lucky enough to have survived, could she have changed her name once again? Could she have left show business behind to live out her days with her husband, cultivating the land of their Campagna home? Perhaps one day Brigitte, or someone who knew her, will come forward to let us all know.

Dave Wakeling, upon learning about the real Beat Girl, stated the following: "Knowing more about Brigitte now is astounding. What are the chances that would

[55] *Diario de Lerida*. 8 Apr. 1976, p.23.
[56] Nash, Marianna. "The Law of Social Danger." *Nashville Review*. 1 Aug. 2019. as.vanderbilt.edu/nashvillereview/archives/15470. Accessed 27 July 2022.

be the photo we picked? A worked with April Ashley at Greenpeace in LA in the '90's, we had a lot of great conversations, and I wish we could have discussed Brigitte! I was also in Spain right before and after Franco's death, so we may even have been in Barcelona at the same time! Grateful of all the research that has been done and stunned that the Beat Girl has become an even more inclusionary icon than ever."[57]

Certainly, Brigitte's life, what we know of it, makes the perfect symbol of ska in the 2 Tone era. Her image, which became the illustration created by Hunt Emerson, represents community, unity, and diversity—all the ideals for which ska stands. The Beat Girl is even more meaningful than anyone could have imagined.

Note: This chapter would not be possible without the expert research, dedication, and collaboration of Joanna Wallace. All of the information contained in this chapter is through a collective effort of continued searching for the woman behind the Beat Girl iconic illustration.

The original photo of Prince Buster and Brigitte Bond, *Melody Maker*, May 19, 1979 (left) and Hunt Emerson's iconic logo illustration of the Beat Girl (right)

---

[57] Wakeling, Dave. Email correspondence with the author, 24 Jan. 2023.

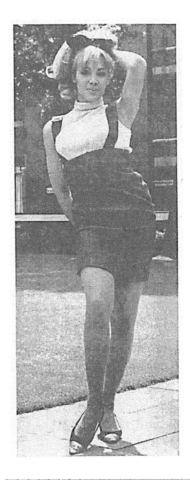

From top left, clockwise, Prince Buster and Brigitte Bond at the London airport 1964; Brigitte St. John defending the mini skirt, *Sunday Mirror*, June 19, 1965; Brigitte Bond in the *Stage and Television Today*, July 30, 1964; and Brigitte St. John on the top of Billy Graham's car in 1965. *Time Magazine*, June 24, 1966.

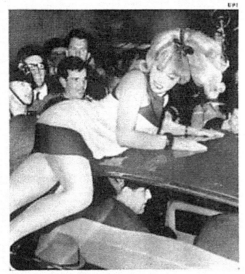

LONDON STRIPPER ON GRAHAM'S CAR
Zealots in the fleshpot.

BLUE-BEAT BOND

Controversial French-Maltese Blue Beat girl Brigitte Bond is currrently scoring in cabaret at Middlesbrough, leaves shortly for an African tour which will take her to Mombasa, Nairobi and Salisbury.

Prince Buster and Brigitte Bond in 1964 (above), Brigitte Bond on the cover and interior of *Tit-Bits*, May 1964 (middle), & Brigitte St. John's modeling shots (below)

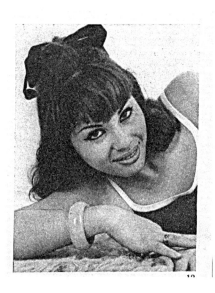

The Selecter

Compton Amanor: guitar

Charley Anderson: bass

Charley "Aitch" Bembridge: drums

Pauline Black: vocals

Desmond Brown: keyboards

Neol Davies: guitar

Arthur "Gaps" Hendrickson: vocals

Juliet De Valero Wills: manager

The Queen of Ska stood before the King of the United Kingdom in Windsor Castle, hands clasped in front of her, clad from head to toe in black and white, smiling, ready to receive the honor. Nearly 50 years after Pauline Black began her music career, her country recognized her, properly, with the award—Order of the British Empire for her "services to entertainment."[58] It was something her fans, thousands of them all over the world, recognized long ago—that Pauline Black is a strong talent, a determined trailblazer, and a helluva badass. And behind the scenes, out of the spotlight, was another woman who became part of the Selecter—as their manager. It was rare for any band during the late 1970s to employ a woman in music management, or heck even today, but Juliet De Valero Wills served as a advisor to the band of young and unruly upstarts. She was a guide as well as a friend, even if managing the group was much more than she ever bargained for. Both of these women were leaders for a band at the start, and heart, of 2 Tone.

If ever someone was destined to be an outspoken representative for unity, as the 2 Tone label proclaimed, it was Pauline Black. She was born Belinda Magnus in Romford, England, 15 miles outside of London.[59] She was adopted by her working-class father, Arthur Vickers and mother, Ivy James.[60] She learned later in life that her biological father, Gordon Adenle, was a Nigerian engineering student studying in London when he met and had a relationship with her birth mother, Eileen Magnus from Dagenham.[61] She had four adoptive brothers, Trevor, Tony, Ken, and Roger and was told that she was adopted when she was four years old.[62] Her adoptive family was white, which presented a variety of problems for Pauline as she explains in her book. "I cannot say that I wasn't loved. I know I was. But I grew up feeling like a cuckoo in somebody else's nest. It's bad enough not looking like anybody in your family, but it is very confusing not being the same colour as them."[63]

It was music that gave Pauline a sense of joy and belonging. At the age of five she began taking piano lessons and throughout her childhood she listened to a variety of musical genres and artists including the Rolling Stones, Bob Dylan, the Supremes, Diana Ross, and Aretha Franklin. "I loved many of the girl singers of the

---

[58] "2-Tone star Pauline Black receives OBE." BBC. 17 Nov. 2022. bbc.com/news/uk-england-coventry-warwickshire-63664426. Accessed 8 Jan 2023.

[59] Black, Pauline. *Black by Design*. Serpent's Tail, London, 2012, p. 4, 29.

[60] Ibid., p. 4, 26.

[61] Ibid., p. p. 5, 29, 374.

[62] Ibid., p. 3, 5.

[63] Ibid., p. 38.

day too, Cilla Black and Sandie Shaw in particular, and even the mysterious French singer Francoise Hardy, who'd just entered the British charts."[64]

Pauline recounts the first time she performed in front of an audience during a family vacation to a seaside town called Llandudno. "Llandudno was my dad's choice of a holiday resort. In between working as a coalman and his present mechanic's job, he had been a long-distance lorry driver. Many of his deliveries were in North Wales and he had grown to love the dramatic scenery. … It was here that I first performed in public, playing the piano in a kids' talent contest in Happy Valley, a pleasure park on the Great Orme. I never won."[65] During her teenage years, Pauline continued to listen to popular music but it wasn't until she was a college student that she performed again. She attended Lanchester Polytechnic in Coventry and says she was "the only black girl there."[66] Needless to say, this likely contributed to her lack of academic and social involvement in the school, so after she flunked her exams for the second time, she dropped out and instead enrolled in a program at the Coventry School of Radiography. During this time, in 1973, she met her husband, Terry Button, a production engineer at Rolls-Royce aero engine division in Coventry.[67] They married in 1980, are still married today, and have never had children.

After graduation, Pauline began working in hospitals as a radiographer and she began teaching herself guitar. She played and sang at local pubs including The Old Dyers Arms on Spon End in Coventry in 1976. "The first song I sang in public was Bob Dylan's 'Blowing in the Wind.' I had typed the words out on a piece of paper and written in the relevant guitar chord changes. My hands shook and my voice wobbled for the opening stanzas, but then I just forgot that the audience was there and performed. I loved it."[68] She performed the next year at the Golden Cup on Far Gosford Street singing Joni Mitchell, Bob Dylan, and Joan Armatrading. "The piece de resistance of my set was a bleak, self-penned song entitled 'A Whore's Life,' about the dreadful spate of killings in and around Bradford, perpetrated by a man dubbed 'The Yorkshire Ripper.' At the time, the killer's name was unknown. The song was written from the perspective of a young prostitute on the streets and dealt with the fear she felt every night."[69]

After one of her gigs, Pauline met Lawton Brown, a politics student at Warwick University who introduced her to reggae and his roommate, Charles "Aitch" Bembridge. Brown took her to see Hardtop 22, Bembridge's band that included members Charley Anderson and Compton Amanor.[70] Brown began songwriting with Pauline and brought in Silverton Hutchinson on drums since he had just been "kicked out of the Specials."[71] According to Specials' bassist Horace Panter, the reason

---

64 Ibid, p. 10, 58.
65 Ibid. p. 68.
66 Ibid. p. 96.
67 Ibid. p. 103.
68 Ibid, p. 111.
69 Ibid., p. 114.
70 Ibid., p. 118.
71 Ibid.

Hutchinson left their band was because "he refused to play ska. He said: 'That's music my parents listen to.'"[72] Clearly he wouldn't last long in the Selecter, soon replaced by Aitch. Aitch's friend Desmond Brown came in on keyboards and the group began to rehearse in a variety of spaces around Coventry. "I was in a reggae band. That was all that mattered. I had some black friends. My dream had come true," wrote Pauline.[73] During an interview in 1997, Pauline recalled that this band "wasn't really named, but we were going to start gigging."[74]

That gigging never had the chance to occur. During one of the unnamed band's rehearsals, Pauline met Lynval Golding who told her he knew a new group that needed a singer. She went to meet this band and was reintroduced to Charley Anderson and Compton Amanor, who she had seen perform with Hard Top 22. Pauline also met Neol Davies and his wife, Jane Hughes, as well as Arthur "Gaps" Hendrickson. They listened to Neol's record with "The Selecter" on the B side of "Gangsters" by the Special A.K.A. since the record with Davies' instrumental had just been pressed and released.[75] The song was written by Davies, who performed on guitar, and the Specials' John Bradbury, who performed on drums. A Coventry trombone player named Barry Jones is also featured.[76] "Then Neol addressed the whole room. 'I need a band,' he said, 'to build on the success of my single. That's why we are all here tonight.' … And thus the 2-Tone band that became known as the Selecter was born. For once I was in the right place at the right time," stated Pauline.[77] She says that the three bands, the unnamed band, Hard Top 22, and Neol Davies' proto-Selecter, all "came together and coalesced into the Selecter."

Pauline had been listening to a wide variety of music during her years, including reggae, and she says that "Long Shot (Kick de Bucket)" by the Pioneers was the first Jamaican song she heard and loved. "I heard Millie Small's 'My Boy Lollipop' first on radio, and same for Desmond Dekker's 'Israelites' and both of them I feel had quite an impact on how I felt about Jamaican music, because it was so fresh. I just really enjoyed it. It was just something that you'd dance to, you talked about."[78] Now Pauline found herself in like company, with musicians who also listened to and danced to and talked about this music, so the folk persona of Pauline's early performance years gave way to the self-styled rude girl that commanded the stage as front and center of the Selecter. "Between 1979 and 1981 everything changed, my identity, my music, my style, in some ways my very being, as I became a fully paid-up member of the 2-Tone movement. Reinvention seemed part of me these days. Perhaps it is easier for an adopted child to adapt to new situations?" says Pauline.[79]

---

[72] Simpson, Dave. "'A blur of legs, arms and adrenaline': the astonishing history of two-tone." *The Guardian*, 30 Apr. 2021.
[73] Ibid., p. 119.
[74] Black, Pauline. All quotations, unless otherwise noted, from interview with the author, 15 Jun. 1997.
[75] Ibid., p. 123.
[76] *The 2-Tone Book for Rude Boys*. Music Sales Corp, 1 Jan. 1981, p. 26.
[77] Black, Pauline. *Black by Design*. Serpent's Tail, London, 2012, p. 125.
[78] Ibid.
[79] Black, Pauline. *Black by Design*. Serpent's Tail, London, 2012, p. 129.

The Selecter officially formed in June of 1979. To help craft Pauline's look, Jane Hughes, Neol's wife, took her shopping at local thrift shops. "Jane had a good eye for stuff and I was happy to follow her direction. We took the 'rude boy' look that Peter Tosh had pioneered in his early ska days and feminized it. It was just a question of changing the proportions of the garments. She picked out some beige Sta-prest for me, which were probably from the previous ska era, circa late '60s. They stopped an inch shy of my shoes, which I was told was 'cool.' An orange, slim-fit, boy's Ben Sherman shirt was poked through the changing room's curtains to cover the upper half of my body. Next she handed me a double-breasted jacket made of shiny grey material. It fitted perfectly. Job done. We sourced a pair of black penny loafers at a downmarket shoe shop, Ravel. White socks took up the spatial slack between the trouser bottoms and my shoes. We decided that my Afro hair did not suit this new ensemble, so I pulled it up into a small topknot. I felt curiously empowered when I tried the clothes on at home and surveyed the result in the bedroom mirror. The addition of a pair of fake Raybans, strictly for posing purposes, finished everything off very nicely," recalled Pauline.[80]

The next change to help create the rude girl image was the bit about Pauline's name, Pauline Vickers. As she tells in her memoir, she decided to take the name Pauline Black as her stage name for a number of reasons. "It was a statement of truth and intent all at the same time. Yes, I was black and I wanted to sing about what it meant to be black. But more than anything I wanted my family to finally say my name. Pauline Black. They could never bring themselves to say the B word. After years of being called half-caste or coloured, I could say it loud and proud, Pauline Black. … As far as I was concerned back then, my adopted name was as good as a 'slave name.' My rebirth was complete. The 'rude girl' I had invented had a new name, Pauline Black. Black by design!"[81]

Their first gig was in Worcester on July 2, 1979 and both Pauline and Gaps harmonized, danced, and played off of one another's energy, as Pauline explains. "Gaps and I had the words taped across the front of the stage, just in case we forgot them. This led to a lot of movement on our respective parts as we followed the words along the front of the stage. Thus developed our style of running and skanking anywhere and everywhere."[82] After the Worcester gig in July, the Selecter immediately penned their first single and recorded "On My Radio" with the B side, "Too Much Pressure" at Horizon Studios the following month. The single was released on September 28, 1979 on the 2 Tone label.[83] It was an instant hit and so the Selecter hit the road with the Specials and Madness on the first 2 Tone Tour, a 40-date whirlwind that kicked off on October 19, 1979.

Before they embarked on the tour, the members of the Selecter realized they would need a manager to help navigate all of the elements that were outside of their

---

[80] Ibid., p. 138.
[81] Ibid, p. 149.
[82] Ibid., p. 137.
[83] The Selecter. *Too Much Pressure deluxe edition*, Chrysalis Records, liner notes, 2021.

purview. They were musicians, they were novices, and they had just accumulated a fan base bigger than anything they could have possibly imagined. "We got ourselves a manager. Her name was Juliet De Vie and she was twenty-one years old, a bottle-blonde puppy of a girl, but beneath the puff-candy exterior lurked a will of iron and a mind like the Enigma machine at Bletchley Park. When we first engaged her, she was working at Trigger, a PR company that by then had become the 2-Tone HQ, in Camden, adjacent to the tube station."[84]

Juliet De Valero Wills, who took the professional nickname Julie De Vie, was born in Trinidad and had a rather idyllic childhood, as she explains. "The reason we were there was that my father was actually a doctor and he had previously been in the army. I'm from a family of six. He's half Spanish—Catholic, of course, which explains the six children. Because he was an army doctor, various kids got born in various countries. By the time Trinidad happened, he was leaving the army and he actually went to work for Shell Oil. They're one of the major employers on the island, and it was so huge that they had their own hospital that they built for all the workers. He was one of the doctors working at the Shell hospital. I was born in the Shell hospital. I have a younger sister, and she was born in Trinidad as well. So that's why we were there."[85]

When Juliet was five years old, they left Trinidad in November 1963 and moved to England, but the culture of Trinidad had made an impact on her that would last forever. "The music and the culture that we knew at that point was ska, blue beat, and American radio. We were living the expat life and there weren't that many Brits there, actually. And mostly it was either Trinidadians or there's a huge multicultural identity with the Asian community—Chinese community, and lots of Americans as well. So that was very much our influence, and not particularly urban either. And we spent most of our time on the beach, really playing around on the beach, onto boats. We did go briefly to a kind of a school, sort of, which was like a shack. So that upbringing, we didn't realize how free it was until we came over. We came over on the boat called the SS Gothic which was like a sort of passenger cargo ship, and so we got to run wild on there for several weeks and then had a very rude awakening arriving in England in November. Dark. Cold. Misty. I mean, we'd never seen cold before. That was one of our really huge memories is seeing what cold looks like. And it was just the mist and the first lights we saw, sailing past Southampton, although we docked in London in Tilbury. We weren't sure what was happening then, but now we know that was right in the middle of what was and has become known as the Windrush Generation," she says.

That connection to Caribbean culture and immigration created a deep empathy and appreciation in Juliet. "What's interesting is our experiences as children were exactly the same as all these other Caribbeans in general were experiencing at the same time. We had that similar experience of coming to England and feeling

---

[84] Black, Pauline. *Black by Design*. Serpent's Tail, London, 2012, p. 150-151.
[85] De Valero Wills, Juliet. All quotations, unless otherwise noted, from interview with the author, 26 Aug. 2021.

completely alien, not fitting in at all, but with a huge caveat, which is we're white. I never ever forget the difference. So our not fitting in was more cultural. It was more do to with the fact that we had literally not worn shoes for—my entire life. I hadn't worn shoes at all at that point. We had our mom trying to put jumpers on us, and hats and scarves and caps, and as fast as she was putting them on, we're just tearing them off. They were scratchy and horrible. Suddenly you're covered up, buttoned up, shoes, the whole lot. And it's just a whole new thing—it's not just a new country, not just new schools, it's just everything and you're just getting used to seasons and people being much more formal. We hated it. We weren't happy."

The family settled in Bristol, which Juliet describes as being "very political and very art driven. It was probably the most radical city in the UK at that point. It was the center of what was then the burgeoning feminist scene in England at the time." When her father was called to do work in Saudi Arabia at that point, the rest of the family stayed in Bristol and her mother embraced feminist culture. "She completely embraced this whole other person she always had repressed, which was this radical feminist writing poetry, out there protesting and getting heavily involved in that scene. So we, of course, by default, got swept up in all that as well. So we went from this quite strict, austere sort of home, to a completely mad home life. We'd have endless parties, a house full of people, and we went back into this quite bohemian life for a while. And music was a big part of that," Juliet says.

The music that Juliet heard in her home and her community was the music she loved as a young child in Trinidad. "The whole bluebeat ska side of things, we never really left behind. Living in Bristol, we would still regularly take the curtain poles down and practice calypso [limbo is the dance, calypso is the music typically played during limbo]. To us, it was really competitive—who could go the lowest, and who could go under it. And it still really still mattered to us that we could dance properly to calypso and we could also dance ska properly. And also, what coincided with that was there was a whole chain of venues that were very big at that time in the UK— Top Rank venues, the cinema chain—they own all these venues and they often used to put on discos in the afternoons for underage groups. In that period, they were playing a lot of ska and bluebeat. By then, I had decided that I was actually a suede head so I was wearing the loafers and having the tonic dress and looking pretty sharp and was rebelling against the hippie hold that was going on in Bristol at the time, which was mom and all her friends. It didn't work for me at all. So that was my rebellion. So ska was always a thread, and to me it always set us apart."

Juliet says that her mother and father had a strained relationship, to say the least, which added to the disfunction of the family. "It got worse because when I was 11, dad had come back from Saudi and he'd gone straight to Scotland to a locum up there without bothering to tell mom or us that he was back in the country. So we just went straight up there and things were bad between them. We were told that they were getting back together and we were being moved up there, which was kind of really hard. I was very academic and was very focused, had a strong work ethic. So the plan was, I was going to complete grammar school and then go to university and study English. I wanted to be a journalist or lawyer, or someone something in the middle. I'd loved English, which I got from my mom, because she was writing reams of poems. She then, many years later, in her late 50s after dad died, because they never got around to getting divorced, she actually went back to university to do the English degree she'd always wanted to do. She worked so hard at it. Anyway, that was going to be the plan."

"But then all of a sudden, we were taken up to this godforsaken place in Scotland at a place called Whitburn, which the kids actually called Shitburn, and of course it lived up to all our worst expectations, because we were not accepted at all. There was a lot of violence in school, a lot of bullying. The thing about all those villages at the time was they, all of them, had their own gang. And there was a hell of a lot of violence at the time, and all the gangs would deliberately do raids on other villages. It wasn't just the guys either—the girls were as bad. Rather than carry knives or knuckle dusters that the guys used to carry, they used to have a metal comb, a metal handle, which usually came to a sort of a point and they used to file it down to make it super sharp. And that was their weapon of choice. And the girls were just, you know, you just look at them in this, what they were considering, the slightest wrong way, and they were just as bad. And they were always looking for an excuse to find something. So you weren't going to be accepted at school until you had your first fight, and so our oldest sister, she was a tomboy. And she was sort of goaded into picking on this girl to start a fight. And to this day she feels really really bad about it, but it was this kind of do or die, and we are never going to be accepted and we're going to be bullied constantly. And it's the sort of environment where you can't just leave it at school, because it's such a small village. Everywhere you go, if you even tripped up, kicked, or anything else, you're going to have to somehow become part of the gang and be accepted. But in order to do that, we then had to completely deny who we were. So everything that would have gone before, none of that could come into it."

"Mama hadn't quite got the memo. She was wearing her kaftans and black kohl eyeliner and one night she'd gone for a walk and said she was just picking flowers or something, nothing too radical, and the next thing you know, there's this entire rumor going around the village that she was a witch. She was a witch and she was collecting and making potions. This is the mid-1970s. This is where these people were at. I'm not kidding you. So the long and short of it is that basically I got thrown out and I was 15." Juliet then moved from place to place in Bristol and London, and although her father was required to provide child support of five pounds a week, he never did. Though she was supposed to be in school, according to the law, she dropped out and took small jobs to support herself, including work at a bakery, and then at a stationery store that had a record store in the back.

"It was the first time I was able to just think I can make this my own. I was still only 16 or 17 and trying to earn a living, trying to support myself, but I really wanted to finish my education. So I enrolled at Kingsway Princeton College. It was the college that Sid Vicious was at when they were forming the Sex Pistols. So that was the kind of scene that was going on there. Through meeting friends there, I started squatting in North London. I was waitressing at night, trying to do that, but then trying to get up for 9 a.m. lectures after not finishing until one in the morning and being late. I was not doing as well as I should have done. So by starting to squat, I could make less money and still sort of just survive," says Juliet.

She continues, "With a friend in college, we started going around the pub scene quite a lot which was incredibly important. All the bands who became huge, they all had a start in the pub circuit. So we just started doing that quite a lot, just getting into the bands. Back then, bands didn't get paid to perform. They would actually go around with a big pint mug at the end. Technically, my very first job in the industry was, there was a woman who was a big sort of player in that scene at the time, and her name was Penny Jacobsen. She was Swedish and she previously made her money as a porn star in Sweden quite successfully. So she'd be putting on a lot of bands at all these pubs. It was at one of the places I'd go to where most of her bands were that I met her. I just started helping her out a lot. I was just like, 'Do you want me to take a mug around?' And she's like, 'Yeah, sure.' So I kind of started collecting for the bands with a pint mug at the end, and that became a thing. I was doing that more and more and doing more gigs with more shows and was getting involved in the admin and trying to help her book stuff. And because I was squatting, she then had me move into the flat."

Perhaps Jacobsen's porn past is what the notoriously sexist Garry Bushell was referring to when he wrote that "… the radiant (cough) Juliette [sic] De Vie, a refugee from PR-prostitution …" in noting she had joined Trigger to manage the Selecter.[86] Trigger was the music promotion and management company started by Rick Rogers in the late 1970s. Juliet met up with Rogers through her connections in the music scene during this time, as she explains. "Everybody knew everybody. That was back in the Stiff days when Elvis [Costello] was just starting out, Nick Lowe, Lemmy [Ian Kilmister] as well. It was at the Windsor Castle, the Hope and Anchor, the Red Cow—she [Penny Jacobsen] had bands at all of them at different times. Miles Copeland, because their [Stewart and Miles] dad was CIA—they were living in the UK and Miles started this independent label—well, two, actually. One was called Step Forward, which was sort of a punky label, and then there's one called Faulty Products. And so there was a guy called Nick Jones who was doing press for them. I knew Nick and he brought me in to help him with press. So I had my first proper job in terms of working in the indies, and that is working for Miles who, weirdly despite the family reputation, and despite his reputation for being quite difficult and quite loud and quite antagonistic, I just thought he was great because he was this real kind of get-things-done, just get-shit-done king of guy. So he really didn't look after us, actually, but he always, without fail, at the end of the working day, he would take us all out and he would feed us, for the staff meeting. So we would go around the corner, usually to an

---

86 Bushell, Garry. "2-Tone: Ska Authentic And More." *Sounds*. 6 Oct. 1979.

Italan one, and we would eat, so at least you knew you're going to get this one hot meal."

"We were in an office called Dragon Chambers. Miles had his offices there. And, Mark Perry, who started Sniffin' Glue, he had his office there as well, and another agency where John Giddings was one original agents. So lots of little indie music things going on there, and it meant that we were well placed to be in the heart of what was going on. It meant that you had the Roxy, you had the Marquee down the road, you had the Vortex, 100 Club, everything was within a walk. So the reason we would have an eat with the staff was because the rest of the night would be going to the clubs, all of them, because there was always either someone playing or often, at that point, American bands coming over. And so we would do that pretty much till about one, two in the morning. There was the Speakeasy and always around the corner you'd be greeted with Lemmy and later on in the evening, more than once, I'd go from the bar to the loo and be stepping over Sid Vicious slumped on the floor, which was his kind of favorite position. If anyone was playing in town, chances are they'd bump into the Speakeasy later, so you never wanted to not go because there's someone amazing, so then you'd stay there until, god knows, at least three, and then you'd go down Regent Street to a place called Mike's Diner, which was an all-night diner, which was very unusual in London, and you'd go there and have a stomach liner breakfast and you would go back to the office and have a quick kind of hose down in the loo and then go straight back and start working. We didn't do this naturally—it was all done with the aid of a fair amount of speed, at the time, which was how everybody lived. And so you could to that for, three days maybe, and then at some point you'd go back to the office and sleep on the sofa, recharge your batteries a little bit. But there was probably a two-year period where we barely did anything other than shows."

Juliet started promoting the bands that Miles Copeland had on the roster of his two companies. "Faulty Products had Squeeze, and because Stewart was his [Miles] brother, Stewart had this little band called the Police. And so the first review I ever managed to get them was because it was our job to try and get them press. But as it has been said in other places, it was actually very very hard because the Police were not seen as cool at all. Not at all. When they first started, the real punk scene just didn't take them seriously because it was a bit of a joke. They were too old and they had this sort of bottle bleached hair, but it was all sort of too good, almost trying too hard. Sting had been a teacher and they were seen as just old, middle aged, and basically just jumping on the bandwagon. So it was incredibly hard to get any press to take them seriously. And my best memory of that period was that they were playing the Hope and Anchor and we had about four people in the audience, two of which was me and a very good friend of mine at the time. I literally pleaded with him, like my job's on the line, please, please, just come and review this band for me. I know they're really uncool, but please, I just need something. So he did, like a tiny little review. But fortunately, that night was the first time they played 'Roxanne.' He was able to write a review for *Sounds* focused on 'Roxanne' and just pull that out as a standout song. Once they stopped trying to be part of the punk scene and be mainstream, that's when it started to take off. It took a long time to be accepted."

"There were a million other things that happened during that period, and at that point I stopped squatting and I'd got this little council flat in northwest London. And that that point I was sharing it with a guy called Ray Stevenson. He is the guy who pretty much took all those very kind of important photos of the whole punk era. His brother Nils [Stevenson] managed Siousxie and the Banshees and he was involved in the Sex Pistols as well. He [Ray Stevenson] was the connection with the Damned and Rick [Rogers] was managing the Damned. We were all interconnected in that scene, but that's how I got to know Rick. He was starting up publicity and wanted my help. Most of the jobs in the industry back then you kind of just made up. You decided what you're good at and you just made the job up. No one had studied at college to learn it. They got involved because they wanted to. They'd stuck at it, which you had to do because you went through a lot of shit for a long time, and you didn't get paid for a long time, so you had to really want to do it. And through that you got a vast amount of experience that I'm not sure you can ever teach someone. So there are an awful lot of people in the industry with a lot of street smarts and a lot of innate sensibility," says Juliet.

"So I started helping him there and he had an office above, what then became very famous—next door to the Camden tube station there's a shoe shop called Holt's Shoe Shop, which you will have come across in most of the Madness biographies. It features quite largely and turned up in a load of their videos and stuff as well. Holt's was the one place where everybody—all the skins, but also all the people who were getting into other music—went to buy their DMs [Doc Martens] basically. It was a kind of crappy little shoe shop. So his office was above Holt's Shoe Shop. That's how Madness came to be involved in 2 Tone because they would come into Holt's Shoe Shop already as this skinhead band, but just before that all happened, we set up a company that we agreed between us to call it Trigger, and we had both set it up as sort of joint partners in it. And the original artwork for it was actually a woman, because I'm saying to Rick, I'm just fed up with us being anonymous all the time. So actually we agreed it was going to be a woman with a pistol. But we ended up dropping it because we thought it was too specific. Then next door, you had an incredibly important records store at the time called Rock On Records where everybody would go and congregate. And they would go there for all the old American imports that would come in, but also for the new pop records as well. And Camden at that point was a gathering point for skinheads, for the whole music scene. And above that was another independent label called Chiswick Records and they specialized in importing American labels, R&B and stuff, but they were also signing some new stuff, and one crucial new band was the 101ers, and in the 101ers was Joe Strummer. They also signed this punk band called Riff Raff which was Billy's band." Billy was none other than Billy Bragg, Juliet De Valero Wills' life partner, though they didn't meet during this time. "We could have and should have met then and we never crossed paths!" she says.

Trigger started doing publicity for many of the bands on the Chiswick label, as well as Stiff Records, including the Damned. They promoted Toyah Willcox, Wayne County, and then one day, Jerry Dammers and Neol Davies walked through their door. "There were these old rickety stairs and halfway up was a disgusting little bathroom. I was in the loo and I could hear this incredible ska beat coming up from downstairs. … I launched myself down the last couple of stairs and cracked my head on the top of the door frame and landed in the office. That was my introduction to Jerry Dammers, who had come down with Neol to play 'Gangsters.'"[87]

A short time after the Specials enlisted the help of Rick Rogers and Trigger, so too did the Selecter. And booking a 40-date tour, that first 2 Tone Tour, was going to take a lot of expertise and tenacity. "We desperately needed someone to manage us," said Neol Davies, "so I said to the band, 'Let's invite Juliet,' which we did in the dressing room in Brighton on the first night of the tour. It was an obvious thing to do because she'd been involved right from the beginning. She was really clued-up, very young, very competent and a very attractive blonde girl who was really fired up managing a black band with a white guy in it. We didn't have a standard record company acceptably suited manager type, quite the opposite, and I'm proud of that. And Pauline was very comfortable that she had another woman on the road."[88]

Pauline Black agrees that having Juliet to help support the band was invaluable, especially in these early days where there were so many unknowns. "Juliet was very important to us. She was fun and bubbly and seemed very capable. She was doing PR stuff and getting us interviews and it went from there. It was unusual to have a female manager. The tour was like a school outing. It was an old bus that as schoolkids you might have gone to the swimming baths in; you just had a bit more luggage with you and instead of getting in the pool you got on stage and did your thing."[89]

Juliet definitely garnered press right from the start for the Selecter, as well as the whole 2 Tone Tour. These reviews were largely favorable. One reviewer, Giovanni Dadomo of *Sounds*, wrote that he had "three whiskeys" before entering the gig at the Electric Ballroom in Camden and complained throughout the article about the heat in the venue. Of the Selecter he wrote they "… have two all-action vocalists in their all-dancing line-up. One of these wears a Bluebeat hat, mohair jacket and roll-up jeans and introduces the songs in a squeaky oop north accent somewhat reminiscent of the late Clitheroe Kid."[90] Clitheroe Kid was a British comedy sitcom that ran mostly throughout the 1960s and featured the title character, a northern school boy. Clearly, Dadomo missed the fact that Pauline was female. Perhaps this is because she intentionally chose her look to capture more Peter Tosh than sexy posh. He wasn't the only one who took Pauline's androgynous look for male. "A lot of people thought that I was a boy because I wore a pork-pie hat, jacket and trousers. … Wearing dresses

---

[87] Rachel, Daniel. *Walls Come Tumbling Down*. Picador, 2017, p. 249.
[88] Ibid., p. 254-255.
[89] Ibid., p. 255.
[90] Dadomo, Giovanni. "The Specials, Madness, The Selecter: Electric Ballroom, London." *Sounds*. 4 Aug. 1979.

made me feel unpowerful. To go on stage I had to feel powerful. I wasn't the backing singer or one of Bob Marley's I Threes. I made a very conscious decision that I did not want to be like that. … a bit of androgyny never hurt. … Dave Wakeling thought I was a boy when he first saw me."[91] Reviews of their performance, however, were very favorable. "They're infectious ska-based reggae rockers who on present form alone would give any club level outfit a run for your money," wrote one journalist. "There's never been a British band like them."[92]

The tour, as Pauline describes well in her book, was full of cavorting and debauchery. Horace Panter also recalls the wild environment and says, "That first 2 Tone tour was 40 people on one bus for 40 nights. It was like a school trip with no teachers."[93] Neol Davies recalled there were "two thousand people plus, every night. Fire limits obviously being exceeded. Such a thrill."[94] But for Juliet De Valero Wills, organizing all of the publicity and logistics for such a large entourage and ambitious schedule, to say the least, was a massive undertaking. "Organizing the 2 Tone tour was crazy. There was going to be forty-odd people out on the road. I had drafted in my sister Sarah to help out and we stayed up until 2 a.m. stapling and assembling tour itineraries by hand. There were stacks of paper and we had to use the copying shop down the road. This was the night before because the arrangements had been changing constantly and the bands weren't exactly organized or easy to pin down. So, as we were launching off up the motorway, I was completely exhausted, and then seeing everybody not giving a shit about the itineraries and tearing off bottoms to make roaches with, I was like, 'Great. Thanks. Cheers.' But for them it was like a load of kids going on a school outing, all really excited. There was a lot of laughing and joking and a lot of energy. They'd all come from nowhere not long before: shitty jobs living in shitty bedsits, no money, trying to get things off the ground. There was a fabulous sense of unity and starting an adventure. The whole 2 Tone ideal was about to be lived and borne out in these dance halls across the country. I had just a flash of that moment before I went back to being tired and worried."[95]

Pauline Black says that the choice to have Juliet manage the band was a strong decision, even if now, looking back, she realizes that Juliet was young. But they all were. "I feel back in those days, to a certain extent, I wouldn't say we were naïve, but it was definitely a very very steep learning curve. … and she asked, when it looked as though we were going to get signed, whether she could manage us and we thought, yeah, that would be a really good idea. She was only 21 at the time. Now I mean, lots of people might—she had no experience in managing a band, so people would say we were absolutely crazy allowing such a thing to happen. You know, you're supposed to go for much more tried and tested older person, you know, who has experience of

[91] Rachel, Daniel. *Walls Come Tumbling Down*. Picador, 2017, p. 256.
[92] Rambali, Paul. "The Selecter: They Still Bear The Skas." *NME*, 8 Sept. 1979.
[93] Simpson, Dave. "'A blur of legs, arms and adrenaline': the astonishing history of two-tone." *The Guardian*, 30 Apr. 2021.
[94] Ibid.
[95] Rachel, Daniel. *Walls Come Tumbling Down*. Picador, 2017, p. 253-254.

dealing with lawyers and accountants and things like this. But yeah, we just jumped in the boat and said, come on board. That sounds really good. We're all learning, you learn too. So maybe that was slightly insane but it made for some interesting times." In her book, Pauline also says that Juliet provided her with female friendship, as the two were the only women on the bus of 40 men—or at least the only two who were on the bus for the long haul and not temporarily. "The Selecter's manager Juliet De Vie and I were the only women on the 2-Tone bus who were gainfully employed and not giving gratis blow-jobs. The fragrant Juliet was a welcome respite from the sweaty-boy smell that infiltrated the bus after very hot gigs," Pauline states.[96]

In September 1979, Pauline Black resigned as radiographer since she was calling off of work for her tour dates.[97] The shows were incredibly well attended and incredibly well reviewed. "We were playing venues like 1500, 2000 people, I guess, and they'd be absolutely packed out. There'd be sweat dripping off the ceiling, people jumping off balconies. I mean, they were like all kinds of dance halls and there's a whole load of those kinds of clubs that were still around then. It was just absolutely crazy because we'd each go on and do like an hour set, so that was three hours of music that people got to listen to, all high energy. It was just a really really crazy time. The bands, all three bands, had seven people in them, plus all the other roadies and hangers on—they were fairly crazy times and we all traveled in the same bus and it was good," Pauline says.

While Pauline departed her job at the hospital, Juliet departed the tour, though she continued to manage the band. She had to return to the Trigger office to help promote and manage the other bands on the roster of their new startup company. Plus, she had started a relationship with the tour manager, according to Pauline in her book, which was a "definite 'no-no' and undermined her authority."[98] Would a man who committed the same act of forming a lateral long-term relationship, amid a bus full of blow jobs and hotels overflowing with orgies, be subject to the same derision? As Juliet reflects, "I may have been only twenty and appeared to be a 'fluffy bottle-blonde,' but I had a very clear idea of what I wanted to do as a proper manager, but had to square that with all the youthful testosterone unleashed on tour for the first time, with inevitable results. … this was the late seventies and deeply sexist attitudes were the acceptable norm; it was as if the female empowerment of the sixties had never happened. You're on this rollercoaster and you've got to live with these people and you're sharing profoundly formative experiences together. So it gets laughed off. Rock 'n' roll was, and is, a deeply macho culture and universally accepted as a lifestyle. There was no sense of accountability because there was no sense of accountability in wider society towards those attitudes. In the same way as there was casual and institutionalized racism everywhere, there was also casual and institutionalized sexism."[99]

[96] Black, Pauline. *Black by Design*. Serpent's Tail, London, 2012, p. 176.
[97] Goldman, Vivien. "The Selecter: Survival Inna Suburbia." *Melody Maker*. 23 Feb. 1980.
[98] Black, Pauline. *Black by Design*. Serpent's Tail, London, 2012, p. 199.
[99] Rachel, Daniel. *Walls Come Tumbling Down*. Picador, 2017, p. 308.

Despite the inevitable challenges of coordinating 40 twenty-somethings, the tour was a wild success. The press that Juliet secured embraced 2 Tone and the Selecter. Garry Bushell's review of the 2 Tone Tour in October of 1979 claimed "an earthquake is erupting, but not on Orange Street,"[100] which was astute that he had picked up on the Jamaican origins while others did not. He noted that the tour, which had "Dexys Midnight Runners taking over for Madness half way through" since Madness had signed to Stiff, aimed to "keep ticket prices around the two quid mark" so that it was accessible to all people. He also noted that three bands on the 2 Tone label might appear to provide fans with "much too much of a muchness," or the same sound, given that "what they share is a basis in the first original Jamaican music, ska or bluebeat, which developed in the early sixties," but then he captured the distinct angle of each band—The Specials' vocals were a "post-punky whine," Madness was a "distinctly nutty sound and are more humorous," and the Selecter "have Pauline's feminine touch and she and Gaps could well develop into a fine singing duo."[101] Despite not being able to identify Pauline as a woman, Giovanni Dadomo gave a favorable review of all bands—"Five stars each."[102] And Paul Rambali's second review of the tour for *NME* called the Selecter a "bright, alert, untiring pop band" that "tend to understate the intelligence beneath their boppy, poppy surfaces."[103]

What Rambali had caught in this review was at the heart of ska since its origins. The tempo, lively horns, and overall tone of a song could feel celebratory and spirited, but the lyrics or even just the title of an instrumental tune reflected the socio-political struggles of the people seen, heard, and recognized. This was always at the heart of 2 Tone ska as well. "The 2-Tone logo and identity attached to each of our respective singles was like a corporate kinship, a unique vision that people could buy into, not only with the product, but with a dress code and most importantly an ethos, that of unity and harmony between races and between men and women," said Pauline in her book.[104] Or, as she told Daniel Rachel for his book, "Music wasn't worth doing if you weren't dissenting about something. You didn't waste your time doing loads of love songs and crap like that. If you were going to write a song you made it about something."[105]

That "something" that the Selecter and most 2 Tone bands were writing about was race. Political leaders of this time, like Margaret Thatcher and Enoch Powell, had pointed to race as the reason for their society's ills, further inciting the National Front and British Movement. Suggs of Madness reflected, "It was a heavy time. Margaret Thatcher was talking about the demise of 'society' and the white working class were divided between left and right. At some early gigs our audience

[100] Bushell, Garry. "2-Tone: Ska Authentic And More." *Sounds*, 6 Oct. 1979.
[101] Ibid.
[102] Dadomo, Giovanni. "The Specials, Madness, The Selecter: Electric Ballroom, London." *Sounds*, 4 Aug. 1979.
[103] Rambali, Paul. "The Specials, The Selecter: Lyceum, London." *NME*, 15 Dec. 1979.
[104] Black, Pauline. *Black by Design*. Serpent's Tail, London, 2012, p. 174.
[105] Rachel, Daniel. *Walls Come Tumbling Down*. Picador, 2017, p. 236.

were sieg heil-ing."[106] Jerry Dammers, who had the initial vision to make a statement about race with the composition of his band, said, "We would take our anti-racist message to kids who might be vulnerable to the NF [National Front]. A lot of people over the years have told me that they might have become racists if it hadn't been for 2 Tone."[107]

Juliet agrees that this vision was important for music and culture in that pivotal time. "It was like for the first time the black and the white youth had found a language they could talk to each other in. And to see young black and white guys on the stage together was like a little microcosm of what was starting to happen in society. Punk had been very white. And even though the punks latterly started getting into reggae and embracing black music, there was still 'punk bands' and 'reggae bands.' 2 Tone was trying to make a statement about literally mixing black and white cultures and making music out of the two. And if you do that, can you therefore break through deeply rooted cultural racism? It sounds quite grand but in Jerry's mind I think that's what he wanted. All the bands totally believed in that. It was about them thinking, 'If we do this, we're helping ourselves, too.'"[108]

The issue of race was not characteristic of the UK alone. When the Selecter toured the United States in the spring of 1980, the band was met with racist ignorance and violence. "We went to America just 10 years after a black person would be hosed down for sitting at the same lunch counter as a white person. At a photo shoot in Dallas, a flatbed truck came along with white guys on the back with a baseball bat, saying: 'Get those N-words out of here.'"[109] There was also a cultural barrier to receiving the message Pauline sang in their songs. "The vast expanse of 'good ole boy and girl' ten-gallon hat wearers and wet T-shirt bosom jigglers inhabiting the Midwest and beyond thought we were a bunch of aliens that had just landed in their backyards."[110]

The Selecter had gone to the United States to promote their newly recorded album, just after the Specials, the Beat, and Madness had ventured before them. But before they tried to crack that nut, they appeared on *Top of the Pops*, recorded a Peel Session, and entered the studio just after the first 2 Tone Tour, in December 1979 to January 1980, to record an entire album worth of material. "We recorded in Horizon Studios, a converted stables near to Coventry Station. It was demolished in the late 80s and a car park and shopping centre occupy the site these days. The recording sessions were long and quite arduous, using an old style 24 track, 2-inch tape, reel-to-reel system, but the results were well worth it," said Pauline.[111] The album, *Too Much*

[106] Simpson, Dave. "'A blur of legs, arms and adrenaline': the astonishing history of two-tone." *The Guardian*, 30 Apr. 2021.
[107] Ibid.
[108] Rachel, Daniel. *Walls Come Tumbling Down*. Picador, 2017, p. 241.
[109] Simpson, Dave. "'A blur of legs, arms and adrenaline': the astonishing history of two-tone." *The Guardian*, 30 Apr. 2021.
[110] Rachel, Daniel. *Walls Come Tumbling Down*. Picador, 2017, p. 206.
[111] Morgan, Adam. "Interview: Pauline Black of The Selecter." Surviving the Golden Age. 18 Jul. 2019. survivingthegoldenage.com/interview-pauline-black-of-the-selecter. Accessed 24 Oct. 2020.

Pressure, was a mix of original songs, two of which were written by Pauline ("They Make Me Mad," and "Black and Blue"), as well as covers of Jamaican songs. The black and white front of the album "originated from a sketch drawn by Charley Anderson of a man holding his hands to his head against a wall. … 'We had a model to assume the same pose,' Neol remembers, 'but he couldn't get it. So, a friend of ours, Steve 'Cardboard' Eaton, who was with us, said, "Let me have a go,' and that became the famous shot.'"[112] The production was led by Errol Ross, and Rico Rodriguez and Dick Cuthell added their horn arrangements.[113] According to *The 2-Tone Book for Rude Boys*, the album was "rushed, partly because Chrysalis wanted to get some product out as soon as possible to cash in on the waves of publicity," and the members of the Selecter "were disappointed in the final result."[114] If that was the case then, it would be curious to see if that's the case now, because *Too Much Pressure* is the very definition of classic album. The songs capture the zeitgeist of British music subculture, mixing punk, pop, Jamaican ska and rocksteady, race, sex, class, and politics to provide listeners with the feel of all of that. It's a timeless time capsule.

The album garnered good reviews, including one from Garry Bushell who first provided the disclaimer, "I didn't want to give this album five stars, honest I didn't. A nice 3 ½ or 4 would have done. Anything to avoid those eyes and those accusations of 'fawning adulation,'" and although he didn't much care for the cover songs of Jamaican tunes, writing that the Selecter's interpretations "piss all over the original versions," he did enjoy the work of Pauline Black. "The other originals see Pauline emerging as a formidable song writer. Her 'Black And Blue' has a soulful, almost jazzy feel, while 'They Make Me Mad,' co-written with Desmond, features some nice tempo/aggression changes."[115] Vivien Goldman said of the Selecter that they had "something for everyone—a touch of Dread, some equally natty baldheads, a white boy, plus the most militant black woman singer in the land. Their eclectic personnel fuses into a distinct personality."[116] She too was drawn to the two songs penned by Pauline. "The most specific, not to mention the most original element in the Selecter's music is Pauline Black's songwriting … It's such a *relief* to hear Pauline just get mad, and trace the reasons why—the girl who never had the chances, whose friends get nervous as she stops being placid, submissive, eager to please, and sparks start to fly. It's now accepted that white women can display a range of emotions musically; it wasn't, really, pre-'77 or so … to hear Pauline sing 'THEY MAKE ME MAD … I shake my head and frown, I'm getting off my knees, I'm gonna teach myself a new philosophy…' is crucial."[117] The song addressed the sexist lyrics in reggae. No wonder Vivien Goldman gave it a standing ovation—she certainly had to put up with a sexist lyric or two in her many years covering reggae music. Garry

---

[112] The Selecter, *Too Much Pressure deluxe edition*, Chrysalis, liner notes, 2021.
[113] Watts, Peter. "The Selecter." *Uncut: Ultimate Genre Guide*. June 2019, p. 52.
[114] *The 2-Tone Book for Rude Boys*. Music Sales Corp, 1 Jan. 1981, p. 26.
[115] Bushell, Garry. "The Selecter: Too Much Pressure." *Sounds*, 9 Feb 1980.
[116] Goldman, Vivien. "The Selector: [sic] Too Much Pressure. *Melody Maker*, 9 Feb. 1980.
[117] Ibid.

Bushell commented, "… those proud assertive lyrics, such a welcome antidote to the to the standard Rasta attitude to women."[118]

After the album's release on February 8, 1980, the Selecter again hit the road for the second 2 Tone Tour from February 14th through March 20th of 1980. They were accompanied by the Bodysnatchers (see also the Bodysnatchers chapter) as well as the Beat, the latter of which left after forming their own Go Feet label. Their slot was taken up by Holly and the Italians (see also Holly and the Italians chapter) and when they didn't go down well with 2 Tone audiences, they were replaced by the Swinging Cats. Because things were moving fast, things were also always changing. There were 35 dates and the Selecter's album was ranked number five in the charts.[119] When they embarked on that tour of the U.S. in Mary, performing in cities like Los Angeles, New York, Chicago, Dallas, and places in between, 2 Tone ska didn't yet translate for U.S. audiences. Richard Harrington reviewed a performance for the *Washington Post* and explained that ska, an "imported music phenomenon," is "basically a reggae rhythm spruced up with a bigger, heavier beat and played by racially mixed bands. The Selecter is the third major British ska group to tour America (after the Specials and Madness) and for them, rhythm is all. Unlike a mystery, you can walk in late and miss the plot, leave early and miss the denouement and not even attempt to decipher the words. But can you dance to it? (This is, after all, rock's only eternal question.) Yes, you can dance the night away. Selecter is graced by vocalist Pauline Black, who at least convinces one that all ska bands aren't drawn from the same music and dance school. Choreography for a ska band consists of jumping up, down and about, like someone with his shoes tied together trying to get out of a too-tight suit on a trampoline. Wardrobe may be the group's downfall, though. Ska encourages a salut Partiste mentality in which homage becomes imitation. Dancewise, it's no problem, and fans can find plenty of white shirt/narrow black tie variations. But there are precious few pork-pie hats to be had these days. Since fashion competes with rhythm in the group's acceptability, expect Selecter to disappear with autumn's leaves."[120]

When the movie *Dance Craze* was released in the US, it also received strange reviews from confused reviewers. Director Joe Massot filmed numerous UK shows for the 2 Tone film during 1980, including performances by the Specials, Madness, the Bodysnatchers, the Beat, Bad Manners, and the Selecter. It was released in the UK in 1981, and in 1982 in the US. Janet Maslin of the *New York Times* wrote that it was "sloppy but cheerful" and painfully claimed "the English bands featured here owe a lot to reggae—the best-known British band rockers playing anything of this sort are the Police, who do not appear in 'Dance Craze'—but have added a thing or two of their own. Flat tops. Checked jackets. Persistent hopping, preferably from one foot

[118] Bushell, Garry. "The Selecter/The Bodysnatchers: Live Injection." *Sounds*, 1 Mar. 1980.
[119] Ibid.
[120] Harrington, Richard. "The Selecter." *Washington Post*, 23 May 1980.

to the other. An overall spirit of jubilation. … The personnel is racially mixed—which is part of why the music is nicknamed 'two-tone.'"[121]

In the summer of 1980, the Selecter enlisted the help of Roger Lomas to produce the single "The Whisper" with the B side "Train to Skaville." Though their previous work had always charted well, this single did not. Added to this, the members of the Selecter grew frustrated over the lack of voice they had in the direction of the 2 Tone label. When the label started, the agreement was the members of both the Specials and the Selecter were all supposed to be directors, involved together in creative decisions. But that had not come to pass. As a result, the members of the Selecter left 2 Tone in July 1980 and issued the following statement: "2 Tone was intended to be an alternative to the music industry, a label that took risks and, we hope, injected some energy into what had become a stale music scene. The time has come when we want to take risks again."[122]

Pauline states, "We put it to the Specials that perhaps it was best to stop 2 Tone whilst it has 100 per cent success and go on to something different and just use that as an era you can look back upon and expand on those ideas. But they wanted to continue, so we thought we'd leave and progress from there. When it first came out, 2 Tone was basically about black and white people playing together. It had a certain dress-style and a readily identifiable musical style in that the music was dance music. To a large extent, that's still there: the dance music is still being produced. But, as it always does, the media has tended to snatch it up, blow it up out of all proportion, and then straitjacket us."[123] The members of the Selecter decided to create a deal similar to the one that The Specials had created from the start. "The Selecter stayed with Chrysalis but started their own label and distribution—a deal very similar to the one Chrysalis had with 2 Tone—enabling the Selecter to release records by other bands. Unlike 2 Tone, however, it didn't have a name: it was just a logo."[124]

Pauline explains, "The logo was adapted by Jane Hughes, who was at the time the wife of Neol Davies. It was adapted from a government utility sumbol that was used in Britain during the Second World war. It was decided that the logo was a kind of trademark for an 'of the people and for the people' kind of idea. The colors of black, white, and red summed up the racial configuration of the band and the color of our particular brand of politics at the time. We didn't have the chance to sign any other bands to our label because we split up nine months after signing to Chrysalis. We signed to Chrysalis because we felt we were being stifled within the 2 Tone label. It was sad, but it was necessary to gain some independence from the Specials and the original idea of all 14 members of us and the Specials being creative directors behind the label had got lost somewhere along the way. We tried to stay true to the idea, but in the end we were cutting off our noses to spite our faces, as they say."

[121] Maslin, Janet. "Dance Craze." *New York Times*, 25 Apr. 1982.
[122] Rachel, Daniel. *Walls Come Tumbling Down*. Picador, 2017, p. 312.
[123] *The 2-Tone Book for Rude Boys*. Music Sales Corp, 1 Jan. 1981, p. 30.
[124] Ibid. p. 31

But all was not copasetic within the band. Desmond Brown had behaved irrationally since their first tour, and only later would he be diagnosed with a serious mental illness. Until then, however, his aggression and disappearances created discord among members. "It's mainly white people who say, 'I thought you were all about being together and unity,'" said Pauline. "We were continually arguing. The mix of the Selecter was such that all our problems were like a microcosm of society. But I think that's cool. It's how you deal with those arguments. But it's no damn use if people are arguing and being destructive, which went on within the band."[125] As the band manager, Juliet De Valero Wills tried to assist. The week of Christmas, 1980, after three shows supporting Ian Dury, Juliet issued her rules to try to help the band members coexist. It was based upon a Prince Buster song that all of the band knew. "It was shit, so I wrote the 'Alternative Ten Commandments (or) The Selecter Shake-Up Manifesto,' based on Prince Buster's 'Ten Commandments of Man,' which I sent them all in the post in hope that the humour of it might cut through some tension. Commandment Ten was: If you care about THE SELECTER then you must care about each other. The idea was to let everybody simmer down over the holiday, get some rest and hopefully be able to commit to each other and to the venture in general in the new year. It didn't fucking work," Juliet said.[126]

```
                    THE ALTERNATIVE IO COMMANDMENTS  (OR)
                    'THE SELECTER SHAKE UP MANIFESTO'

I.You are seven individuals all with your own individual requirements.
2.You are also seven grown up,supposedly mature and responsible people.
3.This being so,anybody who rightly expects to be accorded the respect and
condsideration of the above,must therefore accept the responsibility and
expectations that come with it.
4.although you are seven individuals,you all have in common the basic human
requirements of food,sleep etc. Now as you all do mostly the same thing at,
the same time it is not unreasonable for you all to be tolerant of each others
needs.Beyond that i.e. relaxation/entertainment.This is also something you
all share as a common need.What you do not all share is in what form you
need it.Consequently,you must accept the individual responsibility of
what you want to do.This also includes the acceptance that no matter what
you do or how late you do it, you will still get up and do what needs doing
the following morning,and not expect others to sit about accomodating your
antics.
```

[125] Rachel, Daniel. *Walls Come Tumbling Down*. Picador, 2017, p. 306.
[126] Ibid., p. 314.

5.As several individuals you make up a whole, creative,working entity.So you all need and are responsible for each other.
DICTIONARY DEFINITION OF GROUP : The combination of several figures or objects to form a single mass.A number of persons or things classed together on account of certain resemblances.To bring together so as to produce a harmonious whole or effect.
6.This basic fact being accepted (and if it isn't you mi.ht as well stop now) it is quite logical and important that everybody,whenever and wherever possible tries to understand more than their own point of viewand is prepared where neccessary to make concessions and compromises for the common good.
7.Which leads to the 'Democracy'.This situation is at present a farce and is currently being abused.The right to have your equal say,is not the same thing as presenting what is at any given time convenient to you persoally.To expect your opion to be heard you must be prepared to participate;to put yourself out and be involved.A Democracy,in your sense is the right to contribute and is not to be used for private retribution.
8.You have the rare oppurtunity of realising your ideas and ideals.But it is not a self generating force,nor manna from Coventry.It relies completely on your accepting it's potential and going all out to fulfill it.
9.Because of your current success ther are new and greater pressures on you. One of which is 'professionalism' (not a dirty word).Professionalism is in fact the only way to cope,combat and alleviate those pressures.Purely because the smoother things are done the less general and personal stress ther is.It is also the only way of retaining let alone developing your current success if you wish to do so.

IO.If you care about 'THE SELECTER' then you must care about each other,because you are 'THE SELECTER' and you rely on each other for that future.

SOME MORE DICTIONARY DEFINITIONS : Band, A uniting influence.A pledge.
Compromise, A settlement by mutual concession.
Adjustment of a controversy or of antagonistic opinions.
Professional,Of or pertaining to a profession
as opposed to amateur.

HAPPY CHRISTMAS
LOVE JULIET XXXXX

P S.ARGUEMENTS BY APPOINTMENT ONLY.

127

---

127 Provided by and used with permission from Juliet De Valero Wills' personal artifacts.

Despite attempts at peace, the band decided to change course with their lineup. "Desmond Brown quit and bassist Charley Anderson was sacked. 'We knew we had the songs to make a really good second album,' said Pauline Black about the sacking, 'and in certain areas the musicianship didn't hold up to exactly what we wanted.'"[128] Anderson and Brown then formed their own group, the People, along with Silverton Hutchinson, which were signed to John Bradbury's Race label. The remaining members of the Selecter also fired Juliet De Valero Wills and opted instead to manage themselves. Pauline states it was a "big mistake. Needless to say, we were not very good at it."[129] They went back into Horizon Studios to record their second album, *Celebrate the Bullet*, with two new members, Adam Williams on bass and James Mackie on keyboards and sax. They wanted to forge a new path for their music while still appealing to their fanbase. Pauline Black changed her look to coincide with the change in sound on the album. "The music had started to change, and I'd started to sing more than in the early days, and I just began feeling different. My hair had started growing, so I thought I'd try wearing a dress and see what happened. And it was all right. It didn't seem to set off any reaction, so I had a go at wearing dresses for a bit. I just felt it was time that you could go out and perform as 'a girl' and be seen as 'a girl,' I suppose," said Pauline.[130]

This album featured a red television on the cover and a red inner sleeve, which coordinated with the red of the Selecter's new logo. It was all a vision of Jane Hughes, Neol Davies' wife, and although Pauline said at the time that red was a reflection of their anger, stating, "We are quite an angry band. I feel all we're doing is reflecting what's going on in society anyway. … The use of the logo, the whole utility thing, is everything being taken down to its barest minimum. We're having to do it, but we're angry about it and wish to do something,"[131] Lyrics of many of the new songs dealt with social issues, political issues, issues of struggle. It was a darker album, not as upbeat in tempo and tone as its predecessor. It was produced by Roger Lomas and although the title of the album made it difficult for success at the time, released on February 6, 1981, two months after the assassination of John Lennon and two months before the assassination attempt of President Ronald Reagan, the album has since aged very well. Pauline wrote of the album, "I think *Celebrate the Bullet* is a forgotten classic of 2-Tone, on par with 'Ghost Town' in terms of orchestration and arrangement, but with a more oblique message. It was an own goal for Neol Davies. Without a hit single, both the British tour and sales of the album were in jeopardy. Neol had told us to prepare for success. Now we silently stared into the abyss while arguably making the best album of our careers. I stand by *Celebrate the Bullet* wholeheartedly. It is a proud album by a proud band. We were rowing against the tide

[128] "Selecter back with a new line-up." *Bracknell Times*, 5 Mar. 1981.
[129] Black, Pauline. *Black by Design*. Serpent's Tail, London, 2012, p. 239.
[130] Steward, Sue and Sheryl Garratt. *Signed Sealed and Delivered: True Life Stories of Women in Pop*. South End Press: Boston, 1984, p. 53.
[131] Hanna, Lynn. "Who Knows the Secret of Black's Magic Pop?" *NME*, 28 Feb. 2021, p. 21.

and ultimately were swamped in the mighty swell of the '80s pop market. There was no place for us in the musical world anymore."[132]

The Selecter split up not long after the album was released and Pauline Black embarked on a solo career, also on the Chrysalis label. She recorded a cover version of Frankie Miller's song, "Shoo Rah, Shoo Rah," which she disliked,[133] but Miller had been an artist also signed to Chrysalis so it was likely a matter of money. Label executives restyled Pauline's appearance yet again. "The record company seemed to feel, 'Well, she's gone solo, we'll make her wear dresses and get some Brian Aris photos done of her.' I was very disoriented at the time about what I wanted to do, and I was getting sucked into something that just wasn't me. I spent another year trying to put it all back together again," Pauline said.[134] She recorded a couple of other singles while turning her talents to theater.

In the summer of 1982, Pauline became a presenter for *Hold Tight*, a kid's TV quiz show, the same summer that she had her solo career.[135] She was 28 years old and was the "first woman regularly to present a nationally-networked quiz."[136] Three months prior she had starred in two plays, *The Trojans* and *Love in Vain* at the Black Theatre Cooperative in London.[137] In November 1983, Pauline became a presenter with Louise Simone Bennett-Coverley, better known as Miss Lou, the Jamaican icon, on the television show *Black on Black* for BBC's Channel 4. Pauline and Miss Lou hosted the live show with guests like Nina Simone, Coretta Scott King, Yellowman, Fela Kuti, Gil Scott Heron, Amazulu, Linton Kwesi Johnson, Miriam Makeba, Aswad, Afrika Bambatta, and others.[138] According to Pauline, when BBC officials decided that "Louise Bennett's style wasn't working for the show," Pauline began as sole presenter.[139] She was sent to America to cover the 1984 Democratic Convention and interviewed Jesse Jackson. Pauline wrote, "He spent most of the interview admiring my legs between questions, even giving my left knee a bit of a squeeze before he left to catch his plane. I have to confess I was smitten. How I wished that I could have become one of his interns on his campaign trail."[140]

That same year, in 1984, Pauline Black joined with Lynval Golding and Neville Staple after Terry Hall left Fun Boy Three.[141] They recorded and released a single as Sunday Best, a group of the three along with Wayne Lothian on bass, Phil Graham on drums, and Jeremy Edwards on guitar and keyboards, the latter of whom

---

[132] Ibid., p. 241.
[133] Steward, Sue and Sheryl Garratt. *Signed Sealed and Delivered: True Life Stories of Women in Pop*. South End Press: Boston, 1984, p. 54.
[134] Ibid.
[135] Black, Pauline. *Black by Design*. Serpent's Tail, London, 2012, p. 267.
[136] "Granada has this one wrong." *Aberdeen Evening Express*, 7 Sept. 1982.
[137] Ibid.
[138] Ibid., P.268
[139] Ibid.
[140] Ibid., p. 273.
[141] Daily Mirror, 31 Mar. 1984.

penned the song.[142] The song, wrote author, historian, and musician Marc Wasserman, was "Pirates of the Airwaves" which "heralded pirate radio stations like Radio Caroline and others that broadcast music illegally from ships moored in international waters outside the U.K."[143] Cue the Toasters a couple of decades later. One reviewer at the time commented, "The respected Ms Black of Selector [sic] fame sounds able as ever on vocals as she fronts for two of the Funboy [sic] Three who've taken yet another turn in their career. It's bright Caribbean fun which may make a slight impression on the chart."[144]

Pauline performed in a number of television and stage productions during the mid-1980s through the 1990s. In 1983 She starred in *Blue Angel* at the Liverpool Playhouse, playing Lola Lola, a character once portrayed by Marlene Dietrich. "Her stage presence is amazing, she really does knock people out with her ability and we didn't think it made any difference to the play her being black, because there were a lot of black entertainers around at that time," said Geraldine Morris who directed the play.[145] In 1988, Pauline played Marsha in Anton Checkov's *Three Sisters* at the Donmar Warehouse,[146] and that same year played Madame Defarge in *A Tale of Two Cities* at Newcastle's Tyne Theatre.[147] The following year she portrayed Billie Holiday at the Tricycle Theatre and reviews were positive, as they typically were of her acting and singing talents. "Pauline Black plays the part of the legendary black singer better than any director could have wished for in his wildest dreams. There are several moments in her performance when she captures the essence of the singer's genius— an extraordinary gift of phrasing which lent depth and feeling to songs that other vocalist have sung sweetly but without feeling. Most remarkable of all is Miss Black's portrayal of the singer's sad demise, as the ravages of drink, narcotics and bad marriages take their toll."[148] In 1990 she acted and sang at the Croydon Warehouse in *Sugar Hill Blues*, a play about New York's jazz scene.[149] Three years later she performed in *From the Mississippi Delta* at the Cochrane Theatre[150] She starred in countless other plays including *The Cape Orchard*,[151] *Love in Vain*,[152] *Wilderness Road* portraying a stripper,[153] *Edward the Second*,[154] *Sitting in Limbo*,[155] and she portrayed Cleopatra.[156] She

---

[142] Wasserman, Marc. "Rare 2-Tone Spin-off." Marco on the Bass, 29 Jan. 2013, marcoonthebass.blogspot.com/2013/01/rare-2-tone-spin-off-pauline-black-with.html.
[143] Ibid.
[144] *Kilmarnock Standard*, 18 May 1984.
[145] Thomas, Angela. "Following in Dietrich's steps." *The Stage*. 1 Sept. 1983.
[146] Chand, Paul. "This sister version sticks close to home." *The Stage*. 25 Feb. 1988.
[147] *Newcastle Journal*. 2 Sept. 1988.
[148] "Thurlbeck, Neville. "Blues out of the ashes." *Harefield Gazette*. 27 Sept. 1989.
[149] Rohumaa, Lisa. "Remaining idol." *The Stage*. 5 Apr. 1990.
[150] Charles, Louise Stafford. "Through life's compelling journey." *The Stage*. 6 May 1993.
[151] *The Stage*, 19 Nov. 1987.
[152] *The Stage*, 29 Apr. 1982.
[153] "Pauline Bares All!" *Daily Record*. 18 Aug. 1986.
[154] *The Stage*, 23 May 1996.
[155] Forsberg, Bob. "No holds barred in women's jail drama." *Pinner Observer*, 23 Apr. 1998.
[156] *Observer*, 4 May 1989, p. 15.

also acted on television, starring in a series called *Shrinks*, playing the part of Leixi.[157] She hosted a number of shows on music and race as well.

But Pauline always continued her involvement in music, whether it was singing in plays, or on other stages. In 1986, Pauline supported Coventry's SportAid event along with Jerry Dammers and other musicians. This was a "fun run" that supported the Coventry Youth Council.[158] And in in 1988 she performed with dozens of other notable musicians, including Miriam Makeba and Hugh Masakela, Jerry Dammers, Sting, and Whitney Houston, for the Nelson Mandela 70th Birthday Concert at Wembley Stadium, the now-legendary anti-Apartheid event that raised the world's consciousness to the plight of black South Africans and put pressure on the South African government to free Nelson Mandela.[159]

Throughout 1986, while still continuing her theater work, Pauline formed her new band, the Supernatrals (yes, that is the proper spelling!) and supported the Communards on tour. The band included Pauline on vocals, John Shipley of the Swinging Cats and the Special AKA on guitar, and on drums was Everett Morton, formerly of the Beat, among others. But the group had difficultly landing a recording contract. Then the relationship between Pauline and Shipley took a turn. As Tony White, who performed guitar with the band for a period of time, explains they "fell out, everybody took sides and it got a tad nasty."[160] As a result, the band split. At the time, White said, "The split was very amicable. There was a personality clash between Pauline and the rest of the band. The tour was a success and we were all very happy with the music. But our living conditions were very cramped and tempers frayed. When we got back we had a meeting and decided we would be better off with a new singer. At the end of the tour Pauline had said she was leaving anyway. She put a hell of a lot of work into the band and was a talented lyricist. We are keeping the name and the music. We have already played one show in Manchester without Pauline. John Shipley and I shared the vocals but we will be recruiting a new singer in the coming weeks. This is a setback for us. We had record company interest but we can bounce back."[161]

Pauline next stood in for Sarah Jane Morris with the Communards for a few performances, and the rest of the Supernatrals reformed with Valerie Webb who had been vocalist in the Swinging Cats (see also the Swinging Cats chapter).[162] "We only did a few gigs," said Valerie Webb, "but they were well received. John wrote some excellent stuff for the band. I sent a cassette to Trev Teasdel, which he managed by magic, to transfer onto a CD. Unmistakable Shipley wonder stuff. They are, in fact,

---

[157] *Evening Herald (Dublin)*. 13 Jan. 1993.

[158] "Fun run backed by a bevy of pop stars." *Evening Telegraph*, 17 May 1986.

[159] *Aberdeen Evening Express*, 11 Jun. 1988.

[160] "The Supernatrals." Hobo—A to Z of Coventry Bands. sites.google.com/site/bandsfromcoventry/coventry-bands-a-to-z/coventry-bands-s/the-supernaturals. Accessed 15 Nov. 2022.

[161] Taylor, Jim. "Pauline quits—and spots a vacancy." *Evening Telegraph*, 3 Jan. 1987.

[162] "The Supernatrals." Hobo—A to Z of Coventry Bands. sites.google.com/site/bandsfromcoventry/coventry-bands-a-to-z/coventry-bands-s/the-supernaturals. Accessed 15 Nov. 2022.

my proudest moments."[163] The group had to rename themselves after a dispute with Pauline over the band's material and brand. "Guitarist John Shipley claims he wrote songs like 'Happy End' virtually single-handed, and wants to record them with other former members as the Unnatrals. 'John wrote the material and we all had a hand in arranging it, says fellow Unnatral Robin Hill. 'Pauline just stood at the front and sang.' But Pauline has hit back at the band's 'hands off our songs' message by saying: 'As far as I'm concerned, I wrote half of them, just as much as John Shipley wrote half.'"[164] The name of that band, the Unnatrals, then changed again to the Great Escape, but they too split for good later that year.[165]

In 1991, the Selecter reformed with Pauline Black and Neol Davies, along with Nick Welsh and Martin Stewart of Bad Manners.[166] One article stated that they were "taking up where they left off."[167] "The duo who were one of the prominent bands of the SKA era … are enticing skinheads with Sta-Prest trousers and shiny braces out of the woodwork. Pauline, who hasn't aged a day they say, is full of her legendary energy and it looks like SKA music is still as popular as ever. Said Pauline at one of her recent gigs, 'It's been a long time.'"[168] In 1993, Neol Davies left the group over differences with Pauline and in 2011, Pauline won the legal rights to continue to use the name the Selecter after Davies continued to use the name for his version which toured at the same time. "We're in the music business, and the Selecter is a name, a recognisable name from over 30 years ago. From that point of view, it had never been trademarked and I felt it was necessary to do that," stated Pauline.[169] The Selecter with Pauline and Gaps back in the position of united vocals, continued to perform.

"And then in 1993 we took part in the Skavoovie Tour," said Pauline, "which was the Skatalites and the Special Beat, which was an amalgamation of some of the members of the Beat and some of the members of the Specials and sundry other people. And we would alternate the bill. Some nights we'd headline, some nights Special Beat would headline, some nights the Skatalites would headline. I think pretty much the Skatalites were still intact. Roland [Alphonso] was still there, but he had a stroke by that time too and he wasn't too well. That was the first time I had seen the Skatalites play and it was the first time I'd ever met Prince Buster. It was overwhelming." The Selecter recorded *The Happy Album* in 1994, *Pucker* which was released outside the UK as *Hairspray* in 1995, *Cruel Britannia* in 1998, *The Trojan*

---

[163] Clemons Pete. "From the Albert Hall to the Snooker Hall." Coventry Music Articles. 28 May 2020. coventrygigs.blogspot.com/2020/05/from-albert-hall-to-nothing-at-all.html. Accessed 14 Nov. 2022.
[164] "Discord in battle of songs." *Coventry Evening Telegraph*, 10 Jan. 1987.
[165] "The Supernatrals." Hobo—A to Z of Coventry Bands. sites.google.com/site/bandsfromcoventry/coventry-bands-a-to-z/coventry-bands-s/the-supernaturals. Accessed 15 Nov. 2022.
[166] Black, Pauline. *Black by Design*. Serpent's Tail, London, 2012, p. 310.
[167] "The Selecter blasts from the past." *Evening Herald (Dublin)*. 25 Apr. 1992.
[168] Ibid.
[169] "The Selecter: Pauline Black Interview." Female First. 15 Aug. 2011. femalefirst.co.uk/music/interviews/Pauline+Black+interview-97747.html. Accessed 15 Nov. 2022.

Songbook in 1999, *Kingston Affair* in 2000, *String Theory* in 2013, *Subculture* in 2015, *Daylight* in 2017, and numerous live albums, acoustic albums, and compilations.

Pauline also formed the group 3 Men + Black comprised of JJ Brunel of the Stranglers, Nick Welsh of Bad Manners, and Jake Burns of Stiff Little Fingers. The lineup also included others from time to time and they toured each year since 2001 for a few years.[170] Pauline worked with numerous musicians including Geno Washington, the Ram Jam Band, and Eddie Floyd.[171] She has recorded the Amy Winehouse song, "Back to Black," prior to Winehouse's death as "a little doff of the hat back towards her and saying I think you are a great songwriter too,"[172] and she performed with Gorillaz on their Humanz tour. Pauline Black was appointed as a Deputy Lieutenant of the West Midlands in May 2022 and she was appointed Officer of the Order of the British Empire (OBE) in the 2022 New Year Honours for services to entertainment. She wrote her memoir, *Black by Design*, in 2012.

Being so successful, so experienced and versatile hasn't been easy for Pauline. "Ska music wasn't necessarily known for bringing its ladies to the fore. As a woman, it's a different fight to get yourself heard, and it still is," she said in an interview with Rhoda Dakar in 2021.[173] When asked if, after all of her experience, she has seen access and opportunity for women expand over the years, she responds, "There's still a huge amount of work to be done in order to effectively break down the traditional gender stereotypes, but I see some progress being made. I hugely respect the new DIY ethic among young female bands … if the boys won't let you join in their game, then sometimes it's best to invent a new one of your own."[174]

And this is precisely why Pauline Black deserves to be called the Queen of Ska, and deserves to be recognized with her contributions to her country, and deserves to reign in the spotlight—to show girls, women, people of color that there is space for them. If Jerry Dammers made 2 Tone about racial equality, Pauline Black also made it about gender equality. She has retained her crown, still standing some five decades later while countless others have left the stage.

---

[170] "Black to the days of 2 Tone." artists2events.co.uk/artists/Black_to_the_days_of_2Tone.htm. Accessed 15 Nov. 2022.

[171] Ibid.

[172] "The Selecter: Pauline Black Interview." *Australian Musician Magazine*. 23 Nov. 2015. australianmusician.com.au/the-selecter-pauline-black-interview. Accessed 24 Oct. 2020.

[173] Interview with Rhoda Dakar. "Pork Pie and Mash Up." Podcast, 5 Apr. 2021.

[174] "If ever a message of unity was required in the world, that time is now." Band on the Wall. 5 Sept. 2017. bandonthewall.org/2017/09/interview-with-pauline-black. Accessed 24 Oct. 2020.

Juliet De Valero Wills with husband Billy
Bragg (left) and with Rick Rogers (right)

Pauline Black (left), Julie De Valero Wills (center), and Rhoda Dakar (right)

Pauline Black, photo by Heather Augustyn, Riot Fest, Chicago, 2013

Pauline Black having received her
OBE (left) and on the set of Black
on Black (right)

The Bodysnatchers

Stella Barker: guitar
Rhoda Dakar: vocals
Miranda Joyce: saxophone
Penny Leyton: keyboard

Sarah-Jane Owen: guitar
Nicky Summers: bass
Jane Summers: drums
Judy Parsons: drum

On May 26, 1979, Nicky Summers, a fruit and vegetable vendor at the Rupert Street market in Soho in London, placed an advertisement in the *New Musical Express* that would change her life. The four small lines of ink on newsprint would also undeniably change the lives of six other young girls at the turn of the decade, as well as countless others on the receiving end of their energy and talent for decades to come.

Growing up as an admittedly "bored" teenager, Nicky was eager for excitement and a creative outlet. "The 70s, I remember, were a dark period musically and culturally," Nicky recalls.[175] "I felt I was desperate for something incredible to happen and in early '76 you could almost sense it in the air, the restlessness of a generation." That inexplicable something that Nicky sensed in the air was the collective spirit that brought together politics, race, gender, art, culture, and yes, music. It was a comingling of people in urban centers where reggae and punk amplified and charged the atmosphere.

"I got into punk by accident in the autumn of 1976. The Sex Pistols had appeared on the Bill Grundy TV show. I didn't watch it as I wasn't into Bill Grundy, but the next day it made front page news and people were talking about it at school. Coming home from school, people in the street were calling me a 'punk' due to my dress sense and the way I had 'doctored' my school uniform in general. I had my hair in a crew cut, cut by a Soho barber, a knife-pleat skirt and plastic sandals. I think I was around 17. So as I was being referred to as a 'punk' in the street, I decided to check out some of the band, thinking the whole scene might be something I might be into," she says.

It is almost impossible to convey today the intensity of the punk movement in the late 1970s. As one writer put it, "Punk does look a little different through a 2022 lens."[176] The history and complexity of what led to the punk era is best left to other analyses, conversations, and books. Suffice to say that for Nicky Summers, an immersion into the culture that produced such a movement was deeply felt, and much more than a mere expression of fashion. Nicky Summers was the embodiment of

---

[175] Summers, Nicky. All quotations, unless otherwise noted, from "The Bodysnatchers Early Days and Anecdotes by Nicky Summers." nickysummersthebodysnatchers.blogspot.com. Accessed 23 June 2022. Used with permission.

[176] Rappaport, Sarah. "The Sex Pistols Are Back With a Disney Vision of Punk," *Bloomberg*. 25 May 2022, bloomberg.com/news/articles/2022-05-25/disney-hulu-pistol-review-sex-pistols-return-with-danny-boyle-vision-of-punk. Accessed 28 June 2022.

punk. She was young and working class, she was DIY, and she was obsessed with music.

Nicky says, "The thing about punk is that it gave a sense of empowerment to a young generation initially through music and subsequently art, fashion, film, etc. Punk opened the doors for the future and the next decade. It kicked out the stale, dead stuff that had to go. …The list of bands I saw in punk days is endless. … I remember the first band I saw was the Damned (late '76), can't remember where, and I also went to the Roxy club a few times. I had the great opportunity to see many bands including the Clash (several times), Damned, Buzzcocks, Subway Sect, John Cooper Clarke, X Ray Spex, Penetration, the Jam, and the Slits." Seeing an all-female band like the Slits certainly made an impression on Nicky who, for the first time, realized that women could have space in this movement at the intersection of music and identity. "I saw the Slits 2 or 3 times and found them really inspiring as they were female and challenged the general ethos of what being in a band and making music was about and for me, being a female member of the audience, it was a different thing watching them than a male band," she says.

Nicky assembled her first group of musicians after purchasing a guitar and teaching herself to play. "Around this time [late 78/early 79] I purchased my first bass guitar. I chose bass because though I wanted to make music as part of a group I had no desire to be centre stage, so I thought bass guitar would suffice. I was also intrigued by melodic bass lines and inspired by reggae bass rhythms. The first one I bought randomly while passing a guitar shop on Shaftsbury Avenue. I picked one off the wall, couldn't play it and asked the guy behind the counter to play it for me. It sounded ok so I bought it. 30 quid. I rehearsed with a punk outfit but we had never gigged," she says. Motivated by the Slits, Nicky sought to form an all-female band of her own. "I was looking to put an all girl group together. I was inspired by punk, reggae/dub, Motown, Bluebeat, 1950s RnB, and Stax-60s girl groups and singers such as Aretha Franklin and Nina Simone, but it was quite difficult to get together."

The musical sounds that influenced Nicky also included David Bowie, Lou Reed, The Rolling Stones, Marc Bolan, as well as those she heard in Soho while working in the market. "I was listening to reggae more at this time, mainly dub such as Joe Gibbs' 'Majestic Dub' and 'African Dub,' U Roy, Augustus Pablo, and slower paced rocksteady as well as some early bluebeat and ska such as Don Drummond who I believe was way ahead of his time. I worked in Rupert St. market in Soho and opposite was a record shop, now defunct, known as Cheapo Cheapo records that was filled with albums passed on by the nearby record companies and music journalists. The owner Phil would let me 'borrow' records, listen to them and if I didn't like them I could return them to him. I was able to be exposed to a lot of music this way and heard some rare sounds and short-lived bands who never made the mainstream," says Nicky.

In the course of her musical consumption, Nicky came across a band that had just formed—the Specials. She saw them perform, not as the Specials, but as the Special AKA the Automatics whilst supporting the Clash on their On Parole Tour in

1978.[177] She wasn't overly impressed at the time and says she thought they were "interesting" and "a bit art school to be honest," but a year and some change later, during a show at the Hope and Anchor, Nicky says they made quite an impression on her. "…my friends and I went to check them out and they had really transformed into an amazing live band—blew themselves off stage really … Apart from their music and animated performance, I was also inspired by the ethos and ideas behind the Specials with relation to both black and white musicians and artists working together. I saw this as a positive direction forward both musically and socially."

So Nicky began to assemble a band of her own—one that brought together the ethos and energy of the Specials, the confidence and liberation of the Slits, and the musical cultivation that was solely Nicky Summers. "I had been wanting to be involved with music since I was about 13 but frankly had no idea how to go about it. … I met up with Jane Summers (no relation) who played drums and had come up to London from Portsmouth to join a band. I met her on the platform of Highbury and Islington tube and she was wearing a fake leopard skin coat and bright red lips and looked like a young Shirley MacLaine. She moved in and slept on my floor with her drum kit and stash of *NME*s and the rest of the Bodysnatchers came together in late summer 79." Nicky herself filled the position of bass guitarist and she now had a drummer, and it was through that aforementioned advertisement that she recruited the remaining musicians. "I did place a few ads in the music press for band members, (as my girlfriends at the time didn't seem to get it together to come to rehearsals or find instruments to play) in the *NME* and *Sounds* (not *Melody Maker* which in those days was for old fogeys and was anti punk). My criteria to join the band seemed to be that you turned up regularly to rehearse with a musical instrument." Nicky also told music journalist Adrian Thrills that the advertisement was slow to recruit women who were genuinely interested in the opportunity. The ad "brought only three months of dirty phone calls," stated Thrills, an ironic testament to the need for such a band.[178] The full advertisement from the *NME*, May 26, 1979 read: "RUDE GIRL types (guitar(s) with noisy vocals, drums) sought by similar bassist (rudimentary but improving) Ska, rock, reggae, early punk ideas for fast, emotive, danceable stuff. Sharp Brains. Around 20 years. 01-886 9775 (Nicola)."

One of those women responding to the advertisement was Sarah-Jane Owen who was employed in the fashion industry at the time. "I was dating a musician and he was in a band that was kind of quite controversial, I suppose, and I was very impressed with what he was doing and he knew I played guitar and he had a newspaper that he would subscribe to called *New Music Express*. And they had an ad in the classified section that said, 'girl guitarist wanted for all-girl dance and beat band.'"[179]

[177] Weir, Jason and Peter Walsh. "The Specials." 2-tone.info/the-specials/. Accessed 28 June 2022.

[178] Thrills, Adrian. "Rude Girls and Dirty Phone Calls." *NME*. 26 Jan. 1980.

[179] Owen, Sarah-Jane. All quotations, unless otherwise noted, from interview with the author. 4 June 2020.

Sarah-Jane had grown up in Southsea, Portsmouth in Hampshire and says she grew up in a household that embraced music. "I was into music, I suppose, from a young age. It was definitely encouraged in our family. Our family was quite musical. Both of my parents played the piano and both of them could whistle a tune and sing really well and so music was definitely something that was around. I was so inspired by Bob Dylan and Joni Mitchell, artists that were activists—Joan Baez, people like this. I was so inspired by them that I wanted to get a guitar for my 12th birthday so that's how I became interested in the guitar, but at that point it was kind of folk music and activist songs and Leonard Cohen and that sort of thing. So I started off playing in a folk club with a friend called Tessa," Sarah-Jane says. Over the next few years she would learn to play her instrument through watching others and through friends who expanded her musical horizons and exposed her to further musical genres, including reggae. "For my senior thesis at school, I wrote on Rasta roots and reggae. I still have it! So clearly I was into how music played a role in religion in the Rastafarian tradition. And of course, ska is from the same island, so in truth I was already interested. It's like I was destined to go that route."

Though Sarah-Jane continued to play guitar when she went to college, she went to study art rather than music, and her two interests would soon dovetail. "I very much had to put my guitar to one side and concentrate on my studies," she says. "So it kind of collected dust for a little while. I studied art and fashion design at my first school and I got a B.A. there and it was suggested to me by a professor at that college, which is now Portsmouth University, that I should apply for the Royal College of Art in London. I did and was able to get in. It was very fierce. It was a three day interview to get into that college and I was a country bumpkin and a lot of the people that were applying were already at colleges in the London area, so it's a very prestigious college. [David] Hockney went there and other various people. I had no idea at the time just what the wonderful ramifications were for attending a college like that, but that's where I did my master's degree. It would behoove me in my later years because I was able to teach with a master's and of course I did that, in between and after and before I was in all these musical groups." At first, Sarah-Jane's family wasn't so sure about the idea of her being in a band, especially since she had been pursuing a different path in life. "I was teaching at three schools, and of course, mother was just mortified. I was the black sheep. I was going to get into sex, drugs, and rock and roll. So that was a bone of contention, but it was a choice I had to make," she says.

While Sarah-Jane Owen joined the Bodysnatchers as lead guitarist, Stella Barker joined as rhythm guitarist when she too saw that advertisement placed by Nicky Summers in the spring of 1979. Stella, also a self-taught musician, came to the band through a rather circuitous route. She explains, "I grew up in a very rural situation. My family are agricultural farmers in Yorkshire, so I had a very idyllic childhood, I would say—outdoors, climbing trees, and riding ponies until I was sent to boarding school when I was 10, which was a bit of a shock to the system. But actually, even though I was kind of homesick at first. It was a convent boarding school, so in the 60s, life was quite strict at school, but I also think it was very good for me because I forged some great friendships there and I learned to stand on my own feet and not have my mom hovering around all the time, kind of making sure I was okay. So I feel that in the long run it was a very good experience for me to have had that sort of education."[180]

Stella gained a music education in much the same way as Sarah-Jane—through her love of folk music rather than music in her home. "I didn't come from a musical family, although my mum played piano by ear. She couldn't read a note of music but she was very gifted. She could hear a tune once and then play the whole thing, the left and right hand as well. It was quite a gift—not one I inherited, unfortunately. But I was always intensely interested in music. From a very young age, I loved the Beatles, I loved the Stones, and I saved up to buy 45 singles and what have you. And then going on to boarding school, me and my friends at school were very into music and we had a record player in the common room and music was very very much—I guess it was our life, really, because we didn't have anything else. We didn't have boys, we didn't go out, we didn't have any fun, so we loved our music. When I was 14, and I don't really know why this happened, but probably because I loved music and was listening to Joni Mitchell and other female musicians—I got an acoustic guitar. I can't remember how I acquired it or if my dad bought it for me or whatever, but I taught myself to play guitar. I got a guitar book and learned to play Simon and Garfunkel songs and Bob Dylan songs and I just taught myself to play, in my bedroom. And I strummed away," Stella says.

After boarding school, Stella went to university and like Sarah-Jane, the guitar was set down for a period of time. "Life went on," she says. "I went to university in Edinburgh. I studied French and Spanish. I was always strong at languages, so that's what I did there. I wouldn't say they were the happiest years of my life, my university time, but I think it was just the age I was and struggling to find my own identity. I had weight issues—all that sort of awful stuff in one's late teens, early twenties. But I did continue to listen to music. I went to some gigs but not that many. I didn't really know anybody that was going to gigs, particularly, so in my university years I would say I was more sporty than getting involved in the music scene. When I graduated from there, I went to Cambridge to do a bilingual secretarial course, not at the university, but at the technical college which happened to be in Cambridge."

She continues, "There I got together with a very good school friend of mine who was in her last year at Cambridge Uni, and so we met up and she said, 'Come, come with me, I'm going to see a band tonight,' and that was it. As soon as I saw this band on stage, I just thought, 'This is fantastic! This is me—this environment.' It was like a lightbulb moment. It was a local band called the Soft Boys. They were very cult. They were one of my favorite bands. It was their music, it was going to see them in a small venue, John's College Cellars, and the atmosphere—I just felt elated. I felt high

---

[180] Barker, Stella. All quotations, unless otherwise noted, from interview with the author, 27 Oct. 2020.

in that environment. So I continued to go and see them and other local bands and got to know them and got to know people who were friends with them and that became sort of my entourage. And then my friend Beverly, who was in her last year at Cambridge, a friend of ours said, 'Oh, do you two want to do backing vocals in our band?' So that's what we started doing in this very local band. We just played a few gigs at Cambridge and we did backing vocals, Beverly and I, so that was my first experience on stage. Archie Pelago and the Kamikaze Surfers. That was it. No looking back."

Although she had found the calling of her heart in music performance, Stella still proceeded with the plans she had set out for her career. She graduated from her secretarial course and began working in an antiquarian book shop. Not surprisingly, she found this work unfulfilling. "This same friend of mine that I had gone to school with, we were sitting in the pub one night and she had just graduated. I was not really thrilled with what I was doing and so we just decided we would go to America!" she says, laughing at the impulsivity of her decision. "We decided we would go to San Francisco because at the time, my sister was living there. So we thought, at least when we get there we'll have someone we know. We wanted to go and just see what happened, so we went. Who knows how much money I had in my pocket, not a lot, but we flew to New York and we got the Greyhound bus all the way across the states. I was 23. A crazy baby. Another school friend, she heard that we were going and she said, 'Can I come with you?' So there were three of us."

The late 1970s in San Francisco was a prime time for the birth of punk music. Stella found herself in the middle of the nebula. "I was going to see lots of punk bands. The Mabuhay was run by a guy named Dirk Dirksen and I saw bands like Devo there and the Dead Kennedys, the Talking Heads, Blondie, so some great gigs." When Stella returned to the UK after one year in San Francisco, she definitely did not want to return to a life of dusty books and she instead pursued her passion—music. "I thought, I need to go to London if I want to be involved in music. I didn't at that point know that I wanted to be in a band, but I knew I wanted to be involved in music. So I moved then to London and I managed to get a job at EMI Records. Those were the days when you could go into the phone directory and look up record companies and ring the HR department and say, 'Have you got any jobs going?' And I just happened to be ringing EMI at the right time and they said the international guy is looking for a P.A. [personal assistant] and that was very interesting," says Stella who secured the position.

At EMI, Stella was exposed to all sorts of musicians who were just beginning their careers, including one incredibly influential woman. "I learned about the business and it was a very exciting time because Kate Bush was the big signing there and she was just embarking on her *Wuthering Heights* tour and so I saw dress rehearsals and things. Imagine me, looking at women making music! I mean she was just absolutely phenomenal!" Stella says.

Although supporting musicians in the promotion of their work was a bit more exciting than dealing in old books, after a year and a half at EMI, Stella became restless. "I just felt that the artists are having a much better time than me, stuck in this office, and I actually left the job without any plan and I thought vaguely of going back to San Francisco but I had no plan. So I was flipping through the *Melody Maker* one day, looking at the ads, and there I spotted an ad. Nicky, the bass player, had put in an ad saying she was looking for female musicians to form a ska/bluebeat band. Reggae was not in my sphere at that point, but definitely ska and bluebeat, and I thought, well, I can probably play on the offbeat," she says, laughing.

The audition to be part of the band wasn't anything formal by a long shot. Stella says, "It was not a proper audition, no. I had this chat with Nicky on the phone and she said, 'Come down and meet at such-and-such a pub at 7:30 or whatever and I turned up at this pub and there's Nicky there and Jane, the first drummer before Judy. So we got drinks and this was back in the day when you could smoke in pubs and we were smoking away and just chatting and so at the end of a drink or two she said, 'So do you want to join the band then?' I didn't even take my guitar, but I said, 'Well, do you want to hear me play?' and she said, 'No, you sound like you've played a bit,' because I did play a little bit of guitar in that same Cambridge band. When I came back from San Francisco, the guy who had recruited me and Beverly to do backing vocals, he said, 'I know you do acoustic guitar—why don't you go electric?' And I did have an electric guitar by then, but when I say a little bit—it was like four chords."

Penny Leyton also saw that advertisement for "rude girl types," though she says it took her three times to get up enough nerve to respond. Growing up playing the piano as well as a multitude of other instruments provided Penny with the talent for performing, but still she had apprehension, as she explains. "I grew up near Oxford in England and my grandfather was a singer—not that any of us inherited his voice. We all played the piano from like about the age of eight or nine. And then I played the cello. I always wanted to be in a band. But this is the kind of world it was back then—I had a friend who was a bass player in a band, and I asked him to teach me how to play the bass and he said women don't play the bass. So that was like, you know, a challenge to me, to play the bass. As soon as someone tells me I can't do something, it makes me want to do it even more."[181]

Penny did learn to play the bass but the Bodysnatchers already had their bass player, Nicky Summers. Instead, Penny would join as the Bodysnatchers keyboardist. She says, "When I left art college in Canterbury, I moved to London and continued to do art courses at St Martin's college of art. That's where I saw the advert for the Bodysnatchers. I saw it three times before I had the courage to answer it. It was on the notice board at St. Martin's College of Art because Sarah-Jane taught there and had put the little advert up on the notice board saying they wanted a keyboard player. They also put a notice in Rough Trade records in Notting Hill, which was a record shop that kind of like, had alternative music. I never played an electric instrument in my life. I just played the piano for years. So I went to the audition. And they had a

---

[181] Leyton, Penny. Interview with the author, 20 Dec. 2020.

piano in the practice room where they were. And I just played and they could obviously see I could play piano so they said, 'Yeah,' without actually playing any of the music that they played."

Fortunately, Penny was familiar with ska music and considered herself a fan. "When I was at Canterbury, the Specials came to play there. For me, it was just like, wow, just like an awakening—like, what is this music? I love this music. And I'd always liked ska music, because in the '70s it was kind of a ska thing. I knew that I really liked it. I mean, my parents listened to classical music. But sometimes we have a love of music that is not something we grew up with and we just hear it and it's like, that's the music for me."

Miranda Joyce joined as the Bodysnatchers' saxophonist when the group recognized the need for horns. Sarah-Jane Owen recalls, "We knew we needed horns and so gradually and slowly we managed to procure Miranda because there was a band rehearsing next door that heard us and knew we were looking for other players. And I think it was Miranda's brother said, 'My sister might be interested. She's about to go to art school.' So she came in and she said, 'What instrument do you need?' and we said, 'Well we need sax,' and she said, 'Well I don't play it yet, but I'll see what I can do.' And literally she went away and she came back I think three or four weeks later with a Salvation Army saxophone that she got and she was able to play them the tune to Hawaii Five-0—roughly, you know what I mean."

Stella Barker recalls how Miranda joined the band too. "I found Miranda," she says. "I remember her [Nicky] saying to me, 'I'm looking for a sax player—do you know anybody?' and I knew of somebody in Hampstead, but I hadn't ever met her. A friend of mine, I said, 'Oh, I'm joining this ska band and we're looking for a sax player,' and he said, 'Oh I know somebody, Miranda—she's in Hampstead, but she's still at school.' I think she was 16 at the time, nearly 17. So I must have rung her up and said, 'Do you want to come to this rehearsal, this audition?' And I think she could play one song and that was Hawaii Five-0."

"Now we've got most of the band," said Sarah-Jane. "We had Miranda, we had Penny, we had Jane on drums, Stella and me on guitars, and then Nicky on bass—now we were looking for a front person. So Nicky, ever the leader again, says, 'Why don't we go down to the Camden Palace and see what music scene is happening down there?' So we all went as a group." Camden Palace was a live music venue in London which featured bands like the Clash and the Jam. It was a place to see and be seen. "The world's media and photographers learned this was the fashionable place to find the next big thing," said one writer of the iconic venue.[182] "There on the dancefloor" recalls Sarah-Jane, "was this very tall mulatto girl with a beehive who was really dancing up a storm, and that would be Rhoda and the story goes something like this—Nicky goes right up to her and says, 'Can you sing?' Rhoda turns around and says to

[182] "1982: Strange takes UK clubbing mainstream." Shapers of the 80s. 22 Apr. 2022. shapersofthe80s.com/2022/ 04/22/1982-%e2%9e%a4-strange-takes-uk-clubbing-mainstream. Accessed 30 June 2022.

her, 'Yeah, what's it to you?' And so that's how that happened. It's classic! Classic! So we then procure Rhoda who can dance and sing and now we've got a front person and that's how it began."

Nicky Summers remembers seeing Rhoda at a different venue and recalls a different encounter. "Rhoda was the last to join us. I met her at a gig in Fulham and I was intrigued by her (and beehive!) and asked mutual friend Shane MacGowan to introduce us," says Nicky who had known MacGowan, later of Pogues fame, from the Soho Market where he worked at a record stall. Nicky and Shane MacGowan were part of a group of friends who met up after work for drinks and to attend gigs. Whichever venue, and whichever encounter, the Bodysnatchers had found their charismatic frontwoman, Rhoda Dakar.

Rhoda E. Evans de Dakar was born in London and grew up in Brixton, though her roots are in Jamaica and Panama. She explains, "Well, my dad was born in Panama, not Jamaica. He was born in Monkey Hill, which is now part of Colon, because my granddad was working on the Panama Canal, as lots of Jamaicans do. So lots of Jamaicans went to Panama and worked on the Panama Canal. So my dad, and I think maybe eight of his siblings, were born in Colon and one uncle was born in Jamaica. And there was one who was adopted and I don't know where he was born."[183]

Rhoda's father was a tremendous influence on her growth in music as he himself was a performer of some renown. His name was Andre Dakar, birthname Rudolph Bayfield Evans though he changed his first name to Andre and last name to Dakar after "he decided that our family came from Senegal because there is a, what they call the tribal mark, there's kind of a resemblance. There's a tribe in Senegal called the Peul and we look like them very much. … So when he was acting, he called himself Andre Dakar. But it was never officially part of his name. But when I was born, he registered me as Evans, which is the Jamaican family name, Evans de Dakar." Andre Dakar was indeed an actor who had appeared in a number of films including, *All Neat in Black Stockings* in 1969 as the man with a parrot; *Never Take Candy from a Stranger* in 1960 as Olderberry's Chauffeur; *Our Virgin Island* in 1958 with Sidney Poitier; and numerous television shows including *the Avengers* in 1961.[184]

"He was a singer in Paris in the 20s and 30s," she says. "My dad had been in the great jazz age in Paris with some of the greatest artists that jazz produced, from its grand era. … He made a record. It was called 'My Little Lulu.' And I think it was John Brown and His Boys. But he wrote the lyrics, because he used to write lyrics and he used to translate from French or into French, whatever was necessary. 'My Little Lulu' was his wife at the time, whose house I was born in. And her name was Germaine Louis, so he used to call her Lulu. She was known as Lulu, and that was the song he wrote, 'My Little Lulu.'" Rhoda's mother was "a white woman from Bristol. Her family moved to London during the Second World War. Why that would

---

[183] Dakar, Rhoda. Interview with Junor Francis on the History of LA Ska podcast, 11 Apr. 2021.
[184] IMDb, imdb.com/name/nm0197469. Accessed 30 June 2022.

be, I don't know. But she met my dad because he had a nightclub in London during the war. And she used to go to his nightclub, so that's where she met him."

Rhoda was influenced by her father's music as well as his character. She says, "I liked him very much. Because obviously you love your parents, but I liked him very much. He was a very nice man. He was very easy to get on with, he was very charming, he was quite funny. And what I liked about him is that he encouraged us, and me definitely, to argue. Because if you're Jamaican, you don't just put up with stuff! Plus, he lived in France, so it made him doubly argumentative. So if you had an opinion, you had to voice it. And he taught me to play cards and drink coffee. He didn't believe in Rastas, no. He didn't believe in Rastas. He knew Marcus Garvey and he wasn't a fan. And he also met Haile Selassie and he didn't like him either. He sang at a Royal Garden Party and Haile Selassie was a guest. So, he met him. He [father] was charming. He could talk his way into anywhere, anything. He knew all kinds of people, met all kinds of people. … He was friends with Josephine Baker, and he was friends with Louis Armstrong. And I know he was friends with Louis Armstrong because my mom said that they went to see him play in London and she said she didn't really believe that my dad knew him until he introduced her to him. She said, 'I had to believe it then!'"

Because Andre Dakar was a vocalist during the jazz era in Paris, the music he played in his home was also jazz. "I was exposed to jazz because my dad only believed in jazz," Rhoda says. "He didn't believe in any other type of music. Because if you said to him, 'What sort of music do you like dad,' he would say, 'Jazz, naturally,' and there would be no other answer. So, you could ask him until you were blue in the face. Jazz. He only believed in jazz," she says. But Rhoda had her own musical interests which were largely influenced by the songs she heard on the radio. "It'd be the Monkees probably, and the Beatles," she says, though she was largely a fan of Elvis Costello, the New York Dolls, and David Bowie in the later years.[185] "And in '69 as well they started to play Desmond Dekker on the radio. I mean, we knew about reggae because it was around us all the time."

Reggae was part of the culture of many neighborhoods in England in the late 1960s and 1970s as the Windrush generation (the ship that brought West Indian immigrants to help rebuild a post-WWII England in June of 1948) settled in the land that had once colonized them, and in many ways, continued to. Brixton was in the center of this cultural influx and was therefore a hotbed for reggae. "Sound systems replicated the Jamaican model—basically huge mobile discos with live entertainers rhyming or singing on the mic. 'Sounds' were central to black life in the UK in the 80s. As Linton Kwesi Johnson said of their earthquake power, they would shake

[185] "Rhoda Dakar—Musician London." Fred Perry. fredperry.com/us/subculture/articles/rhoda-dakar. Accessed 1 July 2022.

'down your spinal column/a bad music tearing up your flesh,'" wrote radio producer Brent Clough of his memories of Brixton as a youth.[186]

But the exposure to such exciting music and culture came with tremendous social and political oppression. Immigrants were not welcomed with open arms, to say the least—not even by the government that had once invited them. "People are really rather afraid that this country might be swamped by people with a different culture," said a racist Margaret Thatcher in 1978, some 16 months before she took over as prime minister of England.[187] For Rhoda Dakar, she experienced this oppression firsthand as a young child. "There weren't that many black kids in my primary school in the '60s and when I went to secondary school there were five of us when I first went there. There were five of us out of 500. Because it was a working-class grammar school in South London, we weren't expected to go to university. We were expected to join the civil service. We weren't expected to do too much," she says.[188]

Rhoda saw an opportunity for herself, not through school, but through the stage. Though she may have been inspired by her father's career in acting and singing, Rhoda had to fight for the opportunity to train as a performer. "I had to beg them to go to dance lessons," she says. "Well, I had to beg my mom because it wasn't really my dad's decision. So I had to beg my mom and my mom finally said yes, after about a year. And she let me go to dance classes. So I did my first public performance in 1969." She continued to pursue her passion for performance and was inspired by other family members as well. "My grandmother had been a theatrical costumier. She taught me how to sew, so I got a job in theatre wardrobe and I was there for a couple of years. And in all that time there was one mixed race actor who came in for one play. I had been in the Youth Theatre and we'd done Shakespeare at the Old Vic and I went to the Young Vic, which is just across the road, working professionally. And I suddenly realized I'd be playing nurses and prostitutes for the rest of my life. I just had to re-evaluate what I wanted to do. I went into the civil service but I was only there for about six months," she says.[189] Rhoda Dakar's service was cut short as a result of her joining the Bodysnatchers as their vocalist.

Now that the group was assembled, the women sought to put together their repertoire of songs, which consisted largely of ska and rocksteady covers. Sarah-Jane Owen recalls their process and practice. "So we rehearsed and rehearsed and we basically taught ourselves. I had a Dansette record player that we plugged in—they're like a little portable thing. We plugged it in where we rehearsed and we would play

[186] Clough, Brent. "What happened to Brixton's reggae revolution?" ABC Radio National. 13 Nov. 2013. abc.net.au/radionational/programs/archived/360/what-happened-to-brixtons-reggae-revolution/5107636. Accessed 1 July 2022.
[187] Trilling, Daniel. "Thatcher: the PM who brought racism in from the cold." *Verso*. 10 Apr. 2013. versobooks.com/blogs/1282-thatcher-the-pm-who-brought-racism-in-from-the-cold. Accessed 1 July 2022.
[188] Dakar, Rhoda. Interview with Janine Booth, 13 July 2000. janinebooth.com/content/video-janine-interviews-rhoda-dakar. Accessed 1 July 2022.
[189] "Rhoda Dakar Speaks to Eyeplug." 23 Feb. 2017. eyeplug.net/magazine/rhoda-dakar-speaks-to-eyeplug. Accessed 1 Jul. 2022.

ska music that existed because we knew that that's what the Specials and the Selecter were doing and they were already making headway in the music scene, so we studied it. We would listen to these songs and dissect them, because none of really knew music—none of us had a degree or studied what a song was. It was a mixture of 'Time is Tight,' things like that which was not ska music but was more R'n'B. We did listen to some ska music too and we figured out that the music that the Selecter and the Specials was playing was definitely Jamaican oriented music."

The decision to cover Jamaican songs, and specifically rocksteady songs, was certainly based upon the music that bands like the Selecter, the Specials, and others were recording, but it was also an aesthetic that the women in the band enjoyed. Leader Nicky Summers says, "I didn't want a ska band," she says. "I did not consciously form one. I was looking for some sort of musical hybrid of punk, reggae, bluebeat, girl groups, Motown, etc. but that is just how we played. It came out to be a modern take on rocksteady. We were new to playing so it came out slower." Penny Leyton says the writing process, aside from their cover songs, was a collaboration for the most part. "We all tried writing and sometimes it worked out and sometimes it didn't. Rhoda was great at writing lyrics. She had an incredible talent for that. Sometimes also if we'd just come up with like backing music, she'd come up with a tune as well. So, I think we sort of wrote songs jointly. Sometimes one person would write the songs and sometimes it would work and sometimes it wouldn't and at that point it was pretty collaborative," Penny says.

The writing process was a group effort, agrees Sarah-Jane Owen who recalls those early rehearsals. "Some songs started with an intro and there would be like a verse and there would be maybe a bridge before a chorus and there would be a middle eight or an instrumental, so we learned literally by listening to songs, how song structure was formulated. So mostly we were playing covers, and that's how we began—playing covers and emulating what we heard, trying to pick out the bass line, helping Nicky work out what the notes were of the bass line, and then figuring out what the chords were, and I think our most musical person at that time was Penny—she knew her way around a keyboard so she was helpful. She was also a good songwriter and when it came to writing our own self-penned, she really paved the way for us with quite a few songs in the Bodysnatchers."

That name, the Bodysnatchers, was also a collective effort and though quite a few of the suggested names received a veto by one band member or another, it was largely democratic. Rhoda recalls, "We were called the Bodysnatchers because around this time there was a new version of the 'Invasion of the Bodysnatchers,' the film, out at the time. We voted and it was the name everyone hated the least. There was a name that was quite popular, but I said, 'If you call yourselves that, I'm leaving.' So you know, we weren't post-feminist and we couldn't really call ourselves those sorts of names. I think it was Pussy Galore, they wanted to call us. They said, 'No, but it's James Bond,' It's like, yeah, not in the music business it isn't, love, you know, so I had to say no. You can call yourselves that, but without me. So, we were the Bodysnatchers," says Rhoda.

Penny Leyton says they named the band the Bodysnatchers "because it is body-snatching music"[190] and Sarah-Jane echoes Rhoda's recollection. "Stella's boyfriend said, 'You're rehearsing and rehearsing—have you come up with a name yet?'" remembers Sarah-Jane, "And of course we couldn't agree on a name. I think we had 60 or 70 names and we decided that we had to be democratic, so we had to have total agreement—unanimous. So six of us would think it was good, others wouldn't and it just went on and on and on like this." They finally settled on a name, says Sarah-Jane, when they had to have one for their first gig which forced their hand, but that name wasn't the Bodysnatchers yet. "We went out as LaRude Galore because we didn't have a proper name yet," says Sarah-Jane.

The first gig the group played was at the Windsor Castle and Nicky Summers recalls how it happened. "We rehearsed for about seven weeks," Nicky says, "and in November '79 our first gig was supporting Shane's [MacGowan] band The Nips at the Windsor Castle pub along the Harrow Road. It was for us a try out gig and we were fairly ramshackle. We were having a laugh." Nicky, as mentioned prior, was friends with MacGowan so she arranged the event. Sarah-Jane remembers it a bit differently, though no one disputes the memories and impact of that important night. "I supposed it was Stella's boyfriend who just decided it was time and booked us a gig at the Windsor Castle to get our feet wet. ... It was a little tiny pub gig on Harrow Road. When we showed up, the place was packed," she says.

One member of the audience that night was Stella Barker's father who had come down to witness his daughter play. Though she had experience in the music industry, working for EMI, she was still fairly unacquainted with the protocols of performance. "We were all so new to everything, all of us ... because we were naïve and inexperienced, we didn't even know how to set up a backline on stage, and my boyfriend at the time and Sarah-Jane's boyfriend sort of acted as our roadies almost. They said, 'We'll set you up, you need to plug that in there, and stand there,' and what have you. ... I do remember that first gig which was at the Windsor Castle on Harrow Road and my dad, my Yorkshire farmer dad, he bought me a VW van because we didn't have anything to shunt the gear around with and he very sweetly bought a van. He probably got it for a good price up north so he drove it down to deliver it to me and it was the same night as this gig, and when we were up on stage and playing, the pub was absolutely jam packed. And I could see my dad at the back of the pub and there was a skinhead on one side of him and a punk on the other. My dad is standing there with a pint. It was very sweet. And the other thing I remember about that gig is we'd rehearsed about ten numbers or so and we'd played them all and got huge applause at the end and my boyfriend at the time and Sarah-Jane's, they were sort of in the wings going, 'Come off stage! Come off stage!' because we were just sort of standing there like lemons, and off we went. And the audience were going, 'Encore! Encore!' but we haven't got anymore! So the guys said, 'Well just do one or two again,' so we did two songs."

[190] Silverton, Peter. "Invasion of the Bodysnatchers." *Sounds*. 22 Dec. 1979.

But there were other members of the audience that night. These members had either been invited to the gig, or had heard about the unusual aggregation of this ska band, or any band for that matter. No one had blinked at an all-male line up, which had been typical since, who knows when. Even today, an 18-piece ska orchestra features not a single female member, so in 1979, an all-female ska band was, frankly, a novelty. "I mean, most boys had been playing instruments since they were really young," says Penny, "but the attitude was that women don't play in bands and that was still very prevalent at that time. Most women had only started learning their instruments as adults and had not played in bands so we were kind of learning as we went on. I mean, because I was classically trained, I knew a lot about music, but playing in a band was very different." Plus, as Pauline Black pointed out, "It's hard to play instruments when it's mostly men standing around."[191]

The Bodysnatchers all hoped, and proved, to the members of the audience that night and for the next year of non-stop gigging, that they were much more than an all-girl band, despite their excusable inexperience. "So the place was packed and I said to Stella, 'What in the world? How many people did you invite?'" says Sarah-Jane. "And she said, 'Oh, about four or five,' and I said, 'I invited probably the same, but that doesn't explain why there's so many people here.' Well what happened was her boyfriend had leaked it to the press that a girl band was going to debut. He was a clever boyfriend, I guess, because he had invited the Specials and the Selecter had heard about it. So here we are our first-ever gig. We played our gig and we were so nervous that we don't even know at the last applause to get off the stage because we were so in shock that they like us, so we're standing there like absolute lemons, wondering what we should do next. Somebody tells us to shuffle out, so we shuffle out into a back room. They're still applauding, we go back out and we had to play our first number again because we didn't have any extra numbers to play. As we play that number, through the crowd, literally squeezing through the crowd and spitting as he comes toward us, was Jerry Dammers, because he doesn't have any front teeth, and he says, 'You girls are great! I want to sign you for our tour!' And that was that. I'm telling you, no lie—this is exactly how it happened."

Nicky Summers recalls those members in the audience as well as a few others as well. "The pub was packed. Just about everyone turned up including Gaz Mayall who was a friend of the band, Pauline Black from the Selecter, and Jerry Dammers. Richard Branson was also there running around shrieking, had anyone signed us yet. I recall we always ended our set with Booker T and the MG's 'Time is Tight.' Our playing was so loose this number always fell apart—it was an anarchic version. When we improved our playing and tightened up, audience members were disappointed, though we were more musically competent and improved with every performance," says Nicky. Gaz Mayall later co-wrote "Ruder Than You" with Rhoda Dakar, side B of their first single on the 2 Tone label with the A side "Let's Do Rocksteady."

---

[191] Rachel, Daniel. *Walls Come Tumbling Down: The Music and Politics of Rock Against Racism, 2 Tone and Red Wedge 1976-1992.* Picador, 2016, p. 286.

Pauline Black may not remember being in attendance at that gig, or perhaps Nicky remembers incorrectly, but it's not an important detail since Pauline was ultimately in support of their participation. "The Bodysnatchers had first come to my attention when they had supported us at a gig," Black writes in her autobiography.[192] "I loved the sheer chutzpah of their lead singer, the gorgeous, tall and tanned Rhoda Dakar, who sang with a charmingly idiosyncratic, richly nuanced voice, perfectly suited to their somewhat shambolic rocksteady sound. Her style was Mod-inspired but nonetheless highly individual. Her hair was a glorious Mr. Whippy, gravity-defying beehive. She was completely at odds with, but a perfect foil, for my rude-boy image. The Selecter suggested that they were signed to the 2-Tone label, which didn't meet with universal approval within the 2-Tone camp. Some voiced concern about the band's relative inexperience. They had only done their first gig in November 1979. By their own admission, they were not competent musicians and they were about to jump under the media spotlight, which by this time was waiting patiently for the label's first failure. Ironically, Roger Lomas was drafted in to produce their first single, the Dandy Livingston song, 'Let's Do Rocksteady,' backed with an original composition, 'Ruder Than You,'" Pauline Black states. Rhoda recalls, "We wrote 'Ruder Than You' when I was round Gaz Mayall's house and he said, 'You guys need an anthem, let's write one!' so me and him sat down and wrote a statement of intent."[193]

Just two days after that single was recorded, the Bodysnatchers immediately went on tour with the Selecter. "I remember the Selecter telling us that we needed to practice if we went on tour," says Penny. The tour with the Selecter began on Valentine's Day, 1980 with a gig at Darby Kings Hall. Prior to the tour, the Bodysnatchers gigged and solidified their image. According to Penny Leyton's personal diary, she and Sarah-Jane Owen designed the badges and posters for the Bodysnatchers which they got to the printer in early December 1979. They then performed another gig at Windsor Castle supporting the Nips on December 4, 1979; a gig at the Nashville supporting the Mo-Dettes (see also Mo-Dettes chapter) on December 8, 1979; at the 101 Club with Scottish musician Bobby Henry on December 13, 1979; and then on December 29, 1979, the Bodysnatchers had the opportunity to perform at a rather notable event at the Embassy Club.[194] "We would gig fairly regularly around London, including Debbie Harry's birthday bash organized by Chrysalis," says Nicky.

Blondie had already established themselves in the UK since their first album, *Private Stock*, was released in 1976. British journalists seized on the opportunity to promote the band thanks to the allure of their leader, Debbie Harry. "Surely no red-blooded male can resist the appeal of the delectable Debbie," said one rag's writer.[195] Blondie had sold out the Hammersmith Odeon in 1978, and in 1979 in London to

[192] Black, Pauline. *Black By Design: A 2-Tone Memoir*. Serpent's Tail, 2011, p. 196.

[193] Beaumont, Mark. "We Were Intent on Making Our Mark." *Uncut*. 24 Apr. 2019, p. 121.

[194] Entries from Penny Leyton's personal diary, courtesy Penny Leyton.

[195] Wheeldon, Mark. "Big Hit for Delectable Debbie?" *Burton Daily Mail*, 12 May 1979, p. 6.

promote their new album *Eat to the Beat*, appeared on television shows like *Multi-Coloured Swap Shop* on BBC1, *Top of the Pops*, and attended parties hosted by their record label.[196]

The following year, Blondie released the massive hit, "The Tide Is High," a song originally penned and performed by the Paragons. It is fair to say that Blondie's time in the UK during this era likely inspired their interest in this otherwise rare tune. One unverified source claims, "[Debbie] Harry and [Christopher] Stein heard the song on a compilation tape they picked up in London; they thought it was too good not to record."[197] In a 1981 interview, Blondie guitarist Chris Stein says he actually tried to involve the Specials in recording the tune. "Actually, I asked the Specials to back Debbie up on 'The Tide Is High' and they didn't wanna do it! I don't know what happened with them. Linval [sic] wanted to do it!" says Stein.[198] On another note, Stein was also a fan of movie themes, though it's not certain if he knew of the Jamaican link to one particular song. "Chris learnt to play the guitar when trying to pick out the melodies of movies, 'The Guns Of Navarone' being his particular favourite (which, ironically, has now been released by the Specials as a single)," wrote journalist Tony Horkins in 1980.[199]

The Debbie Harry party at the Embassy Club was certainly an important opportunity for the Bodysnatchers, but it was one of many significant gigs during this blip of time. Three days after the Debbie Harry party, the Bodysnatchers supported Madness at the Lyceum on December 30, 1979 and on New Year's Eve they supported the Selecter at Dingwalls. The new year, 1980, was no less frenzied for the Bodysnatchers with gigs on weekends as well as weekdays at clubs like the Hope and Anchor, the Moonlight Club, Rock Garden, and on February 3, 1980 at the Lyceum supporting Lene Lovich.

On February 12, 1980, the Bodysnatchers recorded their first single on the 2 Tone label at the Music Works studio at 23 Benwell Road. The deal that the Bodysnatchers signed with 2 Tone was dictated by Jerry Dammers. Nicky Summers told music journalist Daniel Rachel, "Jerry was in America but the message was, 'It's a two-single deal.' So we recorded 'Ruder Than You' and 'Let's Do Rock Steady' with Roger Lomas [producer] to sound good on the radio. We did twenty-six takes and he kept saying, 'Play faster.' It wasn't the point of punk to be a proficient musician. It was about getting your thoughts across or your attitude or energy or fury or whatever it was. That was a large feature of the Bodysnatchers."[200] The single was pressed on February 27, 1980 and released on March 7, 1980. Four days later it entered the charts

[196] *The Kilmarnock Standard*, 21 Dec. 1970, p. 40.
[197] "The Tide is High." Songfacts. songfacts.com/facts/blondie/the-tide-is-high. Accessed 2 July 2022.
[198] Needs, Kris. "Debbie & the Koo Koo Clocked." *Zig Zag*. 1 Sept. 1981.
[199] Horkins, Tony. "The Boys Behind the Blonde." *Beat Instrumental*, 1 Mar. 1980. thebestofblondie.com/1980/03/01/beat-instrumental-2. Accessed 2 July 2022.
[200] Rachel, Daniel. *Walls Come Tumbling Down: The Music and Politics of Rock Against Racism, 2 Tone and Red Wedge 1976-1992*. Picador, 2016, p. 287.

at number 44, a week after that went up to number 31, and finally up to 16, securing the Bodysnatchers an appearance on *Top of the Pops* on March 19th.

All of these accomplishments and appearances coincided with traveling all over the country on the 2 Tone tour with the Selecter. "It was all very fast," says Nicky. "Within two weeks we had to make a decision who to sign with and find a lawyer. 'Shit, I'm out of my depth here.' We voted between EMI and 2 Tone. I didn't vote for 2 Tone because it was the safe option and predictable," Nicky told Rachel.[201] There was one other opportunity that presented itself, Nicky says, but that opportunity was democratically voted down by band members. "Richard Branson [Virgin Records] offered us this album deal but the rest of the band wouldn't meet him. … Branson wanted to take us to Memphis where Aretha Franklin used to record. I've no idea why we didn't do that? Five people refused to play ball. How can you let that go? We didn't need a manager for direction or content but we needed somebody who had links to business," said Nicky to Rachel.[202]

Penny says that she has no recollection of ever being offered a deal by Richard Branson, though she does recall having dinner with a Virgin A&R executive. "I'm pretty sure we would have wanted what would give us the best chance of success so why would we turn down an amazing opportunity? It doesn't make sense, so there must have been strings attached that are not mentioned here, or the offer was not as good as it sounds. I do remember voting not to be signed with Virgin; perhaps Nicky's confusing 'meeting Richard Branson' with signing to Virgin. However, saying we 'refused to play ball' is a little petty. If you have a democratic set up and the vote goes against you then you have to live with it. I'm sure we all had situations where the vote went against us and we didn't tell people they weren't 'playing ball.' We were not an autocracy however much some people may have wanted it that way," says Penny.[203]

The band, however, did have a manager, like it or not. They were assigned a manager by Rick Rogers, manager for the Specials. Rogers appointed Frank Murray who had been tour manager for the Specials during their American tour, had previously managed tours for Elton John and Thin Lizzy, and subsequently managed the Pogues. Murray was less than enthusiastic about the band he once was tasked with supporting. "The funny thing was, none of the girls were telling me they'd just learnt their instruments. They were walking around as if they were queens of the castle and they seemed to think they knew an awful lot more than they actually did," Murray told Rachel.[204] One can only speculate if the band's gender helped to shape his rather scathing and sexist opinion.

Murray's dismissive attitude toward a band of all "girls" is not uncommon. "I can remember our first gigs on that tour and the lighting crew and the roadies that were on that tour were sniggering in the back like, 'Oh my god! What's this? All girls?'

---

[201] Ibid. p. 288.
[202] Ibid. p. 288.
[203] Leyton, Penny. Email with the author, 27 Oct. 2022.
[204] Rachel, Daniel. *Walls Come Tumbling Down: The Music and Politics of Rock Against Racism, 2 Tone and Red Wedge 1976-1992*. Picador, 2016, p. 287.

They couldn't fathom—we were such a novelty. It's hard to believe now because there are so many girl bands now, it's not unusual. But then, especially in such a male dominated industry, and especially for guys who are already jealous of anyone who's playing, because they're not the players—they're the lighting techs, they're already sort of wannabees, and here's this troupe of girls trying to be something, so we were kind of marks, behind our backs. But very soon, and at the end of that tour, we were so tight that we were gaining their respect because they could see that we were sincere and determined, so the next tour we did, it was so much better, the relationship with any male counterparts," Sarah-Jane says.

It's no wonder that the Bodysnatchers gained respect since they performed 26 times during that tour with the Selecter—from February 14 through March 20, 1980. The lineup on this tour included the Bodysnatchers who performed first, followed by Holly and the Italians, then the Selecter. When Holly and the Italians didn't go down well with audiences on that tour (see also Holly and the Italians chapter), they were replaced partway through the tour by the Swinging Cats. Once the tour ended, the Bodysnatchers kept going. That spring they appeared on television shows like *Alright Now* and *Tiswas*; they performed on prominent radio shows for Kid Jensen, Mike Read, and John Peel; and they performed with Bad Manners and the Swinging Cats. In April through June of 1980, the Bodysnatchers toured with Bim supporting them. Bim was a five-piece all-male new wave band who had a small hit in 1982, "Blind Lead the Blind," which was produced by Mick Jones of the Clash on the Swerve record label.[205] Rhoda says that there were some good times on tour. "I mean, we did a lot of kind of mad stuff like water pistols, apple pie beds. We did lots of pranks. We were known for our pranks, which was quite funny," she says.

But tensions started to surface throughout the band that spring into summer, which is not surprising, seeing as the group of seven women was assembled without established friendships and, for that matter, no relationships at all. The women came from different backgrounds, different classes, different races. Important decisions and the direction of the band revealed these differences as fissures. Penny Leyton's diary notes problems such as, "Jane leaves drumkit during Rock Steady encore to throw water over Dougie of Bad Manners—obviously more important," for a gig at the Electric Ballroom on May 31, 1980. There were also issues with touring in general, some of which may be associated with gender, like "slimy promoter," "bad, not many ppl, no advertising, kitchen to change in, creepy hotel," and "really crummy place, dressing room about 4ft squ but useless anyway cos no light. Good fun tho. T-shirts arrive."

As will be discussed more in the Belle Stars chapter, a dressing room was important to women, especially women in the Bodysnatchers, many of whom came from an art and fashion background. Fashion, it goes without saying, was a large part of the 2 Tone era and ska as a whole. For women, it was an opportunity for self expression and empowerment. "The thing about those times," reflects Nicky, "was

---

[205] Discogs. discogs.com/release/587407-Bim-Blind-Lead-The-Blind. Accessed 3 July 2022.

there was a different take on feminine style, i.e. you could wear a binbag or have spike hair. There was a different take on 'femininity' and appearance and image. You were not dressing for men. It was always about creativity and expression and what ideas were going on. And the guys at the time supported you in that." She says this freedom is much different than the norms today. "I am disappointed nowadays that in the last 10 years women seem to be tremendously limited in the mainstream as to their appearance—almost obsessed with ultra-grooming as a kind of pastiche or augmented type of femininity as if to be feminine meant only one thing and everyone's visual appearance is similar and manicured/curated by what they have been told to wear or what they should look like by the media or peer group. It has never occurred to me that I had to take my clothes off to make music."

While fashion was important to most members of the Bodysnatchers, for one it was also a profession. Sarah-Jane most definitely had a background in fashion. Not only had she obtained an undergraduate and graduate degree in the subject, but she also worked in the fashion industry prior to becoming a musician. "I had my own line and I was quite successful. I had the front page of *Vogue* doing fashion design with my own collection and I was doing well. It was just under my own name, Sarah-Jane Owen, and I sold to boutiques in London and abroad and had a good agent so I got a lot of press. It's a tough business though because you have to fork out money to develop a line that you then sell from. So there's a lot of money up front of investment and you're not sure if you're going to sell it. So I was getting a little disillusioned with the fashion industry, that it wasn't the magic that it's sort of supposed to be," she says. Instead, she turned her talent towards herself and her bandmates, helping to shape the image of the band as well as her subsequent bands (see also Belle Stars chapter).

Miranda Joyce and Stella Barker also contributed to the style of the Bodysnatchers with their interest in art and fashion. "Miranda was about to go to art college when she joined the band," says Stella. "So you've got three very artistic people, and Sarah-Jane was doing fashion at art college, so we had a really good selection of people for clothing ideas and also for design," she says, though a more formal approach to designing the look of the band would come later with the Belle Stars. Rhoda had already developed her own sense of style as she recounts to Daniel Rachel, "I used to dress in old Sixties clothes from Kensington Market and wear a white ribbon in my hair. At Chelsea College of Art they had this thing where you had to dress up like the Sixties and I won. I remember Gaz [Mayall] saying to me, 'Oh, it looks like fashion's catching up with you.'"[206]

The Bodysnatchers recorded their second single on the 2 Tone label the weekend of May 17 and 18, 1980 at Wessex Studios in Highbury New Park with Jerry Dammers producing. The members of the band had some disagreement with the selection of the songs for this release, as Penny notes in her diary entry, "We have

[206] Rachel, Daniel. *Walls Come Tumbling Down: The Music and Politics of Rock Against Racism, 2 Tone and Red Wedge 1976-1992*. Picador, 2016, p. 286-287.

vote on single. SJ and I are really unhappy about it. Jane very rude just because we happen to think differently from her. Big upset." The women chose the songs "Easy Life" and "Too Experienced" for the A and B sides respectively, but the recording didn't go as well as they had hoped. Penny notes, "SJ and I decide single can't go out as it is. Ring Frank [Murray]" in her diary on June 1, 1980. The next day the entry reads, "Meeting with lawyer. lawyer doesn't like single. group agrees to remix. To Chrysalis; Selecter put stop on single. Everyone says production is bad. Agree to remix with, if possible, Dave Jordan." Jordan had produced a number of the Specials' singles and worked extensively with the Pogues.[207] The single was remixed on June 14, 1980 and Penny writes, "Day off to remix single. Bad start, hotel doesn't wake anyone in time for 10 am start. Back to London in minibus straight to studio (Wessex). Single much better." The single was officially released on July 11, 1980.

"'Easy Life' was produced by Jerry and suddenly it came across as an anthem with this very slick production," Nicky told Daniel Rachel.[208] "We were taken aback. The riff came forward and it had this catch-line. Rhoda wrote the lyrics. It was about not taking the easy option and girls doing something more challenging, more creative than going for the safe norm. I did modern languages at school and was told the best I was going to be was a bilingual secretary." Rhoda Dakar wrote the song when she was 20 years old and faced the decisions and limitations on those decisions that many young women face. Author, podcaster, and musician Marc Wasserman offered the following insight on the song, "Despite not breaking the top 40, 'Easy Life' may be one of the most deceptively revolutionary 2 Tone songs of all time. Though it sounds like an upbeat feminist ditty and it is remarkably catchy and danceable, a close read of the lyrics reveals some real layers to the song. 'Easy Life' addresses and rejects the pressure and refusal to conform to pre-determined—often media driven—constructs of femininity. Dakkar [sic] sings: we are near to an equality/girls and boys with pay parity/we are near to an equality/the law says there is equal opportunity/but still it's a struggle/yes life is still a struggle."[209] Nicky says of the song, "Easy Life was received well because of its feminist lyric."

"For me, I always preferred Too Experienced," said Nicky. "Jerry Dammers produced them both. A couple of weeks after we had recorded them, he became fixated about the timing on Too Experienced and rebooked a studio for the weekend to add a tambourine (on the offbeat). I recall he, Jane, and I in the studio recording over the track. The other members of the band had gone off to the launderette. Jerry ended up playing the tambourine himself, just ahead of the offbeat to speed up the song a fraction. Later I remember hearing Too Experienced for the first time on acetate. It was the closest thing to the original sound I had always had in my head for the band. I think Jerry did a great production on it. When it was reviewed in the *NME*

[207] Discogs. discogs.com/artist/139030-Dave-Jordan. Accessed 3 July 2022.

[208] Rachel, Daniel. *Walls Come Tumbling Down: The Music and Politics of Rock Against Racism, 2 Tone and Red Wedge 1976-1992.* Picador, 2016, p. 289.

[209] Wasserman, Marc. "2 Tone Legacy - Easy Life." Ska Boom - An American Ska & Reggae Podcast. 26 May 2022. Accessed 4 July 2022.

they wrote that we sounded like a cross between PiL and the Supremes, recorded in an aircraft hanger. I think that was the coolest compliment."

"Too Experienced," while a cover of a Bob Andy song, is an interesting choice when presented by seven women, especially when the lyrics are subtly and cleverly modified. Penny says that Rhoda is the one who came up the new lyrics. "I believe the lyrics differ because we couldn't actually work out what the lyrics were! We were listening to old 45s with scratches, probably not on great sound systems. I seem to remember having a discussion about what the words actually were and then Rhoda decided to sing what she then sang," Penny says. Instead of Andy's statement that he is "too experienced for someone to rock and roll," Rhoda sings she is "too experienced to let someone wreck my soul." This change reflects wisdom and independence and rejects the plethora of "you're mine" songs for more of a "you don't own me" proclamation. "The original version was recorded by a man, but changing the words so that they're sung from a woman's point of view makes all the difference," wrote one journalist in 1980. "Men have always been able to brag about their sexual sophistication, but you'd never get women singing about being 'too experienced' in the early 60s."[210]

Meanwhile, the Bodysnatchers left at the beginning of June in 1980 to accompany the Specials on the Seaside Tour. For three weeks the two bands traveled and performed together at venues such as the Colwin Bay Pier Pavilion, Aylesbury Friars, Hastings Pier Pavilion, Margate Winter Gardens, and Portsmouth Guild Hall, to name a few. Members of Bad Manners appeared from time to time to join in the festivities, though not the performances. According to Penny's diary entries, and as one might assume, the off-stage antics were quite raucous. Her notes include the following entries: "Jerry [Dammers] put his foot through Stella's [Barker] ceiling (June 6); Sugar cube fight after gig. SJ [Owen] went to sleep on table with bowls on her (June 6); We throw water out of window onto Jerry and fans standing below (June 9); Jerry claims Roddy [Radiation] tried to push him over a cliff (June 10); Specials have big argument. Roddy smashes guitar over keyboards saying 'better than over Jerry's head.' Melody Maker guy there. Moody scenes in hotel lounge afterwards (June 11); Roddy exchanges Patrice [his model girlfriend from the U.S.] for wife who he doesn't speak to [who came to visit unannounced, resulting in a quick scramble to get Patrice out without notice]. Jerry walks off. Possibility of gig not happening but it does (June 12); Skinheads outside climb up to our window. Sort of party afterwards but not very lively. Bar closed early. Jerry rearranges hotel signboard (June 19)."

There are a few significant points about this tour with the Specials, other than the obvious historical appeal of the entire event itself. First is the appearance of the Go-Go's during this tour. The Bodysnatchers had first performed with the Go-Go's at the Electric Ballroom on May 31, 1980 along with Akrylykz. Akrylykz was a ska band fronted by Roland Gift who later went on to Fine Young Cannibals fame. Akrylykz supported a number of 2 Tone-related bands during this time including the

210 "Bodysnatchers." *Spare Rib*. Nov. 1980, p. 13.

Specials, the Beat (the Beat bassist David Steele and guitarist Andy Cox would join Gift in 1984 to form Fine Young Cannibals), the Reluctant Stereotypes, Dexys Midnight Runners, and they also supported the Clash. They had a small hit with the single, "Spyderman" with the flipside "Smart Boy" and were signed to the Polydor label.[211] The Go-Go's performed on a number of the gigs during the Seaside Tour which helped them to gain exposure and experience touring and performing as an all-female group (see also Go-Go's section in Specials/Special AKA chapter).

Another item to note is that during this tour, the Bodysnatchers made the decision to fire their drummer, Jane Summers, and pursue a replacement. As previously mentioned, the band members began to have disagreements with one another and Penny had alluded to difficulty with Jane Summers' performance, stopping to pour water on Buster Bloodvessel's head. And Jane's subsequent contributions on the tour didn't improve, leading one friend to comment to Penny, "She's crap and the band won't last 3 months with her," according to her diary entry on June 16. That same night, band members called a meeting to discuss her participation in the band and made the decision to remove her. "Nicky tells Jane she's been sacked," reads Penny's entry, though Jane agreed to fulfill the rest of the tour dates, culminating on June 19th. Penny writes of that performance at the Portsmouth Guild Hall, "Last night of tour. Gig—Jane awful—reinforced our decision about her."

"I felt it was a great loss," says Nicky Summers, "as we were good mates and I had always been happy with Jane's drumming and input in the band, though earlier in the year we had Sex Pistol Paul Cook come to a few rehearsals to offer drumming tips. We auditioned many drummers." Those auditions took place at the end of June through July before they found the right person. There were women named "Sacha" who was "pretty average," and "HM girl from Birmingham," according to Penny's diary entries, as well as one named Carla who rehearsed a number of times with the band before absconding with £100 they gave her as a deposit on a flat and a drumkit, never to be seen again. On August 7, 1980, Judy Parsons officially had her first gig as a member of the Bodysnatchers when they performed at the Birmingham Cedar Ballroom with 21 Guns supporting. 21 Guns was a group signed to Neville Staple's new label, Shack Records, which he established with his then-girlfriend, Stella Barker (see also Splashdown chapter). This one-release wonder was comprised of Trevor Evans and Johnny Rex, two roadies for the Specials, along with Kevin Tanner, Stuart MacLean, and Gary Chambers. Pauline Black writes of Trevor Evans and Johnny Rex in her book, "Much is made of Neville Staple's sexual antics and those of his procurers, the rude-boy roadie duo, Rex and Trevor. Yes, all of that is true, I saw many a silly young girl backstage being groomed by the duo for future sacrifice on the altar of Nev's cock."[212] In his book, *Original Rude Boy*, Staple also confirms Trevor and Rex were groomers for him. "…their real role was to make sure I had some fun

[211] "The Akyrlykz." boredteenagers.co.uk/akrylykz.htm. Accessed 3 July 2022.
[212] Black, Pauline. *Black By Design: A 2-Tone Memoir*. Serpent's Tail, 2011, p. 178.

afterwards. Trevor would spot some totty who could be 'fished out of the pool,' in his words, and then I'd move in for the kill after the gig."[213] The point in mentioning this here is that there are zero comments from music critics or fellow musicians that Trevor Evans and Johnny Rex were "inexperienced" or "needed to practice" or not "competent musicians" or were "inept" or had "total musical inability."[214] They were predators, not musicians, yet as men, they faced none of the judgment unleashed on a group of seven women who were admittedly novice but had tenacity, creativity, style, and skill.

The newest member of the band, Judy Parsons, was 28 when she joined as drummer and had no idea that the group was about to implode. Judy, whose last name is now Hancock, was raised in the Blackheath area in Southeast London. She says that growing up, her household was not a musical one. "My mom hated music. She loved talking. Music gets in the way of talking. I don't know about my dad because my parents are separated so I lost touch with him completely. But my brother is also very musical, actually. He plays pedal steel guitar, drums, and double bass in a country-western band. He also plays guitar and mandolin and can play by ear. Which makes me jealous that I don't have this musical ability!" she says.[215] As for Judy herself, she had no formal musical training, as such, though her brother did. She always wanted to sing but was not given the opportunity. "I was the only person that wasn't allowed into the senior school choir. I love singing. Love singing. But I didn't sing in tune or something," says Judy.

Her break came, like many others in the band, and like many other women in general at this time who were faced with few other options, from her boyfriend. "I went to university and went out with a musician who used to play guitar and he could play anything, and sing, and I love that. Acoustic guitar and singing is just heaven. Then one day he came back home and he said, 'I've joined a country-western band.' So it's just like, 'Oh, you're gonna kind of go away in the evenings and weekends.' So I'm going along, watching him play in this band in Oxfordshire, going to the gigs, and it was boring. I thought, 'I'd like to be in the band.' And when you watch someone drumming, you just sort of think, 'Oh, I could do that.' But you can't. And in fact, the drummer in that band kept his drum kit in our house. So, he gave me a couple of lessons. And also at the time, I talked to a percussionist who was going to come and teach me percussion, which I would have preferred, because it's just bongos and that sort of thing, but he never appeared. And drumming is so difficult because you split your body into four parts. One hand is doing something and then the other hand is doing something completely different, and then the legs are supposed to be doing something as well, so it's very mental."

Judy had attended Sussex University and obtained a degree in mathematics and logic. Still, she found time for her music. "When I started drumming, I was

[213] Staple, Neville. *Original Rude Boy: From Borstal to the Specials*. Aurum, 2009, p. 146.
[214] Kelly, Ryan. "Girls Talk." *Smash Hits*. 1 May 1980, p. 13.
[215] Parsons/Hancock, Judy. All quotations, unless otherwise noted, from interview with the author, 9 July 2022.

working as a scientist—a government scientist in the Department of the Environment looking at river mud. It was in a large ground with lots of building and little wooden huts. I was living in a flat at the time where I couldn't drum, so I put my drum kit in one of these wooden huts and I waited until six o'clock at night and that's where I practiced drumming," she says.

Clearly, the few lessons and ample practicing paid off. "I eventually got into the country-western band, but then weeks later, he [boyfriend] left the country-western band to join a rock band, which was not the idea. So then at the weekends, we had to get two vans and I'd go to my gig, and he would go to his gig. That's how I got in. I was bored of watching my boyfriend at the time. Bored watching him playing and then all the other women had to get up and dance, and as soon as the band's women danced, everyone danced. Well, why do you have to wait for us to show you that you can dance? And then you sort of say afterwards, 'Oh, you played really well, darling, you were lovely.' It's more fun being in the band than sitting with the women looking at the band," says Judy.

That country-western band, called the Countrymen, despite the female drummer, lasted about two years, Judy says, and she was then fired. "We had outfits—tangerine silky shirts and turquoise bottoms. I didn't wear mine. I wore a Fenwicks, that's a posh shop, sleeveless t-shirt and they sacked me after a bit because I wasn't dressed properly. Also, it was very unprofessional. But I also had more fun when we were playing rock. At a certain point at the end of the evening, it's 'Rock Around the Clock.' So they actually sacked me."

Hancock had other plans, at that point. She says, "I wanted to play with better musicians. And that's when I saw the Mistakes advert. They were wanting a girl band." The Mistakes was a five-piece punk band from Oxford who played mostly small gigs or political festivals since they were feminists and their songs featured feminist lyrics. They included Georgina Clarke (who went by George) on bass and vocals, Ali West on keyboards, Mavis Bayton on guitar and vocals (she later wrote the book, *Frock Rock*, about the dearth of women in music), Penny Wood on guitar and vocals (sister of British comedian Victoria Wood), and Judy Parsons on drums. They were managed by Jill Posener and they had one recording, a single on Oval Records in 1979—a song called "Radiation" with the flipside "16 Pins." Song topics included nuclear weapons, police powers and state control, environmental decline, and women's issues. "Penny Wood put the adverts in—it's Penny's band. And so I went along and I really wanted to play with good musicians to help me become a better musician. Penny could play piano and guitar. And the others couldn't play. But then we went to the pub. After sort of sitting down and chatting, they were such nice people that I thought, I want to join you anyway. We only played tiny audiences but we were good fun as a band," Judy says.

Judy says that she was in the band for two years before she left to join the Bodysnatchers. She tells the story, "So in the Mistakes, when we started recording, it got a bit more serious. We would all be there whist the tracks are being mixed, and people get a bit kind of like, 'Oh, you need to turn me up in the mix,' and another says, 'You need to turn me up in the mix.' And it's like, well, we can't all go up in the mix. People have opinions—I don't like that, someone else did like that. It brings a rift. In some bands, it's all casual and fun and then suddenly, you're making records and the differences come out. So I wasn't really happy in the band. But I wasn't thinking of leaving the Mistakes."

"And then at a certain point there was an advert in the *Melody Maker* for girl band looking for drummer, which was the Bodysnatchers. And my memory of it is that actually, I told the same boyfriend, I said, 'I'm interested to know who they are,' because I knew all the women on the circuit—it's not Jam Today, it's not the Slits, the ones that you know—this was another one. And he was only meant to find out who they were. But when I came back from work, he says, 'Your audition is at 10 o'clock tomorrow in London.' And it was just like, 'My audition?!' So for some reason, I went along, which is strange. And I drove down to London with my drum kit and I did the audition."

"And they had sacked Jane and they were about to embark on a tour, which is like stupid of them. And I hadn't actually booked my summer holiday and the gigs were quite separated. I was still carrying on working, but I said, 'Okay, I'll do the tour for you.' And I would get a train up to Manchester, go over to the Manchester Apollo, which is a big place in England, where a roadie had set up my drum kit, which was like, amazing. So in the Mistakes, I drove our big van, I had a transit van. So when we went to women's gigs, sometimes my boyfriend couldn't come, he was doing mixing, he was a sound engineer. So I had to set up all the bloody equipment, drive the bloody van, do everything. So to turn up at a gig and a roadie had already set up the drum kit and tuned it, it was just like heaven. I'd do the gig, walk away, get on the train back to Oxfordshire, and go to work. I'd never played big places like that. There were 3,000 people. In the Mistakes, we were happy if we got 80 people in the local pub. And I had no idea how to do ska and reggae music. I remember Lynval from the Specials teaching me the reggae one." She joined the Bodysnatchers in time to accompany them on a short supporting tour of Scotland with the Specials in late September. But on September 23, 1980, she and the rest of the women in the band played at the Leicester De Montfort for a performance that will forever be re-experienced by audiences. This performance was filmed by cinematographer Joe Dunton for American director Joe Massot as part of the 2 Tone classic documentary, *Dance Craze*.

"*Dance Craze* was an idea from the director's son who was at school," says Dunton in an interview during the Bradford Film Festival in 2011. "He had seen the bands at that time at college and he had said to his dad, Joe Massot, 'You have got to make a film of these bands.' Joe Massot had directed the picture *The Song Remains the Same* with Led Zeppelin. I had met him when he used to come into Samuelsons when he was making *The Song Remains the Same* and we used to chat. I was basically an engineer and camera person."[216] The film was screened in the UK in spring of 1981

[216] "The Making of 'Dance Craze' by Joe Dunton." in70mm.com. 26 March 2011. in70mm.com/news/2011/dance_craze/index.htm. Accessed 4 July 2022.

and the following year in limited release in the US. Denton says the film was different because it wasn't a "'third row film,'—not shot from the audience, from the third row; everyone shot concert films from the third row, and it does not mean anything, and because the bands were young bands I ended up being on stage with them. ..."[217] This perspective attempted to capture the energy and excitement of the band with as close to a live experience as possible, and, as Producer Gavrik Losey stated, "... to give kids otherwise too young to attend concerts the chance to see the bands perform."[218] It also furthered the ethos established by the Specials of removing the barrier, and therefore hierarchy, between audience and performer as they typically did during their legendary stage invasions.

The Bodysnatchers performed three songs for *Dance Craze*—the Desmond Dekker classic, "007," their first single and Dandy Livingstone cover, "Let's Do Rock Steady," and their second single and original composition, "Easy Life." Still to this day, the Bodysnatchers endure questionable judgment over song selection and performance. "Here were the bands doing what they did best," writes Horace Panter of the Specials in his book.[219] "Admittedly the Specials and the Beat were the only bands who didn't doctor their soundtracks like the others appeared to. (Where do all those backing vocals come from on The Bodysnatchers' tunes?)" he writes, as if that petty inquiry really matters. Incidentally, the audio was produced later for the film, as it was for many of the other bands. Penny notes in her diary on October 27, 1980, "Over to Ayr recording studios to overdub on film sound-track (backing vocals and keyboards)."

Rhoda Dakar has never watched the film, she says in a 2019 interview. "I've never seen it. I don't know, I can't watch it," she states, though members of the Interrupters tell her they were inspired by her performance. "... *Dance Craze* particularly inspires us. We listened to it pretty much every day, before we go on stage we watch it, we see Rhoda, we see Pauline and that energy inspires us to get up on stage. That punk rock energy that you can dance to, it inspires in the studio and on stage," says Aimee Interrupter.[220] Rhoda does acknowledge that *Dance Craze* is "the reason, I think, pretty much, why people remember us."

Four days after their *Dance Craze* performance, the Bodysnatchers supported Split Enz at the Hammersmith Odeon and then the next day, on September 28 through October 1, 1980, they accompanied the legendary Toots & the Maytals on a mini-tour. The only notes that Penny makes of this tour is that there was "no soundcheck" on each night, that there were "not many ppl." at the Coventry Tiffanys gig, and on the last night at Brighton Top Rank there was an "argument over paying PA and lights." Nicky Summers says that performing with Toots & the Maytals was one of her fondest memories.

---

[217] Ibid.
[218] "No Substitute for a Live Gig," *Marylebone Mercury*, 27 Feb. 1981.
[219] Panter, Horace. *Ska'd for Life: A Personal Journey with The Specials*. Pan Books, 2007, p. 261.
[220] "People Get Ready." *Vive Le Rock!* Issue No. 61, Vol. 3, 2019, p. 53.

Set lists for their gigs throughout the year the band was together include their recorded singles along with "Monkey Spanner," "Double Barrel," "Time is Tight," "Long Shot Kick De Bucket," "Ruder Than You," a reggae version of "London Bridge is Falling Down," their own "Ghost of the Vox Continental," and the powerful song, "the Boiler" which wasn't recorded by the Bodysnatchers. It was recorded after the breakup of the band, in 1982 as "Rhoda with the Special A.K.A. featuring Nicky Summers" with John Shipley on guitar, John Bradbury on drums, Dick Cuthell on cornet, and Jerry Dammers on organ and producing. "That song is very personal to her," says Sarah-Jane of Rhoda. "We related to it and felt like it was something that we wanted to say. Of course, most people in the audience didn't quite get it at first because the song is jogging along and it tells the story and you don't get until the end what is happening. So I think it really gave us an edge because we weren't afraid to say how things really were and I think we gained the respect of so many more women at that point who became part of our fanbase because of what we were standing up for."

Stella says that though this song was difficult in terms of content, it was important to expose the reality of date rape that many women experienced. "Rhoda wrote the song. I thought it came from, and when I say personal experience, I don't mean Rhoda's personal experience, but probably somebody that she knew or some second-hand interpretation of it. That was a very difficult song to perform. I think a lot of the band members felt that—not that we didn't want to perform it, but it was a difficult song and it was challenging sometimes for the audience and for us, but it was certainly very compelling," Stella says.

Nicky recalls the way the song was written and later recorded. "Bodysnatchers songs came about with the music first. We would generally collaborate and jam on pieces of music or someone would have a few chords, bassline, or keyboard line. Rhoda would then be inspired by our musical output and put the lyrics to it. She would listen to us play in rehearsals and write while we played. The Boiler—we used to jam around a 1960s' sounding keyboard riff and gradually this piece of music grew. I remember coming out of Gaz Mayall's club, Gaz's Rockin' Blues, one night and asking Rhoda to put lyrics to it. She came along to the next rehearsal and improvised over the music an experience of a rape. The song title was called this because the manager of the Nips, a guy called Howard, used to refer to women as 'Boilers.' I think we were being ironic when we called the song that," she says. Rhoda told Daniel Rachel the following about the title: "'Old boiler' was a phrase Nicky told me she'd hear men use to describe ugly women."[221] In the same way that other victimized groups reclaim the derisive and abusive language that is used upon them, so too did Rhoda seize and recode this term, thereby removing power from the oppressor.

---

[221] Rachel, Daniel. *Walls Come Tumbling Down: The Music and Politics of Rock Against Racism, 2 Tone and Red Wedge 1976-1992*. Picador, 2016, p. 290.

Nicky continues her recount of the song, "The audience reaction was generally stunned silence. They didn't used to even clap hardly after we played it, but they were always definitely transfixed by the song. Jerry Dammers did a different treatment of the song and I rewrote the bass line when we recorded it with Rhoda and the Special A.K.A. I like both versions of the song. The Bodysnatchers version was more of a 60s R'n'B thrash. It was powerful to play live. It's challenging song for any audience, I think more powerful live than Dammer's version which is manicured with production. The song itself had to be written, played, and recorded and I'm glad and proud to have been a part of it."

Pauline Black has also expressed her respect for Rhoda, saying of the song, "We're talking unreconstructed male personages who might have been able to take on board the black-white thing, but expecting them to do anything else? No. Rhoda has my undying admiration for the song."[222] Juliet De Valero Wills, manager of the Selecter, reflects, "Rhoda had total balls to do that," using a male expression since a female version does not exist.[223]

Rhoda had a background in theater, so portraying the real emotion of a first-person account of rape in song was a comfortable and convincing platform for her. She told Rachel, "If you read Stanislavski [co-founder of the Moscow Art Theatre] there's a technique called the 'emotion memory' where you take something that has made you terrified and you reuse that feeling using the words you've got to speak. That's all it was. The rape recounted in the song didn't happen to me. I was used to acting so therefore I was used to having an effect on the audience. I would have been more horrified had it just gone over their heads and they didn't react to it."[224] In an interview with Marc Wasserman in 2009, Rhoda says the song was more inspired than mere theatrics. "A friend had been raped a couple of years earlier and I supposed I was thinking of her at the time," she said.[225]

When the song was recorded and released in 1982, it received little to no airplay (for more on this, see section on the Special AKA). Silencing the voice of this song further demonstrated the problem behind the subject matter, as Rhoda observed. "In Britain, rape is something that you don't talk about, even if it happens to you," she told Thrills. "The attitude of a lot of people is that girls on their own are just asking for it by the way they dress or the fact that they are walking around late at night … we are almost conditioned to think that if a girl is raped, then it's her own fault, which is ridiculous. A woman walking around late at night is somehow regarded as inviting some sort of approach. They just assume that you're looking for a bloke. It's the same stupid attitude."[226] Despite the lack of airplay, and the commentary from critics like Garry Bushell writing that the song "sticks out in a set of general good

[222] Ibid.
[223] Ibid.
[224] Ibid.
[225] Wasserman, Marco. "Exclusive: Interview with Rhoda Dakar of The Bodysnatchers, The Special AKA & Skaville UK." Marco on the Bass. 13 Jan. 2009. marcoonthebass.blogspot.com. Accessed 23 Feb. 2022.
[226] Ibid.

cheer like a clown at a wake,"[227] "The Boiler" reached number 35 on British singles charts.[228]

Rape is predominantly an overt display of misogyny—power and violence of the typically male aggressor over the typically female subject. Less overt misogyny, however, is also painful and powerful and comes in many forms. All of the members of the Bodysnatchers recall experiencing the latter form of misogyny during this era in the form of sexism. "Being taken seriously, being listened to, especially when it was around executive ideas or decisions that need to be made," Sarah-Jane listed as some of the general sexism she experienced. Adrian Thrills wrote in 1980, "And what of those ever-present nagging doubts of sexism in the ska field? One wonders if Prince Buster would appreciate the ironies of the Bodysnatchers tampering with a genre that has produced such pearls of wisdom as 'The Ten Commandments' and 'Wreck a Pum-Pum.' Nicky is philosophical. 'Obviously things like that get up your nose if you're a girl, but we don't push it. We just want to be up there helping people to enjoy themselves.' Stella takes the sexism question a stage further. 'The links we do have with ska music are through the things in it that we can use to our advantage. It's the music we are using, not the lyrics [though they certainly did]. I mean stuff like Prince Buster's 'Ten Commandments' is so ridiculously sexist that it's hysterical. It must be tongue-in-cheek.' 'I bet it isn't,' Rhoda muses—a little closer to the mark, methinks."[229] As a sidenote, it took over five decades for a response come to that song, "the Ten Commandments," delivered by activist Saffiyah Khan backed by the Specials. "It got better and better as the years went on," said Sarah-Jane. "You could see with the movement of more and more women musicians coming to the forefront, it wasn't a novelty anymore and people would take women more seriously." Certainly, the Bodysnatchers have a hand in that evolution.

Critics were certainly sexist, writing comments like "The Bodysnatchers are nothing if not ambitious. Apart from throwing themselves in at the deep end as far as writing and playing go, they do not as yet have a manager to keep them on the straight and narrow."[230] This kind of subtle sexism is perhaps most dangerous of all because it is slight and enters the subconscious of the reader where they may be less likely to critically question it, and more likely to accept and repeat it. It is a microaggression. To remove the veil of this comment, consider if it would ever be lobbed at an all-male, or more accurately an "all-boy" band. Other critics were sure to point out that Miranda was a "schoolgirl,"[231] and described Sarah-Jane as "delicious."[232] Using the schtick of an alien abduction to cue the Invasion of the Bodysnatchers film, the notorious Garry Bushell nauseatingly uses phrases like, "my suspicions were first

---

[227] Bushell, Garry. "The Selecter/The Bodysnatchers: Live Injection." *Sounds*, 1 Mar. 1980.

[228] Wasserman, Marco. "Exclusive: Interview with Rhoda Dakar of The Bodysnatchers, The Special AKA & Skaville UK." Marco on the Bass. 13 Jan. 2009. marcoonthebass.blogspot.com/2009/01/exclusive-interview-with-rhoda-dakar-of.html. Accessed 23 Feb. 2022.

[229] Thrills, Adrian. "Rude Girls and Dirty Phone Calls." *NME*. 26 Jan. 1980.

[230] Kelly, Ryan. "Girls Talk." *Smash Hits*, 1 May 1980, p. 13.

[231] "Bodysnatchers." *Ska 80: The Beat from the Street*. SB Publishing, No. 1, 1980.

[232] Nicholls, Mike. "Bitching Bopper." *Record Mirror*, 23 Feb. 1980, p. 32.

aroused…" and "when they penetrated Top of the Pops …" to describe his lead up to an interview before writing that his "companion" named "Gross Halfwit" made "requests for photos 'naked in showers,' 'down the ladies loos.'"[233] In one article, Bushell commented about Sarah-Jane Owen, "I clapped till they encored, but was this only to get another glimpse of SJ, a woman so moodily beautiful that I couldn't believe Playboy talent scouts weren't camped out in front of the stage."[234]

Sexism also exists in the repeated statements from critics underlining the point that the musicians in the Bodysnatchers were inexperienced. By their own admission they were, but this was not uncommon for an all-female group. It was the frequency and the volume of these comments from male music journalists that hints at something deeper. "… the Bodysnatchers suffered in the press because of their lack of playing skill; it appears from music press reports of female instrumentalists that the writers became obsessed with the concept of women players and their lack of skill …" says author Helen Reddington who writes much more about this phenomenon in her work.[235] Mavis Bayton, guitarist with the Mistakes, sociologist, and author studied and wrote her dissertation focused on the imbalance of female musicians during this era. She observes that because young girls were not encouraged to learn music in school nor from their families in the 1950s and 1960s in England, but boys were given opportunities to learn instruments, women during the punk era felt empowered to level the playing field. That, however, came with a publicly visible learning curve. She states, "For some the very rudiments of playing their instrument are learnt within the band."[236] Therefore, male journalists who would "obsess" with the lack of musical ability of a brand new all-female band were simply observing the process of righting the ship.

Lest we think that all sexist comments were from male critics toward the female lineup, female music reporters, what few there were, could be just as harsh in allowing gender to taint their opinion. "I found the sight of five girls standing in a line (Jane's sat at the back, and Nicky a bit behind the offensive like a mother hen) stomping up and down vaguely hysterical," said music reporter Jane Garcia of *New Music News*.[237] Never has a male been compared to a mother hen. Nor has Terry Hall's pogo been described as vaguely hysterical—well, at least not often.

Also counter to the bouncy tone and fun-girl image was the social environment of violent racism that presented at many 2 Tone shows, including those of the Bodysnatchers. The aforementioned music critic Jane Garcia accompanied the Bodysnatchers on tour in 1980 where she witnessed, "a lot of trouble and fighting between rival gangs of [racist] skinheads, some of whom had made the trip from London for the punch-up/gig. The Bodysnatchers got their fair share of gob and

[233] Bushell, Garry. "Ruder Than the Rest." *Sounds*, 26 Apr. 1980, p. 14.
[234] Bushell, Garry. "The Selecter/The Bodysnatchers: Live Injection." *Sounds*, 1 Mar. 1980.
[235] Reddington, Helen. *The Lost Women of Rock Music: Female Musicians of the Punk Era*. Equinox Publishing, 2012, p. 150.
[236] Bayton, Mavis. *Frock Rock: Women Performing Popular Music*. Oxford University Press, 1998, p. 84.
[237] Garcia, Jane. "Girls Keep Skanking." *New Music News*, 1980, p. 13.

Seigheils and even Rhoda's sharpish tongue, which had silenced the obviously weedier Aylesbury skins the previous night couldn't shut this lot up. In the end, Jane, an impulsive little creature ran down from behind her drumkit and gave everyone standing at the center front a Coca-Cola shower and they took the hint. That apart, it was a good set."[238]

Stella recalls, "My memory of it was that it was quite anarchic. Firstly, the whole [racist] skinhead movement was very strange, if you think about it, because the bands on 2 Tone had black members and white and there's a very strong Jamaican influence and a strong representation in bands, and yet you have this [racist] skinhead British Movement, National Front, and we had some nasty clashes at some of the gigs when we were supporting the Specials, for example, and were quite scary. It was not so much us. But spitting was a thing and there was some of that coming our way and you had to look out for it flying, so that was a bit unruly."

It was more than unruly for Rhoda Dakar, the one member of the band who felt these attacks deeply as a black woman. "My most remembered gig was Guilford where the audience seig heiled for so long there, it was like proper NF times, National Front. So there was lots of seig heiling in the audience and what we did is when people started to seig heil, you'd walk off until they stopped and then come back on. But I remember at Guilford, they didn't stop so I had to come back on and shout at them until they stopped in order for us to carry on the gig. Otherwise, you know, we'd have to abandon set," she says.

Though the members of the Bodysnatchers were united against fascist and racist violence at their shows, division within their own ranks began to widen. "It was what they call band differences, I believe," says Penny, laughing. "There were definitely divisions in the band. I mean, I think I could see that they were very much along class lines, looking back on it. It's very prevalent in England especially. There's definitely a sort of working class/middle class divide." Stella says that the band started to have larger problems after Jane Summers left the band. "There was a very definite conflict of interest between the five of us and then Rhoda and Nicky. Because by that time Jane had left and then Judy was in the band. So it was a very different view on things—what we should be doing, what we should be singing, who we should be supporting, and it seemed like every discussion we had, it was Rhoda and Nicky on one side of the line and the five of us on the other. And it got worse and worse. We were young and we were headstrong and opinionated. I think the deciding thing was that the five of us wanted to play more than just reggae. We wanted to evolve and to play some punk, some pop or whatever, and the other two were just adamant that they wanted to continue to play ska and reggae. It wasn't that we five people left the two—it was just we can't carry on. We want to make more music, so we'll splinter off and we'll do that," she says. And splinter off they did, forming the Belle Stars (see also Belle Stars chapter). Rhoda told Daniel Rachel, "Five of the Bodysnatchers wanted to be pop tarts and Nicky and I wanted to keep going in the same tradition.

---

[238] Ibid.

They endured the politics but that wasn't their motivation. Life had been good to them; they didn't really need to change stuff. We played at the Oxford Ball where Penny's dad was a professor. It was like, 'What do you need to change, particularly? Your life's OK.' There was no reason to swim against the tide."[239]

Penny Leyton clarifies that Rhoda's recollection is "completely untrue." She states, "Rhoda is mistaken in this: my dad was never a professor, he was not connected to the college at which we played the ball, and the Oxford ball gig was booked through our agent as all our other gigs were booked—in the same way as pretty much all the bands that played at Oxford college balls. Neither I nor my family had anything to do with the booking of this gig. It's a long time ago but I believe that doesn't mean lies should prevail. I have to say that this was typical of the huge chip Rhoda had on her shoulder; without actually finding anything out about other people in the band, she made assumptions based on her prejudices and treated us accordingly. My dad was so poor when he was growing up his parents had to send him to more well-off relatives to be looked after at times. We grew up not in indulgent richness as Rhoda seems to think but with very limited means as he had to support his parents and brother. But Rhoda loved to create a narrative in which she was the victim. She was an amazing performer, but horrible to work with when she couldn't get her own way, and the rest of the time she spent making sarcastic comments to (and about) the rest of us (those of us who were not Nicky or Jane). What's more, she says 'your life's ok' and 'there was no reason to swim against the tide'—what a load of prejudiced rubbish. We were all swimming against the tide just playing music. Of course we wanted to change things. Just being a woman, of any race or class, playing in a band was a challenge. I think many, if not all of us, wanted it to be easier for women and girls to be able to play in bands and not be mocked."[240]

An additional reason the members of the band had different opinions on musical direction is that appeal in 2 Tone began to wane in the fall of 1980. Since the first 2 Tone release in July 1979 (The Specials "Gangsters"/The Selecter "The Selecter"), the label had received tremendous publicity in music magazines, bands had exposure on television shows, and most releases had ample airplay, with the exception of the aforementioned "the Boiler." Music journalist Jane Garcia grew to hate the music she said sounded like "a cross between a washing-machine and a waste disposal unit, plus a hatred for most things 2 Tone and Go-Feet, born of having it rammed into my ears every day for the last 12 months by the media."[241] Many of the bands that signed to the 2 Tone label at the tail end of its tenure were not ska bands at all. And those that were, and hoped to remain relevant, had to consider new ways to approach the material. The Bodysnatchers found themselves at the end of that 2 Tone era and like the label, the band suffered from the decline in popularity. Their second single didn't chart well, many gigs had low attendance, and support from the label was

---

[239] Rachel, Daniel. *Walls Come Tumbling Down: The Music and Politics of Rock Against Racism, 2 Tone and Red Wedge 1976-1992*. Picador, 2016, p. 311.
[240] Leyton, Penny. Email with the author, 27 Oct. 2022.
[241] Garcia, Jane. "Girls Keep Skanking." *New Music News*, 1980, p. 13.

weak, to say the least. "Everyone up until us, everyone just had a one single deal," says Rhoda of the agreement with 2 Tone. "So you did one single, it usually did very well, and then you got to sign an album deal. You go make your album somewhere else. But for us, they decided that we should have to do two singles. So we had one single, it did very well, and then the second single didn't really do anything. So at the end of it, we were left without an album deal, without the possibility of an album deal. So it actually made things very difficult for us. It wasn't good for us at all."

No one had told Judy when she auditioned shortly before the breakup that there were problems simmering. Needless to say, the split came as quite a shock. "I had left my job as a civil engineer scientist and joined the Bodysnatchers, only to find out that they split a few weeks after I'm finished working my notice. There were internal arguments in the band. It was like, I hadn't realized you had problems. I hadn't realized there was actually a deep hatred between two factions," she says.

The official announcement of the breakup came, according to Penny's diary entries, in mid-October 1980. "Thu Oct 16: Goldsmith's College. Nicky tells us that band is splitting up after 31st. Too many support bands booked," she writes, which is why the band had to continue to fulfill their obligations. Her entries indicate they could have, perhaps even should have, separated sooner. Nicky herself recounts the breakup of the band. "Later during the year, around October 1980, during a sound check, I recall, in Manchester (it was raining!) a couple of band members fell out and it appeared to be irreconcilable differences. The band split up and we booked a farewell concert at Camden Music Machine in November, exactly one year after our first gig," she says.

The incident that led to the breakup of the Bodysnatchers was not a good one, to say the least. In short, there was violence, but to protect the identities of those involved, and to prevent any distraction from the impact and meaning of this powerful group of women, specifics will be omitted here. Perhaps this tumultuous ending is why when male interviewers repeatedly ask Rhoda if the "girls" are going to get back together (as if it were normal to call a 50- or 60-year-old man a "boy"), she replies with curt frustration, "No."[242] She is reluctant to talk much about her time with the band, perhaps due to the way it all ended. "I don't remember looking back and thinking, 'Oh, we had some great times.' Well, no, we didn't. I mean, I was in the Bodysnatchers for 13 months. If you were great friends, you would have lasted longer. We weren't great friends. So it didn't last longer. So I don't look back on the Bodysnatchers with any fondness whatsoever. I just think, yeah, done and dusted, you know. Onwards and upwards."

Others look back at their time with the band more favorably. "It was totally exhilarating. It really really was. I sort of—well my feet didn't feel like they had touched the ground. Everything happened so quickly—from meeting Nicky, then the gig, and sometime very early on we were asked if we wanted to record a single on 2

[242] Joachim. "This is Not a Bodysnatchers Reunion—The Rhoda Dakar Interview." Reggae Steady Ska. 31 Oct. 2014. reggae-steady-ska.com/bodysnatchers-reunion-rhoda-dakar-interview. Accessed 23 Feb. 2022.

Tone and then to go on tour with the Selecter—it was all such a whirlwind, but it was so exciting and I feel very very lucky to be in that situation," said Sarah-Jane.

Nicky Summers, the juggernaut behind the whole expedition, also has good memories but says the ending came because the direction of the band had just strayed too far from her original idea. "For roughly a year we toured consistently in Britain and Ireland and had the opportunity to support great bands such as Madness and Toots and the Maytals as well as supporting the Specials on the Seaside Tour in the summer of 1980 alongside the Go-Go's," says Nicky. "We rarely had time off and I remember I wanted us all to take a break and write some new material, experiment more, but some members of the band were afraid we might lose the momentum we had achieved. We had signed to 2 Tone but it seemed we were managed by Chrysalis (the record company 2 Tone was affiliated with) who, for my part, appeared to wish to market us as a pop girl band and for me I felt I was losing my original intention of why I had formed the band from a creative (and social) point of view."

The impact of an all-female band at a particular point in time cannot be fully understood. It transcends geography, transcends that period of time, transcends the very sounds that came from the instruments they played and the presence they offered. "It was great to have girls in the audience from different backgrounds," says Nicky. "It meant in a way that we had reached out and inspired young women in a way to do something more with their lives—to take action for themselves. I always think that when you are in a band that has some success that you have some sort of influence, even subtle, on the public. And I always think, what message to give especially young women. To be in a band is to maybe acquire a certain role, so what would you do with it? What is the best way? How do you want to encourage support, and inspire other women to be independent, confident in themselves, creative, start initiatives, be more respectful of their gender."

Sarah-Jane Owen, Penny Leyton, Miranda Joyce, Judy Parsons, and Stella Barker all left to form their own band, the Belle Stars, along with Lesley Shone on bass and Jennie Matthias as lead vocalist, later joined by Clare Hirst on saxophone and keyboards (see also Belle Stars chapter). Rhoda Dakar continued to perform and record with the Specials and the Special AKA (see also the Specials and the Special AKA chapter). Nicky Summers worked briefly with Rhoda and the Special AKA for the recording of "the Boiler" before leaving music altogether. She says, "I realised I had spent about 4 years hanging out on the music scene and spending most of my time in clubs or recording studios and decided I wanted to see more of the world. I was still very young, about 22. I played with a few bands briefly but over the next few years put more energy into travel, holistic healing, painting and photography—went to Art School (Chelsea) and became a Buddhist. In 1986 I officially joined the Buddhist group SGI-UK. I have chanted the mantra Nam-Myoho-Renge-Kyo (the title of the Lotus Sutra) daily ever since and it has answered all my questions about life and more. I do not regret anything."

The Bodysnatchers: (left to right) Jane Summers, Nicky Summers, Rhoda Dakar, Penny Leyton, Stella Barker, Miranda Joyce, Sarah-Jane Owen

RUDE GIRL types (guitar(s) with noisy vocals, drums) sought by similar bassist (rudimentary but improving) Ska, rock, reggae, early punk ideas for fast, emotive, danceable stuff. Sharp Brains Around 20 years. 01-886 9775 (Nicola).

Original advertisement for Bodysnatchers, *NME*, May 26, 1979

(Above, L to R) Rhoda Dakar, Miranda Joyce, and Sarah-Jane Owen, (below) the Bodysnatchers and the Specials on the Seaside Tour, courtesy Penny Leyton

Bodysnatchers and the Go-Go's (above) and Miranda Joyce with Lynval
Golding (below) on the Seaside Tour with the Specials, courtesy Penny Leyton

Members of the Bodysnatchers and the Specials on the Seaside Tour,
courtesy Penny Leyton

Debbie Harry's rude girl look (left) and
Penny Leyton's backstage pass for Dance
Craze premiere, from her personal
archives (right)

The Belle Stars

Stella Barker: guitar
Clare Hirst: saxophone
Miranda Joyce: saxophone
Penny Leyton: keyboard

Jennie McKeown/Matthias: vocals
Sarah-Jane Owen: guitar
Judy Parsons: drums
Lesley Shone: bass

It may seem strange to begin a chapter about the Belle Stars with a bit of background on canboulay. Allow a little latitude here, but canboulay, a derivation of the French words cannes brulees meaning burning canes, was a procession of celebration during festivals in the Caribbean. These processions featured masked characters representing people and animals in a theatrical dance that entertained festival goers and lampooned life. But there was a serious side to canboulay as well. The very origin of the burning canes recalled the centuries of slavery and occasions of revolt when slaves destroyed the enslavers' plantations with canes of fire. During canboulay, a kalinda, or stick fight, was part of the celebration and featured a group or band of some two dozen men led by a "big pappy" who directed their crew through the streets until they encountered a rival group. There each group would boast of their prowess, issue challenges to one another, and engage in a mock battle, all accompanied by music. These processions date back as far as 1774 in Jamaica where carnival was called jonkunnu. Stick fights, incidentally, are also central to sound system clash culture in the 1950s forward.[243]

The canboulay is the foundation for the Belle Stars most popular song, "Iko Iko." It was not their original creation and was instead a cover of the version recorded by the Dixie Cups, another all-female band, in 1965. The original song was written in 1953 by New Orleans native James Crawford, better known as Sugar Boy and his Canecutters, and the song was originally titled "Jockamo." Crawford says that this word was a chant he heard during processionals in his city during Mardi Gras.[244] Could this be a mutation of jonkunnu? The lyrics of the song certainly tell of a canboulay with the big pappy represented by the "flag boy," the presence of fire, and boasting. And Crawford said his lyrics were written to describe the Mardi Gras processionals which share roots with the processionals of jonkunnu and carnival.

All of this is a rather lengthy verbal Venn diagram that aims to show the connections between, well, a myriad of cultural phenomena—geography and history and, of course, music. But none of this was apparent to the Belle Stars when they chose this song as their pièce de resistance. No, it was nothing quite so overt as that. The song came to them via an audition of their new lead singer, Jennie McKeown, better known as Jennie Bellestar.

---

[243] Augustyn, Heather. *Ska: The Rhythm of Liberation, Rowman & Littlefield*, 2013, p. 8.
[244] "Behind The Song: Sugar Boy and his Canecutters / The Dixie Cups, 'Jockamo / Iko Iko.'" American Songwriter. americansongwriter.com/behind-the-song-sugar-boy-and-his-canecutters-the-dixie-cups-jockamo-iko-iko. Accessed 13 July 2022.

To say that Jennie Bellestar had a rough childhood is putting it mildly. According to her own book, *Surviving the Storm*, Jennie was "born out of wedlock to an Irish/English mother and Jamaican father, both of which were poorly educated."[245] Her mother's last name was McKeown and her father's was Matthias, both of which she took as her surname interchangeably. Her given name is Eugenie Theresa, though she's always gone by Jennie. Jennie's mother was violent to the extreme, as she unveils, therefore Jennie left the home regularly. "My early years were spent in poverty, and by the time I was three, my Mother bore 3 children. Bernadette, who was originally the eldest, died before I was born, then came me, and a year later my little sister Elaine. When money was tight, moods ran high, and tolerance of anything slightly annoying to my Mother became very low. It was on one of these low days that Elaine had been crying incessantly, and her high-pitched tones were too much for my Mother's short temper. She just snapped, grabbed a pillow, put it over her face while I looked on in helpless horror, terror, fear, anger, and sadness. After a short while, Elaine cried no more, nor would I ever see or play with her ever again in this lifetime. I was left alone with a Mother aware that I had witnessed her actions and, boy, I was going to pay in later years for that involuntary intrusion," she writes.[246] Jennie's only happy memories of childhood were times she lived outside of her mother Margaret McKeown's home. She was sent to a convent by social services and to a children's home before being placed back in her mother's home at age eight. Here she "spent the following years there as a slave and a punch bag for my Mother's moods," as Jennie was forced to cook, clean, wash, and care for an additional six children in the home. When her mother suffered a nervous breakdown, social services sent Jennie and her siblings to childrens' homes or boarding schools. Placed in one of these boarding schools, Jennie was expelled and returned to her mother's home, though that was short-lived, and she entered yet another children's home. Jennie was only 15 years old.[247]

At the age of 16, Jennie began working at a factory laboratory and moved in with a boyfriend. They were together for five years and the relationship was healthy for her. Her next relationship, however, was not so healthy. "I then met Steve, became attached to him and hung with his friends who introduced me to recreational drugs, which went with being young, free, and punk. I lived a freedom I had never known before, and as this was during the punk era, anything went. Music, gigs, and fun were my pastime," she writes.[248] It was during this time, at the age of 21, that Jennie McKeown became the lead vocalist of the Belle Stars.

The five members of the Belle Stars that transitioned from the Bodysnatchers needed to augment their band with a charismatic lead singer and a skilled bass player, so they did what initially brought many of them to the group and placed an advertisement in music magazine. "We were a bit older and wiser at this point," recalls

---

[245] Matthias, Jennie. *Surviving the Storm*. Breakfree Forever Publishing, 2019, p. 23.
[246] Ibid, p. 24.
[247] Ibid, p. 25-26.
[248] Ibid, p. 26.

Stella Barker.[249] "We advertised and asked around to get a bass player and a singer. We knew what we wanted by then, so we auditioned quite a few bass players and a few singers and Jennie was the one. When we met up with her, she was the obvious one," Stella says.

Jennie recalls that audition and says she came at the behest of a friend. "So, I'm hanging out with a young lady. And she was just someone random that I'd met in the apartment, we became friends. And she said to me, 'Jennie, I'm going to do some singing in a studio, will you come with me?' And I was just like, 'No, really, I've got a cold,' this and that. And she's like, 'Jennie, I need some support.' So, I thought, well, I'll go there. So, I went there and I hung out in the studio and I watched these people singing. I was waiting for her to do the backing vocals. The producer guy, and the guy that was running the studio, I think his name was Ian, a really lovely guy, we were chatting and getting along really well. And then the track, by the way, was called 'Iko.' This is, this is a fairy story. All of a sudden, the lead singer has come out and the producer guy says to everybody, 'Thank you,' and then he said to me, 'Why don't you give it a try?' I said, 'Oh, no, I can't sing!' He says to me, 'You've got a great speaking voice, give it a try,' so I gave the backing vocals a try and then I came in. I'd seen what they'd done, but I'd never sung before in the studio. And I said, 'I told you I couldn't sing,' and he said, 'Oh no, you're wrong there. Do you think you could do the lead part?' I was like, 'Excuse me?' Now I kind of had an idea what the lead part was because I'd been watching for an hour what was going on, so I said, 'Okay okay, I'll give it a try.' I'm in there singing this song, singing pretty bad, but I did it and the next thing you know, he put it on a cassette and he said to me, 'Here it is, keep learning and come back to the studio.' Anyway, I went home that night and I passed it to my boyfriend at that time and Paul said to me, 'I didn't know you could sing.' And I said, 'No! Nor did I!'"

She continues, "The following day, his ex-girlfriend, who used to be in a band called the Bodysnatchers, Sarah-Jane [Owen], she said, 'Paul, I don't know, it's a long shot, but I don't know if you know of anybody, but we just lost our singer, who's Rhoda, she's black, right? And we're looking for somebody, you know, black, mixed race, and everything else.' He says, 'Look no further, she's sitting right next to me on the bed.' She said, 'What are you talking about?' and he then described me, and she said, 'I've seen her at Gaz's Rockin' Blues! I love the way she dresses—can she sing?' So, he said yeah, and she said, 'You think she'll come down?' And he said, 'Yeah, I'm sure she will.' He didn't even ask me, he just said, I'm sure she will. Anyway, so I go down there to this audition. I've never been to an audition in my life, and out of 26 people, they gave it to me, bearing in mind that in them days, I was really shy and I sang to the wall because it was the only freaking song I had sung in my life. That's why 'Iko' is in the band and as you know, 'Iko' has been the most important song of the Belle Stars," she says.[250]

[249] Barker, Stella. All quotations, unless otherwise noted, from interview with the author, 27 Oct. 2020.
[250] Matthias, Jennie. Interviewed by the author, 12 Dec. 2020.

Incidentally, "Iko Iko" failed to chart when the Belle Stars released it in in 1982 because it was usurped by a version recorded by Natasha England that reached the top ten. Jennie also explains how that happened. "The Belle Stars were playing 'The Venue' which was quite a prestigious gig, and the place and atmosphere were jumping. Dave Robinson's [Stiff Records] wife Anne was in the audience and had brought her friend Natasha down to see us. On hearing our version of 'Iko' Natasha asked about the track and Anne said that we were recording it as our next single. Natasha wasted no time, went home and mentioned to her husband who happened to own Bell Records at the time, that she would like to record 'Iko' and that time was of the essence as we were recording it. Natasha sneakily got hers out there first because we were so busy with other stuff and gigs that she pipped us to the post. What proceeded from there was a competitive playoff. It seemed like the radio stations were lapping up the whole 'whose version is better' malarkey and who is going to reach highest in the chart. Sadly Natasha's version reached higher than ours but we had the last laugh when ours was chosen to be featured in some of the coolest films and adverts. Natasha's version has been lost in the channels of time whilst our version remains alive and has been sought after by many film-makers and advertisers since."[251]

Sarah-Jane Owen also recalls how the Belle Stars acquired Jennie to lead the group. "The story of how we found her [Jennie] was I asked an ex-boyfriend if he knew of anybody that he felt was a good singer and he said, 'Well actually, I'm dating a girl that sings well but I don't know whether she's ever performed in front of anybody.' I can remember she came to the interview and she was embarrassed and she said, 'I'll sing but I'm going to sing over here. I'm going to sing to the wall, if you don't mind.' She was so shy at facing all of us and singing, but she had this smoky voice, throaty voice. And you can see how she moves on stage. I think she just wasn't confident at the time she joined the band but she soon found that she was accepted. She found her confidence to really be that front person," Sarah-Jane says.[252]

Through auditions the members of the Belle Stars also found Lesley Shone on bass. "Penny Leyton and me were the organized people in the band," says Judy Parsons, "so we put out the advert that we needed a bass player and a singer and in fact, the singer Jennie came through a friend of Sarah-Jane, and Leslie came through a *Melody Maker* advert."[253] Lesley says she was influenced by listening to great bassists in music she listened to during her youth. "Being a bass player, Sly and the Family Stone's Larry Graham and I used to listen to a lot of Weather Report," she said in an interview in 2010.[254] Stella states that Lesley was good for the group because she fit in well personally, and she was a talented musician. "Les was such a great bass player. She was, well, not a lot better than us, but compared to our musicality, she was really

[251] *Belle Stars Turn Back the Clock*. Liner notes.
[252] Owen, Sarah-Jane. All quotations, unless otherwise noted, from interview with the author, 4 June 2020.
[253] Parsons Hancock, Judy. Interviewed by the author, 9 July 2022.
[254] Shone, Lesley. Interview on Edith Bowman's Album Show, 1 Dec. 2010.

up there. So having recruited those two, we really knuckled down and started writing and playing different styles and listening to lots more music to get ideas and things."

Before they played their first gig as their new incarnation, the women needed to find a new name. Miranda Joyce tells the story of finally selecting the Belle Stars for their moniker. "It was almost impossible to find a name. We ended up writing all our favourite words down on pieces of paper and shuffling them around, but Judy didn't like a lot of the connotations. We thought about the Coconuts, but she didn't like the hair and milk connotations," to which Sarah-Jane Owen replied, "and Crazy Cactus wasn't any good because of all the prickles connotations."[255] So Belle Stars became the name as a mash up between words they could agree upon. Setting out to showcase their new sound and new look, they did perform a few selelctions from their old repertoire. They transitioned with one or two Bodysnatchers tunes, like "Too Experienced," but they added "Iko Iko" to the mix. Another original, "Hiawatha," addressed the right-wing nationalistic movement they had witnessed at Bodysnatchers gigs. Because popularity in ska had started to wane, the Belle Stars wanted to expand their musical repertoire and their new songs showed the direction the new lineup was headed. Penny Leyton states, "We started off playing a lot of the music that the Bodysnatchers played, but we changed … because then, the ska days were kind of over. People were wanting different things."[256] But the women had to maintain the momentum they gained in the Bodysnatchers so they didn't have to start from scratch with the music industry and fanbase. "We used the fact that we were a spin-off from the Bodysnatchers to begin with, to get gigs or interest from record companies and agents," said Judy.[257]

Having just come from an imploding band, Judy says she was surprised that riding that wave was still possible. "When they [Bodysnatchers] split they said, 'Oh, we'll make it again, Judy, we'll make it again.' And I thought, 'Oh, you're so arrogant! You know nothing of the real world!' I'd just come from the real world where you were really happy to get a gig in a local pub, and they'd just risen up to fame from nowhere. The first gig they [Bodysnatchers] played, they got signed up. They don't know real musicians and the slog that it is to try and get a gig and no one likes you. And then the first time we [Belle Stars] played a gig, there were three record companies there trying to sign us up, and it's just like, they were right! Arrogant, but maybe it's part of their arrogance which is what made them successful, just the assumption that they would make it again!"

Among those three record companies was the one to which the Belle Stars eventually signed—Stiff Records. Dave Robinson had been seen at their gigs, scouting the band, but the women took their time making a decision. One thing they knew for sure—they wouldn't be signing to 2 Tone. "We'd be handicapping ourselves if we re-

[255] Millar, Robbi. "Stripe Teasers." *Sounds*, 14 Mar. 1981, p. 20.
[256] Leyton, Penny. Interviewed by the author, 20 Dec. 2020.
[257] Staunton, Terry. "The Bodysnatchers." *Uncut Magazine: The Ultimate Genre Guide 2-Tone, The Specials and the Full Story of the 2 Tone Revolution,* 2019, p. 81.

signed to 2 Tone," said Miranda Joyce.[258] "Y'know people would be saying 'Oh, just another one-off or two-off single deal and it'd be the same all over again." Penny adds, "Besides, we want to get away from everything, from the image that the Bodysnatchers had."[259] Jennie says that one of the ways they got away from the 2 Tone and ska image was through the other bands that had signed to Stiff, which is the main reason they chose the label. She says, "Though we did a bit of ska, we also did pop music because things were changing then. Although we did do gigs with Madness and the Specials, we also did with Elvis Costello and all those kind of people too because we were on Stiff Records, so then we would go and support the bands of that era. There's an iconic venue in Camden Town called Dingwalls—a very popular venue. And we had a gig there, and it was our debut gig, to show the world, and we were looking for a record label. And so in those days, record labels used to hunt bands. Seven women, we can all play our own instruments and there weren't any girl bands at the time. Bananarama went out, none of these bands are out, and here we are, seven women, a proper band, everybody's a musician, and we're going to play a gig. Every single record label was there. Who do we go with? Stiff Records. And the reason is it's the smaller one but the largest independent. Because Madness were on the label, Ian Dury and the Blockheads, you name it, all the best artists, all the artists that were credible were on that label. And Stiff Records also had a really good marketing program. They would do some weird stuff, you know?"

Stiff Records was founded by Dave Robinson and Andrew Jakeman, also known as Jake Riviera, in 1976. They "started fly-posting London with posters declaring 'If it ain't Stiff It ain't worth a fuck.' They also signed the Damned, whose single 'New Rose' became the first officially recognised English punk rock record."[260] They were known for their unconventional promotional antics, including one that landed Elvis Costello in jail overnight, as well as producing picture discs and package tours, the latter of which helped to build success for all bands on the roster and were popular with audiences.

The Belle Stars signed to Stiff in April 1981. "The only time I remember we were all unanimous was about Stiff Records," said Jennie. Sarah-Jane says that the new label dictated their decisions from the get-go as Dave Robinson directed the Belle Stars to perform covers at first, rather than their own songs. "When we got signed to Stiff from 2 Tone, he [Dave Robinson] said, 'No, not yet. You will do better if you do covers first, until you get notoriety, and then you'll hit them with your own, and he was right. So we had to kind of take a lot of flak from him at first," says Sarah-Jane. There were plenty of cover songs in the Belle Stars playlist including "Iko Iko" as well as "The Clapping Song" recorded by Shirley Ellis in 1965, "Mockingbird" recorded by Inez Foxx and her brother Charlie Foxx in 1963, "Needle in a Haystack"

[258] Millar, Robbi. "Stripe Teasers." *Sounds*, 14 Mar. 1980, p. 20.
[259] Ibid.
[260] Bell, Max. "The story of Stiff, the most anarchic record label of all time." *Louder*. 28 Mar. 2018. loudersound.com/features/the-story-of-stiff-the-most-anarchic-record-label-of-all-time. Accessed 18 July 2022.

recorded by the Velvelettes in 1964, "Harlem Shuffle" recorded by Bob & Earl in 1963, and "The Snake" recorded by Al Wilson in 1968. Performing these cover songs wasn't by choice of the band members, but as women they had little choice and little voice. "Record companies do, of course, package male bands too, but the range of images and options is much wider. It also seems that women's bands may be easier to manipulate. The Belle Stars went along with what was happening partly because they lacked confidence in their own songs, ideas, and musical skills and because they were, as explained, disunited, and failed to present the company with any cohesive alternative strategy which they all believe in," wrote Mavis Bayton.[261] Judy says, "We could have said, 'No, we will not do one of your shitty, horrible covers,' but the band do what we're told by the record company. The record company books all our radio, press, TV type things and we do whatever they say."[262]

Just one month after signing, in May 1981, the Belle Stars toured in support of the Beat with fellow supporting band the Mood Elevators (see also Mood Elevators chapter) and Linton Kwesi Johnson. The Belle Stars' first single was the original, "Hiawatha," which was produced by Clive Langer and Alan Winstanley who produced for Madness. Their second single, "Slick Trick," was also produced by the same team. Since Madness was signed to Stiff Records, the two bands toured together. Belle Stars performed to promote the singles, as well as others on their *Another Latin Love Song* four-track EP released that same year. Before that, though, in early May 1981 they toured in support of the Clash for three shows in France and Belgium.

Stella recalls the tour. "We couldn't believe we had been booked to do a few European dates supporting the Clash! We could barely contain our excitement. However, we were brought resoundingly back down to reality finding ourselves meeting at the bar at Victoria Station at 8:15 p.m. to take the train down to Dover to catch the overnight ferry. My memory recalls that we didn't even have the budget for sleeping cabins and that we slept on couchettes on the upper deck. Rock 'n' roll! In some ways the gig was less terrifying than the sound check. We were so far away from the audience that we were able to concentrate on playing our best and moving around on the huge stage. The audience, who clearly were all there to see the Clash, were nevertheless gracious and gave us a good applause at the end. Phew! It was an exhilarating feeling to have played to such a big crowd. Even more exhilarating was getting on the same coach as the Clash for the next day. It was almost dream-like and so exciting for us girls, making our way in the world of rock 'n' roll. The next night we played Lille and went to a bar with some of the Clash after the gig and drank champagne. We were getting a taste for the high life! Joe Strummer referred to Judy as 'the wild woman of Borneo' all night which we thought was hilarious and that moniker stuck with her for the rest of the tour. Jennie and Paul Simenon started to get friendly that night too. I think love was in the air. I think it took all of us a while to come down from the high of being with the Clash for those few days. It was a time

[261] Bayton, Mavis. *Frock Rock: Women Performing Popular Music*. Oxford University Press, 1998, p. 84.
[262] Ibid.

that I will try to remember so that I can tell my grandchildren what I did for a few very special years when I was a young woman."[263]

The Madness tour in October and November of that year brought them to Scotland and England. They churned out releases quickly to capture the momentum of the publicity. "Stiff Records were known for doing this stuff straightaway and getting it out there immediately. They want it out like yesterday. From an artist's point of view as a songwriter, that's what you want. And also we knew that we would get very good shows, you know, get good, very good gigs because we could support many of the artists. They knew what they were doing when it came to tours and stuff," says Jennie of Stiff.

The Belle Stars did pen most of their own songs. Jennie recalled the writing process during an interview for the *Record Mirror*. "Once I get up I go to our rehearsal studios up the road. If we've got different ideas—as we quite often have because there's seven of us—we compromise. I usually write songs when I'm on my own. I'll pick up a pen and paper and try and write a song. When we're rehearsing, the sax player teams up with the piano, the guitars with bass, and little old me gets left on her own minding her own business. When they're working parts out there's nothing I can do apart from read comics. We carry on rehearsing for a couple more hours," said Jennie.[264] Stella recalls the process, "I tended to write a lot of lyrics, usually, with a very basic kind of melody and I would work usually with Miranda and Sarah-Jane. I don't know how that happened, it's just how it came about. So we would arrange my original song, the three of us, and then record it on a tape and take it down to rehearsal and everyone would get involved that way. Other people like Jennie, she would write a song and then we would arrange together. Clare came later, after Penny and she was a good song writer and she would write pretty much entire songs because she was a keyboard player and a sax player. She was very good musically. She could sort of arrange the whole thing almost." Judy Parsons says she remembers her contribution to the band's compositions. "I wrote 'Burning' which is about consuming all the world's resources."

Critics were typically favorable of their recordings and performances. Even before they had signed to Stiff, performance reviews were supportive of the "defunct Bodysnatchers"[265] or the band that rose "out of the ashes of the Bodysnatchers."[266] Reviews stated that "Jennie, the irrepressible mouthy lout with a heart of gold, bounds around. She keeps the audience on their marks and demands attention. Lesley, calm and watchful builds a solid bassline, Sara-Jane [sic] and Stella laugh and dance with their guitars. Miranda moves her hips and lips ... on that sax. Penny plays her keyboards, and Judy, the drums."[267] This review, penned by a female critic, is unusual in that it matches the women in the band with their musical instruments and

---

263 *The Belle Stars Turn Back the Clock* box set. Liner notes.
264 Soave, Daniela. "A Life in the Day of Jennie McKeown." *Record Mirror*, 9 Jan. 1982, p. 14.
265 Amos, Sharon. "The (ap)peal of Belles." *Sounds*. 28 Feb. 1981, p. 50.
266 Ibid.
267 Hu, Laura. "The Belle Stars." *NME*, 8 Aug. 1981, p. 39.

comments on their playing said instruments. "As most journalists are male," writes Mavis Bayton, "a hegemonic masculine view tends to predominate in the music press. Women, who are not presented as artists in the way that men are or to be taken seriously as musicians, are often viewed as just puppets, moulded by record companies, rarely asked about playing their instruments and often presented in sexual terms rather than as craftswomen, serious about their work."[268]

Another positive review came after a performance in Bristol in early August 1981 when the Belle Stars performed with a local ska band called the Rimshots. The journalist, only identified by the initials RAB, wrote of the Belle Stars, "They're bright, poppy and perspicacious—seven young women of distinction, and I mean the music above anything else. Everybody is walking around going, 'Wow! It's not like the Bodysnatchers, is it?' Of course not. I remember the Bodysnatchers as uncertain and faltering. These girls practically swagger."[269] This journalist went on to also describe the musicality of the women in the band. "Jenny [sic] the vocalist is the obvious centre of attention with her remarkable presence, wit, and big, big voice. None of the others possess quite the same dynamism as she, but they make up for it in the playing. The sax player's tone reminds me of Saxa and the bass and drums are certainly snappy but the guitar sound was a bit thin, no doubt due to the fact that one of the guitarists had injured her wrist." The article further highlights a few of the songs with positive analysis.

Yet another reviewer, writing with the initials SJK, stated that the Belle Stars were "embracing styles from ska/rock to reggae dub and blues, and with backing vocals that can (and did) cope with anything from Red Indian whoops to be-bops a la Shangri-La's, the band have an infectious charm which had everyone smiling in a few seconds. ... Suffice to say that I have not heard a new band of either sex for a long time that can beat their performance."[270]

Even with the positive reviews and the growing popularity of the band, in late 1981, keyboardist Penny Leyton made the tough decision to leave the Belle Stars. She explains why. "We started off playing a lot of the music that the Bodysnatchers played, but we changed and I think, personally, I felt that we tried to go down too many musical avenues. It's like every time there was a new sort of style of music, like, 'Oh, look, funk is trendy right now, let's write a funk song.' And I felt, honestly, that we'd lost a bit of musical direction." Penny says it wasn't easy to leave the band, but she has never regretted her decision and she went on to other musical and artistic endeavors, including performing with the Deltones (see also Deltones chapter). "I was just exhausted, you know, just tired. And also, at the time I had a really serious relationship and I just didn't want to be away from my boyfriend and it was a really hard decision to make, to leave. Obviously, I could see that the Belle Stars were having

[268] Bayton, Mavis. *Frock Rock: Women Performing Popular Music*. Oxford University Press, 1998, p. 3.
[269] RAB. "Sweet and dandy." *Sounds*. 8 Aug. 1981, p. 38.
[270] SJK. "Belle Star Charmers." *North Wales Weekly News*. 28 May 1981.

a lot of success. But we went on a six-week tour with Madness and I felt like, I mean it's ridiculous, but like I was in prison. You know, we were playing six nights a week."

Clare Hirst then joined the Belle Stars on keyboard as well as saxophone. She grew up in a musical household and learned to play multiple instruments as a child. "I'm from Appleby, which is in the Lake District up in Cumbria, so I'm a northerner. I think I was the most musical of everyone, but my mom has always been a very keen amateur violin player. I just loved playing music and I always played but because I was in the middle of the countryside, there weren't many opportunities really to go in orchestras or all of that. I left when I was quite young. And I started learning piano when I was very young. My brother used to have piano lessons and I always just copied him, you know? And then I started having them. And so I played the piano, and then I played a bit of clarinet and a bit of flute. And my mom and dad would say to me every year, 'What do you want for Christmas? What do you want for your birthday?' And I said, 'I want a saxophone,' and they'd be like, 'Oh no, there's no one around here who can teach you,' and 'no, no, no.' Anyway, eventually when I was 16, they said, 'Okay, well there you go. We'll buy you a saxophone,'" says Clare.[271] When asked what it was about that saxophone that appealed to her, Clare doesn't hesitate to answer. "I can tell you what it was. It was a picture of David Bowie wearing this zoot suit with his orange hair and the saxophone and I was like, 'Ah, I've just got to play that thing. It sounds so amazing!' And I was a huge Bowie fan. The first three albums I bought were like *Ziggy Stardust*, *Hunky Dory*, and *Aladdin Sane*," she says.

Clare left home at the age of 16 to become an au pair for her young cousins in York. It was there she saw an advertisement for an all-female band called Sphinx and she auditioned and joined as saxophonist. "We were playing the Doobie Brothers and Chaka Khan, Beatles, all kinds of stuff. We had nice harmonies, there was lots of singing going on and I mean, I didn't have a clue what I was doing but it was just so fun," says Clare, noting that there were no recordings made of the band, just live performances. The bass player for that band was Sara Lee who went on to perform with Gang of Four, the Indigo Girls, the B-52s (she appears in the video for "Love Shack"), and the Thompson Twins, among others.

Clare moved to London where she took up residence in Shepherds Bush and befriended a number of musicians and became a member of the band Shriekback. "I was playing with them a bit and I was playing with a few other bands. And then I saw this advert for the Belle Stars, and so I went to audition for them. And I knew they had this record deal and I was like, right, well, I'm just gonna go and do that anyway. To be honest, there was one other girl that came to the audition. I think if you had an audition now there'd be about 500. But then it was just like two of us and I think the reason I got the job was they said to me, 'Oh, what star sign are you?' and I said 'I'm a Leo,' and they went, 'Oh, that's it! You're in then.' They were all Leos and Virgos and this poor other girl must have been something else!" she says.

---

[271] Hirst, Clare. Interviewed by the author, 8 Feb. 2021.

Clare Hirst and Miranda Joyce were both saxophonists in the band, Miranda on alto and Clare on tenor as well as keyboards. "We worked every day for about five years," Clare says. "It was absolutely full time. We piled in the minibus in Camden Town and then took off and just went wherever we were taken and eventually we'd pile back out again. And it was great fun. It was really good fun. We toured a lot. And because we had a lot of hit records, we used to get flown to Europe a lot. We'd even go to France for a day to film TV and then fly back again and that kind of thing. A lot of that went on. We had a lot of fun. Nobody had been in famous bands before—we were all just in it together."

The touring and recording schedule was certainly a busy one. In 1982 they performed at the Théâtre des Champs Elysées in Paris in support of Elvis Costello and the Attractions; in the US, including Philadelphia and two dates at the Danceteria in New York City; and throughout the UK. Of the performance with Elvis Costello, Judy Parsons remarked, "I was so chuffed that after our gig, his band the Attractions complemented me on my drumming. Not sure now exactly which members of the band did that. But Costello and that band were gods in my eyes at that time and still are. I was so chuffed."[272] The US shows were the only time the Belle Stars visited the states as a band. Stella recalls, "Driving out of the Queens Tunnel with the whole of Manhattan's skyline in front of us was one of the most exhilarating vistas I had ever seen. I had been to the States before but it was so wonderful to be there with the band, some of whom had not been out of Europe before. The excitement was contagious. The Danceteria in Manhattan, where we played two nights, was a nightclub built over several floors with the stage on one of the floors. I remember Nina Hagen coming backstage after the gig and being very unusual. ... We drove in heavy snow conditions to Philadelphia in a mini-van. The Philadelphia gig was in one of the tiniest venues we had ever played and in a basement. We wondered why we had driven all that way to play to such a small audience. However it turned out to be a cracking gig with a very enthusiastic audience who seemed to be swinging from the rafters, it was so tightly packed with a great crowd. Hot and sweaty gig!"[273]

Jennie recalls the New York gigs rather well because of the hotel in which they stayed. "I don't know whose idea it was for us to go to that hotel of horrors [The Iroquois Hotel] but it was an experience I shall never forget ... We were living in a hotel with uninvited guests that made their emergence after lights were out and we were all in bed. I know this because when I went to put the light on to look for the toilet there they were as plain as day running all over everything and I remember screaming the place down. Everything was covered in cockroaches. It was a nightmare and I never slept well that night. And the only reason we stayed there was because the Clash had stayed there. I will never forget that place for all the wrong reasons!"[274]

[272] *The Belle Stars Turn Back the Clock* box set. Liner notes.
[273] Ibid.
[274] *The Belle Stars Turn Back the Clock* box set. Liner notes.

That same year they also recorded an additional four singles including "Sign of the Times," released at the very end of that year. It reached number three on the UK charts, number two in Belgium, and only 75 in the U.S. The song was produced by Peter Collins who had produced for the Lambrettas and later produced for Rush, Suicidal Tendencies, Alice Cooper, and Jane Wiedlin of the Go-Go's, in addition to others. The flip side of "Sign of the Times" was the song "Madness" which was in no way related, in lyrical content nor tone, to Prince Buster's nor Madness's eponymous tune. The Belle Stars continued to record singles which culminated in the release of their first, and only, album in February 1983. It was self-titled and included twelve songs, many of which had been released previously as singles. "At the moment we're having a bit of trouble with our producer David Robinson," said Clare in 1983.[275] "He's the sort of guy who wants twelve hit singles from the album, but I don't agree with that. I feel an album should mean that you can experiment and change your style a bit. Hopefully if the album does do well though we can then start planning some live dates."

Those live dates to promote the album included a brief tour with the Police during their Synchronicity Tour on December 13, 1983 in Leeds, and December 14, 1983 in Nottingham. Lesley Shone recalls this show because of different treatment they received as all women. "When you turn up for soundchecks, like when we were on tour with the Police, I think the sound crew looked down their noses a little bit at us, but we proved ourselves in the end that we were players. That shut them up, didn't it, girls?!" she said.[276] Mavis Bayton notes that sexism from audio crews is common for women and the impact is deeper than just disrespect. "Sexist attitudes of the sound crew lead to women's bands being undersold on time and attention. Sexist prejudice acts as a handicap. Male bands do not face the same kind of hostility, sneering, or jokes, but even women in mixed bands are singled out for different treatment."[277]

The members of the Belle Stars had to endure sexism in newspaper reviews as well. For example, Richard Cook, writer for *NME*, stated, "They take the inconsequence and blankness of chart music, tut-tut over it in front of a mirror, spray on some cosmetics, dress it up and give it an encouraging shove on to the dance floor."[278] Another by Mitchell Cohen in *Creem* magazine called their songs "dumb-ditties that are inspired nonsense," compared the women's vocals to a "parochial school cheerleader," and called their overall appeal to be "innocence mixed with sexiness," though he aptly attributed that to the overt marketing of the record label.[279] This is precisely why Judy Parsons says she decided to leave the group.

Judy states, "We'd performed a song called 'The Snake' and the record company man, David Robinson, Stiff Records, he got in the photo shoot with snakes. And I said, 'I'm not going to have photographs of snakes anywhere near me,' because

[275] "The Bellestars." *Chart Beat Magazine*, No. 9, 1983, p. 25.
[276] Shone, Lesley. Interview on Edith Bowman's Album Show, 1 Dec. 2010.
[277] Bayton, Mavis. *Frock Rock: Women Performing Popular Music*. Oxford University Press, 1998, p. 122.
[278] Cook, Richard. "The Belle Stars." *NME*. 5 Feb. 1983.
[279] Cohen, Mitchell. "The Belle Stars." *Creem*. Aug. 1983.

it's so sexist. … I said to the band, 'If this goes ahead, I'll leave the band.' And that was the turning point. It went ahead. I didn't have any snakes near me. I didn't touch them. But I was there beside them. And that, I thought, that's just going too far. You know, we'll do anything for fame. They weren't feminists, as such, except in their own quiet way, they did demonstrate that women can do it. They wouldn't articulate it in a way that I would articulate it. I think they were proud of what they were doing," she says. This sort of sexism is commonplace for women in the music industry, and many industries, for that matter. Bayton observes, "There is a tendency for women's bands and female performers to be trivialized in the media, being presented as sex objects in glamour shots, and as scatty girls in interviews."[280]

Jennie says any sexism she may have experienced was all taken in stride. "That whole thing about men don't take you seriously, I found that kind of boring, yawn. You know, I take things with a pinch of salt. If you look at my life, nothing compares to what I've been through. It's just like water off a duck's back. I don't give a shit what you think, we're going out and doing it anyway, whether you like it or not. I personally came from a really kind of like shitty upbringing and I'm passed this on a plate. I'm having to grow into it. I was always ready to meet the audience, because I knew the power of that. It's a great privilege to be there on that stage."

The women definitely took advantage of the larger stage that was available to them in the early 1980s—the broadcast stage, via television and video. They appeared on *Top of the Pops*, on *The Tube* hosted by Jools Holland and Paula Yates, television and radio shows in France and Germany, and a television show in the UK that Stella remembers as rather surprising. "We performed 'Sweet Memory' for TV at an outside broadcast that was filmed at Alton Towers. What we didn't know at first was that the individual platforms that each of us was given to stand on moved up and down on hydraulics during our performance. We suddenly found ourselves going up and down with all the punters shouting below. What's more, the set builders had only just finished painting the platforms before we went on to perform and the paint was still wet, though drying quickly in the heat of the summer's day. My boots stuck to the platform as I struggled to try and hop about a bit as we performed the song. I remember catching Jennie's expression as her platform started to ascend for the first time up into the blue skies. It was priceless!"[281]

Since MTV went on the air for the first time on August 1, 1981, the Belle Stars found themselves smack dab in the middle of the moment. Eye-catching videos were an essential component of a successful music career and so the band's videos reflected the whimsy, energy, and danceable joy that embodied the Belle Stars. "The Clapping Song" featured, as one would assume, plenty of clapping, conga lines, and costumes like feathered ducks, scuba divers, and a gorilla. "Sign of the Times" was more serious in tone, but still upbeat and full of movement, as the women donned top hats and white suits in front of a field of blue lasers. "The Entertainer" presented

---

[280] Bayton, Mavis. *Frock Rock: Women Performing Popular Music*. Oxford University Press, 1998, p. 169.
[281] *The Belle Stars Turn Back the Clock* box set. Liner notes.

dance sequences in a variety of costumes including military uniforms, bellhop uniforms, and flapper dresses. "Indian Summer" contained Casablanca-inspired images with a smoking Humphrey Bogart character sitting in an outdoor gambling establishment as the band members sang in glamorous costumes before diving into a swimming pool. If any of these scenarios sound strange or silly, try summarizing any video of the early 1980s and one will see that it was more about mood and image than a sensible storyline.

The image the Belle Stars portrayed was largely influenced by their appearance on screen and stage, and so fashion was a large part of their presence. Style, clothing, hair, makeup were all critical in the era of audio now accompanied by visual. Stella says that the women all participated in this effort to sculpt their collective appearance. "Sarah-Jane, she has an art college background, as did Penny, and Miranda was about to go to art school when she joined the band, so you've got three very artistic people and Sarah-Jane was doing fashion at art college so we had a really good selection of people for clothing ideas and also for design. We designed a lot of our artwork, and we even discussed our clothing theme for on stage and that would be based on ideas mainly from Sarah-Jane, Miranda, and Penny and then we would all decide, 'The theme tonight is going to be red,' or 'The theme tomorrow night, we're going to do tartan,' and then from that, each individual just interprets that. It made life easier because you weren't stuck thinking, 'Oh god, what am I going to wear to the next gig tonight,' if we're being told that it's black and sequins. So that's how we did the clothing side of things." Clare adds, "We used to wear really strange clothes. I mean, we'd make a lot of them or get them in charity shops. We certainly had a unique look, I think you'll agree!"

Because fashion was such a part of the performance, having a proper dressing room was essential. That, however, was a challenge. "Oh! Dressing rooms!" exclaims Sarah-Jane. "We were touring up and down the country and most of the dressing rooms never even had a mirror and they always smelled of beer and sweat because it was just such a male-dominated industry. And I'm sure that's probably changed now, and so I feel like if we've done anything, it's improve dressing rooms!" she says with a laugh. Mavis Bayton's research has found that issues with dressing rooms impact women in bands. "As rock venues are organized entirely around the notion that rock bands are male, inadequate dressing rooms are a particular bugbear for women. Well-known and prestigious venues often lack even minimal facilities."[282]

But the Belle Stars faced obstacles much greater than inadequate dressing rooms or cockroaches in hotel rooms. Their charismatic star, Jennie McKeown, had developed a serious drug problem that greatly disrupted the function of the group. In her book she confesses, "Before long, I found myself hooked on heroin; what was once recreation turned habitual."[283] As a result of the turmoil caused by Jennie's habit, Clare Hirst, Stella Barker, and Jennie McKeown herself announced they were no

---

[282] Bayton, Mavis. *Frock Rock: Women Performing Popular Music*. Oxford University Press, 1998, p. 133.
[283] Matthias, Jennie. *Surviving the Storm*. Breakfree Forever Publishing, 2019, p. 27.

longer part of the band, leaving only three remaining members—Sarah-Jane Owen, Miranda Joyce, and Lesley Shone.

Penny, who had left prior to the mass exodus, explains what transpired. "Our singer was a little unreliable. It was very stressful with someone who doesn't turn up to gigs because she's searching for drugs. We had a gig in Cornwall or somewhere like that, or Devon, and she didn't show up for the van. And then we were waiting to play and we didn't know whether she was going to turn up. And she turned up maybe 10 minutes before we were to play, very drug addled. You've got a whole audience waiting for you. And I guess the other people in the band were a little bit more chill about it, but for me, that kind of situation, you know, I feel responsible for the audience and for the fact that they've paid to see us and I could not take that level of stress." Stella Barker says that dealing with the chaos caused by Jennie's habit was too difficult for her and she was the first one to decide to go. She says she didn't necessarily have plans on what would come next, but that didn't matter. "I started to think that I wanted something else, that this wasn't for me anymore. I wasn't sure, but I was the first one to throw in the towel and leave. I knew I didn't want that anymore, that bad feeling and that negativity."

Sarah-Jane says that another habit added to the imbalance in the group. She explains, "That was actually our demise at the end, where she was going with her drug addiction. It was the end of the Belle Stars really, and with what happened with Stiff Records going down the plug hole and we were last on their roster—one of the last acts that Dave Robinson could really slog to another record company because he basically used all the profits and proceeds to do horse betting. That was the downfall of Stiff Records. He and Jake Riviera were a really good team and I think Jake Riviera really kept Dave on his toes and when Jake Riviera left the company, that's when Dave, I think, just got a bit too self-indulgent. He turned all the video editing bays into a way to watch the races round England."

The Belle Stars newsletter, BS Bandits, revealed the band's plans after the split, leaving three to carry on. "Dear Fans," began the statement, "You know the news already, that The Belle Stars are now a three-piece unit comprising of Miranda, S.J., and Lesley. They are at present organizing their career and writing new material for the new line-up. Four people leaving meant a radical change for the band, they no longer could be considered a live gigging band, and do not have an obvious singer. At this stage, rather than looking for replacements for the leaving members, it was decided to keep The Belle Stars as a nucleus of three, work on new material and the existing capabilities of the three remaining voices. This does not mean that we do not intend to gig, but for now we are concentrating on a new look 'Stars.'"[284] The missive continued saying that they planned to use session musicians for their recordings.

Sarah-Jane says this three-piece group was successful, for a time, but it too eventually dissolved. "The latter part of the Belle Stars, after Jennie left, the three of us carried on as the Belle Stars. We recorded with Dominic Bugatti a whole other

[284] BS Bandits Bulletin No. 5.

album and that's *World Domination* and that became a good dance track in America. We recorded with a female producer an album that got shelved." That producer was Anne Dudley and three of those songs, "Crime of Passion," "Is This the Night?" and "Cool Disguise" appear in the box set, *The Belle Stars Turn Back the Clock*, released in late 2019. The three remaining members of the Belle Stars eventually threw in their chic hats and broke up for good in 1986. Jennie tried to hang on to the success she had, but at the expense of the rest of the women. Sarah-Jane explains, "Jennie wanted to go her own separate way and she did, and she did a few things that were upsetting to a lot of us, which was trying to carry on as the Belle Stars and getting imposters to look like us. I don't know if you remember any of that. They played some gigs in England and had somebody dressed up with blonde hair that looked like me and they were basically miming to backing tracks that were our recordings and getting paid for being the Belle Stars, so that was a little upsetting for a few of us."

Jennie's drug addiction only grew worse after the split, but she did get clean. Jennie says, "I became a drug addict. I was like, what am I going to do? Nothing. I'm gonna hang out with my crazy friend, popstar mates, and we're going to take loads of drugs. I didn't exactly go down that road thinking about that, but when you're hanging out with people, you kind of then don't realize that you're forming a habit. So I went to Miami to come off." She ended up getting clean, finding work at a shop in South Beach, and staying for a few years.

While in Miami, Jennie had the surprise of her life while driving down the freeway with a friend. "All of a sudden a song comes on the radio and my friend stopped in the middle of the freaking freeway! She said, 'That's you!' It was me on the radio and I hadn't even recognized it because Tom Cruise and what's his name [Dustin Hoffman] were talking all over it!" That song, "Iko Iko," was used in the opening scene of *Rain Man* as Tom Cruise's character, Charlie Babbitt watches Lamborghinis unloading from a freight ship. The song experienced a rebirth in popularity, reaching number 14 in March of 1989.[285]

As a result, Jennie says she was asked to do the video for the song. She says, "I was at Scratch [restaurant in South Beach, Miami] and I saw a friend of mine from England who was in a band called Visage. And his name was Rusty Egan and he said to me, 'What are you doing here?' I was like, 'I live here at the moment.' He said to me, 'Everyone is looking for you. No one's been able to find you because you're here.' He says, 'Can I take your number and tell somebody? Managers are just wanting to sign you up.' And I was like, 'Really? Why is that then?' He was like, 'Because you have a hit!' I was like, 'A hit? Where?' And he said, 'They picked your song up for the biggest film in the world right now and you don't know nothing about it?' So I get a phone call from a manager and he said, 'Where are you?' And I said, 'I'm in Miami.' They said, 'Okay we want to pass you on to somebody else.' About an hour later I get a phone call from Hollywood. And I know nothing about attorneys but I know that

[285] Whitburn, Joel. *The Billboard Book of Top 40 Hits (6th ed.)*. New York: Watson-Guptill Publications. 1996, p. 57.

the Americans love them, right? At that particular time, I had run out of money. I was living on a sofa and wondering how am I going to get back to England. And then he said, 'Is this Jennie?' I said, 'Yeah.' And he said, 'Would you like to come out to Hollywood because, you know, we understand that we've used your song and you're the lead singer.' And I said, 'Are you trying to work a deal with me on the phone?' And he said to me, 'Well I was gonna suggest,' and I said, 'One moment.' Twenty feet away, which is across the way, there's this guy called Joe and he was an attorney. I knock on the door. I said, 'Joe, come out.' So there he is with a towel wrapped around his private parts and I said, 'I need you right this second,' and he said, 'What's it about?' I said, 'Hollywood's on the phone.' And he said, 'I'm there.' The next thing you know, I'm flying on a plane to Hollywood with my two friends with me. I had to have my friends because I'm not going to come there alone, right? So I'm there in Hollywood and I'm chatting away to these people—there's me on one end of this very long table. It's so surreal, and all these kind of executives on the other end. And I'm sitting there thinking, I'm all alone here—what the fuck do I do? But I'm gonna play the game. So they said to me, 'What do you think?' And I'm thinking, am I supposed to be thinking? I said, 'Think? You mean about the song?' They said, 'Yeah.' I said, 'I kind of like it.' I said, 'I think you like it because you've chosen it.' And then they said 'What do you think about the video? We're just about to do one. Do you have any ideas?' I said, 'I've got loads of ideas.' I had none, by the way, but I said, 'I've got loads of ideas, but I've got to hear yours first.' I don't know why I did it that way, but it all happened. And they said, 'You can audition the dancers.' I said, 'Who are the dancers?' They said, 'Janet Jackson's dancers.' So the only person that you see out of the Belle Stars is me during the 'Iko Iko' video, but you can see the Janet Jackson dancers. I've never auditioned anybody in my life. I didn't know what I was doing."

Jennie eventually returned to England because of the culture and racism in America. "I was kind of homesick and I remember in America they used to have these curfews for certain things that the police had done that were wrong, and I just thought, I can't live in a country like this. I came back to Camden Town where it's all kind of like, everybody knows each other and they're not so prejudiced. It made me really upset. I didn't like that sort of behavior." Prior to moving to Miami, Jennie McKeown formed a group called Dance Like A Mother with Melissa Ritter, formerly of the Mo-Dettes (see also Mo-Dettes chapter). DLAM, as they were known, were signed to Virgin and released two singles "You Ain't So Tough" and "Private Number."[286] After returning to England she formed the band Big 5 with Nick Welsh from Bad Manners and she sang for Skaville UK, a supergroup with members of Bad Manners and the Selecter. She continues to write and has founded and volunteered with a number of not-for-profit organizations.

Sarah-Jane Owen continued to perform in the music industry after leaving the Belle Stars. She performed guitar for Holly Johnson of Frankie Goes to

---

[286] Matthias, Jennie. jenniematthias.webs.com/bio. Accessed 29 July 2022.

Hollywood. "We would fly to Germany, there would be a TV show, we would lay the tracks in a studio and then we would play to playback, and that was very common back then. It was just a given way of getting good sound and not having any issues, so that was fun, and was going out by himself, so he put a band together that looked, for the most part, like a Prince band, so my outfit would be like a little black peaked hat and skirt and cowboy boots and I loved getting up in all this gear and I loved Holly's songs. Then there was a band called One. They were a Chrysalis signing—a boy band that weren't doing great and I was approached to come in and play on a couple of their songs for video to see if I could add some glamour to something they were going to launch, 'Son of the Sun,' but that didn't seem to go anywhere, but that was fun for a bit."

Sarah-Jane continued her other work in fashion as well. She was freelancing for designer Jeff Banks and his team at a company called HQ Design when she had an opportunity to come to the United States. She said, "Of course we had been to the States—we did a track for Whoopi Goldberg [for the movie *Burglar*] and we had a track on the soundtrack of the movie, so we had to come to Cherokee Studios to record that, so we had come out here." But this time, Sarah-Jane made the move permanently. She continued to perform with a band called Light and Sound Band in California, as well as a band called Progression. Since then she had taken up percussion. "I started with a djembe and went on training to learn how to become a drum circle facilitator. I just got completely hooked on drumming and so I've led drum circles and I've been in drum troupes, played at different events, and then I've played percussion with a band called Yesteryear and various different bands locally in L.A. and where I live." She has also taught at the Fashion Institute. "I taught there for 21 years. I'm retired now."

Stella dabbled a bit in songwriting and recording before she left the country. "By that time I had met who was going to be my future husband who's French and lives in Paris, so I thought, here we go again, typical me! I speak French because I studied French at university and that's the romantic notion of living in Paris, so off I went with all my belongings in a car and some songs and demos on a tape thinking, well, I'll see what happens when I get there. And I didn't do much with the songs, if anything at all." She ended up managing a friend of hers who was a makeup artist, which led to a career as a booker in the fashion industry. "I had to take myself away from London to start again," she says. And she did get married, and had a baby, and she's recently become a grandmother.

Clare Hirst has had an incredibly successful career in music since leaving the Belle Stars. "I was covering in Amazulu for their sax player because she was quite ill at one point. So I did that for a bit. And I was playing in reggae bands and then I think I got into playing salsa which was really cool and I loved a lot. And I was working with the Communards, I joined them for a while. I was called in to put a horn section together for 'Don't Leave Me This Way' and then I think I just stayed and ended up working live with them and touring with them and that was really fun. That was a really great band to work with. After the Communards I had a baby. And I joined a salsa band called Candela and that was an all female salsa band, but I was the single parent by that point. I had a son and he used to come along to rehearsals with us. I went on the principle that if the rehearsal was in someone's house, I can bring him along, but if it was paid for in the studio then I would have to get a babysitter, and it sort of worked out." That son is now a sound engineer.

But Clare had her childhood dream realized after just leaving the Belle Stars. She performed with her idol, the one who inspired her to pick up the saxophone in the first place—David Bowie. "I was in the right place at the right time," she says. "My friend was signed to EMI or something with his own band and they said to him, 'We've got a project for you. Can you just be here ready to play, set up and ready to rehearse by eight o'clock on Thursday?' So on Thursday, the guy turns up and he's with David Bowie! And he's like, 'Yeah, I'm looking for a band to play this charity gig with us in North London.' Can you imagine? This is my friend, Kevin Armstrong. He's a guitarist and so I knew that he was working with David Bowie. And then he just rang me up and said, 'Oh, they want a sax player. Do you want to do it?' I was like, 'Oh, let me think about it. Uh, yes! Okay, why not?!'" she says, laughing. "I was playing with David Bowie, like my dream, my dream gig!" That charity gig where David Bowie played and where Clare Hirst performed saxophone on stage with him in the band was none other than Live Aid in 1985. She performed "Heroes," "Modern Love," and "TVC 15." She has since performed regularly with Hazel O'Connor as well as Mike Garson, the piano player from the *Aladdin Sane* album; has recorded and released a number of her solo jazz albums; and had another baby, a daughter who teaches music, plays guitar, and sings. Clare also continues to perform.

Penny Leyton continued in music before she returned to her art background for the next phase of her life. She became a member of the Deltones (see Deltones chapter) and then started working in computer animation. "I did that in London for a few years, doing animation, and then I got an offer from DreamWorks in the States to go work for them. So I did. I worked on *Shrek* and *Madagascar*—lots of the DreamWorks animated films. I specialized in character setup, because after doing my first degree in art, I did a second degree in computer programming. So then I put those two together. And character setup was like making the characters so they're animated but putting all the controls in the character. So It's a combination of art sculpting and computer programming." She left DreamWorks in 2013 and retired and has since moved to Mexico where she plays guitar, is learning to play bass guitar, and she performs Cuban music with a small band.

Judy Parsons, today Judy Hancock, left music though she does stick a toe in the water from time to time. She has been a technical writer for the past 30 years. "I'm still working full time at the age of 70, being a technical writer, and I love it. And I still write occasional songs, and they are political. I sing with a small group and we do a lot of jamming, improvising, just acapella. And I sing my songs, so they still come to me every now and then," she says. She and her husband have a son, Joe, who is not involved in music, but, says Judy, "he's got much better rhythmic skill than me!"

Lesley Shone is owner of a public relations company in London, Indiscreet PR, that promotes musicians and bands. Miranda Joyce is a professional makeup artist whose clients include Marc Jacobs, Miu Miu, Louis Vuitton, Alexander McQueen, Burberry, Prada, and celebrities like David Beckham, Kate Moss, Naomi Campbell, and Bella Hadid. She also did makeup for the cover of the "Shout" single for Tears for Fears.

But the true measure of success is found, not in what the women achieved in their lives or how high their songs reached in the charts—it is something far less tangible and far more important. These women empowered their generation who then passed on that empowerment to the next, and thus evolved culture and society. "There was a space for women," says Stella, "and I think that's a fallout of punk because punk was kind of open to everybody, wasn't it? Men, women, good musicians, musicians that could hardly play—it was just, get up on stage and do it." Lesley concurs and says that this era opened the door for many people who had once found it closed. She credits the era as well as those who provided the opportunity. "In the '80s, it was different times then," says Lesley, "and bands were actually given the chance to grow, unlike today where if you don't have a hit with your first release, then you're consigned to the dustbin, basically. So I think we were really fortunate with Stiff. It was a good time for bands like us to be given the chance to grow and to learn to play our instruments and get tight as well."[287]

Penny recognizes that despite this movement, there still were challenges women faced that could not be easily erased by creative freedom. "Maybe it's not easy for women to do that," she says of becoming a musician, "I mean, it's very hard to make a living out of music, so you can't have too many responsibilities and traditionally, men have been able to get away with having fewer responsibilities. Another thing is, I think there's a whole attitude like, women being strong are considered to be difficult, and men being strong is considered to be bold."

Still, Penny says she feels that continuing that feeling of empowerment for women is crucial for her, for all female musicians, and for the whole of musical output. "For me, it's really important that women play music and we take our share of creating music. Because playing music, creating music is really good for the soul and I think that if they don't see other women doing that, then they feel like it's not something they can do and that it's denied to them. So I think it's important. It's just a feeling like nothing else, playing music with other people and creating music for people to enjoy. Every young girl should feel that they are able to do that and it's not just the exclusive province of men."

Sarah-Jane says that the industry certainly was challenging as a woman, but she has seen much progress. "All of those years, I would have fans come up to me and say, 'Wow, you play so good for a girl,' which was a compliment in their mind, but such an insult. It's just funny. It was very clear that it was a male dominated industry when we first started and we would have to fight tooth and nail for being

---

[287] Shone, Lesley. Interview on Edith Bowman's Album Show, 1 Dec. 2010.

taken seriously and often some of the questions [from journalists] were derogatory or not really about music. Being taken seriously, being listened to, especially when it was around executive ideas or decisions that need to be made was challenging. But it got better and better as the years went on. You could see with the movement of more and more women musicians coming to the forefront. It wasn't a novelty anymore and people would take women more seriously. A lot of women have written to us in our band magazine that we had for a long time saying that we were the inspiration for them to get involved in music. Lots of girls were very taken with the idea that you could be a female musician. It thrills me."

Advertisement for the Belle Stars in 1981, performing with the Beat and the Mood Elevators (above) and publicity photo (below)

The Belle Stars promo (above) and in 1981 at the Wag Club: Jennie Matthias, Chrissy Foreman of Madness, and Jerry Dammers of the Specials (below, L to R)

The Specials and The Special AKA

The Specials:
Rhoda Dakar: vocals
Chrissie Hynde: vocals
The Go-Go's: vocals

The Special AKA:
Rhoda Dakar: vocals
Molly Jackson: vocals
Polly Jackson: vocals
Egidio Newton: vocals
Afrodiziak: vocals

At the very tail end of writing this book, on December 18, 2022, Terry Hall died at the age of 63 from pancreatic cancer—an especially quick and deadly disease. This unexpected event shocked the entire music world, especially the ska community who had a deep love for the front of the Specials and numerous other bands. By all accounts, he was creative, kind, and extremely funny. The women who worked with Terry Hall all spoke fondly of their friend, including those who worked with him in the Specials.

Though her contribution might be only a word or two, or less, Chrissie Hynde of the Pretenders actually contributed to the first album by the Specials. Other women contributed more, but Chrissie had her fingerprint on ska at the very birth of the revival. Born in Akron, Ohio, Chrissie Hynde moved to London in 1973 with an obsession for Iggy Pop and planned to establish a career in music. She started as a music reviewer at *NME*, though she admits, "I really couldn't write. He [Ian McDonald of *NME*] didn't care. He wasn't looking for quality. They were looking for sex. They wanted sex. They wanted a pimple-faced loudmouth to push the male staff around and make them crawl on all fours," writes Chrissie in her memoir.[288] Her next job was as a shop assistant for Malcolm McLaren and Vivienne Westwood. She was with the couple when they went to see the New York Dolls at Biba's Rainbow Room. After losing her job when an ex-boyfriend caused a ruckus in the shop, Chrissie went to Paris before heading back to Ohio. While at home she received a letter from Malcolm, asking her to come back to London to be in a band he was putting together. She said no and instead took up with some musicians in Cleveland to sing in a covers band.[289]

But when opportunities fizzled out, back Chrissie went to London where she met up with McLaren who invited her to hear his new band rehearse. The Barracudas, which featured guitarist Mick Jones, were managed by McLaren who was assisted by Bernie Rhodes. They all wanted to include Chrissie somehow, but she wasn't a musician. She was a singer. "How would I fit into that scenario, I had no idea. It would have to be something that transcended gender. Rock was masculine but its listeners were feminine. It was never gender-restrictive—men loved to see a woman

---

[288] Hynde, Chrissie. *Reckless: My Life as a Pretender*. Anchor Books, 2015, p. 148.
[289] Ibid. p. 178.

play guitar; they always had. I'd have to figure it out, as I didn't want to be a waitress again," Chrissie says.[290] Mick Jones soon jettisoned the idea in exchange for the members of his new band, the 101ers, which became the Clash; Bernie Rhodes "wasn't in favor of me at all," said Chrissie[291]; and so instead she continued to squat, moving into Don Letts's house among others, and living among the nebulae that became the Sex Pistols, the Damned, the Slits, and Motörhead before forming the Pretenders in the spring of 1978.

One year later, perhaps because she was still trying to find her footing in the music industry, Chrissie Hynde performed backup vocals for the Specials. According to Terry Hall, Chrissie "doubles up on 'girls are slags'" during the song "Nite Klub," and according to Horace Panter "that's Chrissie doing the 'heavy breathing' on 'Stupid Marriage.'"[292] Chrissie recalls, "I do remember being in the studio up to a point. Until I got wasted."[293] Terry Hall says, "We must've been introduced through Elvis [Costello] or Jake Riviera [Stiff Records and Costello's manager]. Chrissie agrees, "Right—I knew them because I did my first single with Nick Lowe [who also produced Costello's early albums]. But, you know, I was a fan of the Specials. I thought they were magnificent." Two and a half years after they formed, the Pretenders were also supported by the Beat in the United States. Historian, author, and musician Marc Wasserman has written about this tour in the fall of 1980 after discovering rare live footage of the performance at the Capitol Theatre in the Music Vault archives. "The band receive a muted response from fans of Chrissie Hynde and company who were likely perplexed by the punky reggae sounds of the multiracial septet from Birmingham," writes Wasserman.[294]

Both Chrissie Hynde and the members of the Specials and the Beat continued to perform in recent years, sometimes on the same festival lineup, as Chrissie and Terry Hall did at the Arroyo Seco Weekend festival in Pasadena, California in 2018. Though members of all three bands have died since the early 1980s, the beat goes on.

While 2 Tone started to disintegrate as quickly as it started, the Specials hoped to continue the energy of the movement they started by releasing a second album, *More Specials*. Articulating without foresight in January 1981, Robbi Millar of *Sounds* wrote of 2 Tone, "In 1980, its second year, the battle-scars became more apparent. One by one the Specials' relations fell by the wayside. The Selecter departed and split and are, presently, trying to take the same industry by the scruff of its neck in the search of some more (deserved) acclaim. The now defunct Bodysnatchers fell into a

[290] Ibid. p. 193.

[291] Ibid. p. 195

[292] Pearls, Bill. "The Specials talk debut album, Elvis Costello & more on Tim's Twitter Listening Party." *Brooklyn Vegan*. 18 May 2020. brooklynvegan.com/the-specials-talk-debut-album-elvis-costello-more-on-tims-twitter-listening-party. Accessed 17 Dec. 2022.

[293] Wood, Mikael. "Chrissie Hynde and Terry Hall talk contracts, band breakups ahead of Arroyo Seco Weekend." *LA Times*. 22 June 2018. latimes.com/entertainment/music/la-et-ms-chrissie-hynde-terry-hall-arroyo-seco-weekend-20180622-story.html. Accessed 17 Dec. 2022.

[294] Wasserman, Marc. "Rare Live Footage of The Beat From The Capitol Theatre in September 1980." Marco on the Bass. 28 July 2014. marcoonthebass.blogspot.com/2014/07/rare-live-footage-of-beat-from-capitol.html. Accessed 17 Dec. 2022.

similar shambles after being pumped into the charts on the back of their label—before they'd even had a chance to learn to play their instruments properly!—only to discover that novelties are not the foundation on which to build a strong career. The Swinging Cats crept into view and promptly crept out again. Maybe they'll have another chance. Whatever, it was clear that the wheels of 2 Tone were accelerating too fast, too young and heading downhill. Someone slam on the brakes quick!"[295] But Millar continued, "The brakes were located in the nick of time. They came in the form of 'More Specials,' a startling leap away from the potted ska that was beginning a jolt and bore and drove the doubting Thomasses away. An album of direction and devotion and clear-headed straightforward intent, it oiled the joints and started the wheels rolling again, rolling towards a fresh and fancy dance sound."

More Specials was definitely met with critical acclaim, though Dammers has said he wished he had spent more time crafting some of the songs, like "Stereotype," and "Rat Race."[296] But More Specials did continue the momentum of the Specials with added collaboration from additional musicians and vocalists. Rico and Dick Cuthell were back on horns, but Lee Thompson of Madness and Paul Heskett of the Swinging Cats also joined, both on saxophone. Also new to this endeavor was the addition of female voices on a number of the songs. Adding their vocals from the recently disbanded Bodysnatchers was Rhoda Dakar, and three women also enlisted their voices as backup—Belinda Carlisle, Charlotte Caffey, and Jane Wiedlin of the Go-Go's.

The Go-Go's came to England to try to establish themselves as a band before making it big in the United States. After playing gigs at the Whisky a Go Go in Los Angeles, the band was spotted by members of Madness who came to perform at the venue in December 1979 and invited to support them. The Specials, shortly thereafter in early February 1980, performed at the venue and they too invited the Go-Go's to support them across the pond. The Go-Go's joined Madness in April of 1980, supporting them in such cities as Cheshire, Aberdeen, and they joined the Specials on the Seaside Tour along with the Bodysnatchers for three months in the summer of 1980. Some reviews were favorable, including the *Spalding Guardian* which stated, "The vital, all-female American group 'the Go-Go's' went down well with the ever-increasing crowd."[297]

But most reviews and audience responses were not so encouraging. "We thought we'd go to England and be huge because they'd totally get us," said Go-Gos' drummer Gina Shock. "They hated our guts. Those crowds didn't give a shit about seeing five California girls. We weren't ska! They hated us! At first we'd run offstage crying but after a while we screamed 'Fuck you!' right back. We toughened up because

[295] Millar, Robbi. "No Surrender to Racism!" *Sounds*, 17 Jan. 1981, p. 32.
[296] Ibid., p. 33.
[297] *Spalding Guardian*, 20 Jun. 1980.

we had to. We didn't have a choice."[298] Charlotte Caffey agreed, "That experience was gonna make or break anybody. We hadn't toured before so that in itself was really taxing, and on top of that we were constantly partying and getting crap thrown at us."[299] Jane Wiedlin said, "You've gotta be on your game when you're playing to audiences of National Front Nazi skinheads. Ska had that type of following in London even though Madness and the Specials were not that."[300] For all members, including Belinda Carlisle, the experience was one that strengthened them as a band. "I wouldn't wish what we went through there on anybody. But that tour made us try harder. We honed our skills and it prepared us for what was to come."[301]

Margot Olavarria, bass player and one of the original founders of the Go-Go's, says she loved performing in the UK because it gave her a chance to experience the bands that surrounded them. "I enjoyed touring with the Specials and Madness in 1979 and meeting several members of other ska or 2 Tone artists. I especially liked the Selecter. The time I spent touring in the UK gave me the chance to see wonderful bands. My favorite experience was opening for Desmond Dekker in Shepherd's Bush. I loved the ska scene for its inclusivity and diversity. There was a sense that we were all in this together. I appreciate most the friendships I made with Sir Horace and Bedders," Margot says.[302]

The members of the Go-Go's, as Charlotte Caffey recalls, were certainly enjoying the opportunity and the experience, which included a heavy dose of partying and socializing. This resulted in short-lived romantic relationships, and long-lasting musical output. One of these relationships, between Jane Wiedlin and Terry Hall, produced the song, "Our Lips Are Sealed," which was recorded by both the Go-Go's and Fun Boy Three. "In 1980 we were playing at the Whisky on Sunset Strip and the Specials were in town from England. They came to see us, and they really liked us and asked us if we would be their opening act on their tour. I met Terry Hall, the singer of the Specials, and ended up having kind of a romance. He sent me the lyrics to 'Our Lips Are Sealed' later in the mail, and it was kind of about our relationship, because he had a girlfriend at home and all this other stuff. So it was all very dramatic. I really liked the lyrics, so I finished the lyrics and wrote the music to it, and the rest is history. And then his band, the Fun Boy Three, ended up recording it—they did a really great version of it, also. It was a lot gloomier than the Go-Go's version," Jane says.[303] This song became the first single released in America by the Go-Go's, though not the first single. "We had like a one-single deal with Stiff Records, who were the record company that had signed the Specials [sic, Chrysalis] and Madness—we also toured

[298] Bell, Keaton. "How the Go-Go's Found Their Beat: An Oral History." *Vogue*. 4 Aug. 2020. vogue.com/article/go-gos-40th-anniversary-beauty-and-the-beat-oral-history-belinda-carlisle. Accessed 23 Oct. 2022.
[299] Ibid.
[300] Ibid.
[301] Ibid.
[302] Olavarria, Margot. All quotations, unless otherwise noted, from interview with the author, 13 Dec. 2022.
[303] Wiser, Carl. "Jane Wiedlin form the Go-Go's." Songfacts. 22 Oct. 2007. songfacts.com/blog/interviews/jane-wiedlin-from-the-go-gos. 23 Oct. 2022.

with Madness in England. And then that single was a previous version of 'We Got the Beat.' So I guess technically, that was our first single," says Jane.[304]

UK audiences might not have embraced the Go-Go's, but American audiences definitely did, and shortly after their return stateside, the band was signed to IRS. "They were a completely different band after London. They really gelled having Gina on the drums. They'd gone through the paces quite a bit and they were selling out every club," said Kathy Valentine.[305] Gina Shock contends, "If we could get through London then we could handle anything. We got back to LA and unbeknownst to us, 'We Got the Beat' had started getting played in clubs and became a tiny hit. Kathy was around as a guitar player so she knew the ropes."[306]

Though she was a guitar player, not a bass player, Kathy Valentine joined the Go-Go's after Margot Olavarria became ill and was replaced, against her will. "I found out I'd been kicked out of the band from my good friend Exene Cervenka, from X. The Go-Go's wanted someone with more pop song capability, and the desire to succeed, pretty much at any cost. There was a lack of integrity on their part, and the part of their manager, and their lawyers, who I also sued. I was already in a better band — Brian Brain. The lawsuit took three years," she says.[307] Today Margot Olavarria is an academic and Latin America specialist, writing, editing and translating as a professional.[308] So guitar player Kathy Valentine quickly acquired a bass and began learning to play.

Kathy Valentine was born in Austin, Texas, though her mother was a British expatriate so they traveled regularly to and from England. On one trip, Kathy joined the band Girlschool, and she subsequently returned to Austin to form her own group, the Violators. After moving to Los Angeles where she co-founded the Textones, it was shortly thereafter that Kathy joined the Go-Go's for their New Year's Eve show at the Whisky a Go Go in 1980. "I began to contribute songs as soon as I joined. I think all the Go-Go's material was well crafted and had elements of pop, punk, surf, and in general rock 'n' roll. We could tell if a song was right for us as soon as we started arranging and playing it in rehearsal, and I always thought more about what made the song the best it could be more than what label it fit under," Kathy says.[309] The all-girl band didn't feel any different than any other Kathy had been in, then nor since. "I always feel like a musician playing with other musicians, and while playing or performing my gender never enters my mind, I don't think my instrument can tell either, it just knows it's being thrashed. At the same time, yes we were aware we were

[304] Ibid.
[305] Bell, Keaton. "How the Go-Go's Found Their Beat: An Oral History." Vogue. 4 Aug. 2020. vogue.com/article/go-gos-40th-anniversary-beauty-and-the-beat-oral-history-belinda-carlisle. Accessed 23 Oct. 2022.
[306] Ibid.
[307] Tannenbaum, Rob. "The Go-Go's Recall the Debauched Days of Their Hit 'We Got the Beat' 35 Years Later: 'We Were a Five-Headed Monster.'" *Billboard*. 20 May 2016. billboard.com/music/pop/the-go-gos-we-got-the-beat-35th-anniversary-interview-billboard-music-awards-7378161. Accessed 14 Dec. 2022.
[308] Olavarria, Margot. All quotations, unless otherwise noted, from interview with the author. 13 Dec. 2022.
[309] Valentine, Kathy. All quotations, unless otherwise noted, from interview with the author, 3 May 2022.

all females, because that was the reality. As is fairly commonly known, the band had difficulty landing a recording contract despite having significant popularity—the labels said that there had not been a successful all female band in the past so they passed on signing us."

But, the Go-Go's were signed, and the rest, as they say, is history. They were inducted into the Rock & Roll Hall of Fame in 2021. Kathy Valentine says the legacy of the Go-Go's has been an exciting one, especially since the music industry has evolved to allow space for more bands that feature women. "I believe there are far more women playing music for a career and earning a living doing sessions, touring, writing, composing, producing and what not than there were 40 years ago," she says.

Touring with, mingling with, and composing songs with the Go-Go's has undoubtedly produced results now chronicled in history. But the backup vocals from Carlisle, Caffey, and Wiedlin on the *More Specials* album might still come as a surprise to most fans. Dammers was always a proponent of collaboration, especially in the name of creation and experimentation. So when the Go-Go's found themselves in England in the summer of 1980s, touring with the Specials, it was only natural they accompanied them to Coventry's Horizon Studios for the recording of *More Specials*. The song, "Enjoy Yourself," popularized decades earlier by the likes of Guy Lombardo, Tommy Dorsey, Bing Crosby, Louis Prima, Doris Day, and of course, Prince Buster, appears twice on the album. The first version is twice the speed as the reprise, and listening to the two juxtaposed has the effect of witnessing a carnival ride spinning in slow motion to collision. Nonetheless, the three members of the Go-Go's contributed their light voices to the upper octave of the melody on the reprise. Music maven Vivien Goldman likened the reprise to a "cabaret" in feeling, which seems to capture the mood eloquently.[310]

Also appearing on the *More Specials* album was Rhoda Dakar who had just split from the Bodysnatchers. "Well, they asked me to come and sing on their second album," says Rhoda.[311] "We [The Bodysnatchers] played a gig with the Go-Go's, so they were around at the time. And then we recorded the songs on *More Specials*. Jerry called me up and asked me to come and sing." Rhoda sings vocals, prominently, on the song, "I Can't Stand It," joining Terry Hall. The song strays into Dammers' Musak/electronica experimentation and Rhoda's off-key voice provides an off-kilter approach, giving the song title even more meaning. Rhoda also joined the Specials when they toured during this time. "Their last gig was in Boston, in the US. I was on that tour, so I was there."[312] She continued with the Specials post-split as the Specials AKA.

Another woman involved with the Specials on the *More Specials* album was the very woman appearing on the cover. Music photographer Chalkie Davies who shot the cover of the *More Specials* album recalls, "When I went to shoot the cover for

---

[310] Goldman, Vivien. "The Specials: More Specials." *NME*. 20 Sept. 1980.
[311] Dakar, Rhoda. Interview on History of LA Ska podcast, 11 Apr. 2021.
[312] Ibid.

More Specials, the band's second LP, Jerry told me, 'I'll meet you in this odd little bar in Leamington Spa.' We get there, and it's just the group sitting around having a beer, nothing clever or anything. He comes in and says, 'Can you take a bad picture?' I asked what he meant and he said, 'You know, an out of focus picture? Like a King Tubby sleeve, a Jamaican sleeve. Make it look real.' So I did."[313] The cover features the band gathered around a small table with drinks. It is blurry, indeed. In the foreground is a woman and when asked who she was, Davies recalls, "Apparently the girl on the sleeve is called Pat Bailey. It's thought she was a waitress."[314]

By the time the Specials broke up their original lineup in late 1981, tensions among band members had long been coming to a boil, to say the least. "This group … is coming like a ghost group," wrote Paul Du Noyer in *NME* in August of that year.[315] Their performance of "Ghost Town" on *Top of the Pops* showcased their success as a band with the song reaching number one, but the members of the band were far from harmonious with one another. There had been violence within the band and violence toward the band, issues with power and fame were ever present, and alcohol and drug use only fueled young hot tempers. So when Neville Staple came into the dressing room after their performance to announce that he, Lynval Golding, and Terry Hall were leaving to start their own venture, Fun Boy Three, none of the others were exactly surprised. Still, for Jerry Dammers who had put the whole thing together—both the Specials and 2 Tone—it was shocking. He vowed to carry on.

Jerry Dammers told Pete Chambers in 2005, "Strictly speaking, The Specials didn't actually break up. Some of the band left and said I could carry on the name, which is what happened. I suppose at first maybe it seemed like a bit of a relief, because a couple of the band had become impossible to work with by the end, but deep down it was very disappointing. When the Fun Boy Three went pop and left the Specials, I don't think they really understood the unique position they were in. What they did quite possibly reduced the chances of protest music getting into the pop charts right up to the present day. I also don't think they realise what I was put through trying to keep alive that standard of music, combined with the political ideals, which the Specials had come to represent. I got more than enough grief from a couple of the original Specials for my song-writing and arranging, that resentment was even more crazy from a couple of the replacement members. It was probably a mistake to expect another good live band to come mainly from Coventry, so soon after the Specials and Selecter."[316] Though they might not have been the live band they once were, the Specials in their new incarnation, did go an entirely different direction than Fun Boy Three, though that was not the intent. The intent was to continue the trajectory that the Specials had been on, in Dammers' mind, with bits of innovation

---

[313] Barendregt, Erwin. "More Specials, the best album of 1980?" A Pop Life. 4 Oct 2020. en.apoplife.nl/more-specials-the-best-album-of-1980. Accessed 23 Oct. 2022.

[314] Davies, Chalkie. All quotations, unless otherwise noted, from interview with the author, 3 Jun. 2021.

[315] Du Noyer, Paul. *NME*. "Giving Up the Ghost?" 8 Aug. 1981, p. 19.

[316] Chambers, Pete. "Backbeat." *Coventry Evening Telegraph*, 8 Feb. 2005. rocksgodiva.tripod.com/2tonetrail/id10.html. Accessed 20 Oct. 2022.

and new influence and creation. That path would be a long and winding one with numerous difficulties, including that of the name itself.

The Specials, as they once were, clearly were no longer. Therefore, the name of the band itself needed to reflect this change. Or at least that's what the lawyers said. "Jerry Dammers wanted to continue as The Specials, but legal wrangling forced him to revert to the original moniker of the Special AKA," according to 2 Tone experts Jason Weir and Peter Walsh.[317] Music journalist Neil Spencer also reveals the same, in an interview with Dammers in 1983, stating, "it seems that only legal complications with the name prevented the combo going out as the Specials."[318] So the Special AKA continued the music, and also, in the eyes of the record label, Chrysalis, continued the contract as signed by Dammers for four albums. The first one, and only one, would be *In the Studio*.

Joining Dammers and the Special AKA from the old lineup were John "Brad" Bradbury on drums and Horace Panter on bass. Roddy Radiation left to pursue his own work with bands like the Tearjerkers, and so John Shipley of the Swinging Cats took over the role of guitar. Rhoda featured prominently in the vocals category, as did her good friend she recruited, Egidio Newton. But before Egidio even had the chance to step foot in a studio, the Special AKA recorded their first single, penned by Rhoda, sung by Rhoda, conceived of and portrayed by Rhoda during her days with the Bodysnatchers. Nicky Summers of the Bodysnatchers was featured on bass. The song was "the Boiler," which essentially reenacted a date rape from the woman's point of view. It was harrowing, to say the least, and for Dammers to choose to record the single as the first venture of the Special AKA, it signaled the boldness of his direction for the group.

"Centered around a story about a lonely woman (a 'boiler' is a British slang term) on a date with a man she gradually realizes is dangerous, it's anchored by a pummeling beat, Jerry Dammers' demented-calliope organ and Dick Cuthell's braying trumpet, all of which grow more and more threatening as Dakar's narrative gets increasingly uneasy and frightened, until the song concludes with 90 straight seconds of her horrifying screaming—the kind of 'oh-my-god-call-911-right-now shrieking that triggers the amygdala, the area of the brain that generates a fear response. It's a deeply powerful and disturbing song that you can't un-hear—we can't put enough trigger warnings on it—which was presumably the point," wrote one journalist, four decades after the release of the single.[319]

Rhoda says that the term "'old boiler' was a phrase Nicky [Summers] told me she'd hear men use to describe ugly women"[320] and the narrative of this song was not inspired by personal experiences, but the experiences that many collective women

[317] "The Special AKA." 2-tone.info/the-special-aka. Accessed 6 Jan. 2023.
[318] Spencer, Neil. "The Invisible Profile Shapes Up." *NME*, 8 Jan. 1983, p. 21.
[319] Aswad, Jem. "Kendrick Lamar's Harrowing Song 'We Cry Together' Has a History Far Deeper Than Eminem's 'Kim'." *Variety*, 17 May 2022. variety.com/2022/music/news/kendrick-lamar-we-cry-together-eminem-kim-boiler-1235269707/#!. Accessed 23 Oct. 2022.
[320] Rachel, Daniel. *Walls Come Tumbling Down*. Picador, 2016, p. 290.

experience when faced with male power and aggression. Her background in theater helped her to conjure the role. "I had wanted to be an actress and straight out of school I got a job in a theater. And I'd worked in the theater for a couple of years and realized that I would never play anything other than nurses or prostitutes, if I became an actress. In the UK at the time, that was all it was. I mean, black men could play other roles, but black women were nurses or prostitutes. That was your job. That was what you'd get. And I had been in the Old Vic Youth Theatre and the Old Vic had been the seat of the National Theatre and it was very kind of, you know, old, grand establishment and I'd done Shakespeare on stage at the Old Vic, which is a big deal, and I realized that I would never ever get to do that if I worked as an actress. I'd never get that chance because those opportunities wouldn't be afforded me. So I went into music. So when I was in the Bodysnatchers, I had no experience of writing songs. So what I did was, I started improvising a monologue. And Penny, the keyboard player, started putting a riff behind it. And that's how it came about. So it was improvised every night, really. I mean, but the end, you kind of know what you're going to say, but it was an improvisation," she says.[321]

Though "the Boiler" was improvised on stage during her time with the Bodysnatchers, it was never recorded with this incarnation. Instead, the Special AKA recorded it as their first single. "Jerry has always wanted to record the song. He wanted it to be the Bodysnatchers' first single. Now he's changed the music. The Bodysnatchers' already had music which they put the words to while Jerry wrote this music specially. We just kept the piano riff which was stolen from somewhere anyway. Jerry's music sounds like a soundtrack from a film," Rhoda said.[322]

"The Boiler" was almost immediately banned from airplay. Adrian Thrills wrote in the *Record Mirror* on January 16, 1982, "Radio One last week slipped the disc into their two late evening slots—John Peel and Richard Skinner—but have now dropped from all of their playlists, while one play from DJ Peter Young on London's Capital Radio last Saturday led to listeners jamming the switchboard and a somewhat sensationalist story in the *Sunday People*. A Radio One spokesman denied on Tuesday that the record had been banned, though the BBC have not played it since last weekend. … But Chrysalis Records, 2-Tone distributors, maintain that this constitutes a ban—a claim refuted by the BBC. 'It isn't a case of the BBC ignoring the record,' continues the Radio One man. 'It has been played as a review record. But the general feeling is that it is unsuitable for normal radio play. The final decision is still up to the producer of each individual show, but it is unlikely that they will decide to play it.'"[323] So radio didn't officially ban "the Boiler" from airplay. That would have been a good move, said Dammers. "I wish they'd ban our songs, but they don't—they just ignore them! The best thing that can possibly happen is to get a record in the charts and then get it banned."[324] Rhoda agrees, stating, "The BBC don't make outright bans anymore

[321] Dakar, Rhoda. Interview on History of LA Ska podcast, 11 Apr. 2021.
[322] Cooper, Mark. "Being Boiled—Rhoda Dakar." *Record Mirror*, 23 Jan. 1982.
[323] Thrills, Adrian. "The reality of rape that they're trying to ban." *Record Mirror*. 16 Jan. 1982.
[324] Fletcher, Tony. "The Special AKA: The Skars Have Healed." *Jamming!*, March 1984.

because the last time they did that, it was 'God Save The Queen' which went to Number One. They will play it in connection with 'relevant discussion' on the grounds that if you're discussing something that people consider offensive to begin with, they needn't listen. They believe that if the record just comes up in normal airtime, it'll surprise and offend."[325]

But even record stores were reluctant to carry the record. The Boots pharmacy chain in England once had a record department in some of their locations. A spokesman from one told the *Record Mirror* on January 23, 1982, "'Some shops have the record in stock and they will be selling it. But in view of the publicity the record has got I don't think that we'll be ordering any more.' And it looks as if other major chains will be following suit, which could completely outlaw the disc in some towns. The moves by the radio stations, and now the shops, confirms the criticisms of Rhoda herself that rape is something that should not be talked about."[326] Journalist Mark Cooper hit the nail on the proverbial head when he wrote, "And so the voice of sanity and the voice of women is silenced. Instead we are offered a diet of make-believe or the pornographic fantasies of heavy metal; clever lads like Phil Lynott describing himself as a 'Killer On The Loose', while the Ripper is murdering women. Women who supposedly want it. Who is obscene, the rapist or the victim? You tell me."[327]

Perhaps the song hit too close to home for Britons. That year, 1982, saw a number of rape cases in the UK that drew public outrage. One of these cases involved Judge Bertrand Richard of the Ipswich Crown Court who found a man guilty of raping a 17-year-old hitchhiker. However, the judge only gave the rapist a $4,000 fine and no jail sentence, claiming that the victim, hitchhiking at night in a rural area, "was guilty of a great deal of contributory negligence."[328] Rhoda commented, "It just leaves you speechless when you hear things like that, but it seems to sum up the reaction of a lot of people to the crime of rapists. It certainly isn't treated with the seriousness it should be, not in this country anyway. In America, for example, it is taken a lot more seriously, maybe because it's more of a problem out there. In Britain, rape is something you don't talk about, even if it happens to you. The attitude of a lot of people is that girls on their own are just asking for it by the way they dress or the fact that they are walking around late at night… we are almost conditioned to think that if a girl gets raped, then it's her own fault, which is ridiculous. A woman walking around late at night is somehow regarded as inviting some sort of approach. They just assume that you're looking for a bloke. It's the same stupid attitude."[329]

The Special AKA released a number of other singles before hunkering down for a proper LP. Among these was Rico's "Jungle Music" with the B-side, "Rasta Call You." Another single, "War Crimes," addressed the topic of Palestinian refugees in war-torn Beirut using a 5/4 time signature. The song featured both Rhoda Dakar and

---

[325] Cooper, Mark. "Being Boiled—Rhoda Dakar." *Record Mirror*, 23 Jan. 1982.
[326] "Shops black boiler." *Record Mirror*, 23 Jan. 1982.
[327] Cooper, Mark. "Being Boiled—Rhoda Dakar." *Record Mirror*, 23 Jan. 1982
[328] Borders, William. "Britons Outraged Over 3 Rape Cases." *New York Times*. 24 Jan. 1982, p. 4.
[329] Thrills, Adrian. "The reality of rape that they're trying to ban." *Record Mirror*. 16 Jan. 1982.

Egidio Newton on vocals and it was the first single that Egidio appeared on, as she was brought into the fold.

Egidio Newton lived in South London and was friends with Rhoda. "The two had met when teenage Bowie fans, both camping on the doorstep of David's London homestead. Egidio had sung with several local bands before joining Animal Nightlife, only to exit a few months later and gain a free transfer into the Special AKA on backing vocals," wrote journalist Neil Spencer.[330] Animal Nightlife was a jazz-funk band with an ever-changing lineup that eventually signed to Island Records in 1985, but none of their recordings feature Egidio. Egidio did, however, go on to perform with the legendary Gil Scott-Heron as a backup singer. The two began a relationship and Egidio mothered his child, Chegianna Newton, the last of his four children from four mothers. This has resulted in a number of lawsuits over the rights to his estate, and according to legendary Jamaican percussionist Larry McDonald who performed and toured with Scott-Heron for years, the legal disputes and ugliness has had an emotional impact on Egidio.[331] As a result, she has largely left public life. Her daughter Che, however, has been involved in continuing her father's legacy to activism.

For Dammers, bringing both Rhoda Dakar and Egidio Newton into the regular mix of band members for the Special AKA was crucial. It may have been a decision inspired by the turmoil in the Specials lineup, as well as one about sound. "It definitely gives more balance, just gets the group away from that macho thing," said Dammers.[332] Rhoda commented that being in a band with men was good for music, and the industry, but it wasn't without its challenges. She joked, "It just seems sensible, though personally it seems funny to be in a group with a load of blokes. I never thought I'd miss female company but I do. Everyone starts hiding in the corner of the changing rooms. I'd never realised before how shy men are."[333]

The next single released by the Special AKA was "Racist Friend"—a song that Dammers described as "saying goodbye to a few people. If you're with friends who keep on making racist comments, however jokey, I think you have to make a personal decision. It didn't get played on the radio because it was accusing everyone."[334] The song called upon listeners to cut ties with racist sisters, brothers, cousins, uncles, lovers, and friends. It was an important song then; it's an important song now.

More women were added to the Special AKA's lineup to produce a fuller and more African sound for the powerful single, "Free Nelson Mandela," a song that became an anthem in the anti-Apartheid movement. It cannot be overstated how important this song was to the awareness of South Africa's Apartheid regime and the life of Nelson Mandela himself. Dammers explained his inspiration and intention for the song, "I went to a concert at the Alexandra Palace to celebrate his sixtieth birthday

---

[330] Spencer, Neil. "The Invisible Profile Shapes Up." *NME*, 8 Jan. 1983, p. 21.
[331] McDonald, Larry. Conversation with the author, 2 Apr. 2021.
[332] Spencer, Neil. "The Invisible Profile Shapes Up." *NME*, 8 Jan. 1983, p. 21.
[333] Ibid.
[334] Bell, Max. "The Special AKA: Still Special (After All These Years)." *The Face*, June 1984.

[five years prior] and at the time I didn't know anything about him. However, since then, I've read a few books about him, and I just think that the situation in South Africa is going on and on and on and nobody's doing anything about it. The rest of the world has got to do something about it, otherwise nothing's going to change, because the people in South Africa haven't got the power. The point of the song is really just to say what I feel about it, in the hope that other people feel the same."[335]

In addition to Rhoda and Egidio, three singers that had formed their own group called Afrodiziak joined the vocal ensemble—Caron Wheeler, Claudia Fontaine, and Naomi Thompson; as well as two sisters, Polly and Molly Jackson. A lead vocal, Stan Campbell, also joined, as did Gary McManus on bass, Lynval Golding on guitar, David Heath on flute, Andy Aderinto on saxophone, and Paul Speare on penny whistle. Dave Wakeling and Ranking Roger were brought on board for additional vocals. "Jerry asked me and Dave to sing. I'd been hearing about Mandela since the '70s. All the punks used to rage about how he was a political prisoner. And I'm glad at some point Mandela heard my voice. Wonderful!" said Roger.[336] The song was produced by Elvis Costello. Sleeve notes for the recording educated listeners to the history of Nelson Rolihlahla Mandela and the plight of South Africans who suffered and died at the hands of the Apartheid government, as did the lyrics of the song itself.

Polly and Molly Jackson joined the vocal lineup through connections in the tight-knit musical community and they had already established careers singing. "My sister and I were both born in London of mixed parentage," says Polly Jackson.[337] "Our father was Jamaican and our mother Burmese, more correctly Karen. The Karen is a tribe from Burma—Myanmar—who do not consider themselves Burmese. Our mother had a musical background and could play harmonica and guitar and was also an amazing artist. Karen people are known for their artistic and musical background. Our father loved music and we grew up in a house full of music, dancing, and singing. He had a large music collection and among the many musicians he loved were Nat King Cole, Fats Domino, Ray Charles, Otis Redding, and Bob Dylan."

With a family that placed importance on music, developing their daughter's education in the arts was fundamental. "From the age of seven onwards, my sister and I had private piano, singing, drama, and speaking of prose lessons. We were graded by the Royal Academy of Arts. At this time we both soloed in school assemblies and shows. My sister, Molly, who is two years older, and I have always done things together. Later, as children, we immigrated with our parents to Zambia in Central Africa where we attended convent and continue our musical training there," Polly says. The reason the family moved to Zambia was because the girls' father, Wilston Samuel Jackson, was a train engineer. In fact, he was the first black train driver in Great Britain, and as such, he has been honored with a Blue Heritage plaque

[335] Fletcher, Tony. "The Special AKA: The Skars Have Healed." *Jamming!*, March 1984.
[336] Hasted, Nick. "The Special AKA — The Making Of 'Nelson Mandela.'" *Uncut*. Jan. 2010.
[337] Jackson, Polly. All quotations, unless otherwise noted, from interview with the author, 26 Nov. 2021.

which hangs in London's Kings Cross Station, erected there on October 25, 2021. Born in Portland Jamaica, Wilston Jackson emigrated to London in 1952 as part of the movement to rebuild the UK after WWII. He experienced terrible racism in his pursuit to become a train driver, which he did in 1962. He moved to Zambia in 1966 to pursue a different lifestyle for his family and there he continued to drive trains and later became a farmer and helped his neighbors erect an iron bridge over a river.[338]

"Molly and I returned to the UK in the seventies as early teenagers and started writing and playing acoustic songs together," Polly says. "We joined a couple of bands doing original music, mainly a fusion of reggae, funk, and ska. We did some backing vocals for Osibissa and some song writing with Vangelis, as well as backing vocals with Vangelis. We were never credited for this. We then got a record deal of our own with an independent label which didn't come to anything. By this time I was playing keyboards and Molly playing bass and guitar, but we never stopped singing or songwriting, which we did from when Molly was around 11 years old and me 9. We continued doing backing vocal sessions with a number of bands and travelled to France and Italy a number of times to work on various albums or singles. We met Big George, a bass player, on a session and he introduced us to Brad who was part of The Specials."

Big George was George Webley who had formed a group, the Blitz, during the punk era in London. He was a successful session bass player and he later became a composer and musical director, writing the opening theme to the UK version of *The Office*, among others. After Webley introduced Molly and Polly to John "Brad" Bradbury, the connection to the "Free Nelson Mandela" session was secured, but Polly says the experience was not a good one. "We did some backing vocals and TV with Brad in a band he had formed called J.B.'s Allstars. He was a really nice guy and a true gentleman. He wanted us on the 'Free Nelson Mandela' single even though Elvis Costello, who was producing the single, tried to scupper this, for his own reasons. But Brad was adamant we be on the single, and so we were. Later on, Brad introduced us to Jerry Dammers, who was also a very nice man, even though he had no front teeth. They were very nice to us. Elvis Costello had us waiting in Abbey Road and Air Studios for several days, waiting to sing on the "Free Nelson Mandela" track. We guessed he was hoping we would become infuriated and leave, which we nearly did, and would have done, but for Brad asking us to stay and invoice the record company for the hours that we had waited and were available. We believe that EC is a racist and this has been confirmed by many other black musicians. He could not look us in the eyes and while we were recording and mic'd up, he (and the rest of the people in the control room) overheard us slagging him off and calling him names. The rest of the people in the control room were very amused (although EC just kept quiet) and told us many years later they had heard everything we said. What a rookie

---

[338] "Wilston Samuel Jackson—The First Black Train Driver." blackhistorymonth.org.uk/article/section/bhm-firsts/wilston-samuel-jackson-the-first-black-train-driver. Accessed 24 Oct. 2022.

mistake, but we were very young and angry. After the record's release, we did a video with the band and some TV, but never spoke to EC again," Polly says.

The sisters continued their careers in music for as long as they were able, before they had to turn to other employment. Polly explains, "We continued to play music and do backing vocals for around another ten years, after which, although we thoroughly enjoyed ourselves, we decided to move on and now have our own law practice. Manoeuvring in the music business as strong women, unwilling to compromise our beliefs by refusing to jump into bed with men just because we want the job or deal is something we will never regret. Because of this, not all our dreams came true, however, when we look in the mirror we know who we are and are proud that we held firm. The advice we give to other women, and even men, is that never do what in your heart you know is wrong just for the monetary gain, fame, or misguided respect, because when you go home at night, you only have yourself to face and you must be able to love yourself. Furthermore, nine times out of ten, those promises are not upheld by the person. Nothing is worth losing your self-respect. We have never stopped composing songs and still play music and sing for pleasure. That will never change."

Caron Wheeler, Naomi Thompson, and Claudia Fontaine also joined the vocal ensemble on "Free Nelson Mandela" as the vocal trio Afrodiziak. Caron Wheeler, born in London to Jamaican parents, had performed as a youth in another vocal trio called Brown Sugar. The group won a number of local talent competitions and even recorded a single, "I'm in Love with a Dreadlocks," a lover's rock tune that was popular with sound systems. They toured with Dennis Brown in 1978 and released a number of other singles the following year. After they disbanded, Caron Wheeler formed Afrodiziak. She had met Claudia Fontaine while singing, as Claudia was a backup singer. Claudia also performed lover's rock tunes. Her first song was a solo, "Natural High," released in 1981. At first, Afrodiziak was just Claudia Fontaine and Caron Wheeler and the two performed on the Jam's *Beat Surrender* album, and on Elvis Costello's song, "Everyday I Write the Book." Through Costello, they, along with Naomi Thompson, were brought into the studio for the recording of "Free Nelson Mandela."

"Thank goodness Elvis brought in Afrodiziak, the bit they did at the beginning made the record," said Dammers.[339] It's true. The female voices definitely elevate the song to a powerful level. That was the intent, said Caron. "It was like, 'Wow, we're trying to spring this man from jail via musical powers! Do it right, make 'em feel it!' Like creative visualisation. If you see it, it makes it real. That conviction came across in everyone's playing. You couldn't be thinking about doing the laundry. It was important to belt it out, but sweetly. We were there for that, we were hired for that. We flew through those recording studio doors. Somehow, Jerry and them captured the essence of the South African rhythm. Between the girls and the horns, we tied it up like gravy! It was first-class casting. We thought about the South African

---

[339] Hasted, Nick. "The Special AKA — The Making Of 'Nelson Mandela.'" *Uncut*. Jan. 2010.

140

accent as we sang. Stan looked like he could have been from there as well. There were a few things that made it seem authentic."[340]

A music video and television performances of the song followed the recording, as the song became popular on radio. "We had a big session with everyone at the end so they could film the video. I didn't know our vocals were going to be upfront and a cappella at the start 'til we saw it. Performing it to TV audiences when it was in the charts felt like a Fight the Power thing. It was a rare black British thing we could latch onto then, in a mixed-race band who all felt the same way. People wanted to support it, because dancing to it felt really good. That lifted the message up to a power where people really took notice," said Wheeler.[341]

"Free Nelson Mandela" brought awareness to the brutality of Apartheid and made Nelson Mandela a household name. It held governments, like Great Britain, responsible for conducting business with the racist regime. It shined a spotlight on events like Margaret Thatcher entertaining South African Prime Minister P.W. Botha in the English countryside, even when British media barely noticed, and encouraged questioning why one's own leader would engage in diplomacy and merry making with an ally of Hitler and his ideological successor.[342] One journalist wrote of the song that it was "a seamless marriage of heartfelt protest and surging hi-life exuberance, its effect was simple and direct. I know it made at least one person want to find out more about the man and the regime that had systematically robbed him and his people of their dignity and basic human rights. It also caused Chrysalis' South African office to forward a telegram to London requesting that on no account should they be sent any copies of the record, as possession would be a prisonable offence. The more you find out about South Africa, the more you see how firmly entrenched we in the 'free' world are in bolstering its heinous racism, how entertainers like Elton John and Millie Jackson play for outrageous sums of money in the Sun City entertainment capital, the more sickening the whole thing becomes."[343] Linton Kwesi Johnson observed, "'(Free) Nelson Mandela' made an incalculable cultural contribution to the anti-apartheid struggle. It should never be underestimated the impact it had not only on the consciousness of people in this country but all over Europe."[344] It could certainly be argued that the song had an impact globally.

Caron Wheeler went on to sing for Erasure, Aswad, and Phil Collins, before joining Soul II Soul with Jazzie B and singing the hit songs, "Keep On Moving" and "Back To Life" which won a Grammy Award for Best R&B Performance by a Duo or Group with Vocal in 1990. They have sold over 30 million albums worldwide. She has also had a successful solo career and in 1994 moved to LA. She began her own production company, Power Phoenix Entertainment, providing music for such movies as *Mo Money* and *How Stella Got Her Groove Back*. She has one daughter, Asha

---

[340] Ibid.
[341] Hasted, Nick. "The Special AKA — The Making Of 'Nelson Mandela.'" *Uncut*. Jan. 2010.
[342] Martin, Gavin. "The Special AKA: 26,732 Hours In The Studio with Jerry Dammers." *NME*, 18 Aug. 1984.
[343] Ibid.
[344] Rachel, Daniel. *Walls Come Tumbling Down*. Picador, 2016, p. 521.

Star. Claudia Fontaine backed Madness on the *Keep Moving* and *Mad Not Mad* albums, Pink Floyd on their *Division Bell* tour and their live album *Pulse*, and she backed Robbie Williams, Geri Halliwell, and Will Young before passing away in March of 2018.[345] Thompson, who also went by the name Naomi Osbourne and Nao Mi Osborne, performed backup for Howard Jones on the song, "Things Can Only Get Better," as well as Betty Boo, Vince Watson, Sam Brown, S'Express, Primal Scream, and others. Of the experience, Caron reflects, "The country that imprisons Mandela one day makes him President—and this is, maybe partially, a result of charting this song."[346]

For all the impact that "Free Nelson Mandela" had, the *In the Studio* album was fraught with turmoil. The numbers that circulate regarding cost and time spent in production of *In the Studio* are mythical in proportion, though many are likely close to accurate. "I learned so much from doing *In the Studio*. Like how not to make an LP," Dammers said.[347] One journalist who wrote about the album just after its release, crystalized the making of the album perfectly. "With more than a little irony AKA's LP was titled *In the Studio*, since that's mostly where Jerry had been for 24 months, spending a fortune on sculpting his vinyl child to perfection. Unfortunately, though as compelling and artistically complete as any debut LP of recent times, the record was not as mega-successful in Britain as 'Mandela'. To complicate matters the band weren't functioning. One of the lead vocalists, the very talented Stan Campbell, had departed and Dammers had to rely on videos rather than live performances to keep AKA's profile high."[348] Incidentally, in April 2002, Stan Campbell "was sent to psychiatric hospital indefinitely after a jury at Warwick Crown Court found him guilty of kidnapping and indecently assaulting one teenage girl and assaulting another."[349]

For Rhoda Dakar, who sang of most of the songs on *In the Studio* with Egidio Newton, the experience was a disaster. "We spent two years just doing overdubs. But we only made two or three songs from scratch, and 'Nelson Mandela' was one of them. I don't know which harmony is mine. Quite likely mine was mixed out, to be honest, because I was persona non grata by that time. I wrote a verse for the song, which you can hear in *Play At Home*. And then when we got in the studio, Jerry changed it all around. And I mean, essentially tried to erase everything I'd written, and thought he had," says Rhoda. When asked why she thinks Dammers did this, she replies, "You've have to ask him. Because he does like his name on a record. So I don't know you'd have to ask him. So when I saw the record and realized my name wasn't on it, I called the record company and I said, 'My name is not on the record, so either you put my name on it, or I'm going to sue you.' So I was given some of the publishing. And then it still came out without my name on it. So I called up the record company and they pressed some with my name on it. So there are some versions of

[345] Binnie, Steve. "Afrodiziak's Claudia Fontaine dies, aged 57." Sound of the Crowd. soundofthecrowd.org.uk/news/afrodiziaks-claudia-fontaine-dies-aged-57. Accessed 18 Mar. 2021.

[346] Hasted, Nick. "The Special AKA — The Making Of 'Nelson Mandela.'" *Uncut.* Jan. 2010.

[347] Irwin, Colin. "The Special AKA: Memoirs of a Survivor." *Melody Maker*, 19 Jan. 1985.

[348] Barron, Jack. "The Special AKA: Jerry Can." *Sounds*, 19 Jan. 1985.

[349] Barry, Paul and Steve Chilton. "The Rise and Fall of a Pop Star." *Coventry Evening Telegraph*, 17 Apr. 2002.

that record with my name on them, and some don't. I dealt with the record company, and I dealt with lawyers. That's how that got sorted. But yeah, it was a real fight. I mean, it took ten years for me to get any royalties at all. I didn't get any money for years. And it's actually quite funny because everyone thinks that 2 Tone was like, 'Oh yea, but it was great.' It's like, 2 Tone was run really only by one person. And yeah, I didn't make any money out of it, so I don't know where it went. Not in my pocket."[350]

Dammers didn't make money either, as he was deeply in debt to Chrysalis who had contracted three more albums that would never come. Instead, he went on to lead the Anti-Apartheid movement in England. He explains, "At that point, the son of Oliver Tambo, the head of the ANC in exile, asked me to approach musicians for Artists Against Apartheid. Because I couldn't do anything in my career, I thought I might as well. The gigs got bigger and bigger, until my proudest moment, the free concert on Clapham Common with Peter Gabriel, B.A.D., Hugh Masekela, the Style Council, Boy George. Quarter of a million people. The whole point of a song like 'Nelson Mandela' is you're one cog in a wheel, but one thing leads to another. Julian Bahula's song led to mine, which led to the Mandela concert at Wembley, which went to 600 million people around the world, more than Live Aid. Before that concert, Margaret Thatcher was referring to Mandela as a terrorist. After it, she wanted to be his friend. The weight of popular opinion must have affected negotiations behind the scenes. But all I did was write a song. People in South Africa gave up their lives."[351]

Rhoda has continued her career in music since the end of the Special AKA and the end of 2 Tone. She sang a duet with Suggs, "On the Town," which appeared on *the Liberty of Norton Folgate* album in 2009, and worked with Nick Welsh, the Communards, Apollo 440, and Skaville UK. She has her own band, LoTek Four and has recorded a number of solo singles including four during the pandemic. Her album *Cleaning in Another Woman's Kitchen* was released on the Moon Ska World label in 2007, and her 2014 album, *Rhoda Sings the Bodysnatchers*, was crowdfunded. She has been a DJ all over the world including for tours of the Specials, the Selecter, and the Interrupters.[352] She says she has "done all sort of things. I've worked in fashion, I've done a bit of graphic design, and now as an elder stateswoman, I'm a kind of a serial committee member, so I'm a patron of the Music Venue Trust which is desperately trying to negotiate with government to explain to them what culture is and why we need it; I'm an ambassador for Tonic Music for Mental Health which is a music charity down on the south coast; I'm an all-around troublemaker and a musician."[353] She is mother to a daughter and son, the later of whom is also a DJ and musician.

[350] Dakar, Rhoda. Interview on History of LA Ska podcast, 11 Apr. 2021.
[351] Hasted, Nick. "The Special AKA — The Making Of 'Nelson Mandela.'" *Uncut*. Jan. 2010.
[352] vivelerock.net.
[353] Dakar, Rhoda. Janine Booth. 13 July 2000. janinebooth.com/content/video-janine-interviews-rhoda-dakar. Accessed 1 July 2022.

Afrodiziak (L to R), Claudia Fontaine, Caron Wheeler, & Naomi Thompson

Clockwise from top left, Rhoda Dakar &
Egidio Newton; Molly & Polly Jackson at
the recognition for their father; Molly
Jackson, Rhoda Dakar, and Polly Jackson;
and Chrissie Hynde and Egidio Newton.

Fun Boy Three

Nicky Holland: keyboard, musical
  director
Caroline Lavelle: cello
June Miles-Kingston: drums
Bethan Peters: bass

Ingrid Schroeder: keyboard, vocals
Annie Whitehead: trombone
Bananarama: Sara Dallin, Siobhan
  Fahey, and Keren Woodward

With a name like Fun Boy Three, one might get the impression that men were at the center of this band. One might also think that there were three members. And that they were enjoyable and amusing. That last descriptor may be true, but the former two assumptions were not. There were certainly more than three members of this collective, and most of them were women who had, and would go on to have, arguably, more impressive careers in music than the three boys. Yet they are largely invisible in the lineup—relegated to the back line in appearances, absent from photos and press, and gone entirely from interviews. These are the women of Fun Boy Three.

Fun Boy Three formed somewhat clandestinely while the Specials were still very much a band, touring and recording though not in perfect harmony, to say the least. As a result of discontent over unequal treatment in the Specials, largely at the hand of Jerry Dammers, the group's founder and assumed leader, Terry Hall, Lynval Golding, and Neville Staple decided to leave the group on a high note, just after their last song, "Ghost Town," became a hit in the summer of 1981.[354] The trio was managed by Rick Rogers and produced by Dave Jordan, who also left to join the new venture. They signed to Chrysalis, the parent company for 2 Tone, since the popularity of Fun Boy Three was all but ensured. Hall said he had been planning the departure for some time, though they didn't have a clear vision of what their new formation would sound like. "We knew a year ago [1981] what we were gonna do but didn't have everything set out in the normal way. We'd rather just work from the title when we go into studio. Some of the rhythms started from a cha-cha or mambo, but they've been crossed with a reggae beat or something. It's all our influences coming out naturally, without forcing 'em," Hall said.[355] The beats, the rhythms, and the sound laid on top of them, came through collaboration with a number of women who had established careers in music, as well as those who were brand new. The result was a marked pivot from the Specials.

Press that reviewed the output of Fun Boy Three described the approach which unsurprisingly minimized the roles of the women involved. "The basic format should be familiar by now," wrote Gavin Martin in *NME*.[356] "A drum machine lays down the rhythm track and Lynval, Terry and Neville place lead and vocal harmony lines over the top along with any augmenting instrumentation." This "augmenting

---

354 Green, Jim. "Fun Boy Three." *Trouser Press*, June 1982.
355 Ibid.
356 Martin, Gavin. "Fun Boy Three: *Fun Boy Three*." NME, 13 Mar. 1982.

instrumentation" came via six women who provided the music for the boys' vocals, augmented by Lynval's guitar.

The first women to join the Fun Boy Three were the members of Bananarama—Sara Dallin, Siobhan Fahey, and Keren Woodward. They were asked to join the band after coming to the attention of Terry Hall who saw their photo in a magazine and liked them for the way they looked. But lest we discount such a reason for musical membership, remember that the early 1980s were the heyday of music video and visual interpretation of the music was just as important, if not even more important, than the sound itself. And, as will be discussed, Hall was a strong proponent of art and imagery. "Our first photo shoot was with Derek Ridgers ... he shot us mucking around in the sea in the polka-dot catsuits Siobhan had picked up while she was on holiday, and on the pier in our second-hand shirts and trousers and current favourite choice of footwear—moccasins," wrote Keren Woodward in the book *Bananarama: Really Saying Something*.[357] Sara Dallin picks up the story, "Somehow one of the photos ended up in the *NME*, and another in the fashion bible, The Face. And, as it turned out, Terry Hall, ex-frontman of The Specials, also favoured moccasins. When he spotted our picture in the *NME*, he apparently took a shine to us. Indeed, Terry later said in an interview that he "'liked our shoes,' and, more importantly, had bought our single after hearing it on John Peel's show, where he championed new artists."[358]

Keren Woodward and Sara Dallin were childhood friends who grew up with a love for pop music and strong women like Diana Ross, Patti Smith, Debbie Harry, Polly Styrene, Siouxsie Sioux, Viv Albertine, and Gaye Advert. Sara says they all "made me feel there was a place for women in music. They opened my eyes to a new and exciting world and I had an unquenchable thirst for it."[359] They clubbed in London and moved to the city at age 18. After Sara met Siobhan Fahey in a class at the London College of Fashion where they were both students, the trio frequented clubs like the Blitz and Studio 21 as part of the scene. They befriended Paul Cook of the Sex Pistols who introduced them to other luminaries and arranged a squat when Sara and Keren were about to become homeless. The squat, the Sex Pistols old rehearsal space, was in the heart of Soho and provided more connections to musicians and artists. Inspired by their love for music and the music all around them, they began to dabble on their own. "We each bought a Dictaphone to warble our early attempts at songwriting into. Meanwhile, I asked Paul if we could use Denmark Street to try a few of the ideas out," says Sara.[360] Not long after, the trio performed at a club called the Wag. Through a connection they came to the attention of Clash manager Bernie Rhodes who "suggested we go underground for a year to learn our craft," but they rejected this advice.[361] Instead they "approached future DJ and presenter Gary

[357] Dallin, Sara and Keren Woodward. *Bananarama: Really Saying Something*. Hutchinson, 2020, p. 85.
[358] Ibid., p. 85-86.
[359] Ibid., p. 42.
[360] Ibid, p. 79.
[361] Ibid., p. 80.

Crowley, who, at the time, was dating Siobhan's sister."[362] This resulted in recording a demo of "Aie a Mwana" which appeared on John Peel's show.

When Terry Hall brought Bananarama into the fold of Fun Boy Three, Sara says the initial gathering was a bit uncomfortable. "It was quite an awkward meeting, with the three of us sitting shyly on the sofa, while Terry sat on the chair opposite, his teacup rattling while he hid behind our fringes. The conversation was pretty monosyllabic. But the upshot was that Terry had formed a new group, Fun Boy Three, with Lynval Golding and Neville Staple from the Specials, and he wanted to ask if we would sing on their debut album. Once the initial excitement of the offer evaporated, we went into a panic, worried that he'd thought we were professional session singers. We needn't have worried. Terry, Lynval and Neville were utterly inclusive from the start and being in the studio, watching them putting tracks together, turned out to be a great learning experience. That said, I was mortified when I pulled out a tube of Rolos and offered one to Terry, only to realise I was offering him a Tampax. He politely declined," said Sara.[363]

The result was the Fun Boy Three's eponymous debut album and the single, "It Ain't What You Do (It's the Way You Do It)." Sara says, "The recording sessions had a DIY feel that seemed fresh and relaxed. As well as singing, they got us playing all kinds of percussion instruments, with each of us on a drum working out the rhythms together."[364] Fun Boy Three had already released their debut single, "The Lunatics Have Taken Over the Asylum," later re-recorded by the Specials nearly 40 years later for the Specials' *Encore* album. Bananarama, which had named themselves after the Roxy Music song "Pyjamarama," adding a little more, ahem, appeal, now appeared in music videos and on television and radio shows to promote the collaboration. The song was a hit and their performance on *Top of the Pops* propelled them into the spotlight. Bananarama signed to Decca Records to record a single of their own, "Really Saying Something," and Fun Boy Three reversed roles, performing backup singing and backup instrumentation. The career of Bananarama was thus launched. In 1989 they obtained the Guinness World Record for the "most worldwide chart entries of any all-female group."[365]

While Fun Boy Three involved the three women of Bananarama for backing vocals on their debut album, they sought to further that vision with their second album, *Waiting*. This vision required enlisting the help of female musicians, including vocalist and keyboardist Bethan Peters who came to Fun Boy Three after establishing herself as the bassist with Delta 5. This band originated in Leeds and was comprised of two men and three women. One of these women, Ros Allen, recalls how the Delta 5 formed. "Julz and Bethan, who were Mekons girlfriends at the time, decided to form a band and asked me if I'd like to play bass (I'd already left the Mekes supposedly to concentrate on my degree—ho hum!). I thought it might be fun so I did and it was

---

[362] Ibid., p. 80.
[363] Ibid., p. 86.
[364] Ibid., p. 86.
[365] Ibid., back cover.

sometimes. We asked Jon Langford to play guitar and Simon Best, who was then the Mekons's soundman, to play drums," said Ros.[366] Both she and Bethan played bass in the band which provided a punk-funk sound. "Because neither of us played guitar and we thought it would make the music more exciting with two different bass sounds, one trebly and funky (Bethan) and one more double-bass-like (me). It definitely enriched the sound of the band. We also had two guitars sometimes as Julz played occasionally. Come to think of it, we doubled up the vocals as well," Ros said.[367] Both Bethan Peters and Julz Sale wrote most of the lyrics, according to Allen, and in 1979 they had a hit with the single "Mind Your Own Business" which was used in an Apple commercial in 2021. They signed to Rough Trade records and toured Europe and the U.S. but soon lineup changes began to fragment and fray the band. Jacqui Callis performed with Delta 5 for a period before performing with the Deltones (see also Deltones chapter) and other members filtered in and out before they disbanded in 1981 after their album, *See the Whirl*, failed to achieve success.

Bethan Peters joined as bassist for Fun Boy Three, likely cultivated for her talent and her politics. Delta 5 had been involved in the Rock Against Racism movement, as was the Specials, the Beat, the Clash, and others. Rock Against Racism was formed in response to Eric Clapton's proclamation of support for Enoch Powell. In 1968, Powell, a Tory, delivered a racist speech in Birmingham that is now referred to as the "Rivers of Blood" speech. His tirade decried immigration for all the woes of England. Powell and his speech empowered the fascist National Front and British Movement organizations which were further empowered by Eric Clapton in 1976 during a gig, also in Birmingham. Clapton bellowed, "Stop Britain from becoming a black colony. Get the foreigners out. Get the wogs out. Get the coons out. Keep Britain white. I used to be into dope, now I'm into racism. It's much heavier, man. Fucking wogs, man. Fucking Saudis taking over London. Bastard wogs. Britain is becoming overcrowded and Enoch will stop it and send them all back. The black wogs and coons and Arabs and fucking Jamaicans and fucking… don't belong here, we don't want them here. This is England, this is a white country, we don't want any black wogs and coons living here. We need to make clear to them they are not welcome. England is for white people, man. We are a white country. I don't want fucking wogs living next to me with their standards. This is Great Britain, a white country. What is happening to us, for fuck's sake?"[368]

Politics was always at the heart of Fun Boy Three's music, as was politics the heart for the Specials, and for 2 Tone and ska, for that matter. So Bethan Peters and her involvement with Rock Against Racism was an ideal fit. Other members of the band were chosen not only for their politics, which aligned with the message of the

[366] Appelstein, Mike. "Delta 5." *Perfect Sound Forever*. Spring 1996. furious.com/perfect/delta5.html. Accessed 15 Sept. 2022.
[367] Ibid.
[368] Meara, Paul. "Eric Clapton Has Been Exposed As A Giant Racist And His Apology Will Make You Laugh." *BET*. 14 Jan. 2018. bet.com/article/gw1oko/eric-clapton-has-been-exposed-as-a-giant-racist. Accessed 15 Sept. 2022.

music, but their talent as well. June Miles-Kingston had just broken up with her band, the Mo-Dettes (see also Mo-Dettes chapter), and word was out. "That's right, so I just split up with the Mo-Dettes because it wasn't happening for me, and I was like grieving. I was in bed for two weeks with the cover over my head thinking, what am I going to do? You know, that was my life. I want to play music. I didn't know where to go. And the phone rang late one night and it was Lynval [Golding]," says June.[369]

Growing up in working-class East London, June Miles-Kingston says her parents didn't exactly expose her to music through lessons, but music was in her family blood. "My mom was a singer, only semipro. She used to sing in pubs and clubs and funny enough, we used to all trot around every weekend, sitting in smoky pubs and things, you know. Even though my mom was a singer, she wasn't a professional singer. And she was frustrated because she wanted to do it all her life. And she couldn't, because she had a family. She had three kids and she had a husband who went off to work. She could never do it," she says. That experience certainly stayed with June as she made her own choices on career and family.

In her teenage years, June was influenced by the music surrounding her, which was largely Jamaican music. She explains, "I was born in 1955 and when I was a teenager, ska music was so unusual. It was like exotic. And I was at school and my parents were quite typical parents at the time, postwar. They didn't quite understand different races and things like that. They weren't racist or anything like that—they just didn't get it. But I was at school at a time when people were coming over, like the Windrush movement, they were coming over from Jamaica. So I went to school with all these kids and it was perfectly natural for me. But what an introduction to music!"

She continues, "I used to have a Saturday morning job along the high street and I used to rush from there at lunchtime to spend my wages on records, of course, like we all did. And I went to this specialty shop down the road. I wish I could remember the name, but it just sold Jamaican imports. So I knew all the guys there. I was always a bit of a tomboy and I knew all the guys there and we'd just stand around, skanking around to all this new stuff. That was a big part of my upbringing and my musical influence. That music was ingrained in me—those beats and the off beats, the use of the rimshot and the use of the tom like the little, bam! I listened a lot to, as I got older, people that were using stuff like that. And as much as I didn't like the Police, I used to love some of the rhythms Stewart Copeland used. They were far more complicated, as far as I was concerned, but I used to listen to it in the bath and when I was first playing music with the Mo-Dettes. I thought, that's what I want. I love that. I love that!"

So how did June become a drummer? That story may just be the most fantastical and unusual alignment of stars, for the path to a music career like this could never be replicated again. "I was always interested in film because I love stories. I didn't know a girl could be a musician and go on the road and do that kind of stuff. I had no idea. I was always working and I used to go up to the National Film School. I

---

[369] Miles-Kingston, June. All quotations, unless otherwise noted, from interview with the author, 18 Dec. 2020.

had a boyfriend at the time that I lived with and he was doing a film course at the National Film School. He was doing screenwriting. And I used to go out there just for something to do, and hang out there and I used to help out on student films and things—dress sets, do costumes, whatever they wanted, I would do for free, just because it was interesting. And I went through a lot of the workshops. I used to sneak in the back and watch workshops and things like that with famous directors or writers or whatever. I'd just sit in the back and hide and listen. And I thought, that's what I want to do. I was desperate to work in film somehow. So working on all these films, I then met Julien Temple, who directed the Sex Pistols film. He was at school and he was a friend of my boyfriend at the time. And it was Jubilee—the Queen's Jubilee—and Julian said, 'I'm going to go film all the street parties in West London. Do you want to come and take some photos?' And I said, 'Yeah, sure I will.' So we went out for the whole day and took pictures. I just found them the other day. At the time, he was working on the script with Malcolm McLaren. They got a few different people to write it, and he said, 'Look we need help on the film. You want to come and be production assistant? We could pay you?' I said, 'Yep.'"

The casual connection led to June's involvement in that film, *the Great Rock 'n' Roll Swindle*, as well as put her in the orbit of the Sex Pistols themselves. She continues, "So I started in the office and it was just off Oxford Street, answering phones, organizing things, getting people where they should be. But they wanted me to go on set because I really got on with the guys, with John [Lydon], Steve [Jones], and Paul [Cook]. Sid was in a few scenes. He was really out of it and didn't want to do much. But some of my work was to get Sid [Vicious] out of bed and into the set. Nancy [Spungen] was with him then as well. So that was really really hard. I used to have to scrape him off the mattress and get him into a taxi and get him to filming and look after them. And they gave me hell. They gave me—because they didn't know who I was. They had no idea—some stupid bird, you know? But I got on so well with Steve and Paul and I used to hang out at their flat with them, and Helen [Wellington-Lloyd, aka Helen of Troy], who is in the film, Helen is a very short person, I call her, and we talked about doing some stuff together. I don't know what we were going to do. Helen said, 'I'd like to be in a band,' and I said, 'Well, let's form a band.' But at the same time, we filmed some stuff and Kate [Corris], Kate who plays guitar [Mo-Dettes], we filmed some stuff in her squat and I moved into a squat with her. And funny enough, Joe Strummer lived in the same squat. I was kind of thrown into the thick of it all."

She then arrives at how she came to be a drummer. "Paul came into the office one day and said, 'Oh, I want some cash,' and I said, 'I can't give you any cash. I have to account for every penny. I can't do it.' And he said, 'Oh, I've got a drum kit. You know anybody wants to buy a drum kit?' And I said, 'Yeah, I'll buy it, how much you want for it?' And he said, '40 quid?' And that's quite a lot of money then. And I said, 'Okay, I'll give you 40 quid for it,' because I've got two brothers and they were trying to get a band together. So I thought, well, they could use it or whatever. So he delivered it round to the squat and we set it up in the basement. And I just started playing and Steve would play along with me and then Strummer would come and play along with me. That's how I learned to play. It's ridiculous! Ridiculous! The first song I learned to play was 'Teenage Kicks.'"

June went on to form and play with the Mo-Dettes (see also Mo-Dettes chapter), and upon breaking up, Lynval Golding sought her involvement in Fun Boy Three. She says, "The phone rang late one night and it was Lynval and they were in the studio and they pretty much recorded the album *Waiting*, but they didn't have a drummer. Because they'd heard the Mo-Dettes split up, they phoned up and said, did I want to come, and I said, 'Look, well call me in the morning and we'll talk about it.' So we did. And I went down that day with my sticks and stuff, and there was this lovely studio in North London and it was in like an old church and there was a drum kit in the middle of this big church room and they were behind the glass in the control room. And I kind of waved and they said, 'Just sit down and play along. We're going to play you a track.' When I looked, David Byrne was on the controls. And I thought, 'What the fuck?' So I put the headphones on and tried to act cool and listened to the track. And this track started and I just went rup bup bup bup. Everybody behind that glass erupted! It was so funny. That track was 'The More I See.' So I think it's the second track on the album. And I thought, 'Yeah, oh my god, I'm home. I'm home,' because it was just so punchy and the song was all about Terry being on a trip to Belfast and he met all these kids on the plane who lived like in the bombings of Belfast and he was chatting with them and it was all about that. And I thought, yeah, this is it. So they wrote songs about drug culture, they wrote songs about, I don't know, it was like early '83, Thatcher was in and we had lots of stuff to kick against."

June says she was with Fun Boy Three as a drummer for just over a year. She was with them for their British tour, as well as one in the U.S. Assembling the all-female band was part of establishing a new direction for Fun Boy Three as a pivot from the Specials. Terry Hall had designed a change in both the look and the sound of the new band. June explains, "Because they came after the Specials, there was still all that 2 Tone feel. And I think Terry was trying to escape that a little bit and do something a bit new. And I think it was political to have all females. I think it was a little bit romantic for Terry as well because he was kind of thinking of like, what's that movie with Marilyn Monroe where you've got all the women on tour? [*Some Like It Hot*] I think he kind of liked that imagery. He's really into his imagery stuff. And so it would kind of shake it up a bit and it is a bit political in that way. But we didn't feel like that. We just thought, well, we're good musicians!"

In addition to contributing to the musical and political output of the band, June says that the opportunity was one of personal growth for her. "What I loved was all those coaches. Like there's Lynval with his kind of chunky rock and roll guitar, but a brilliant rhythm player, absolutely gorgeous, and then Neville who like skanked over stuff and played percussion, bongos, oh my god it was so much fun playing with them. It was so much fun," she says with electricity in her voice. "I think it was the most exciting album I've ever worked on."

151

"But it was hard work," she adds. "I mean, Terry was going through a breakdown. He didn't know what was going on, and now we know, he was bipolar. We didn't know at the time. It was difficult, but he's an amazing performer. He's great. All that miserable stuff is because that's how he feels. And yet, you know, when he's in private, he's the most funny person you've ever met. I mean, he's absolutely gorgeous." June says she and Terry were in a relationship which ended around the same time as Fun Boy Three ended. "When we came back from America, it was a very difficult tour. Terry and I were still seeing each other then, which was nice. I mean, we had lots of nice times together. But it's unfortunate because his previous girlfriend was on tour, one of the managers, and so that was a bit awkward. That's what happens in music, I mean, we get used to that. But when we came back, we flew back and Terry had already decided to split the band up. I wasn't part of that decision, but he told me that's how he felt. He'd had enough. And I think it was too close to the Specials—I think he needed a break. He was ready to kind of move on and make something new, something different. And he knew he couldn't do that with Lynval and Neville because they were hanging on to those things that they'd gleaned from the Specials. So he was already thinking, and I know he already set it up, because as soon as we got back, he went into the studio with the Colourfield."

The end of the relationship soon followed and June moved on with her career. She says, "So he was up in Manchester doing that. I was in London kind of recovering from the tour, and I thought, I'm going to have to duck out of this because he's already gone on to the next project. I can hang around, and whatever, but like I wanted to play and I wanted to move on and do stuff. As a woman, you can't just be the girlfriend because it's not enough. I was really brave and at Christmas, I spent the whole Christmas alone and so I started writing my own stuff. And I went and got a little solo deal with Go! Discs. I was friends with Juliet [De Valero Wills] for quite a while because I'd been going through a lot of Billy Bragg. I love Billy Bragg and I went to a lot of his gigs and hung out with them a lot. And he was on Go! Discs. I actually got a little job in the office at Go! Discs, answering the phone through one summer, and then they said, 'Let's listen to what you've got.' And they put me in the studio and I did a single, which was great. But I needed more people around me. So I got a letter from Ben Watt from Everything But the Girl, and I had been a fan of them as well, asking me to come and join them. So I did that."

June was with Everything But the Girl for a number of years, recording an album and touring the UK and Europe. She then toured with the Communards and forged a life-long friendship with Jimmy Somerville. "Jimmy is a bloody joy to work with. He never turns up for rehearsals. He never turns up for soundchecks. He just lets things happen. So we were like his backing band, in a way, but he's so adorable. His voice is incredible. And I did a lot of the backing vocals with him and I could do whatever I wanted. And sometimes, some nights, I would take it off on a tangent and then he'd go with me. And it gives you that freedom and then the audience feels that, they can grasp that, they kind of feel the excitement of it, go with it."

She also performed backing vocals on *The Seer* album by Big Country, as did Kate Bush. "It's Scottish, and the Scottish kind of sound and because they're so authentic it worked so beautifully. They're really lovely people. Stuart [Adamson], oh I feel so sad about him because music claims a lot of people for the wrong reasons." Stuart Adamson, the brilliant songwriter, guitarist, and vocalist of Big Country, previously of the Skids, died by suicide in 2001. "Tragic because he was a beautiful singer. He had that tone, that kind of clear bell tone. It was impeccable." June also sang and performed with Microdisney, Prefab Sprout, and Aztec Camera, but today she has left music behind to pursue making film. She and her husband, Simon Mawby of the Woodentops, live in Brighton.

Caroline Lavelle began playing cello as a child, but it was only because it was one of two instruments left to select. She grew up "right out in the middle of nowhere," she says, and first learned to play the recorder, as many schoolchildren do. Whereas many kids, and more so their parents, detest the recorder, Caroline says, "I absolutely loved it."[370] It only fed her desire to learn to play a musical instrument, as did her family heritage. "My mother's father was a conductor and he used to hang around with all these famous musicians and conduct their music and actually, because of her passion for the music, I and my brother and sister, we all learned instruments. Unfortunately, I wanted to play violin and I was so chaotic that when we were told to get to the music cupboard at a certain time when the instruments were being given out, and I turned up at what I thought was a good time and I had got the wrong time. I was late and the only thing that was left was the trombone and the cello. I chose the cello because it was the nearest thing to a violin. Anyway, I'm very glad I chose it."

Caroline left school at the age of 15 to attend the Royal College of Music in London and completed her education there by the time she was 18. It was then that one of the other members of Fun Boy Three, keyboardist and musical director Nicky Holland, found Caroline who was performing in public. "I used to do a lot of busking in Covent Garden with some friends of mine who were fiddle players, Anne Stephenson particularly, and Gini Ball [Virginia Hewes], and they went off to join the Communards. Great, great players, especially Anne's kind of explosive virtuosic kind of playing. I absolutely love that. We would be there [Covent Garden] at the sort of market area. We would be there a lot and doing it when it was freezing cold. We would try to play in fingerless gloves, freezing to death, then to lovely summer days. And I used to do the 'Can Can' and stuff. Oh, I got a policeman to do the Can Can with me, which usually brought in a bit more money! So we were playing with Siouxsie and the Banshees and people like that, working with them, and busking in Covent Garden and that's where Nicky saw me busking. They were looking for a cellist and she suggested me and I don't know how they tracked me down, but they did, and that's how I joined Fun Boy Three."

Caroline says that performing with Fun Boy Three, Siouxsie and the Banshees, and later Del Amitri and an Irish group, De Dannan, was helpful for her

---

[370] Lavelle, Caroline. All quotations, unless otherwise noted, from interview with the author, 14 Jun. 2021.

153

creatively since her background up until that point had been very different. "Coming from a really rigidly classical music background, it taught me a huge amount. Like try new things. Try things. See if they work. And I remember one time somebody had suggested something in the studio and I was thinking to myself, 'Oh wow, that isn't going to work,' and it really did. And that was a huge learning thing for me. It stuck with me ever since. And some of the musicianship I saw in these people from a completely different background, and the freedom and the sort of questioning attitude, the curiosity that they had musically, was fantastic. It was quite different from how I'd been sort of brought up," Caroline says.

The two worlds of classical training and popular music came into view when presented to Caroline through the eyes of a beloved teacher. "I had a fantastic cello professor at college who was not only a great man—he was a great pedagogue and was a scientist as well, so he was really into physics and math and stuff and he seemed to know everything. He was called Christopher Bunting and he was an amazing cello player. After a while when I'd been off playing with Fun Boy Three and De Dannan and who knows who, I'd go back to him now and then for lessons, just for a private lesson. And he was great because in college at that time, all these things were really frowned upon. You would not go and sort of ruin your technique or aesthetic. It has been completely changed now, but then that was really bad and you wouldn't get taken seriously. I would go and play for him and he was such a great guy and he would say, 'Oh, you can really hear it in your playing—the influence is coming from here, and that's making your playing more rich.' And he had this very forward-looking attitude to music. I'd be playing with African musicians and Chinese musicians, and I'd learn the whole time. That's the beauty of music. It opens your eyes and your heart and your mind to all the stuff you know nothing about."

Caroline says she has learned much from fellow musicians over the years and she has performed with countless artists. But she has also written and performed her own music, including recording her own albums. Doing her own writing didn't come without a bit of struggle, though. She says, "I didn't actually start writing until my very late 20s because I had a boyfriend who told me that I couldn't write music, and stupidly, I believed him. How foolish. Very very foolish. So now, well, I spend my days writing, really." Since the mid-1990s she has collaborated with Loreena McKennitt from Canada and lately she has started working with John Reynolds, producer for Sinead O'Connor. As a woman, she has had to make the choices that resulted in this life—choices that men do not have to make, as she explains. "Choices like family and things like that, that really doesn't come up for men. And that is obviously a deeply profound choice that any travelling musician would have to make. And unless you're very successful, you couldn't afford to have a child as a single musician or as a woman on her own. It's still pretty unusual to find a chap who is going to be happy staying home and looking after the children," she says with a laugh. "There's a big choice to make." As a result, Caroline has chosen her passion—music. "I'm really happy with having dogs, so I'm quite lucky from that point of view, and I'm a very solitary person."

Ingrid Schroeder joined Fun Boy Three on the *Waiting* album as a backing vocalist and keyboardist just after graduating from college. She grew up in England but was born in Nova Scotia, Canada where shed lived until she was 10 years of age. Ingrid's mother was born in Java and spent three years incarcerated in Japanese prisoner camps as a child, barely surviving. After the war, Ingrid's grandfather sent her mother to boarding school in Australia and speaking little English, she struggled to have a normal childhood. As a result, Ingrid's mother was focused on making her own children's lives as supported and nurturing as possible. "I feel she wanted to recapture a bit of what she'd lost through us, her own children, vicariously. Whatever interests or talents we had she encouraged and facilitated, always making us feel we could do anything, and we wanted to please her. For all that, whatever low points or pain we might have thought we were experiencing, they could never compare to what she went through."[371]

Ingrid's father was a member of the Royal Canadian Navy, training as a Fleet Air Army Pilot in Nova Scotia. While he was on Naval business in London, he met Ingrid's mother, "married and started a family in Canada. They were a glamorous couple and always very popular. During my childhood my dad was often away at sea, so my mum was the main caregiver to my three brothers and myself and we were a very close unit," she says.

"So I was born in Nova Scotia and we moved around a fair bit through its coastal villages and towns to a military college in Kingston, Ontario and then Toronto. By the time I was eight I had already been to three different schools, so there was no time for sentiment! Although, I think it was inadvertently confidence building because I had to keep making new friends. Our move to England came about because my dad had become disenchanted with the way things were going in Canada and wanted a change. So he managed to get a naval posting near London with NATO. I was just about to turn ten and was instantly enamoured by London and the beauty and charm of the surrounding countryside," says Ingrid.

"My older brother Mike was a naturally gifted guitarist and on dull rainy days, of which there were many in England, we would often sing together, always harmonising. Otherwise we listened to the radio and played our records. I was often competing in a music festival somewhere nationally after school or on Saturdays, and there was no place too far to travel for my mum when it came to driving me there. I amassed quite a collection of cups and medals for singing, piano and recorder and she was very proud and supportive. At weekends my parents' friends always seemed to be dropping by and more often than not a party atmosphere would develop—my dad playing jazz and blues on the piano in a haze of cigarette smoke, with me sitting beside him absorbed in the magic. My mum encouraged all the kids to take piano lessons but I was the only one who stuck at it. From early on I felt drawn to the piano, and still can't pass one without wanting to lift the lid and play a few chords. There was nothing more rewarding than finally being able to play a piece all the way through without

[371] Schroeder, Ingrid. All quotations, unless otherwise noted, from interview with the author, 29 Oct. 2022.

making a mistake after the hours of practice I'd put in. I worked hard at passing my grades, but by the age of eleven my own practice time at the piano gave way to improvising around melodies and I started to write songs about emotions and experiences I was yet to have and could only imagine. Alas, I eventually decided to give up lessons. But I'm grateful I got as far as I did because the beauty of a piano is that you can encompass a complete arrangement in the one instrument, you have it all at your fingertips."

She continues, "My mum would tell anyone who would listen about my songwriting and finally at a party she engaged the interest of a music business manager who put me together with a record producer. I recorded my first songs in a professional studio in London when I was thirteen. This led to more recordings with Will Malone (who would go on to work with Massive Attack and the Verve) and singing on other artists' tracks through my senior school years. I always enjoyed coming up with parts and harmonies—it came easy to me—and I looked forward to any opportunity to be in the studio as it was exciting and so different from my ordinary life. Sometimes I even got paid! I remember finishing an important exam and rushing off to London to sing backing vocals and getting back in time to revise for another exam the next day."

"When I was seventeen I met a songwriter who was living in London, and I spent most weekends up there experiencing a musician's life and going to recording studios. I decided to apply to a music college instead as there were large gaps in my formal music education and I knew that if I wanted to carry on with music as a career it would be more useful. I managed to get a place on the strength of my songwriting and performance to study singing and piano at the Maria Grey College near Richmond which shared a campus with the Ballet Rambert Academy and the Drama Department, and it turned out to be a highly interactive creative community. I had never been in a situation where I performed together with orchestral instruments before, so being in that environment opened my eyes and ears to arrangement possibilities for my own songs," says Ingrid.

She then began performing as a session vocalist while in college and even traveled to Rockpalast to sing with the legendary Jack Bruce and Friends as a backing vocalist. She would perform there again with Fun Boy Three a few years later. She explains how her connection to the group took place. "I was recording vocals for Mike Scott on the Waterboys' album *A Pagan Place* and my friend Nicky Holland told me Fun Boy Three were putting together an all-female backing band. She had been working with them and encouraged me to audition. They were looking for a backing singer who played keyboards and I sent along my demo tape. The response was really positive and we got on great when we met, so they offered me the job. We were all pretty much strangers when we started the album but gradually got to know each other through the recording process when we were called in to lay down our parts and waiting round playing pool. It was amazing being produced by David Byrne. We were all big Talking Heads fans and he didn't disappoint. He brought out that slightly edgy quirkiness to the sound and was easy to work with. Always understatedly stylish—he would turn up in his belted trench-coat and fedora hat like a private eye from a '40's film noir. We often talked together when we had breaks in the pub. We were both North American and his intense looking, enigmatic stage persona belied a warm and funny side. He got me to sing on a couple of things he was working on at the time."

"I was excited to be doing a big tour which would ultimately take me back to New York and California," said Schroder. She had recreationally traveled to the United States and South America after graduating from college, but this time she went for her career. "The band were having hits and I got a taste of what success—and all its pressures—felt like. We even did *Top of the Pops* many times. Live and in the recording studio I sang the high parts, and on stage I also played keyboards and percussion and danced around a lot. I shared a small, raised space with Nicky and her Rhodes piano, so I had to be careful not to bounce her off the podium! We rehearsed for the upcoming tour in Camden Market during a particularly cold winter in a freezing studio where most of us, one by one, got ill! We went to the nearby café for lunch to warm up and after rehearsing headed for the pub, often ending up at The Funny Farm with Bedders from Madness and his mates for some of Frank's lethal cocktails."

"When Fun Boy Three did gigs in France," says Ingrid, "we were based at a hotel on the outskirts of Paris just as there happened to be a municipal strike. So, galleries, museums and sights were closed and public transport was severely compromised. Consequently, on days off we had to entertain ourselves in spite of being in the dream cultural location with time to kill! Nonetheless, we walked around the famous streets and markets, hung out at the hotel and looked forward to evening meals where Neville would order for us in English with a French accent. There was a lot of silliness and drinking back at the hotel and I remember it turning out to be a bonding and fun time. By the last leg of the tour, we got to New York in July when most people leave the city if they can because of the heat and humidity. I recall having a few baths in the hotel with ice cubes from the machine down the hall! It didn't get off to the best start as our first gig was out in New Jersey and there was an angry group of G.I.s in the audience who'd had too much to drink and were spoiling for a fight. Threats of shooting followed, which was pretty scary, and next thing fists were flying as our valiant roadies managed to contain the situation and get the troublemakers out of there. Then on the long drive back to New York the bus driver fell asleep at the wheel. Luckily, the manager realised in time and kept him talking!"

"All was well again when we played the Ritz in New York. In fact, there was a real buzz in the club before we went on. I'd heard there would probably be a lot of well-known people there that night and as I was singing and playing I suddenly clocked Andy Warhol in the audience looking at me—it felt very surreal! There was a lot of anticipation leading up to the gig and there was a huge sense of relief when it was over. When we got off stage the whole band headed for Paradise Garage to catch the New Order gig, and then afterwards we hung out at Danceteria til the early hours. It was a memorable night! Fun Boy Three were at the height of their popularity and had a number of high charting singles from *Waiting* with lots of TV appearances, interviews and more recording sessions during a year-long tour on the road. It was quite full-on and maybe it got to them—even Lynval's tireless energy and enthusiasm couldn't hold them together! Shame though, as it looked like they were about to break America just as they split up," Ingrid says.

After Fun Boy Three, Ingrid carried on doing sessions before writing and recording her own material. She utilized new technology of the time to explore the possibilities of mixing up her songs and lyrics with beats and samples. Over the years, Ingrid has gigged and recorded with bands such as the Higsons, Brilliant, Dream Academy, and Tears For Fears. She sang on "Beat City" for the movie *Ferris Bueller's Day Off,* toured with acid jazz band Incognito, and collaborated with Dharma B. "I always kept writing and recording and subsequently signed a solo deal with East West on Warner Bros Records for her album *Bee Charmer* and subsequent album, *Love Runs Faster*. More recently she co-produced a country indie album with her brother Mike's band and an EP for one of Caroline Lavelle's projects. "Yes, we are still friends after all these years!"

Ingrid says that her experience working in a male-dominated space has been eye opening. "Being brought up with three brothers and a father in the military meant I was used to living in a male dominated environment with a certain pecking order. But it always bothered me, and I found it unfair, that things were different for me in some instances. However, in music I hadn't felt any of this and never thought about it until I was in my first band with another female and a guy. And suddenly it seemed there was this preconception when meeting some male sound engineers or men in the record company that the guy was somehow in charge and inquiries or compliments were directed towards him. I was quite shocked, particularly as in this case it couldn't have been further from the truth. I would have been happy for no one to be singled out, but I was the main songwriter and in fact it was largely through my efforts and contacts that we managed to get the professional studio demos made and secure the record deal. I have heard so many similar stories from other women in music. Going solo I had none of these issues. That said there were other power struggles that were not limited to gender. As an artist you're not always going to agree with the record company on musical direction or your vision and it can be exhausting sometimes standing your ground when facing such resistance. But if you stay true to yourself the twists and turns can also deliver opportunities you may not have considered. I have had a lot of good times being in predominately male bands, but when I chose musicians for my backing band I was determined that at least one would be a woman. It was a good decision and added a positive, more balanced dimension to the mix."

Annie Whitehead may have been recruited for Fun Boy Three because of her talent on the trombone, but her interest in ska and Jamaican music occurred long before she had even heard of the Specials. Her musical education came from her family, her friends, and even her town. "I grew up in Oldham in the north of England, so there are brass bands up there," she explains.[372] "Every town, every village, every mill has got a brass band and that's part of my legacy and heritage, really. I grew up listening—every kind of Whitsun, celebrations, Christmas and all that—there were brass bands playing all over the place. So that's what I heard and saw. And then when I was 11 and I went to senior school, we were offered instrumental lessons, and that was just brass instruments. I wanted to play the tuba, going for the biggest one, and they wouldn't let me because I was tiny. So they gave me a tenor horn and I played that for a bit. And I was the only one who kind of went home and practiced and came back having kind of mastered the next thing. Everybody else was pretty kind of hopeless, really, so I was definitely the swot and the teacher's favorite. And my teacher played the trombone, so after playing tenor horn for about seven or eight months, I asked him if I could play the trombone and he was just so pleased. He just went and got me one from the school cupboard and that was it. So I started playing the trombone and he really was my mentor until I left school at 16."

Annie was exposed to classical, jazz, and blues from her school and town, but she was also exposed to ska by her friends. "The girl that I sat next to in school, Esther Williams, she came from Barbados. And she lived about four doors down on my street. So we used to walk to school together and back. So her parents quite often had music on and I think it must have been blue beat stuff like that. This is in the Fifties [would have pre-dated blue beat, so likely calypso], so whatever was going on there. And it was so thrilling. I'd go and her mum would be plaiting her hair and had music on. So I got pretty friendly with Esther and I heard that stuff really early on. The next thing I kind of fell in love with was Motown and soul. So northern soul was the big thing, so I heard all that, and brass band music, you know, the hymns and marches. I just loved them. There were incredible hymns and the kind of rising marches," she says.

Armed with a trombone and the music that informed her upbringing and passion, Annie began to participate actively rather than passively. "When I was 14," she says, "I joined a big band in Manchester, which was the Manchester Youth Stage Band. It was the northern equivalent to NYJO, the National Youth Jazz Orchestra. So then we started playing big band things like Count Basie and jazz and swing. So that kind of combination of stuff really set me up. I lived seven or eight miles away, so every Monday night I traveled down to Manchester. We rehearsed with that band and on Sunday afternoons, I'd go up into the Pennine villages to practice with the brass bands. And then Saturday night I'd be up at the disco with the Motown and the soul, so yeah, it was a great time to grow up. Great music."

She continued performing after leaving school at the age of 16. "I joined the Ivy Benson Band, which was this all-women band. It was a kind of cabaret and touring band and we worked in Germany. We did some summer sessions and it was a proper professional band. I just wrote to Ivy when I was 15 because I just saw no future for myself in Oldham. My mother and dad were mill workers, the cotton mills in the

372 Whitehead, Annie. All quotations, unless otherwise noted, from interview with the author, 13 Dec. 2020.

north of England. So I was with Ivy Benson for two years, from ages 16 to 18 and it was an incredible experience because there was a lot of sight reading. She had a huge pad of music—about 500 or 600 tunes, and we never knew what we were playing until we got on the bandstand and she'd kind of call the tunes, three or four at a time. So we had to be pretty hot on sight reading stuff. We had singers, so quite often with the singers, these songs had to be transposed into a different key to suit that singer. We we'd have to do transpositions, just like that."

Annie recalls one summer season when she was with Ivy Benson's band in Torquay—a seaside town with a large ballroom. It was an example of what work with the band was like. "We played for strict tempo dancing all night. We played like three tangos or a tango, a waltz, and a quickstep. Then we'd have a little break and then we'd do some more—a foxtrot and something like that. So it was all strict tempo stuff. And we played those nights from around seven o'clock till midnight. Three or four pieces at a time, then a short break, then three or four pieces at a time. So we got through a lot of music in a night," she says. "In Germany we played in big place in Stuttgart and we played in Switzerland as well. And they were really long sets. We used to play from six o'clock until midnight. But it was good work. I learned a lot."

Even when she wasn't performing, Annie was still absorbing and learning. "I was young and somebody was supposed to be looking after me, but I knew how to give her the slip. We'd quite often go down to the club later and I started sitting in with other musicians because I didn't play jazz at that time, but they were and I was really curious. So they let me sit in and stuff, and that was really nice, kind of trying to find my way through tunes by ear really. I'd never played jazz. I'd heard it and I've played big band stuff, but I'd never improvised. After that period, I went to live in Jersey. I left Ivy's band and I did waitressing for a while and that was a good time for me because that's when I started listening to jazz and going, whoa! I was listening to Mingus and Monk and Miles Davis, J.J. Johnson—lots and lots of people. So then we started getting bands together to play music that we like. So it was jazz and then funk happened, you know, Herbie Hancock's *Head Hunters* and stuff, the early kind of jazz funk."

Annie Whitehead formed her own band and performed in hotels while still working as a waitress in cabarets. She came to London in late 1976 and began playing with Chris McGregor, Dudu Pukwana, and Mongezi Feza in a big band group called the Brotherhood of Breath. "They left South Africa because of the Apartheid regime. Chris was white South African. He was the pianist and the other guys were black and they had so much trouble there. So they absconded. They came to Europe and they didn't go back. So they were in exile in London and they really kind of transformed— they were the early part of world music in London."

Annie also did session work during this time, and then in the late 1970s she moved to the coast in Brighton and began to play ska. "I formed a band with some people who loved ska. They were looking for a trombone player and that band was called Second Nature. Our singer was black, Tony, and he lives along the coast in South Hampton. We're still really close. The rest of us were all white and the drummer was interested in ska drumming and so I joined that band and we started playing reggae and ska. We were doing covers, so we were doing Skatalites numbers like 'Confucius.' We were doing Joe Biggs and the Professionals stuff. I love that. I love that stuff. So that was just before 2 Tone kind of happened. So that band was really popular in Britain and we played loads and loads and loads of gigs. And I started really getting into the music then and especially Don Drummond," she says.

Annie joined another ska band after Second Nature, and it was here that she performed with notable Jamaican musicians. She says, "After I left Brighton and went to live in Bristol, that's when I met Nightdoctor [on Race Records] and they were a multiracial ska and reggae band in London at that time, and Vin Gordon had been playing trombone with them. There was this guy called Charley [Wood] who ran the band, the guitarist. And half the band lived in High Wycombe and came from St. Vincent. The organ player, Sister Caroline [Caroline Williams], she was married to, somebody, I can't remember [Horace Andy]. And there was a toaster called Polish. He was just fantastic, and a singer called Robbie. I played with them for years and we made a record as well. And we started writing some of our own stuff, but mostly it was covers again—Gregory Isaacs type things, but some ska instrumentals as well. There was me and two saxophone players."

"And then I moved into Tony's place and Vin Gordon was living there as well at the time and I'd kind of taken Vin's place in the band, which I mean, it was alright, but Vin was just kind of going through a kind of, well, he was just being really really difficult. He was making it difficult for the guys in the band because they'd get to a gig and Vin would say, 'I'm not going on stage until I get all my money up front,' and he had more money than other people, so it was just that kind of thing. We all still loved him. But then Vin was playing with Aswad, and the Clash was happening, and I was in the area so both of these were the West London bands and that's where I was living. So I lived for a short time with Vin in that house and that's where I met Tan Tan [Edward "Tan Tan" Thornton] as well as Drummie [Angus "Drummie Zeb" Gaye], the drummer with Aswad" she says. Annie also became a session horn player with the Fashion record label. She performed with Smiley Culture, Maxi Priest, Youssou N'Dour, and she played with Cuban and African bands. "Everybody played together. It was just a really great time. It was wonderful."

Playing with so many people in different forms and genres, it's no wonder that Annie admits that she can't recall how she came to the attention of Fun Boy Three. "I guess I got a call to do that," she says. "It was a session and it was wonderful. I really like the way they used the trombone and the way that David Byrne wanted to use the trombone. I loved the music. I loved Terry's singing and everything. I was really thrilled that they asked me. I went in and did the session," she says. Annie toured with Fun Boy Three and recalls the way the group involved politics not only in their lyrics, but also in their performances. "It was great touring, traveling the world, doing gigs. Terry was great and we did a program called *The Wire* in England and Terry was really disgusted with something that was going on in the States and he burned the American flag live on TV and they shut down the program. Shortly after that we toured the States and we got some static from people in the States because I think he tried to do it one night in a club in New York and the bouncers just jumped on the stage and just kind of wrestled the flag away from him. People in the audience started booing. It was the Reagan times."

David Byrne made quite an impact on Annie who witnessed his unconventional manner of making music. "Working with David Byrne, he was going through quite an odd phase at the time. He wouldn't sit on chairs. So he would either stand in the studio or lie down on the floor or sit on the floor. I don't know what was going on. I mean, it was very eccentric. I loved working with him. He was very clear. He knew what he wanted. And also we were working in one of my favorite studios at the time which was called, what was it called? [Wessex Sound Studios] The church. It was a big church in Highbury. And I worked there a lot."

Two years later, Annie Whitehead collaborated with another member of the 2 Tone label—this time, the leader himself, Jerry Dammers. Annie had been performing with Robert Wyatt in a band called Working Week, a jazz dance band whose lyrics were political. This led to a collaboration called the Winds of Change with Jerry Dammers who produced and performed on a single to benefit the South West African People's Organisation (SWAPO). This organization fought for the independence of Namibia and freedom from the Apartheid laws of South Africa since Namibia was a de facto province of South Africa. The single featured Annie; Jerry Dammers on piano, guitar, and synth; Clare Hirst on saxophone (see also Belle Stars chapter); Lynval Golding on lead guitar; Dick Cuthell on cornet; and vocals were supplied by the SWAPO singers of Namibia. The A side was the song "Winds of Change" with the B side "Namibia." "Lots of people joined forces for that," says Annie, recalling the lyrics, "'The winds of change, running through the African continent,'—the colonial thing was breaking down. Jerry asked me to do that and I think it was because I was around the scene at the time and playing with a lot of people. And I think politically, that generation were misfits and they were kind of embracing me as a misfit in some ways, like this girl playing the trombone, you know? It's a bit against all odds. I was admired for my playing and I encountered so much encouragement from a specific kind of cultural and political side of life, which was the left."

Annie Whitehead and Jerry Dammers also collaborated on another project, Starvation, a benefit for the people suffering from famine in Ethiopia, Entrea, and Sudan. The project involved Ali Campbell, Robin Campbell, and Ray Falconer of UB40; Claudia Fontaine, Caron Wheeler, and Naomi Thompson of Afrodiziak (see also the Specials and the Special AKA chapter); George Agard, Jackie Robinson, and Sydney Crooks of the Pioneers; John Bradbury of the Specials; Daniel Woodgate of Madness; Dick Cuthell; Dave Wakeling and Ranking Roger of the Beat, and Annie Whitehead. They performed on the songs "Starvation," "Haunted" and "Tam Tam Pour L'Ethiopie."

Because of Annie's work with Fun Boy Three, David Byrne put her forward for another project. She recalls, "Another big thing came from David Byrne for me because he knew a film maker in New York called Philip Haas who was looking for a female French horn player to be in his film. And David Byrne said, 'I don't know any female French horn players, but I do know of a female trombone player.' And he was looking specifically for a British person. So Philip Haas got in touch with me. The film never got made, but it was supposed to be with John Law. But through that I met Simon Jeffe from the Penguin Café Orchestra and I ended up playing with the Penguin Café Orchestra from then on [1986] until Simon died in 1998. So that was a wonderful piece of synchronicity coming from David Byrne, from working with Fun Boy Three."

Since the 1980s, Annie Whitehead's work has continued to be in demand. She has worked with Charlie Watts, Jamiroquai, Eric Clapton, Dr. John, Blur, the Spice Girls, and young composers since she taught in London for many years at the Center for Young Musicians. She says she recently went to see David Byrne in London and continues to enjoy his output.

Nicky Holland was at the helm of the musician-ship for Fun Boy Three, hired as their musical director as well as a performer. She grew up in the English countryside with "literally two pubs and a village shop and a bus once a day."[373] Her family was tremendously musical and she was encouraged to appreciate and study music at a young age. Nicky's father was a tax consultant but she says he loved to sing and act and play music, and his mother, Nicky's grandmother, was a pianist who played in theaters for silent films. But Nicky's mother had a profound influence on her music education, as she explains, "My mother, Pixie Holland, or Patricia was her real name, went to the Royal Academy of Music in her late teens and got an LRAM [Licentiate of the Royal Academy of Music] in her early 20s and received a gold medal from the Royal Academy of Music. And during my childhood she played in a trio, and she taught music appreciation classes. She was a pianist. Then she minored in French horn and cello. And in her early 50s she went back to school and became a music therapist and was part of the British School of Music Therapists and worked with autistic children. It was amazing. So she was always playing piano at home. She didn't put music on the stereo. My father did that. But my mother was a real performer. A beautiful pianist."

Nicky's mother taught piano to her two daughters, but when Nicky was only six years old, she outgrew what her mother could teach her. "She got me a teacher and got a teacher for my sister Diana as well. And we both auditioned at our local county council for the Royal Academy when I was nine and my sister was 11. And we both passed that audition and then we went up to London and played for the professors at the Royal Academy and we both won scholarships there. So my sister went from ages 11 to 16, and I went from nine to 18. And I mean every Saturday I had music classes from about 9:30 in the morning until about 3:30, so it was like a sixth day of school, but it was an incredibly comprehensive musical education. So I studied piano and cello and I learned to write for strings and then there was orchestra

---

[373] Holland, Nicky. All quotations, unless otherwise noted, from interview with the author, 29 Jan. 2021.

and chorus and ear training and theory. I studied with a woman who had studied with Olivier Messiaen in Paris and I was gaining skills that I could use for life. I remember my mom, around the time I started writing songs, being unbelievably supportive and saying, 'How do you do that? I've never done that,' and explaining to me the difference between being an interpretive musician and a creative musician. It's just something that I could hear things and just play them back. I didn't have to read them," she says.

The music that influenced Nicky at school was far different than the music she enjoyed socially. "I remember hearing Carole King's *Tapestry*. It was at a dance and it was one of those free expression dance classes in the early '70s. I remember the teacher put on 'It's Too Late' and it was the only commendation mark I ever got at school was for the dance I did to that song. And my friend's older sister had it so she lent it to me and that's when I realized I could play by ear. I learned every song, and I've got a low voice like Carole, so I can sing them all. And so I kind of became obsessed in my teens with American music and singer/songwriters. John Lennon's 'Imagine' I listened to a billion times, Ricky Lee Jones, Tom Waits, Randy Newman, Steely Dan for complex jazz—I listened to a lot of that. And then my mom, she's play Bacharach and David and I ended up actually at some point writing with David, which was amazing, but she loved all that music and Herb Alpert and the Tijuana Brass."

The first record that Nicky remembers buying was Althea and Donna's "Uptown Top Ranking." She says that this song inspired her with its rhythm, which led her to explore other Jamaican music. "I'd never heard anything like that. It was amazing. I couldn't believe it. I think it was a hit around the same time as 'Jammin' and I love that too. I'd heard 'My Boy Lollipop' by Millie a few years before, but 'Uptown Top Ranking,' I thought it was fantastic. Fantastic. It was the lyricism. And the interesting thing was, growing up in England, pop music was a big melting pot. We didn't have these divisions. It was all thrown together. All these musical styles could collide and it was accepted. You'd listen to everything. It was all on the same program on the radio or on the television," she says.

Nicky Holland began to draw upon these musical influences when writing her own music. She studied at the City University in London, obtaining a BSE in music and upon graduation she formed her first band with two other women she met at university. "It was called the Ravishing Beauties. It was me, Virginia Astley, and Kate St. John. We went out and performed and I did an arrangement of 'Greensleeves' and I wrote something else that we did and then we wrote something together and we made an EP. We wore dresses that people called tea bags. Kate played the cor ainglais and the oboe and the Chinese oboe, Virginia played flute, and I played an arp keyboard and a vocoder. We had this revox with sound effects on it. It was one of the more experimental things I've every used, and we got to play with Teardrop Explodes. That was a popular band at the time in Liverpool. They were doing a residency there. And so we got to try everything out while we were up there in Liverpool and it was an interesting time. Echo and the Bunnymen would show up, the Wild Swans, Orchestral Maneuvers in the Dark, and so the Ravishing Beauties got a lot of press. And then we went on tour with Teardrop Explodes and would play the Hammersmith Odeon, but then on our own we'd go and play the Purcell Room on the Southbank. So we played classical and arthouse and pop venues. We sort of covered the gamut and we got a lot of press. And in one of the articles, some journalists wrote that we were the 'thinking man's Bananarama' and Terry Hall saw that," says Nicky.

Terry Hall sought out Nicky, who by that time had finished performing with the Ravishing Beauties and was now performing to earn more of a living. She explains, "I was sort of writing and paying my way by playing four nights a week at the Gatwick Hilton. I managed to negotiate down from six nights a week to four and I got this call from Rick Rogers saying Fun Boy Three would love you to go to Wessex Studios in North London, and there they played me some African kind of drums and percussion and a bassline. And they're like, 'Okay Nicky, we want you to play piano on this,' and I'm like, 'Okay,' and there was literally a bassline and some drums, and so I said, 'What is it?' and they went, 'Oh, it's "Summertime."' I had no idea it was *the* 'Summertime' by Gershwin that I was playing at the Hilton. I had no idea it was that. And then when Terry sort of sang a bit of that, I went, 'Ah, okay,' and I thought this is going to be a very different version. And I played piano on it and they asked me if I wanted to come back and sing on it and arrange some female vocal, so I did that, and I also then wrote a violin part and came back and we got a violinist and recorded that. And when that was all done, and that had gone really well and it was great, they asked me if I'd be in the video and would I be on *Top of the Pops* with them. I was thrilled!"

Meanwhile, Nicky was still working four nights a week to pay her bills. "I was fitting this all in with going down to the Gatwick Hilton and unceremoniously playing the piano for four hours a night. So one night I'm in the middle of my version of 'Summertime" and these pop stars, Fun Boy Three, show up and sit down on the couch and grin and listen and send up requests or whatever. And I'm like, 'Oh my god, what's going on?' So I had to do four sets, four 45 minute sets with breaks in between, so on one of my breaks, I got up and went and said hello. They stayed. They were great. And they said, 'Well, we came down because we wanted to ask if you'd leave here and come and work with us.' Um, yes! So that's how that happened. I had sort of been tried and tested, I guess, with 'Summertime,' and the thing was, they asked me to be the musical director. So basically they told me, and I don't know whether this was for a marketing gimmick or whether it was a reversal of, say, the Supremes—three men, primarily singers up front and a band of female musicians—and I could help them do this. And I'd been an arranger on 'Summertime,' because that was an existing song. But I agreed to be the musical director and they had an arrangement that no matter who did what on their songs, the three of them wrote them as far as, you know," she says. According to Jerry Dammers, "Nicky Holland was credited merely as 'arranger' on the second Fun Boy Three album, but she has told me she was not happy about (obviously because she felt she had contributed to the songwriting)."[374] Clearly, these matters are more than titles. They impact royalties for now and always. Was Nicky taken advantage of, as a young woman? Was it an oversight? Was it by design because of power and position? That may be an answer best left to debate and a matter of a perspective.

When Nicky looks at it today, she seems to be of two minds. "So yes, I became musical director, so what that meant was we did a lot of preproduction, actually, at my flat. I can't remember how long we worked in my apartment—maybe two months, maybe three, something like that. I had a Beckstein upright piano in my apartment, and either the four of us, or just Terry and myself, or Terry and myself and either Lynval or Neville would come and we'd work on the songs. I think Terry was probably the lead songwriter, or he was the one that would communicate with me most directly. He had very specific lyrics and very specific melodies, but there weren't any chords and there sometimes weren't bridges or introductions or things like that, so I provided for most of the songs, other than the couple that were 'Our Lips Are Sealed' and 'Murder She Said.' I wrote most of the chords for those [other] songs, so had I known better at the time, I probably should have been called one of the songwriters. But I was quite happy with my role as musical director and I was thrilled to be working with them. And they had said to me, 'We're going to make you famous.' So that's how that works."

Working with David Byrne was a highlight of the experience, says Nicky. "He was a lovely presence in the studio. Quiet, and very shy. Quite different, actually. I remember him asking me one day to approach playing the keyboard like it was a hot plate on a stove. He'd always try and find different ways of doing things. When we did the track for 'Our Lips Are Sealed,' I remember David sitting in the studio with a bass across his lap and he just sort of was banging on the strings in rhythm, which became this pulsing thing throughout the whole track and we built around that. So he always came at things from a different kind of perspective."

Other songs involved Nicky working with the trio to collaborate and ideate. "'Tunnel of Love,' I think we'd done quite a lot of it before he came and we did that in a more traditional way. I remember I asked if we could bring in a timpanist that I'd worked with in the Ravishing Beauties and he came in and played. So my role, other than sort of writing the harmonies and things like that for the songs, was helping come up with parts or arrange voices or, yeah, we just all pulled it together. Like 'Our Lips Are Sealed,' I sing the background but the actual bit that's the lead, that's June. She's got a great voice and had a great sort of deadpan expression, like Terry had for that song, and it just worked really really well. But the guys always very much told the stories, had the melodies, the rhythms, and I remember Neville having to really help me with how to feel this one particular beat and I just couldn't get it. I couldn't relax and play it right. And he stood behind me and he held each of my wrists in each of his hands and he just moved my hands in rhythm, and we just kind of moved to the track and then I got it. That was how I learned," Nicky says.

---

[374] Letter from Jerry Dammers to the author, 1 Mar. 2010.

One of the songs that Nicky worked on with Terry Hall was particularly powerful for the creators as well as those who receive the output. Nicky recalls the moment of songwriting she shared with Hall which was far more profound than musical construction. "Terry was there with me on his own and he had this song called, 'Well Fancy That.' And he had a lyric and a melody and he was singing it to me, and I thought, well that's a waltz. And then I'm hearing him singing this lyric and I'm thinking, this is a rape. The hair on my arm has sort of gone up—that kind of shivery feeling. And he's just very deadpan, telling me, you know, and this story comes out that is utterly horrifying. This was in 1982 and here I am in a room listening to this story. It was very moving, but I felt like he was sharing and trusting some very personal story to me, to help him tell his story. And I remember thinking it was like a bad fairground ride—a fairground ride that went out of order, you know? I remember in the bridge I went to like a tri-tone related key because I wanted to take it as far away from that safe tonic musical base that you could go to. And that song, I'm really proud of that one and I felt honored to help tell that story. It must have been a really hard story for him to tell. I don't know whether anyone ever asked him about the meaning of it at the time." She pauses and reflects. "Sometimes, you know, sitting in a room with someone, watching a song being born—there's a lot of trust involved."

She looks back upon the experience with fondness and gratitude for the opportunity it provided to springboard her career and grow her personally as well. "It definitely broadened my musical spectrum and my understanding and seeing how they wrote songs about identity and people from a totally different upbringing. Neville and Lynval came to Coventry, I think, when they were 12. And I'd never heard someone break into patois before, and hearing Neville do that was just magical. Whenever he got excited he'd just speak in this other voice. It definitely sort of extended all my musical horizons and it was a great experience to be able to work on an album with a band and see something through from beginning to end, and I got to do that."

Additionally, the experience led to the next. "When I was playing in Germany with them at Rockpalast, that's when I met Roland Orzabal from Tears for Fears. He had been a fan of the Ravishing Beauties and he had come to our last show and had heard the John Peel radio session we'd done. So I'd started working with Tears for Fears at the beginning of 1985 and then I toured with them on the *Songs from the Big Chair* world tour which was for about a year. And then I wrote five of the eight songs on *The Seeds of Love* with Roland," she says.

During this time especially, Nicky was made aware of the gender inequities in the musical space. "When I toured with Tears for Fears there were 38 men and me. It was an eye-opening experience. The music industry is totally male dominated. Record companies, publishers—men; management and legal—men; touring and agencies—men; artists—here you'd find other women and if you weren't the main artist, usually if you were a musician that worked with a number of different bands, very often women were backup singers, not musical arrangers, players, drummers, bass players. So I think any group that's underrepresented always has to try a bit harder to prove their worth than the dominant group. And things definitely came up where

167

a group of men don't necessarily want to deal with an opinionated woman or a complicated woman. And a woman can change the interpersonal dynamic in the studio or especially on the road. So definitely I think until women are more evenly represented, women are always going to have difficulties. So you either have to be really unique and/or really qualified or look the part, or both. Definitely it is challenging. I think that the one positive was there weren't that many musicians at the time who were women and not artists themselves, like me, so a lot of bands approached me to play with them. So that was a positive," she says.

The rest of Nicky Holland's career right up to this day has been nothing short of astounding. She has written for Cyndi Lauper including the song "A Hat Full of Stars," as well as for Oleta Adams, Ellen Shipley, Tina Turner, Celine Dion, Franny Goldie. She has written the orchestral score for the John Hughes movies, *She's Having a Baby* and *The Great Outdoors*. She is mother to two children including a daughter who attended the Manhattan School of Music and is a classical pianist, and a son who works for the New York Yankees. Today she lives in South Carolina and continues to write, record, and play.

Members of Fun Boy Three and Bananarama in 1982, *History of Rock*)

The Fun Boy Three with Bananarama (above) and Nicky Holland with (L to R) Ian Stanley, Roland Orzabal, Curt Smith, Will Gregory, Manny Elias, and Andrew Saunders on the Tears for Fears 1985 tour (below)

Fun Boy Three with their musicians (top left clockwise) Ingrid Schroeder, Caroline Lavelle, Bethan Peters, Annie Whitehead, June Miles-Kingston, Nicky Holland.

Holly and the Italians

Mark Henry: Bass
Holly Beth Vincent: vocals, guitar
Steve Young: drums

Listen to the track, "Tell That Girl to Shut Up," by Holly and the Italians. It's a straight up pop rock song. Three chord guitar structure; drumming that maintains the beat on the first and third count of each measure; a single vocal with harmonies to accent; verse chorus bridge all in the places where they're supposed to be—it's catchy. But it's definitely not ska. So why then did Holly and the Italians appear on the 2 Tone Tour? That's exactly what audiences at those shows wanted to know, but they didn't exactly express that curiosity with an air of inquiry and an open mind. Instead, they threw bottles and spit toward the stage, showing their disdain. Holly and the Italians may not have received support from the audience, but they did have support from fellow bands, fellow musicians, and music industry suits who saw the potential of this charismatic bad ass known as Holly Beth Vincent. That potential would just need to be realized outside of the small world of ska in early '80s England.

Holly Beth Vincent was born in Chicago and her family was incredibly musical, thereby giving her access to explore her own musician tendencies. Her father, Bob Vincent, was born Vincent John Cernuto, and he had established a career as a vocalist during the 1940s big band era. His most notable song, "You Call Everybody Darlin'," was a number one hit recorded by Al Trace in 1948.[375] Her mother, June Vincent, was also a singer. She too sang backup on "You Call Everybody Darlin'" as well as singing in groups such as the Tune Tailors and recording her own solo albums.[376] In 1962, the family moved from Chicago to Lake Tahoe, Nevada and three years later moved to Los Angeles after Bob Vincent started managing the career of Wayne Newton. In 1967 he began his own agency, Mus-Art Corporation of America, managing the careers of numerous musicians and actors.[377] While Holly says that her parents definitely influenced her musical foundation, it certainly wasn't a supportive and pleasant childhood.

"I was born in Cook County Hospital, the one used in the film *the Fugitive*. I lived in a suburb called Park Forest. My family moved to Lake Tahoe just before my 7th birthday. I don't remember much about Chicago. My father became the entertainment director at Harrah's in Lake Tahoe. I attended several shows and met the performers—many iconic people. I was a child and it was an odd experience," she says.[378] With access to music equipment in her home, Holly Beth says that she

---

[375] 45cat.com/record/nc733361us, accessed 1 Aug. 2022.
[376] legacy.com/us/obituaries/latimes/name/june-riddell-obituary?id=17092624. Accessed 1 Aug. 2022.
[377] *Billboard Magazine*, 9 Sept. 1967, p. 30.
[378] Vincent, Holly Beth. All quotations, unless otherwise noted, from interview with the author, 4 June 2022 and 3 Aug. 2022.

naturally began playing with it. "My first bands were a result of my family owning a PA system and a lot of instruments, amplifiers, etc. in our garage and I was fairly popular," she says with a laugh. "I sang or played drums in these bands. It was very fun. It was high school. I started out as a drummer and studied that. I had my own drums."

Holly Beth's mother was also an influence on her musically, though she says the family dynamic was traumatic. "I'm proud of my mother's accomplishments. However she was a domestic violence victim and the trickle down wasn't good. Her taste in music was excellent. I heard the albums of many great singers and musicians of her generation and that influenced me. She was very organized and an officer in the Marines, though she developed emotional problems and I'm not sure the basis of that. I wasn't actually influenced by my father at all, except to get as far away as possible. There was constant domestic violence throughout my childhood and teen years. It actually explains most of what follows, and my decision making. Very difficult."

In addition to the music of her mother and father, Holly Beth was influenced by her own musical tastes. "A lot of 'Top 40' singles were purchased, along with Credence, Zeppelin, Steve Miller Band, Sly, Aretha, whatever was on the radio which was very broad musically at that time. Not like today where it's all one style relatively on each music station. ... I was into the Beatles as a little girl. I wanted to be a rock star like one of them, immediately. I didn't want to be one of their girlfriends," she says.[379]

In order to remove herself from a bad home environment, Holly Beth moved to London at the tender age of 18. "I had to go somewhere to get away from the violence in my home. I was a target of that. And another country seemed like a good idea, and one I felt a strong affinity for. I went alone and met other musicians there. My drums were sent there," she says. It wasn't easy just to grab success by the tail, even if her parents were deeply involved in the music industry. Holly Beth had to forge her own way. While in London, she met a number of musicians, including Mark Knopfler who had just moved to London to also pursue a career in music. Holly Beth says, "I recorded there [in London] with known producers and a girlfriend of mine, Jackie Parsons, played with Michael Corby of the Babys, and we auditioned via the *Melody Maker* for a singer and a guitarist. This is how I met Mark Knopfler. He responded to our ad. He became fairly obsessed with me. We weren't involved however, to clear that up. We became involved much later and briefly." When Holly Beth wasn't able to gain traction with her career as a drummer in London, she moved back to Los Angeles to establish herself there before giving it another go.

Back in Los Angeles, Holly Beth played drums and sang with two bands. She expanded to singing and playing the guitar, first in an all-female punk band called Backstage Pass. She explains, "I'd showed up to be drummer but they wanted another guitarist. So I borrowed one from someone and did that for a few months, not long.

---

[379] "Holly and the Italians." punk77.co.uk/groups/hollyandtheitalians3.htm. Accessed 2 Aug. 2022.

From there I drummed for a punkabilly band the Brothel Creepers with Gerard Taylor. His father was the Beatles publicist. In this band, Gerard let me play and sing two songs, which was the beginning of Holly and the Italians. I was encouraged by his father's reaction. I wasn't the best rockabilly drummer, but I kept up," she says, laughing.

Holly Beth then formed her own band and called upon a high school friend, Steve Young, to play drums, and Mark Henry on bass. They were able to secure a few gigs but no substantial success. Still, she was determined to make it work. She told journalist Mark Mehler in 1983, "I did a lot of things to keep myself and the band together. I was a waitress, and for two months I worked as a dominatrix to pay for rehearsals so we could make the first record," said Holly Beth, to which Mehler added "now it's not everyday someone admits in print to being a dominatrix. It's *National Enquirer* stuff, if Holly could be drawn on it, but as it turns out, she speaks of her adventures in the skin trade as simply a convenient means of making money—you might just as well be talking to someone who's served an apprenticeship in leathercraft."[380]

After Mark Knopfler heard his old friend Holly Beth's new band, he urged her to return to London "He heard a demo I'd recorded with Holly and the Italians and wanted to bring myself and the drummer to the UK to be managed by his management. I'd already at this time been offered a publishing deal with a major label, had interest from Phil Spector to produce Holly and the Italians, and was even stopped on Hollywood Boulevard by screenwriter/director Donald Cammel. He'd written and partially directed the film *Performance* [starring Mick Jagger]. He asked me to audition for the lead in another film he'd written, but I already had made a plan to go to the UK with my band and I told him I probably wouldn't audition. I took his number however. This was a crossroads. But as I said, I made many decisions based on seeking safety and getting away from violence that followed me. Stressful."

Returning to London this time, in early 1979, proved much more fruitful for Holly Beth's career. She and Knopfler began a relationship and she moved in with him. He then introduced her to Charlie Billett, a disc jockey for BBC and owner of Oval Records.[381] Holly and the Italians signed to Oval and put out their first single, "Tell That Girl to Shut Up," and secured a number of gigs at notable venues in London including the Hope and Anchor, the Electric Ballroom, and the 100 Club in mid-December 1979. Unfortunately, critics failed to see the power she had as her own musician, commenting that the song was a "simple, brisk, sharp number that's very much to the point. Written by Holly, former girlfriend of Dire Straits leader, Mark Knopfler. A probable hit."[382] It is doubtful when Knopfler released a single that critics noted he was the former boyfriend of Holly and the Italians leader Holly Beth Vincent.

[380] Mehler, Mark. "'Live Fast, Die Young' Is Bunk: Holly Beth Vincent Survives." *Record Magazine*, April 1983.
[381] "Holly and the Italians." punk77.co.uk/groups/hollyandtheitalians3.htm. Accessed 2 Aug. 2022.
[382] *Daily Mirror*, 29 Jan 1980.

The following month, in January 1980, Holly and the Italians opened for Blondie and the Selecter, which meant that things started to move very quickly. "We opened for Blondie at the Hammersmith Odeon and I was 'discovered' by Lynn Goldsmith [photographer]. She went back to New York and hyped me to my soon-to-be manager Gary Kurfirst," she says.[383] Kurfirst was a massively influential manager. According to Vivien Goldman, "Four artists he managed are in the Rock and Roll Hall of Fame: the Talking Heads, the Ramones, Blondie and Mick Jones, formerly of the Clash. ... he staged the New York Rock Festival at Singer Bowl in Flushing Meadow Park, an open-air event featuring Janis Joplin and the Doors. Its success helped inspire the concert at Woodstock in 1969. ... he cherry-picked talent before it became legendary, giving bands like the Who and performers like Jimi Hendrix their East Coast breaks."[384] As a side note, the Singer Bowl in Flushing Meadow Park was host to "Millie Small Day" on August 12, 1964 during the New York World's Fair when Byron Lee & the Dragonaires performed with Millie Small, Jimmy Cliff and others to showcase ska music to the world.[385] Holly Beth continues, "Gary came to London and became my manager. Pauline Black is awesome of course, and the show that night, the lineup was so strong—all women leading their bands. Debbie is fierce. Both are. I guess I was also."

In her book, *Black By Design*, Pauline Black reflects on this performance. "Holly Beth Vincent, the main squeeze of Mark Knopfler in those days, and I had first met with the Selecter and her band, the Italians, were invited on the bill to play with Blondie at the Hammersmith Odeon on 22 January 1980. It was a big opportunity for both of us. 'Three Minute Hero' was about to be released the following week and Holly was picking up a lot of radio play with 'Tell That Girl To Shut Up.' Ms. Harry even invited Holly and me to her dressing room for a photo shoot to mark the occasion. She was a very gracious lady while the necessary photos were taken and on stage a superlative performer. This was one of the best nights I can remember on stage with The Selecter."[386]

Black says that members of the Selecter felt that Holly Beth and her group would be a good fit for the rest of their tour. Until then, Holly and the Italians had been paired with bands like the Dickies, the Vibrators, and other punk and rock groups. This would be Holly's first alliance with ska, and that would prove too incongruous for fans of 2 Tone. The lineup featured the Bodysnatchers, followed by Holly and the Italians, and headlining, of course, was the Selecter. Black writes, "After seeing their performance, the Selecter decided to invite them on the Too Much Pressure tour because we hoped that they would provide a different sound palette, a welcome respite from the relentless ska off-beat, for the audience. Holly was a pertly pretty Chicago-born singer-songwriter who wielded a deft guitar lick and played music

[383] Ibid.
[384] Goldman, Vivien. "Gary Kurfirst, Rock Promoter and Manager of the Talking Heads, Dies at 61." *New York Times*. 16 Jan. 2009. nytimes.com/2009/01/16/arts/16kurfirst.html. Accessed 2 Aug. 2022.
[385] Augustyn, Heather. *Operation Jump Up: Jamaica's Campaign for a National Sound*. Half Pint Press, 2018.
[386] Black, Pauline. *Black By Design*. 2011, p. 197.

with a punk/pop edge. She looked as though she could more than hold her own on any stage."[387] It was sound reasoning, but audiences weren't feeling the logic. Holly Beth says, "I was into it, my band was into it, and it was exciting. It was unfortunate it didn't work but yeah, the audience was there for a night of ska music and that culture and that rhythm. So I easily understand why it didn't work. My band was placed in the middle of the two ska bands. Musically it didn't work to disrupt that flow. I even tried wearing only black and white outfits," she says with a laugh, "but it was a musical thing. Ska is a very particular musical style. It's not just about fashion, which I knew. So I didn't take it personally, but psychologically it made me anxious to go out on a tour with a new label and have it fail. I felt off after that. It wasn't a good start. The ska bands and Pauline especially were very welcoming and sorry when it didn't work."

Coverage in *Smash Hits* magazine also reflected that the issue was with the reception of the music, not the music itself. It stated, "Ace new band Holly and the Italians were forced to leave the Selecter tour recently because a small section of certain audiences decided that their music wasn't acceptable. Since the Selecter invited Holly on the tour purely because they admired her music, they are bitterly disappointed that some of their fans think that anything which isn't ska or on the 2 Tone label is not fit to listen to. When you consider that one of the main ideas behind 2 Tone is to encourage the maximum integration, musical, racial and otherwise, it's doubly depressing that certain characters are incapable of seeing the wood for the trees. Ah well, bigots are nothing new."[388]

Of the departure, Black writes, "Immediately we realized that we had made a mistake in electing to have Holly and the Italians as second on the bill after the Bodysnatchers. The fact that their music had absolutely nothing to do with ska or reggae—something we saw as a plus—was not enough to stop the diehard, unreconstructed male 2 Tone fan from spitting, bottling and heckling them off the stage every night. Understandably Holly got upset and although they struggled on for a while, their reception got so bad that they were forced to leave the tour. … After Holly and the Italians left the tour, we drafted in another 2 Tone-inspired act, Coventry band the Swinging Cats, to take up the slack. They had formed at the end of 1979, so they had something in common with the Bodysnatchers [see also Swinging Cats chapter]."[389]

There were plenty of other successful shows, however, including support of bands like the Clash and the Ramones. Holly Beth recalls, "My band opened for the Clash several times—about six to eight times. It was around the UK right before the Clash went to America and played those shows in NYC at Bond's. It was when photographer Pennie Smith was on tour with them for her book about them. I think it was called *Before and After*. My band opened for the Clash replacing the Fabulous

[387] Ibid.
[388] *Smash Hits*, 20 March 1980, p. 12.
[389] Black, Pauline. *Black By Design*. Serpent's Tail. 2011, p. 198-199.

Thunderbirds. Honestly, I was told they were getting booed off. And the booking agency, which was the same as my agency, Wasted Talent, decided to try us. We were a hit with their audience, and we even opened the London Palladium show. The last show for them before America. I think. I remember the Fabulous Thunderbirds were at the London Palladium show backstage with the Clash and watched us. I also remember falling backward over a snare drum stand our drummer threw to get our roadies attention because his broke. The roadies pulled me up (embarrassing) and I walked up to the mic and said, 'Well so much for being cool,' and the audience all cheered me, and it broke the ice for us at that show and we did a great job they loved us. There was a lot of smoke onstage and in the venues and we could barely see each other onstage. There was a lot of pogoing, gobbing of spit, beer bottles flying. Dodging spit and beer bottles, I was assured by the promoter that meant they liked us," she says, laughing. "The Clash tour was super exciting, high energy onstage—like going into battle. Funny how me being a female, I don't ever see any photos or anything about this tour. I do think that because we were a three-piece band and doing some pretty ballsy things we weren't, or I wasn't, credited for all I was doing. Certainly all the guy bands were."

She continues, "It was very intense and dramatic and fun. We played a short set of our fastest songs and were aggressive about it which was my strategy and it worked. I remember one time a Clash roadie came into our dressing room to complain about my getting lipstick on Mick's microphone and I remember I said, 'What's the matter, isn't it his color?' I was a brat. I had to be, in that situation. But I loved it and have great memories from that. Very exciting high energy. I also remember seeing Joe Strummer sitting on their tour bus with a boom box on his shoulder listening to our album *the Right to Be Italian*. I'm sure he wanted to hear what we were like. This was at the very start of our being with them and we were in our own van."

That album, *the Right to Be Italian*, was recorded in New York after the band signed to Virgin/Epic in early 1980. Holly Beth says it took a while to record that first album because the label was in no rush to make an album. "Everybody was so busy going around chuckling, 'God, this could be great,' but nobody bothered to do anything about it. I was their precious little thing, you understand. Anyway, eventually I met Shadow Morton (a producer legendary for his work on the Red Bird label with the Shangri-Las) over a couple of Bloody Mary's and we went into Electric Lady," says Holly Beth.[390] Electric Lady Studios in Greenwich Village in New York City had been used to record Led Zeppelin, the Rolling Stones, Blondie, Stevie Wonder, and David Bowie, among a host of others, and was built by and for Jimi Hendrix. Holly Beth's album pooled together members of her band along with a host of notable musicians including Jerry Harrison who had performed synthesizer for Talking Heads; Paul Schaffer on keyboards who was later the leader of "The World's Most Dangerous Band" for David Letterman and writer of the song, "It's Raining Men;" drummer Anton Fig who was also in Letterman's band; strings and brass were

390 Mehler, Mark. "'Live Fast, Die Young' Is Bunk: Holly Beth Vincent Survives." *Record Magazine*, April 1983.

arranged by Torrie Zito who had worked previously with Frank Sinatra, John Lennon, and Tony Bennett; and additional vocals from Ellie Greenwich who had written numerous hits like "Da Doo Ron Ron, "Be My Baby," "Then He Kissed Me," "Do Wah Diddy Diddy," "Chapel of Love," "Leader of the Pack," and others along with arranging vocals for Aretha Franklin, Frank Sinatra, and Dusty Springfield," and others. It was an impressive lineup, to say the least.

Shadow Morton served as producer on the album, and Holly Beth said that the recording process was problematic. She explains, "He kept disappearing in the middle of tracks to go out and talk to friends, or something."[391] During recording, Steve Young quit the band and Anton Fig and Mike Osborn filled in on drums. Richard Gottehrer, who had founded Sire Records and launched the careers of Blondie, Madonna, the Ramones and Talking Heads, was brought in as producer which had to be remixed in the UK. Holly Beth was unhappy with the result, calling it "muddy, drenched in reverb and loaded with the kitchen sink."[392] Gottehrer said the process itself was muddy, resulting in a messy product. "There was plenty of turmoil," said Gottehrer. "She broke up with her drummer and there were other personality things, and when you have flareups in the band, the balance can get thrown off. Holly has a lot of potential and a terrific-sounding voice, but she has to leave it alone. In her desire to get involved in every area of the recording, I think she might have spoiled the record. What does she know about mixing an LP? You've got to let people around you do what they do and just get on with it, and she wasn't able to do that."[393]

Because the process was so lengthy and intensive, it was an expensive production. "Around Virgin, there's a saying that my first album is the only one that cost more to make than the film of Apocalypse Now," joked Holly Beth.[394] It didn't do well. Holly Beth wasn't doing well either. "I began acting very badly," she says. "It was a number of things, really. I've always had problems dealing with companies, institutions, all kinds of authority. I know it's childish, but I'm not going to play the poor, oppressed artist. I brought it on myself. And then there were certain chemical things—I was withdrawing form drugs prescribed by a psychiatrist I was seeing at the time. You know the story of Frances Farmer? Well it's a lot like what happened to me. No, I didn't have a lobotomy, but it was a psychotic time. During one of the worst periods, I did trash a dressing room at the BBC. Meanwhile, my manager was 3,000 miles away in New York and there was nobody in England to be a buffer between my actions and the record company. Anyway, Virgin dropped me, and from their point of view, they were right."[395] She says that she was just mentally overwhelmed at the time. "I just hadn't slept for a few days, my leg was broken in Sheffield at a hotel, a blind staircase and carrying my guitar and not wanting it to

[391] Ibid.
[392] Ibid.
[393] Ibid.
[394] Ibid.
[395] Ibid.

break. My leg was instead. Train ride back to London with said leg broken, ouch. Then a T.V. show to do. Hair appointment. It was the *Old Grey Whistle Test*. Very serious show. Seriously a great music performance show. A prestigious element I wasn't aware of at that moment. Americans. It was supposed to be live performance and I blanked out on lyrics from lack of sleep and injury. Had to stop playing. People were yelling at me. I smashed a dressing room mirror, was surrounded by security and shown out. They said it wouldn't air but it did. It was good. I was good. I'm sorry about their mirror but I doubt it's anything anymore. Life went on."[396] That performance on the *Old Grey Whistle Test* from May 1981 is available via YouTube.

Before she was dropped from her label, Holly Beth recorded another album since she was signed to a two-album deal. With none of her original members, the album was essentially a solo album and was self-titled, *Holly Beth Vincent*. She recorded it in the UK in the fall of 1982 and traveled to the US to mix the songs with producer Mike Thorne. "Upon attempting to return to Great Britain in October [1982] she was turned away at customs as an undesirable, a form of rejection that seemed to cut more deeply than all the other hurts," wrote Mehler.[397] Holly Beth commented, "I may have not been a great human being, but I don't think what I did makes me a 'dangerous' person." [398] Prior to her second album's release, Virgin released a number of singles including the song, "I Wanna Go Home" which was reviewed in *Smash Hits*. Reviewer Mark Ellen stated, "Virgin Boss to Marketing Dept.: 'Could be on a winner here Oscar. Stick these Italian folk in the studio with some Big Name producer chappie who'll make 'em sound like The Glitter Band. Y'know, all beefed up powerchords and team ranting. Then give 'em a chord sequence that's made the Top Twenty at least 4,000 times. Something like 'Teenage Kicks.' Can't fail, old boy.' By rights, it shouldn't. (Had to be re-mixed though)."[399] Ellen's review of her album two months later was more scathing. "Stacking all three of her individually promising singles on side one only serves to expose the shallowness of Holly Vincent's songwriting. They're all the same; rhythm section blustering but drab, guitars smouldering and songs that rest on the barest structures. Her voice is plaintive but limited and she has great difficulty in wresting any kind of melody out of the material. All in all, this is unimaginative, laboured pop obsessed with self-consciously 'teenage' dreams and quite honestly Kim Wilde does it better. (4 out of 10)."[400] Other critics weren't kind either and said that Holly Beth's voice and songwriting was solid, but blamed the tedium of the support band, saying it had "all the panache of a Foreigner or Survivor," but "now and again, enough happens to convince me that inside this stereotyped record there's an original idea struggling to get out."[401]

---

[396] Cortina, Lene. "Holly Beth Vincent—the Interview." 30 Aug. 2018. punkgirldiaries.com/holly-beth-vincent-the-interview. Accessed 3 Aug. 2022.
[397] Mehler, Mark. "'Live Fast, Die Young' Is Bunk: Holly Beth Vincent Survives." *Record Magazine*, April 1983.
[398] Ibid.
[399] Ellen, Mark. "Reviews." *Smash Hits*. 30 Apr. 1981, p. 25.
[400] Ellen, Mark. "Reviews." *Smash Hits*. 14 May 1981, p. 30.
[401] *Harlow Star*, 14 Oct. 1982.

It should be noted that most of the reviews, the critiques, the "challenges" associated with the output of Holly and the Italians concern the production of the recordings and the process of making those recordings. No one is denying Holly Beth Vincent's talent. They are calling her difficult. Step back and see that men are calling this woman difficult. Does she have a right to call the shots on how her band sounds? Does she have the power to say how her song should be played and heard? Does she need permission to push back when the output fails to meet her expectations? Is she allowed into this space of musician and producer? And when that world fails to support her, is it not a surprise when she reacts, grows frustrated, breaks mirrors, breaks down? "She's a perfectionist," said Steve Ralbovsky who went on to manage Holly Beth, "a real artist. And she stuck to her guns."[402]

Holly Beth collaborated with Joey Ramone since the two had formed a friendship during their previous work together since they were both managed by Gary Kurfirst. They had played together in the early 1980s and she says the combination of the two bands was always a good one for audiences. "We were a big hit with Ramones fans. It was a great match and I don't remember how many times we opened for them. It was America only and a lot of Agora Ballroom shows, East Coast touring and West Coast/Texas shows, and the Hollywood Palladium show. I remember in Texas going to a mini go-cart racing place with them and we all raced. We also went to a reptile farm. Funny. In Miami we all went to the beach at the hotel and I remember thinking how funny it seemed to see the Ramones in swim trunks on the beach. We all looked pretty out of place—glow in the dark white. It's Miami after all. I remember the Ramones always played through their whole set in the dressing room beginning to end to warm up. I was impressed by that. They also always had pizza and cereal in their dressing room. I think Froot Loops or something like that. They were all nice to us. They liked our band. I remember the pizza thing because it was like that in the movie Rock and Roll High School. I always went out into the audience to watch their set after ours and that was a big treat to be able to do that. I also always got lots of compliments from people in the audience who recognized me. Supporting the Ramones was great and fun. It was a good pairing. We also opened for them in Central Park NYC and that was amazing. You could see people all around NYC in high-rise buildings watching the show, apart from the regular audience. And also played with them at the Pier 84 show in NYC. Then also the Joey Ramone shows he put on at the Ritz and Irving Plaza—he'd put a bunch of bands on to play three songs."

One of the collaborations with Joey Ramone resulted in a recording of the Sonny & Cher classic, "I Got You Babe." Holly Beth says, "I don't remember who came up with the idea, I think it was a promoter, not sure and wish I knew. Anyway, it was recorded at one of Virgin's studios, the Manor, in the countryside somewhere. It was my song arrangement, and my band, me on guitar, Bobby Collins on bass, and Kevin Wilkinson on drums. I later produced the synth part which was played by Tom Dolby—me and Tom sitting on the couch at the Townhouse studios in London. Joey

---

[402] Mehler, Mark. "'Live Fast, Die Young' Is Bunk: Holly Beth Vincent Survives." *Record Magazine*, April 1983.

was scared at first about adding synth, then loved it when he heard it. He loved the sound on that single, and asked me to join the Ramones as a result of making that single which I turned down because I was about to make the 'blue' album [*Holly Beth Vincent*], and I figured Johnny would hate me the whole time. But he [Joey] did call me from New York and ask me to join. The thing I remember about that session is there were these Irish wolfhound dogs there, and Joey would stand next to one and say he liked them because they made him look normal height. It was cute and funny to me."[403]

Holly Beth has always continued to keep busy with projects. "My management team introduced me to my new band—Jimmy Rip, Jay Dee Daughterty, Fred Smith from the New York band Television, Dolette McDonald, and Mary Davis from the Cissy Houston band. We were a troupe and it was musically great and fun. We never recorded but performed live. There were other bands in New York City and I wrote a lot of songs. I was, at one point, offered a recording contract with Island Records but the company changed ownership and it didn't go forward. Debbie Harry and I were backup singers for Ronnie Spector and for Billy Idol. I also sang with Joey posthumously on the album *Ya Know?* He is very missed. The Ramones were a favorite band of mine since I'd first heard a test pressing of their first album, before my own bands." She also replaced Patty Donahue in the Waitresses; performed with Wild Things, a combo with Anthony Thistlethwaite of the Waterboys; formed the group Vowel Movement with Concrete Blonde singer Johnette Napolitano; and she has recorded a number of songs as a solo artist as well as with her band, the Oblivious, with whom she toured the U.S. twice.[404]

In 1989, Holly Beth Vincent gave birth to a son. She continues to write and perform when able. "I've been autoimmune sick for several years and it's about how much energy I have. I get inspired to write and have ideas," she says.

---

[403] "Holly and the Italians." punk77.co.uk/groups/hollyandtheitalians4.htm. Accessed 3 Aug. 2022.
[404] Ibid.

Holly Beth Vincent with Pauline Black and Debbie Harry, backstage at the Hammersmith Odeon, January 22, 1980.

Cover of the single for Holly Beth Vincent and Joey Ramone (left), Holly Beth Vincent performing with the Italians (right), and from her solo single (below).

Dexys Midnight Runners

Kevin Archer: vocals, guitar
Geoff Blythe: saxophone
John Jay: drums
Helen O'Hara: violin
Jim Paterson: trombone

Pete Saunders: keyboard
Steve Spooner: saxophone
Kevin Rowland: vocals, guitar
Pete Williams: bass
And others

The brass harmonies and bouncy keyboards would lead anyone to believe that Dexys Midnight Runners were bound for the 2 Tone movement. They wore sunglasses and trilbies, they pogoed on stage, they built their sound from punk and northern soul. But Dexys Midnight Runners, just a few years after forming in 1978, were as far from 2 Tone as one might maneuver, donning cropped overalls and red bandanas around their necks, or a few years after that sporting what can only be described as business attire suitable for a bank. And they changed lineups quicker than their attire. So, pinning down Dexys to a single genre, a single moment in time, is simply not possible. And that's just the way they like it.

Dexys Midnight Runners was founded in 1979 in Birmingham by Kevin Rowland and Kevin Archer (nicknamed Al to differentiate between the two Kevins) after their punk band, the Killjoys, broke up. Their new band was fashioned, at first, on the northern soul movement, both in sound and culture. The name itself, Dexys Midnight Runners, is a reference to the use of dextroamphetamine, a stimulant used to stay up and dance all night which was a feature of this subculture. "I was trying to figure out which direction to move in next and one day it came to me: soul music," said Rowland of his decision.[405] To compile the rest of the band, Rowland put an advertisement in the *Melody Maker* and over 30 musicians came to audition. They acquired eight of them, all men, to fill the ranks, including horns which gave them "a brassy sound but the aggression and immediacy that punk rock had," according to their bassist Peter Williams.[406]

As a result of some success with the Killjoys, the new band was able to get the attention of Bernie Rhodes who managed the Clash (and is name checked in the Specials' "Gangsters"). Rhodes helped to shape their sound as Rowland recalls, "We'd done a demo tape that included early versions of 'Tell Me When My Light Turns Green' and 'I'm Just Looking.' Rhodes liked the songs but wasn't too keen on my singing. That really pissed me off at first, then I realized he had a point, so I thought about it and made some changes. When we started recording again, my voice had a

[405] Wilde, Jon. "Kevin Rowland: Classic Interview." web.archive.org/web/20121111024942/http://sabotagetimes.com/music/kevin-rowland-i-ruled-dexys-with-an-iron-fist. Accessed 28 Aug. 2022.
[406] Elwell, Mina. "The Untold Truth Of Dexys Midnight Runners." 27 Feb. 2022. grunge.com/781824/the-untold-truth-of-dexys-midnight-runners. Accessed 28 Aug. 2022.

sort of 'crying' quality to it and that made it sound more emotional."[407] Rhodes produced Dexys first single, "Dance Stance," on Rhodes' label, Oddball, in November 1979.

Their look changed as well, and fashion would always be important to the band throughout their run. They were inspired to rethink their appearance after securing a spot in support of the Specials on tour. "The Specials started happening and they were wearing suits. They asked us to support them on their tour. We'd played with them a couple of times before and, maybe because of the way we looked, their audience didn't take us seriously. I realized that, if we were going to do the tour, I had to find a look that the audience would get. If we didn't get the look right, we'd get laughed off stage. Around that time Jimmy [Patterson] walked into the rehearsal room wearing a woolly hat and a polo-neck sweater. It was so cold that you could see his breath in the air. He started playing the trombone and it hit me that this was a great look. So we got the clothes and took on this look. Maybe we looked like a gang who had attitude. But it wasn't an intentionally hard image."[408]

That tour took place in 1979. Dexys filled the vacancy left by Madness when they signed to Stiff Records and left to tour America. The tour maybe did more for Dexys as a group than it did for audiences who came to hear ska. This is not to say that audiences rejected Dexys—they didn't. But performing for such audiences challenged Rowland to evaluate his creation and iterate the image and sound over and over again. "The 2-Tone tour is a fascinating moment," opines one writer in hindsight.[409] "It made Dexys: it brought them to an audience all too ready for their dour devotions, it spurred them to hone their set into a fearsome testament, and it brought them to the attention of an industry desperate not to miss out on the next big thing from the West Midlands. It also became, in Rowland's mind, something like an original sin, a founding compromise he ever after had to atone for." 2 Tone, needless to say, was a strong subculture that could brand a band. And when that brand was no longer in fashion, the bands associated with it had to fight to remain relevant. "We don't want to become part of anyone else's movement," Rowland said during this era.[410]

While they had supported the Specials while gigging, and they went on the 2 Tone tour, Dexys Midnight Runners never signed to the 2 Tone label. And in March 1980, Dexys proved they were a band in their own right when their northern soul single, "Geno," a nod to soul-singer Geno Washington, reached number one and was released on the EMI imprint Parlophone. Four months later, in July 1980, they released their debut album—an opportunity that surely would never had been afforded them had they signed to 2 Tone. That album, *Searching for the Young Soul Rebels*, received good reviews which further differentiated the Dexys' sound as separate from

---

[407] Wilde, Jon. "Kevin Rowland: Classic Interview." web.archive.org/web/20121111024942/http://sabotagetimes.com/music/kevin-rowland-i-ruled-dexys-with-an-iron-fist. Accessed 28 Dec. 2022.
[408] Ibid.
[409] Trousse, Stephen. "Dexys Midnight Runners." *Ultimate Genre Guide*, 24 Apr. 2019, p. 20.
[410] Ibid.

2 Tone. "Dexys are more soul orientated, heavily influenced by Stax, Mowtown [sic] and the Atlantic labels of the fifties and sixties, and it is this quality which holds them apart from the 'run of the mill' ska bands that are currently dominating the charts," wrote one journalist.[411] Dexys were clear to make the distinction themselves as well. The album begins with an element that one might call a beef. "In one of the most audacious opening gambits in pop history, the album begins with the sound of a radio dialing through the megahertz. Through the static we hear the ghost of Johnny Rotten, lost on the airwaves singing 'Holidays In the Sun,' then Terry Hall, the lonesome wail of 'You're no friend of mine,' from the Specials' 'Rat Race.' The set is abruptly switched off. 'Jimmy? Al?' Kevin Rowland calls to his bandmates. 'For God's sake—burn it down.'"[412]

By the time that Helen O'Hara joined Dexys Midnight Runners, they had already established themselves as a serious soul-influenced band. They had recorded singles and an album, they had toured all over the UK, and they had garnered plenty of good press in newspapers and music magazines. But Helen had never heard of them. So she didn't go looking for them, as a young musician hoping to make a life in the arts—they came looking for her. She was born Helen Bevington on November 5, 1956 and today her name is Helen Stookes. "I grew up in Bristol, in the southwest of England," Helen says.[413] "I had some very young years in Wales in Swansea, but predominantly, it was Bristol. I started playing the violin when I was about nine years old at school. I come from a big family of nine—seven children and I'm number six and all of my family are all very musical. I had classical training, but I was always more interested in pop music. So at any opportunity, I was playing along to pop records on the violin or the piano."

Before studying music at university, Helen joined a number of bands that did fairly well in gaining fans and even airplay. She was only 17 when she joined her first band. "I'd answered an advertisement I'd seen in a local paper about a pop band wanting musicians to audition. That was a group formed by a drummer, which was called the Groundhogs who were a very successful sort of 1970s progressive bluesy group but quite psychedelic. Ken Pustelnik, the drummer, was forming this new group in Bristol and myself and a friend of mine who played viola, we auditioned and we got the job. And it was an instrumental progressive group playing music, sort of prog rock, you know what I mean, sort of Gentle Giant, Van der Graaf Generator, that sort of thing. And I played with them for about a year," says Helen.

"And then I left them and joined another group, mainly on keyboards to be honest, which was just a way of getting into the group. And we supported an American soul singer called Al Matthews, who at the time had a hit single called 'Fool,' which was in the charts in Britain. And then after Al's tour, this group then developed into a sort of punk-new-wave group where I was playing more violin. That group was

[411] "Rare treat in store from the 'Runners.'" *Drogheda Argus and Leinster Journal*, 18 July 1980.
[412] Ibid.
[413] O'Hara, Helen. All quotations, unless otherwise noted, from interview with the author, 4 Dec. 2020.

called Uncle Po. We did quite well. We toured a lot. I basically got a lot of my experience with that. We toured an awful lot and won a lot of competitions. We were on a BBC Radio One competition, it was new bands, voted on by the public and recorded a single, but it never really got anywhere. But that band was so important in terms of the experience for me. But they disintegrated. I think we felt we'd gone as far as we could with trying to get a record deal and nothing happened, band folded," she says.

After that, Helen decided to develop her musicianship more formally. She says, "I felt I was at a bit of a loss and my sister suggested maybe music college and I thought, you know what, that sounds like a really good idea. I can improve my playing. And it just seemed the right thing to do, so about this time, I was about age 21 and I was still keeping an open mind with groups, but decided to really, really work hard at music college and sort of dedicate myself to becoming a better musician. And so I spent four years at Birmingham Conservatoire, which was absolutely amazing, really good training. I learned a lot. But I sort of decided to cut myself off from the pop world because I felt that I could so easily be led back into it. It was in my blood. That's what I really wanted to do."

It was here, at the music college, when Helen says she, despite her promises to herself, was tempted back into that world of pop music. She states, "So basically, the time with Dexys when they were supporting the Specials on the 2 Tone Tour was 1979 but I hadn't heard of Dexys then. I had no idea about who they were or anything. But in 1981, late 1981, after this tour, after their session for *Soul Rebels*, Kevin Archer, who was in the first Dexys group with Kevin Rowland, he'd left the band then and he formed his own band called the Blue Ox Babes. And he wanted to use violin for his new album. And he came to the college and somebody said, 'Oh, you want to ask Helen because she's played in bands before—she'd probably be right.' So he knocked on my practice room door. And it really was like the devil tempting me! I remember thinking, I mustn't do this! I mustn't do this! I've got to stick to it and I've got to be sensible! And of course, I was tempted. I went to the rehearsal and it was just amazing. It was really good. His songs were great, they were really hooky and he was great and that was it really."

Then Helen came to the attention of Kevin Rowland, since he and Archer were still close friends. Archer only left the band because of the rigorous tour schedule. Helen explains, "I recorded some demos with them in Birmingham and then Kevin Archer played those demos to Kevin Rowland. Kevin Rowland had been experimenting with strings as well. He'd been experimenting with violin, cello, viola, those sorts of combinations. And Kevin Archer said to Kevin Rowland, why don't you contact Helen because she'd be good for your group. Kevin Rowland sent Jim Patterson, the trombone player, and Paul Speare, the sax player, to the music college. So I had sort of a second knock on the door. I couldn't believe it. Two groups wanting a violinist! And I went to the demo studio. They asked me to bring along a cellist and a viola player, so I found these musicians at the college and we went along to the demo studio and we played the music. But I could tell that Kevin Rowland didn't

186

seem that happy with what he was hearing. I didn't think it was the way we were playing, I thought it's the sound. Sure enough, he then said to me, 'Can you just come by yourself? Can you come along to Dexys rehearsal in Birmingham?' and so I went along. And then the enormity of how great the group was hit me because I was then in a rehearsal with the band and they just blew me away. I mean, I thought Kevin Archer's group was good, but Dexys were just something else. It was really amazing. And so Kevin Rowland said to me, 'Look, can you find two other violinists and I want to try three violins together.' And so I found two other fiddle players at the college. And when Kevin heard us, all three play together, that was obviously what he wanted. And from there, that's how the *Too-Rye-Ay* sound developed."

Helen officially joined Dexys Midnight Runners in July 1982. She changed her last name to O'Hara to conjure Celtic connections. The horn section was replaced by strings including Helen and her fellow students Steve Shaw, renamed Steve Brennan, and Roger Huckle, renamed Roger MacDuff, all on fiddles in a section they dubbed "The Emerald Express" for Rowland's experiment in what he called "Celtic soul."[414] Helen's contribution to the "Too-Rye-Ay sound," as she calls it, propelled Dexys to absolute stardom. The song "Come On Eileen" went to number one on the charts.[415] The album *Too-Rye-Ay*, originally titled Hey, *Where You Going With That Suitcase*, was recorded for Mercury Records and produced by Clive Langer who had produced for Madness and was a member of the Deaf School with Bette Bright, Suggs wife (see also Deaf School section in Others chapter).

"I was the violinist," says Helen of her now-iconic song, "and Eileen was played in the video by—have you heard of Bananarama? It was Siobhan's [Fahey] sister. I think her name was Maire. She played Eileen. So the first tour was quite soon after 'Come On Eileen' was a hit. Number one in Britain for six weeks. So we did a UK tour which sold out. And some of the performances, we did two shows a night. We went to Europe, toured all around France, Germany, masses of promotion. I mean, it was really a full-on tour." At the end of 1982, keyboardist Mickey Billingham left to join General Public with the Beat's Ranking Roger and Dave Wakeling. Many members of Dexys shuffled in and out as needed, especially since the lineup was large and instruments changed to suit the sound.

It was during this time that Kevin Rowland and Helen began a relationship that soon became serious. "You see in late 1982, me and Kevin got together, as boyfriend girlfriend. Well, Kevin asked me out, sort of thing. I suppose, I think he was more, what's the word? I suppose he was more infatuated with me than I was with him to start with, but I gradually, you know, I sort of, well, I fell in love with him, I suppose. I did. And, and he with me. And in fact, we were going to get married. He'd asked me to marry him, actually. And we moved in together after the American tour in 1983. We moved into a flat together and you know, we were very, very, obviously, very close and everything."

[414] dexys.org. Accessed 28 Aug. 2022.
[415] Ibid.

That American tour took place in February 1983 and by April of that year, "Come On Eileen" had reached number one in American charts. "We did our first tour of the States and Canada, but just sort of mainly around the edges of America—New York, Boston, San Francisco, and then Toronto. And there was a very good response. Very good response," Helen says. "We came back [to England] and then we went [to the U.S.] and did a second tour [May 1983] and by this time, there was a British invasion of bands in America like Duran Duran and Culture Club, that sort of thing. And that tour wasn't so good because we were being booked into places in the middle of America where nobody's really heard of us, which was not great for us. And we were getting a lot of attention through MTV at the time, but audiences didn't seem to know anything else apart from 'Eileen.' It was dispiriting really. And then we were also being booked into places that were too big for us as well. And some of those were cancelled. So, at this point, we weren't being managed very well. Some of the venues were fine, so when we were playing in New York and Los Angeles and those spaces, we could play in quite big places and the audiences were great," she says. One of these performances took place on Saturday Night Live on May 14, 1983,[416] But despite this exposure, it wasn't fulfilling for the band. "It was the sort of middle areas that were wrong for us, so we were sort of getting a bit worn down at this stage. Kevin wasn't really happy with the way things were going. And so, the American tour was the last tour that we did before we took a break and started to write for the next album."

Before that, though, Dexys supported David Bowie in Paris on June 9, 1983 at the Hippodrome D'auteuil. After impatient fans continued shouting for Bowie during Dexys performance, nine songs into their set, Kevin Rowland responded to them, "Who are you shouting for? David Bowie? Didn't you know Bryan Ferry's got three times the amount of talent? Didn't you know David Bowie's a complete fucking arsehole? Well you know it now!"[417] Rowland was known to be impassioned with audiences who he felt didn't really understand their art. He once hit someone in the crowd for "making these weird noises during the quiet bits of the songs," and also hit a *Melody Maker* journalist because "I felt he was attacking the group," both of which he feels bad about now. "I think I was considered a bit of an oddball, a bit of a joke by the music business. I was certainly seen as a loose cannon. I had this me-against-the-world mentality. The more success we got, the more entrenched I got in that way of thinking. My world was getting smaller and smaller. I'd backed myself into a corner," Rowland said.[418]

After a two-month break from the touring, Dexys began composing songs for their new album. They spent many months writing and perfecting the songs for the album, *Don't Stand Me Down*, which wasn't fully recorded and released until

[416] dexys.org/id14.html. Accessed 28 Aug. 2022.
[417] dexys.org/id14.html and tapatalk.com/groups/thefall/dexys-midnight-runners-t17738.html. Accessed 28 Aug. 2022.
[418] Wilde, Jon. "Kevin Rowland: Classic Interview." web.archive.org/web/20121111024942/http://sabotagetimes.com/music/kevin-rowland-i-ruled-dexys-with-an-iron-fist. Accessed 8 28 2022.

September 1985. By then, much had changed including the sound of the songs, the look of the band, the lineup, and the relationship between Helen and Kevin. "Just before we were going to record *Don't Stand Me Down*, Kevin ended our relationship, which was very difficult for both of us. But we, you know, we carried on. At that point, the band really was only Kevin Rowland, me, and Billy Adams, the guitarist, in terms of the old members, although we were putting in different musicians, doing the recording and touring, and so it also didn't really affect anything, to be honest. I'm not even sure that some of the musicians who came in even knew that me and Kevin would have been together I don't think it affected anything. I mean, obviously, it must have. It did play a part in the whole album in lots of ways. In fact, a couple of the songs were about me, so that was kind of surprising, but also rather lovely, you know. And for me and Kevin, we wouldn't have been unaffected," she says.

If they were affected, it certainly didn't show in the creation and production of their music. Helen and Kevin continued to work together in an environment of respect and professionalism and Helen says she always felt extremely valued from every member of the group for her contributions as a musician. "There was never any sexism. I was treated as an equal. I think musicians are very open minded and tolerant and there was never a problem. I was hired for my musicianship, not because I was a woman," she says.

Though *Don't Stand Me Down* didn't have as much commercial success as Dexys' earlier music, this album is still considered by many to be a masterpiece. Their look had changed from "country hicks" to "double-glazing salesman look," as one rather idiotic interviewer put it during what can only be described as a hostile grilling for the Channel 4 show "Bliss."[419] Their new look, which was always part of the art and the concept of the whole of performance, had become so associated with the band that those with a shallow ear seemed more distracted by shiny objects rather than the substance underneath. They couldn't see that it was all part of the package. It was there from the very beginning in who Dexys was as a collection, and who they were as individuals. "Everything from the clothes to the music should all tie in," said Rowland.[420] One writer astutely observed, "As the Specials became increasingly Dammers' studio project, ska became one ingredient among many as he incorporated lounge, library and Latin music. In a similar way, Dexy's notion of soul became more purely conceptual—eventually on the chart-topping raggle-taggle gypsy sounds of *Too-Rye-Ay* and then the well-tailored Brooks Bros pop of *Don't Stand Me Down*, coming to stand almost purely for Rowland's ongoing confessional journey. … The type of shoes you wear, or the cut of your trousers, the look of the video, the typography on the label or the sound of the band—it isn't a matter of life or death. It's much more important than that."[421]

[419] dexys.org/muriel_gray_interview.html. Accessed 28 Aug. 2022.
[420] Mulvey, John. "A Pure Sound." *History of Rock*, 1982. Uncut. Jan. 2017.
[421] Trousse, Stephen. "Dexys Midnight Runners." *Ultimate Genre Guide*, 24 Apr. 2019, p. 20.

Helen O'Hara continued her musical career beyond Dexys Midnight Runners, having left the band in 1986 when Rowland decided to go solo. "I helped Kevin with his solo project. Dexys had sort of disbanded at this point. I did feel a bit of a loss, to be honest. Having worked so closely with the band for five years, it was, well what now? I wrote an instrumental album—it was new world music. That album was called *Southern Hearts*. And I used some Dexys connections on the album, some musicians." Helen then had two children in the 1990s and says she did perform violin for Graham Parker for his *Struck By Lightning* album, but she found it hard to be on the road with children. "I just left the violin, to be honest. It was a difficult time. So I made a choice that while my sons were very young, I wouldn't tour and so really there wasn't going to be as much work, to be honest. And then as time went on, I started to lose confidence. I did lots of other things as my children grew up. I got lots of horticultural qualifications and worked as a gardener and I did volunteer work with food banks and was kind of busy and it was worth it because it fit in with my children."

Helen's sons are both musical as well, a testament to her devotion to them and to the arts. "Both my sons went to the Guildhall School of Music and Drama. One of them is a drummer, and the other got into the theater side. And the more I saw them doing what I used to do, the more I began to get really—well it was gnawing inside me really, that I wasn't doing what I'm about, I suppose. And what sort of got me back into playing was I went to see Dexys play at the Barbican in London with their album *One Day I'm Going to Soar*. Kevin had given me some tickets and I went with my youngest son who's called Billy. One on hand, I felt elated seeing Kevin and the band playing, and I also felt I should be up there. Kevin over the years asked me, 'Are you playing? Will you come back and join the band?' He asked me over the years when he was doing projects, but I wasn't, so I declined. Then one day, it was almost beyond my control, I just went to the back of the cupboard. I hadn't played for over 20 years. I got the violin. I knew it'd be difficult, but my head was ready, to be honest. It led me back to playing with Kevin again."

Since then, in 2015, Helen has worked with Kevin Rowland on his projects including an album of Irish music and pop music called *Let the Record Show*, as well as live performances. She has also worked with Tim Burgess from the Charlatans and other musicians. But in more recent years, Helen has returned to performing with Dexys and has even brought her eldest son into the fold. And in 2022, Helen, Kevin, and others came together for the 40th anniversary of the album that is still cherished today. The text for the music video of "Come On Eileen (As It Should Have Sounded Remix 2022)" reads, "In 1982, on completion of the album *Too Rye Ay* which contained the single 'Come On Eileen,' Kevin Rowland was never happy with many of the mixes on the record. Although he loved the finished version of Eileen, he knew many of the mixes could be better. In 2022, Kevin, Helen O'Hara and Pete Schwier got the opportunity to remix the album. They even gave 'Come On Eileen' a few tweaks." Reflecting on her life and contributions to what began as northern soul but has branched out into so many other experiments, projects, sounds, and even looks, Helen states, "Yeah, I'm in a good place."

Helen O'Hara & Kevin Rowland in 1982, *History of Rock* (above), Helen O'Hara &
Kevin Rowland in 2022, screenshot from video for remix (above)

Dexys Midnight Runners in their *Too-Rye-Ay* era

The Swinging Cats

Jane Bayley: vocals
Billy Gough: drums
Paul Heskett: saxophone
Chris Long: vocals, percussion
Toby Lyons: keyboard

John Shipley: guitar
Steve Vaughan: guitar
Valerie Webb: vocals
Steve Wynne: bass

There are essentially three songs released by the Swinging Cats, and "released" is using the term loosely. Their most well-known song is an instrumental tune, a single released on the 2 Tone label called "Mantovani," though it is more like a catawampus calliope than ska. The B side of this single is a tune titled "Away," and it does feature a proper ska beat, a slower tempo, and the simple and unadorned vocals of Jane Bayley. The third song is a dash through the Connie Francis classic, "Never On A Sunday," and is only available as a video of a television performance on the BBC show filmed at Pebble Mill called *Look! Hear!*[422] Sung by Valerie Webb, this tune resists the ska beat but nonetheless catapults stage dancers into a frenzy, their hips and limbs flailing like inflatable tube men outside a used car lot. Of these three songs, one has no vocals, and the other two have their respective vocalists, which has caused some identification confusion over the years. Perhaps this is one reason that many online posts have only focused on the group's founder and most popular musician, John Shipley.

2 Tone author George Marshall wrote of the Swinging Cats that they "ended up going through more band members than England's had cricket captains,"[423] which has certainly made chronicling their history a challenge. But the band made a lasting mark on the 2 Tone era, having been signed to the label, featured on the second 2 Tone tour, and established fans that still remain today. Jane Bayley was the group's original vocalist. She was friends with John Shipley which led to her joining the group and she always had a background in music and the arts. "I was born in my Granny Lovatt's house in Leek in Staffordshire," she begins, "but from the age of four I lived and grew up in Coventry where my dad got a job in the car industry. My dad played boogie-woogie on the piano in the living room and made up little tunes and songs. There was always singing in the car—old songs and pop songs and our own variations. I liked putting in the harmonies. He sent us kids to piano lessons, but I was terrified of the piano and gave up as soon as I could!"[424]

Jane says that she was a fan of Bob Dylan, Joni Mitchell, and the Incredible String Band as well as "Sixties soul and pop." But she started performing music herself when encouraged by a dynamic teacher. "I played the songs of the day on my guitar

[422] "Swinging Cats." Hobo: A to Z of Coventry Bands. sites.google.com/site/bandsfromcoventry/coventry-bands-a-to-z/coventry-bands-s/swinging-cats. Accessed 27 Oct. 2020.
[423] Marshall, George. *The Two Tone Story*. S.T. Publishing, 1990, p. 64.
[424] Bayley, Jane. All quotations, unless otherwise noted, from interview with the author, 20 Nov. 2020.

and sang at folk clubs in Coventry with a school friend. We had a fabulous singing teacher at school, Mrs. Fitzsimons, who was straight out of college and got us singing challenging ancient and modern madrigals. She was a big influence on me." Another big influence was the Selecter's Pauline Black. "I remember Pauline giving me some hints about singing through a microphone and suggesting I take ginseng for energy!"

Since Jane performed in clubs in Coventry, she crossed paths with other musicians like Black, as well as members of the Specials. "The Specials were already established by a group of people I knew in Coventry and another friend, John Shipley, who had been in school with Jerry Dammers, was a fantastic guitar player. Jerry agreed to release on 2 Tone a song called 'Away' that John had written. John asked if I'd sing it and help him form a band. I introduced him to another friend, Toby, who was in art college in Coventry who played keyboards and had an ironic sense of humour and music. A young and talented bass player, Steve Wynne, had been playing with the Specials' drummer, John Bradbury, who I shared a house with at that time, and The Selecter's Neol Davies in a band called Transposed Men, and John asked him to join us. Billy Gough, a local young and energetic drummer agreed to play with us, and we were a band!" Each member of the band took a stage name: Steve Vaughan was "Vaughan Truevoice," Chris Long was "Craig Guatemala," Billy Gough was "Troy Corner," John Shipley was "Wayne Riff," Paul Heskett was "Vince Laredo," Toby Lyons was "Toni El Dorko," Valerie Webb was "Pussy Purrfect," and Jane Bayley was "Jane De La Swing."[425] As for the name of the band itself, Jane says, "Toby came up with the name, which reflected the kind of music we played—Sixties-influenced Latin pop tinged with ska." Shipley says the name the Swinging Cats was a result of the conditions in which they rehearsed. "We practiced in our drummer Billy Gough's garage, full of canoes and moose heads. There wasn't enough room to swing a cat, and a name was born."[426]

The group officially formed in 1978, according to Pete Clemons, and after some time practicing they entered the Battle of the Bands competition at Lanchester Polytechnic, better known as "The Lanch."[427] Clemons writes, "The prize for winning the competition had been a day's recording at Woodbine Studios in Leamington Spa," but that recording wasn't released until later in 1980 and by that time, the ska pendulum had begun to reverse its swing. Until then, though, the Swinging Cats continued to ride the wave and other 2 Tone bands were happy to have the support. According to George Marshall, "Although the band had a slight ska tinge to it, their biggest claim to a spot on 2 Tone was the fact that they played good time dance music. Ska, Latin, calypso, it was all there in a nostalgic cocktail mixed especially for the danceable Eighties. They also had something of a fetish for Sandy Shaw covers and theme tunes along the lines of the Avengers and Captain Scarlet. The sort of fun band

---

[425] "Swinging Cats." Hobo: A to Z of Coventry Bands. sites.google.com/site/bandsfromcoventry/coventry-bands-a-to-z/coventry-bands-s/swinging-cats. Accessed 27 Oct. 2020.
[426] Ibid.
[427] "From the Albert Hall to the Snooker Hall." 28 May 2020. coventrygigs.blogspot.com/2020/05/from-albert-hall-to-nothing-at-all.html. Accessed 27 Nov. 2020.

that would perhaps go down better at a student ball than a skinhead bash, and not surprisingly a band that had influenced Dammers' musak ideas. 'Hopefully the music stands up on its own as a variation on the 2 Tone theme,' said [Steve] Vaughan. 'I think people will obviously get into it because of the 2 Tone thing, but we hope that they'll take it for what it is after that.'"[428] The sound of the Swinging Cats was characterized by some fans as "easy listening ska."[429]

Dammers certainly had his hand in helping to shape the Swinging Cats, more so than just supporting their musical direction and by releasing their single on the 2 Tone label. He also had a connection to their second lead singer, Valerie Webb, who today is Valerie Haudiquet. Valerie says that she was engaged to Jerry Dammers, which is how she came to sing for the Swinging Cats. Born and raised in Coventry, Valerie grew up with the musicians who formed the backbone of the ska revival. "I was born in Earlsdon, Coventry. Lived there all my childhood. No one was particularly musical," she says of her family.[430] "Neither am I. But music entered my life obviously as I became a teenager. But music really entered my life when Jerry Dammers did. We met when I was 15 in a pub in Earlsdon. We were then together for seven years. So I suppose I was there to see him evolve from playing in some pretty awful bands into the creation of the 2 Tone label."

Valerie stepped into the role of lead vocalist when Jane Bayley stepped out. "The Swinging Cats was a favour to them as their vocalist had disappeared for some reason and they needed someone pronto. I had no experience, but a bit of confidence. I knew John Shipley from old. Jerry and he were at school together. I am only aware of a link on YouTube of us in 1980 on a programme called *Look! Hear!*—two songs, 'Away,' and 'Never On A Sunday.' Didn't know how bad I was till I saw that. Anyway, previous vocalist reappeared and so I went back to oblivion," she says.

This is the same reason why Jane left, she says. "Half-way through our short life, we listened to a live recording on tape and my singing sounded awful. We didn't know at the time that unless I had foldback and hear myself, I couldn't sing in tune. So they replaced me with Val, who was at the time Jerry's long-term girlfriend. But after a tour they'd been on, Val left, so they asked me to come back. I think we must've sorted out some foldback by then," Jane says. It would be extremely difficult to trace which vocalists and which musicians performed at specific shows, sans tour diary. But as a whole, the group performed both in support of other notable acts, and as a headliner at numerous shows throughout 1980.

Significant performances include the second 2 Tone tour when the Swinging Cats replaced Holly and the Italians in support of the Selecter in February 1980. They appeared along with the Bodysnatchers for the "2 Tone 'Pressure Tour' Package" as it was billed in the *Belfast Telegraph*. The following month they toured in support of the Mo-Dettes in March 1980, and that fall they headlined their own small tour in the

---

428 Ibid.
429 Brough Rex. "The Swinging Cats: 2 Tone Records." 2-tone.info/the-swinging-cats/. Accessed 27 Oct. 2020.
430 Webb, Valerie. All quotations, unless otherwise noted, from interview with the author, 18 Jan. 2021.

Midlands and in London. In September and October 1980, the Swinging Cats accompanied the Specials on their *More Specials* tour, appearing at the Hammersmith Palais, Mayfair Suite in Newcastle, and the Cambridge Supertent Show, among other venues.[431] Jane recalls one of the gigs when the Swinging Cats performed with Madness. "We were playing to a big crowd at the Electric Ballroom in London, supporting Madness, and we were in full swing when a friend of Toby's marched onto the stage from the wings and shouted at us for not putting him on the guest list!" she says.

The 2 Tone single, "Mantovani/Away" was recorded after Jane Bayley had returned to the lineup, therefore it is her voice that appears on the song "Away." The single didn't do well, unfortunately, and that combined with the violence at shows led to the band ultimately breaking up. "John reshuffled the band and I was replaced with Craig Guatemala, who was at college with Toby and used to dance and play percussion sometimes with the band," says Jane.

Horace Panter in his book, *Ska'd for Life*, notes that their tour with Craig Guatemala, whose real name was Chris Long, was memorable, but for the wrong reasons. Panter says that Long was singing on the Specials support gigs in September 1980 when audiences became violent. "Chris Long, the Swinging Cats' singer, was punched out by some local Neanderthal pretty much as soon as they got on stage. And this was before we'd gone on. The local security were overwhelmed. Faced with a 3,500-strong crowd, a fair percentage of whom were in a pretty belligerent mood, we basically played background music for fighting (headbutt muzak?). It was appalling," wrote Panter.[432] This violence was reported in the *Reading Evening Post* with the headline "Skinheads on the Rampage." Journalist Terry Kerr wrote of the event, "A mob of chanting skinheads went on a frightening rampage of violence during a Saturday night rock concert. They fought a pitched battle with security men in front of the stage at Bracknell Sports Centre and a young girl had to have treatment after a gang smashed her head against a lamp post. ... The first hint that the concert might erupt into trouble came during the performance by the support band, Swinging Cats. Security men leapt into the crowd from the stage as fights broke out and removed about half a dozen trouble-makers."[433] But one reader, a 12-year-old boy named Tom Thorn, wrote to the *Reading Evening Post* after the story ran to say he was at the show and though there was violence, the bands, including the Swinging Cats, should not be guilty by association. "During the Swinging Cats set, the Cats lead singer said: 'You've come here to hear bands, not have a fight.' The Cats said they wouldn't play, but after a few minutes said they would be generous and play. 'If you're NF, then why did you come to see the Specials.' The crowd gave a loud cheer," wrote Thorn.[434]

Adding to the violence and the constant reshuffling of singers and lineup, another compounding factor leading to the short life of the Swinging Cats was the

---

[431] From various newspaper advertisements via British Newspaper Archive.
[432] Panter, Horace. *Ska'd for Life: A Personal Journey with The Specials*. Pan Macmillan, 2007, p. 249.
[433] Kerr, Terry. "Skinheads on the Rampage." *Reading Evening Post*, 29 Sept. 1980.
[434] Thorn, Tom. "Skinheads 'rampage.'" *Reading Evening Post*, 6 Oct. 1980.

fact that their 2 Tone single just didn't sell well. The single "was eventually released in August 1980. The release of their debut, though representing a great step forward, did not fare well however, despite the first 20,000 copies being sold at the giveaway price of 50p."[435] They did have another song ready to go, and in fact it was recorded, but never pressed. It has never surfaced. It was to be the second release on 2 Tone as promised by their deal with the label. "The second planned single, 'Greek Tragedy,' was finally recorded with a roster of Rhoda Dakar on vocals, Chris Dickie (of Gods Toys) on bass, Rob Hill on drums, Jerry on keyboards, and John on guitar. Sadly, it never reached the pressing plant. 'Greek Tragedy,' however, did get a live outing during the Rock Against Racism gig at the Butts stadium in June '81."[436] The song was only heard by two people in the audience. Greek tragedy indeed.

The Swinging Cats split up and each member went their own direction. Craig Guatemala became a DJ, Steve Wynne joined Dexys Midnight Runners and other bands, Toby Lyons formed the Colourfield with Terry Hall, and Paul Heskett, who performed flute on "Ghost Town," became a member of the Specials playing saxophone, flute, and latterly string synth until they broke up in 1981. He has since performed with Hazel O'Connor and with Lynval Golding in Pama International. John Shipley became a member of the Special AKA and the Supernatrals, both bands featuring other members of the 2 Tone crew. He also performed with Heskett in a collaboration called Electrik Custard, and also joined with Valerie Webb, as she recalls. "Later I had a child and sang again with John Shipley in about 1987 in a band called Great Escape. We were good, but didn't last long sadly. I eventually left Coventry and now live on the coast in Norfolk. I miss Coventry like mad still. It will never be the same as it was then, sadly, but I still keep in touch with Jerry and John Shipley and Roddy Byers," she says.

Jane Bayley continued her career in music as well. "I moved to London and formed a band we called the Round-A-Way Wrong Chamber with my sister Leigh on clarinet, my partner Andre on trumpet, and his sister Francoise on vocals and keyboards. I sang and played the guitar and harmonium. We all wrote the songs together. I think they were great, but we didn't have a drummer and we never really played in time! But we did lots of gigs, though mainly around London, and brought out a single, 'Boy/yoB' on our own label, Wrong Records, which was played a bit on the radio, but we didn't have a manager or record company behind us and just sold the records at gigs. I've still got a box under the bed. After that, for years I played solo at festivals and arts centres around the UK, and had a lot of TV and press coverage when I performed at the Edinburgh Festival."

Jane's performances mix music and art and she has her own café, Bom-Bane's in Brighton, where she serves food and entertainment. "I write and sing songs and accompany myself on the harmonium. A number of songs have mechanical hats that

[435] Ibid.
[436] "From the Albert Hall to the Snooker Hall." 28 May 2020. coventrygigs.blogspot.com/2020/05/from-albert-hall-to-nothing-at-all.html. Accessed 27 Nov. 2020.

illustrate them. I use small motors, batteries, lights, and tiny pulleys. I make most of them myself," she says. The tables in the café also have mechanical features. "I either perform alone, or with Eliza Skelton who works and sings and plays with me at Bom-Bane's. Every year we write a new musical to perform at the café during the Brighton Festival," says Jane. She is divorced and has a son, Rudi. Together with school friends, Rudi founded his own band called Melodica, Melody and Me. "They were great, made a couple of singles and an album and toured all over America and Europe. Rudi now makes dance music and he DJs."

In 2010, the Swinging Cats reconvened for the 30th anniversary of 2 Tone celebrations in Coventry. Only John Shipley and Paul Heskett played from the original lineup. Jane says she has reconnected with Steve Wynne and they plan to perform gigs together in the future. She also states, "I've just made a double album 'Jane Bom-Bane's Songbook.' It's on Bandcamp and on the second album are different versions of two songs we did with the band."

Jane Bayley (left), photographed by Mark Osbourne, and Valerie Webb (right) on the *Look! Hear!* television show in 1980

The Friday Club

Terry Bateman: vocals, saxophone
Andrew Brooks: vocals, guitar
Eddie Eve: keyboard
Anton Hilton: drums

Michael Hodges: vocals, congos
Graham Whitby: bass
Adele Winter: vocals, vibes

It was 1985 and the sun was setting on the dawning of a new era. 2 Tone had two bands left in it, at this point—the Friday Club and J.B.'s Allstars—neither of which were ska. It seemed an almost impossible task to find commercial success on a label known for churning out ska acts five years prior without the support and energy of the 2 Tone juggernaut, but the seven members of the Friday Club took their chances. One might argue that they missed their window of opportunity, but they clearly made their mark on fans. Their single, "Window Shopping," sells for hundreds of dollars today and is coveted by collectors all over the world.

The Friday Club officially formed as a group in 1984, just one year before they recorded their single and supported Madness on their Mad Not Mad tour in the UK and Northern Ireland. Their core band was augmented on their recording by Al Elias on tenor sax and Tony Miller on trumpet. Their sound was categorized as northern soul since Andrew Brooks, one of the main songwriters, was a fan of northern soul and they had all grown up with northern soul sounds in the region. They formed after becoming friends in the town of Scarborough in Yorkshire, as Brooks recalls their origins. "The band was called the Friday Club as we had all met and formed friendships in the early eighties, on the big night out in Scarborough at that time, Friday night. The common ground between us all was that we were the local misfits. Scarborough was very tribal at that time (Punks, Goths, Mods, Soulies, Rockers)—none of us fell into any of the accepted categories—we bonded together very quickly," said Brooks.[437]

Adele Winter, whose name today is Adele Carden, was one of the two women in the band. She was born in August 1959. She recalls those days in her youth after leaving home at age 16, moving from York to Scarborough. Today she struggles to tell the story because her multiple sclerosis has advanced over the decades since she first started displaying symptoms and it greatly affects her speech. "I made friends with some people. They were going to all nighters. I got to know three or four people and they were starting a band and asked me if I wanted to be in it. You know there's another girl called Terry. I heard that she was playing saxophone but wanted to get another band. And so they all knew her. We really got on well and the way that we looked at things. I'm still best friends with Terry," she says.[438]

---

[437] Brooks, Andy. 2-tone.info/display/?123. Accessed 27 Aug. 2022.
[438] Carden, Adele. All quotations, unless otherwise noted, from interview with the author, 17 Feb. 2021.

The band built up a decent fanbase, playing at gigs in Scarborough, Leeds, Hull, Bridlington, and other northern towns. They then made the decision to move to London to pursue a larger platform for their music and they began playing at pubs and underground warehouse parties. According to author Lee Morris, Adele began a relationship with Harry Cooke who then managed the band and ran the illegal warehouse parties.[439] The band made demo tapes in order to try and land a label which proved successful. Brooks states, "In the summer of 1984 we were looking for producers to work with and we found out that Jerry Dammers lived just around the corner from where I (and most of the band) lived in Clapham. We dropped a demo cassette wrapped in a gig flyer through his door and much to our surprise Jerry came to the gig and offered us the opportunity to record a single for 2 Tone at the gig. 'Window Shopping' was recorded in September 1985 in Powerplant and Wessex Studios."[440]

Adele says that signing to 2 Tone was a dream come true. "We were in London doing well with gigs in London. We were meeting people and the partners in the band were all meeting people and what happened was, we all loved 2 Tone. We all loved 2 Tone, we really did."[441] Adele sang on "Window Shopping," and she also played the vibes. "They were used in the 40s and they are like a xylophone," she says, describing her instrument. "They're very spectacular. So we ended up using them and it's very difficult to carry around. And this particular set we got from the drummer's father. And then when we went to do the first recording with Jerry Dammers, we brought it into the studio."[442] Side B of "Window Shopping" is an all-instrumental version of the tune. Both were produced by Dammers.

The Friday Club then went on tour to promote their song and to support Madness during their Mad Not Mad tour. "It was a tour of the UK and Ireland," says Andrew Brooks. "It was 28 dates during October and November 1985. We got the tour because Jerry Dammers' manager had an office that was above Madness's manager's office and when they were looking for a support act for the tour. Jerry's manager [Pete Hadfield] mentioned to Madness's manager that Jerry had just signed a new band to 2 Tone. Madness had also been signed to 2 Tone so it all seemed to make sense. 'Window Shopping' was timed to release during the Madness tour to maximise on the exposure the Friday Club had by being on the tour." Though J.B.'s Allstars' "Alphabet Army" was released after "Window Shopping, the Friday Club's single was the last recorded by the 2 Tone label, securing it an important place in history, and possibly warranting the exorbitant cost to collectors.

Up until that point, Adele hadn't experienced any symptoms of her multiple sclerosis, but they soon began to manifest. She says, "I wasn't really having any problems. I had no idea. With MS you have remissions—long remissions where nothing happens whatsoever and you're normal. So, I was fit as a fiddle and then all

[439] Morris, Lee. *2 Tone: Before, During, & After*. Media House Books, 2020, p. 170.
[440] Brooks, Andrew. All quotations, unless otherwise noted, from interview with the author, 12 Aug. 2022.
[441] Carden, Adele. All quotations, unless otherwise noted, from interview with the author, 17 Feb. 2021.
[442] Ibid.

of a sudden, I'd be laid on the floor and couldn't get my foot to move. And I thought, what the hell is going on here. Then one time I was having panic attacks and had no clue what was going on."[443] Her friends also began to notice strange movement in her eyes. Shockingly, she says she wasn't diagnosed with multiple sclerosis until she was 39 years old.

"But in the meantime, the band was doing the tour, a fantastic tour," Adele says.[444] "Suggs wore a green suit and red gloves for much of the tour and had a thing about asking the audience to look under their seats, only to find nothing there—he loved it! As people, Madness were really friendly and supportive. Suggs, Cathal, and Lee were always making sure things were all right for us and reminding us that they started their first tour staying in tents. They gave away tickets to kids for their concerts, especially in Ireland. After performing in Cork, I was out front watching them when Suggs announced he had been helped back to his hotel after some lads found him collapsed drunk outside a local radio station! Immediately, this lad of about ten said to me, 'That was us, miss!'"[445]

Brooks concurs that the tour in support of Madness was successful for The Friday Club. "Touring with Madness has to be one of the high points of my life. We were so lucky to be playing in support of one of the greatest bands that England has ever produced and also lucky that they were the nicest guys you could ever possibly meet."[446] He continues, "One of the best memories I have of the Madness tour was a gig that Jerry Dammers came along to. The warmth and respect shown to him by the guys from Madness was truly touching to witness. They clearly had not forgotten that he had kick started their career."[447]

Unfortunately, "Window Shopping" didn't chart well, perhaps because Chrysalis, the parent company behind 2 Tone, didn't spend money to promote the song, according to drummer Anton Hilton.[448] Brooks says that it was also because the song was released during the holiday season which meant it had to vie with every other end-of-the-year release. "'Window Shopping' was rush released to take advantage of the Madness Tour support slot. This was a Chrysalis decision and not a view shared by Jerry [Dammers] who knew that any single released by a new band that late in the year would get buried amongst the Christmas releases. The single picked up some air play and entered the top 100 on the first week of release. Gary Crowley in particular played it a great deal, and we were very happy when Radio One's Simon Bates put it on his breakfast show play list. He then went on holiday and as Jerry had predicted the single got lost amongst the Christmas releases."[449]

---

[443] Carden, Adele. Southward Arts Forum, Boundless Event at Fashion & Textile Museum from 2011. m.youtube.com/watch?v=Nob6AeztQil. Accessed 5 Aug. 2022.
[444] Ibid.
[445] Reed, John. *House of Fun: The Story of Madness*. Omnibus Press, 2010.
[446] Morris, Lee. *2 Tone: Before, During, & After*. Media House Books, 2020.
[447] Brooks, Andy. 2-tone.info/display/?123. Accessed 27 Aug. 2022.
[448] Morris, Lee. *2 Tone: Before, During, & After*. Media House Books, 2020.
[449] Brooks, Andy. 2-tone.info/display/?123. Accessed 27 Aug. 2022.

It wasn't because of the onset of health problems or the lack of success of their single that the group split, but right after the tour, Graham Whitby, Anton Hilton, Terry Bateman, and Adele made the decision to leave, according to Lee Morris. But none of the members are willing to really say what exactly caused the separation. "To be honest," says Brooks, "I don't really want to get into the breakup of the band." Adele is also reluctant to give details. "There was myself and Graham and Terry. And myself and Terry wanted to continue but we didn't want to continue the lifestyle. We wanted to continue, but in order to continue we had to have the right instrumentation and the right attitude. Then things went wrong and Terry wanted to leave. I wanted too. And then I left. It's just horrible. We had a good few years, but it did take a turn," she says. Hilton says of the split, "The band just fell apart. We just split up. It was a real blow and we worked hard to get where we were. It was a sad moment being on a high from the amazing tour to splitting up soon afterwards."[450]

The Friday Club continued with fewer members and went on to perform on the Red Wedge Tour in 1986, according to Morris. They had long been involved in supporting workers' rights and the Labour Party, including gigs to benefit the Miners' Strike in 1984, and the Rock for Jobs concert in Liverpool where they were billed as "a soul band with a difference."[451] However, without the same momentum as the original full lineup, in 1988 they split for good. As for Adele and Terry, they continued, forming their own group. "I carried on and so did Terry. We were called the Northern Girls and we went to Scotland," she says.[452] Brooks says he saw them perform in early 1986 and "thought they were really great." Adele also recorded a solo album. "I played piano and wrote songs," she says. The songs came to me in the still of the night. I remember how it came to me because I'd sing about clearings in woods and I had a real thing about it. When I was little, we used to go into the forest and there was a clearing with grass and the sun would shine through the trees and I would write a song about it, about lying in the grass and feeling the ticking of the earth."[453]

Adele then transitioned from music to comedy writing. She explains her interest in the comedic arts and says this interest was inspired by her family. "My grandmother, she used to make me laugh so much. I can't remember when I thought of writing and speaking to people but I did. The quips and the anecdotes, I wanted to bring back what my grandma said and what her friends said."[454] She graduated from Thames Polytechnic with a degree in literature and also writes poetry. She served as director of the Southwark Disablement Association for a number of years before having to retire due to her health. Her advice to musicians is, "Have a special place for friends who will tell you the truth—they won't hurt you, but they'll tell you the truth. Any artist who is writing, singing, performing—ask your friends for comments

[450] Morris, Lee. *2 Tone: Before, During, & After*. Media House Books, 2020.
[451] *Liverpool Echo*, 5 Sept. 1985, p. 12.
[452] Carden, Adele. Southward Arts Forum, Boundless Event at Fashion & Textile Museum from 2011. m.youtube.com/watch?v=Nob6AeztQiI. Accessed 5 Aug. 2022.
[453] Carden, Adele. Southward Arts Forum, Boundless Event at Fashion & Textile Museum from 2011. m.youtube.com/watch?v=Nob6AeztQiI. Accessed 5 Aug. 2022.
[454] Ibid.

and how they feel about your work."[455] For Adele, that friend continues to be Terry who has been by her side from the beginning of the Friday Club.

The Friday Club from the sleeve of their 2 Tone single, "Window Shopping" with Adele Winter (left, sitting) and Terry Bateman (right, sitting)

---

[455] Ibid.

Press photo for the Friday Club, October 1985. Back row Anton Hilton, Eddie Eve, Andy Brooks; middle row Michael Hodges, Graham Whitby; front row Adele Winter, Terry Bateman

The Lemons

Paul Hookham: drums
Darryl Hunt: bass
Tammi Jacobs: vocals, trumpet

Paz Parris: keyboards
David Quinn: saxophone
Ian Roberts: guitar

The review in the *Record Mirror* in February 1981 said it all. "Imagine a bunch of high school kids as *MAD* magazine would have drawn them in the early sixties—all severe crewcuts and well-scrubbed faces. Then dress them up in starched white shirts, black dickiebows and matching canary yellow zoot suits. That was how the Lemons looked at the Greyhound. Distinctive, to say the least."[456] They dressed sharp, for sure, but their sound was also distinct in a sea of ska. The Specials drummer John Bradbury definitely took notice, signing them to his label, Race Records, in 1981. Critics took notice too. "The Lemons quite surpassed themselves," wrote one.[457] "They have a girl singer who is blessed with a powerful, versatile voice, but their music is alive and dynamic, instantly appealing," said another.[458] A third wrote, "The variety of their material still comes through, with every number surviving as an individual song rather than as part of a continuous dancing soundtrack...."[459] Certainly, the Lemons were destined for success. So why weren't they a ska household name like the Specials, the Selecter, or the Beat? Well, lead vocalist Tammi Jacobs says that she's afraid it might be all her fault.

Tamsen Jacobs, who today is Tammy Dixon and went by the stage name Tammi Jacobs, was born in Ilford, Essex, a county just outside of London. "It's sort of where the people from the East End, when they became a little more affluent, went out to live," Tammy says.[460] She had a brother who was 15 years older than her, and a sister 14 years older. "My father was Jewish and he was born and brought up in the East End of London, and I suppose you could say, bettered himself. My parents moved out to Essex and there was quite a strong, flourishing Jewish community in that particular area. And so that was where I was born and spent the first six years of my life. And so at the age of six my parents moved to Nottingham which is in the Midlands. My whole family went to be closer to my uncle."

Tammy says that her home was supportive of the arts and as such, she was exposed to many different types of performance. "I always loved to sing. And my mother sang as well. She wasn't a professional but once I got up to Nottingham, my mum thought it might be quite a nice idea if I took elocution lessons so that I could get up to the microphone, and then joined a dancing school and learned how to dance—specifically ballet. When I got to a certain age, well, around ten, my mother

[456] De Whalley, Chas. "The Lemons: Greyhound, London." *Record Mirror*, Feb. 1981.
[457] Ibid.
[458] Swayne, Karen. "You put your left boot in, you put your left boot out." *Sounds*, Aug. 1981.
[459] *Time Out*, Jan. 1981.
[460] Dixon, Tammy. All quotations, unless otherwise noted, from interview with the author, 27 June 2021.

recognized that I was spending a lot of time outside of school attending dance classes and basically I'd go to school during the day and then I'd go home for something really quickly, and then I'd spend up until ten o'clock at night at the dance school, and this was something like four nights a week. And I loved it, don't get me wrong. There was no show biz push here from my mom, but I loved it. And so I think on advice from, and guidance also, she looked at whether or not I should be attending a stage school—what we in England call the stage school, where I'd get a rounded education but I would also be taught in lots of different disciplines—the arts of theatre, basically. And I auditioned at the tender age of 10 for the Royal Ballet School, which was quite a thing in those days. And so I attended the Royal Ballet School three years until they decided that perhaps I was a little bit too independent for the cour de ballet. So that basically means that when everybody else had to turn right, I always wanted to turn left," she says, laughing. "So, I was dispatched from the Royal Ballet School. However, it was the best thing that anybody could have done for me, really, because I then went on to a school called the Arts Educational School, which was much more broad in its training. So we did learn everything. We learned all of stagecraft, dancing, acting, singing, different styles of dance. And I finished off my schooling with the Arts Educational School, but in rural Hertfordshire, but also I went to the London School. And that's how I sort of got into the London scene, really."

It was 1976 and London was a hotbed of creative activity. At the age of 16, Tammy found herself right in the middle of the action. "I'm not going to mention any names, but when I was in London, we were a pretty hedonistic crowd, even at a young age. And not only that, we were theatrical. So you can imagine, it was amplified several times over again. And as one or the other of us left the art school, we started to find work. My very first professional job, I suppose you could say, as an adult was in a film called *Quadrophenia*," Tammy says, as if one has never heard of the iconic film. "Yes, yes, I had a very small small part. I keep it quiet. I'm ashamed," she says, though it's not apparent why, as she produces the tale of her character and securing the role with a bit of nostalgia and joy.

"I was going out with an actor. He was a fellow student with myself and we were in the same crowd and he got a part in the film. And he happened to mention to the casting director about me and that I was also an actress. So I got carted off to, I don't know, Wardour Street in Soho, London somewhere and I had to go in and say something and say hello, then I never heard anything else. The next thing I knew was I got a phone call saying you need to come and have a costume fitting. And I went, 'really?' I got this part and it's an extra—it's an extra with words. So I played my boyfriend's girlfriend in the film, as well as in real life. And I am in it all the way through, I'm just not one of the leads. There's a small scene where I feature, but I pop up all over the place because in real life we were all a gang, and in the film we were all a gang," says Tammy.

Quadrophenia, of course, is the Roger Daltry-produced cult-classic film about all things mod—scooters, parkas, speed, and rivalries with other subcultures. Tammy played the girlfriend of Spider, portrayed by Gary Shail. The film starred Toyah

Willcox who at that time was a bigger star than the film's other celebrity, Sting. Toyah began acting as a young runaway, first appearing in a BBC production followed by the punk film *Jubilee* by Derek Jarman. At the same time Toyah led her own band and she has had a very successful career in both acting and music. She also appeared in *The Corn is Green* with Katharine Hepburn and has released dozens of albums and countless singles up through today.[461]

When Tammy is asked if she can remember a few of her lines, she responds, "I think they were small ones. You probably have to refer to the film. There was no script. It was very much improvised and a development-type piece. I'm sure that some of it was scripted to keep the boundaries where they should be, otherwise it could go on forever. And I think there were a couple of expletives, probably some stuff like, 'Hiya!' and all this sort of thing. There was a little bit of that and a lot of falling off motor, motor, what were those damn things we had? Scooters! Horrible things. But anyway, that finished and it did lead me on to get other work, which was quite good. Of course, you can imagine at the time, we had no idea how *Quadrophenia* would be received. We didn't. We were kids. We were young. We took the money. We had a good time. We went to the next job. So we didn't think about that."

Tammy and Gary Shail broke up during the filming, as Shail recalled in an interview years later. "Franc [Roddam, director] noticed my girlfriend Tammy, who'd come with me for moral support and offered her the part of my on-screen bird. She eventually dumped me though, ironically for one of the Rockers who beat me up," Shail says.[462] The relationship with this member of the fictional rival gang would lead to the next step in Tammy's life putting her in proximity to the music scene in London and leading to her involvement in the Lemons. Sometimes, life is circuitous and serendipitous. "I met somebody else that was in the cast who I also eventually started to live with, and it was from there, living with him across the road from the Hope and Anchor—and there's the link you see—I met Ian Roberts because I used to drink in the pub. But I ended up working there and Ian worked there, and he heard me singing on the stairs once," she says. That small warbling led Tammy to sing for the band that Ian and "the boys," as she calls them, were putting together. "The band hadn't yet formed. I think it was being brought together in Ian's mind. He asked me and I probably just said, 'oh, yeah, whatever,' you know, a couple of pils, lager, and whatever you want. It's a lark. It was great!" she says.

Ian Roberts may have assembled and managed the success of the Lemons, but it was through the Hope and Anchor that this success was possible. The band formed in late 1979 and had their first gig in early 1980 at the Hope and Anchor. "We were very lucky we were in the bosom of the landlord at the Hope and Anchor at that time. He had one of the best music venues definitely in London, if not in the country. I mean, the extraordinary talent that went through there, we were blessed that he was

[461] Thompson, Elizabeth and Giovanni Dadomo. *New Women in Rock*. Delilah/Putnam, 1982, p. 4.
[462] "Suit Yourself Interview Quadrophenia's Gary 'Spider' Shail." suityourselfmodernists.com/gary-spider-shail. Accessed 6 Aug. 2022.

able to give us the gigging slots that we actually got, and we started to build the following that way. But rehearsals, we'd rehearse wherever we could afford in the best possible sort of places. We were a pretty eclectic mix. So Ian, he was band leader. This was his baby. He wrote the songs and he was the intellectual driving force behind the band. There is no doubt about that. The saxophonist was a chap called David Quinn and as I recall, he was in the banking world and he just had an interest in playing the sax. He wasn't a professional musician. And actually, he was a friend of somebody and they asked him in. There was Darryl [Hunt] and he went on to play with the Pogues. He was our bassist and had been in several successful bands but had never quite broke the surface. Darryl was great fun, loads of experience, and then I think he introduced us to Paz Parris, who was our keyboard player. I'm not quite sure where Paz came from in respect to his music legacy. And then there was wonderful Paul Hookham on the drums who was the most gorgeous gorgeous man and so terribly sensible," says Tammy.

Surrounded by five professional and gentlemanly men, Tammy was the visual leader, the vocal leader, and the centerpiece of the band. She explains, "So I'm basically drawn into this fantastic group of men who treated me like a princess and they gave me the opportunity to shine because they were putting me on a stage in the front. Now, there are not many girls that can say that's what happened—well, now they can—but in those days, I never thought, 'oh this is quite rare to have me as a front person. This is a rarity.' I never thought that. I just thought, 'I'm doing this and it's great.'"

As for the appearance of the Lemons, the "starched white shirts, black dickiebows and matching canary yellow zoot suits,"[463] Tammy says that was a large part of their presentation—a polished, professional look. "I will say this, and this has always stuck with me—my beautiful dresses, I have two beautiful dresses and the boys have beautiful lemon suits, which were all tailor made for them. And it was great. And it was David Quinn who financed that for the band. And I remember being taken down to Kings Road to have a look for stuff to wear. I would never have been able to afford that in '81. I was 21 years of age and an out-of-work actress, so to be able to do that is extraordinary."

Tammy says that the business part of the band was handled by the others and she was along for the wonderful ride. "They sorted it all out," she says of signing to Race Records. "I just went and sung. They picked me up, dropped me off, I sang and I went home again. And it was brilliant. It was just a brilliant time. I don't remember actually recording the single. It was 'My Favourite Band,' which was our A side ["English Summer" on the B side] and I was just in blissful ignorance. I just went along with it, you know?" Race Records released five singles during its short one-year life including those by artists Nightdoctor, Team 23, the People, and the Lemons. According to musician and writer Marc Wasserman, John Bradbury who founded Race Records, launched the label in February 1981 at the Hope and Anchor with a

---

[463] De Whalley, Chas. "The Lemons: Greyhound, London." *Record Mirror*, Feb. 1981.

show of two of his signed bands—Nightdoctor and Team 23.[464] The People was a band comprised of Charley Anderson and Desmond Brown, who had just left the Selecter, along with Silverton Hutchinson, original drummer for the Specials and drummer for Machine (see also Machine chapter).

There were other songs that the Lemons performed live, but they have only the one record to their credit. They performed gigs regularly at the Hope and Anchor as well as at Chats Palace, at the Royal Veterinary College, the Rock Garden, the Marquee, Dingwalls, and the Fulham Greyhound, to name a few. They performed rhythm-and-blues-tinged tunes like "This Little Girl's Gone Rockin'" and "Down in the Alley." Other songs included "Chance," "Club Mexico," and "The Girl Next Door," noted a review from an August 1981 show that also lauded Tammy's performance. "It was difficult for the five blokes not to fade into insignificance because vocalist Tammy Jacobs has such a powerful stage presence. She sings with a completely natural charm and ad-libs and wise-cracks throughout. It was clear that she was going to enjoy herself whatever the audience reaction," wrote the reviewer.[465]

Tammy says she felt a bit anxious about being on stage, though she seemed to compensate quite well. "I was never very good at remembering the words. I would always have to have the words in front of me. So they were always down by the monitor at the front of the stage. I was never overconfident about remembering the words, which is ridiculous. But it was a blissful time, a peaceful time where I didn't have anything, but I didn't need anything and all I wanted to do was art. The whole scene was amazing. I mean, I will mention that the house I was living in at the time was sort of a bit of a drop-in for Madness. We were all connected. My partner at the time, his brother was a roadie for Madness and they started out at the Hope and Anchor. The whole scene was going on at the time so, you know, they were there. They got bigger before we ever did much," Tammy says.

Why didn't the Lemons do much? Well Tammy certainly thought they would, as she tells of a time when it seemed the opportunities might come rolling in. "I remember being interviewed for BBC Radio 1 for their lunchtime slot, and it was a DJ called Peter Powell and if you were invited to speak in that slot as an up-and-coming band, it was almost like, that was it. You'd made it because if you were being interviewed on national radio, on the premier music station people would be listening to your music. I don't know what happened after that—why it didn't take off more than it did."

That's when Tammy made the decision to leave the Lemons. She still feels torn about that decision, though it was many decades ago now. "Well, I left because it was—well, I'm not really sure. I mean, music was my life, but for Ian and the rest of the band, it was even more important than that. And I regret I didn't take it more seriously. But my life took a turn and I went in a different direction. I was still acting

[464] Wasserman, Marc. "Race Records—John Bradbury's Record Label Releases Single by Ex-Selecter Members." 21 Sept. 2008. Marco on the Bass. marcoonthebass.blogspot.com/2008/09/race-records-john-bradburys-record.html. Accessed 28 June 2021.
[465] Swayne, Karen. "You put your left boot in, you put your left boot out." *Sounds*, Aug. 1981.

and continued to act. But you know, my life took a turn where I spent a couple of years out—nothing macabre or dark or sinister—it's just where my life went. I ended up in another part of London living a slightly different life, which eventually it didn't suit me and I needed to get back to my acting and my music. Ian assures me that it wasn't my fault that the band didn't quite make that spark, with the musical hierarchy or with the public or whatever. I think we'd have probably been embraced at that time, but he thinks that the band was fizzling out by that time anyway. And he assured me it wasn't my fault that it ended. I just hope that's not the case. I would be mortified to think it was. You know, you just get on with life and that's one of those things. It was a missed opportunity, but that's life." The Lemons played their last gig on November 16, 1981 at the Whisky-A-Go-Go on Wardour Street.[466]

After returning to her pursuit of acting, Tammy moved from London to Darbyshire and joined a theatrical agency based in the Midlands, carrying on "as a jobbing actress" as she puts it, "working in repertory theater, pantomime, all sorts of things. And then I suppose the next big thing that happened to me, and it was a big thing that happened to me, was I auditioned for the musical *Cats*. Cameron Mackintosh, who is the producer of *Cats*, was putting on a tour of the musical, taking it out into the regions, and I auditioned and I got it. I didn't get a part as a cat, but interestingly enough, I got a part as a singer to, what they called and they probably still use, a booth singer. So there would be four singers with the orchestra, behind the scenes, so we'd be singing all of the parts in order to be able to allow the dancers who all sang live, but it was mixed into the mix, and it just gives a bit of body to these extraordinary young people who are throwing themselves around the stage. And I absolutely loved every minute of it. I loved it. I sang however many shows a week. We went to Blackpool for six months, then I went to Edinburgh, and finally we ended up in Dublin, which was absolutely marvelous. It was almost a year and then one had to move on. I then auditioned for *Les Miserables* in the West End and I spent almost three years in that production playing all sorts of parts. And after that I did a musical called *Which Witch*. It was awful but it was full of marvelous talent and we had a ball."

Tammy continued acting, including productions of *the Snow Queen*, *Sugar and Spice*, *Death of a Salesman*, *the Beggar's Opera*, *Pravda*, and *Great Expectations*. She also continued to perform, even after she became a mother. "It's a mad life. It's a mad life," she says before launching into her next story. "I got pregnant whilst I was in *Which Witch*, and so when they closed the show, which they did, believe me, after only three months, I didn't go back to the theater until I'd had my son. But then I was given an offer I couldn't refuse. One of the cast of *Les Miserables*, which was still running in the West of London, had to take some time off. So I was invited back to take one of the principal roles just for three weeks while they were off. It was Madame Thenardier. In 'Keeper's Wife,' they're the comedy. It's not a glamorous role, but it was fun and I adored it. I loved playing that part and it was great. And then I suppose what happened after that was that I thought that motherhood was quite good fun. My

466 Roberts, Ian. Facebook post, 16 Nov. 2021.

last professional engagement was for a gala performance to celebrate Cameron Mackintosh, and everybody was in it—Julie Andrews was in it, Bernadette Peters was in it—my absolute idol, I mean, she's the most sensational performer, and it was just a celebration of Cameron Mackintosh's productions. And he brought us all together. And on the final performance, Her Majesty the Queen and God bless his soul, His Royal Highness Prince Philip attended the performance and it was magical."

Tammy left acting behind, at that point, saying that she "decided that was that. I couldn't top that." She next became a fitness instructor, "which isn't too far removed from dancing." She has served in this capacity for the past 20 years, working for the British Army as a civil servant. "And that's where I've been ever since and I've loved every minute of it," she says. She and her husband live in Wiltshire, having met during work for *Les Miserables*. Her husband was a sound engineer and their son, Oliver Dixon, is a professional drummer living in London doing session work. "He has toured with various bands. He's in a couple of bands at the moment and he is musical to the core," she says. Oliver recently gifted Tammy with a recording that touched her more deeply than anything in her life. "My husband said to me on Christmas morning, 'Come and listen to this,' and then he starts playing it, 'My Favourite Band.' And I said, 'Why are you playing this to me on Christmas morning? It's my single.' And he said, 'Listen to it, Tammy.' So I listened and then I started to hear slightly different notes being played and I thought, 'Whoa!' My son had listened to it, and listened to it, and he brought a load of musicians together and did the cover version and it was mind blowing!"

Reflecting, Tammy Dixon says she is incredibly grateful to have had her time in the spotlight with the Lemons. "We played in good places, we played in bad places. It gave me a practical education on how to deal with an audience. It was something that, though I probably didn't see it at the time, nor in subsequent years of performance, as the most enriching apprenticeship that one can ever have. I was playing in front of these people that were all jumping up and down and doing the most bizarre things, and you had a control. There was a connection which you don't get anywhere else. I'd been on West End theater for years and you still don't get that connection on a big scale, but on a small scale they hang on your every note. And it teaches you that connection. And even when you're on a much larger forum or big arena, if you can just remember the eye contact, even if it's with someone in the first row of the audience, it can make their lives completely different because they come to see magic. And I learned that in the band. The Lemons hold a huge place in my heart."

Tammi Jacobs in *Quadrophenia* (above) and with the Lemons (below), photo by Jon Blackmore and Nick Pawlak, courtesy Ian Roberts

The Mood Elevators

David Ditchfield: guitar
Noel Green: bass
Jenny Jones: drums

They were called "an attractive three-piece with a girl drummer"[467] in newspaper articles, as if a "boy drummer" had ever been identified outside of a Christmas carol. They were also called "Beat buddies,"[468] with "that certain je ne sais quoi."[469] Their sound is not quite ska, but not *not* ska, which is why they appealed to the Beat who took them on tour, and took them into the studio, signed to the Beat's own label, Go Feet.

That "girl drummer," Jenny Jones, says that she grew up knowing she wanted to become a musician. She just didn't know how to make it happen—that is, until she was empowered, like so many others, by the punk movement. "I was born to a working-class family in a semi-rural suburb of outer Birmingham," says Jenny.[470] My childhood environment, its geography, sharply defined what seemed to me possible in life. An odd clash of rural fields next to high rise blocks of flats and a concrete shopping centre. It was a world of low-paying jobs, limited opportunities. The period, a time before the Internet, shaped a social environment where sexism was mainstream in a way that would seem shocking now, but was normal then. Feminism was something that barely registered in the ordinary world of my formative years. My parents owned a small hardware shop, and we lived in the flat above the shop. They didn't prioritise education, so I didn't really engage much with school. Instead, their lives were driven by a strong, practical work ethic, and growing up, I shared my childhood with an endless stream of shop customers and endless evening trips to the wholesale cash and carry warehouses to restock the shelves."

Jenny continues, "But then in my early teens, I had two deep realisations that eventually changed the course of my life. I don't know where these insights came from as they were not rooted in my day-to-day world and I had no idea what I hoped or expected to happen when I took action. I just knew with a passion that they were two things I had to do. First, out of the blue, I had an epiphany about animal welfare issues. And in that moment, I knew I would never eat meat or fish again. I never have to this day. In this period, in my working-class world, going 'vegetarian' (and eventually vegan) was unheard of, so this newfound moral stance proved to be a huge personal challenge in many ways. The second thing that happened was a sudden desire, a passion, to be a musician, to produce notes, chords, songs, not just listen to it on the radio. My family had inherited an old upright piano and I loved playing it.

---

[467] *North Wales Weekly News*, 3 Sept. 1981.
[468] Aitken, Brian. "Pop Talk." *Aberdeen Evening Express*, 6 May 1982.
[469] Fulton, Roger. "The Mood Elevator." *Harlow Star*, 16 Apr. 1981, p. 13.
[470] Jones, Jenny. All quotations, unless otherwise noted, from interview with the author. 11 Jan. 2023.

I'd spend hours picking out the melody lines from my favourite pop tunes by ear and pestered my parents to let me have piano lessons. Eventually, they let me. That was my big mistake."

The reason Jenny says that piano lessons were a mistake is because it took the fun out of music for her. She felt that playing classical music was "tortuous" and she says she lacked the cultural context to appreciate them. What she really wanted to do was join a band and play pop music. "I wanted to join a band, because music seemed full of promise and opportunity. You could see it in the faces of the musicians on *Top of the Pops*. They looked like they lived a rarefied, magical existence, lives lived to their fullest. I just had to figure out how to overcome the obvious limitations—the pre-internet, pre-streaming, pre-digitised, pre-women-in-music limitations and get past the powerful gatekeepers of popular culture—Radio One and Top of the Pops. All the 'real' musicians were men, white males, long-haired turbo-charged axe-wielding metal heads, permed pop musicians or lanky-haired, preoccupied-looking prog rock virtuosos playing complicated concept pieces with obscure meanings. Birmingham was the epicentre of the heavy metal movement. There seemed no obvious way to gain entry to this exclusively male world."

"Then punk happened. Suddenly the energy of my entire world felt utterly different. The week that the Sex Pistols were at number two in the British pop chart, almost everything else in the top 10 was a novelty song or throwaway pop. A gap had opened, offering the possibility of experiencing a new reality that broke through the constraints of 'normal' social convention. It felt really scary, but something about punk made me feel alive and empowered. Gone were the teenage mags, *Fab 208* and *Jackie*. Now I had something far more dangerous—a new bible called the *New Musical Express* (NME). And the upcoming punk bands started to play at Barbarellas Club in Birmingham city centre. I saw the Adverts, X-Ray Spex, the Clash. And as I watched them all and marvelled, an idea took shape, because for the first time, I felt a sense of possibility, of hope, a vision of what I wanted to do. This wasn't complicated. If they could do it, so could I. Didn't matter that I was a girl. Didn't matter than I wasn't a virtuoso musician. I had a plan," says Jenny.

"I don't remember the exact moment I decided to focus on playing drums. But when the idea took hold, it was bone deep, as though I'd always had it. The clarity of my vision felt thrilling. I would play the drums. I loved the power and exhilaration in the imagined physicality of it. And I had a plan how to get my drums too. I saved my wages from a Saturday job in a local newsagent's shop to buy my very first drum kit, a second-hand, five-shell purple Shaftsbury drum kit, salvaged from someone's shed. I managed to get the dismantled drum kit home and after my parents had shut the shop for the night, I laid out all the parts on the shop floor. I had no idea what any of the components were or how it all went together, and it took me ages to figure out how to set the snare stand up. Even longer to assemble the very complicated foot pedal. Then, slowly, I taught myself to play by pounding along to my brothers' prog rock record collection night after night in my parents' shop after hours. 'Crash, bang, thwack.' Each evening, I couldn't wait for the shop closing time so I could begin. I have no idea how the neighbours coped with the noise. They never said anything but I have a pang of guilt whenever I remember it to this day. I had no idea how to play so I listened to each record and picked out the drums by ear and stumbled slowly into the dexterity required to coordinate two hands and two feet simultaneously. At first, I just hit the hit hats and snare, because that was all I saw drummers hitting when they mimed on *Top of the Pops*. It took a few weeks to realise that the bass drum pedal was there for a reason, it wasn't just a foot rest. It was the dull thud I could hear on records. It was for hitting the bass drum. 'Thud thud thwack. Thud thud thwack.' I could now play a proper beat."

Jenny was now ready to join a band—or at least a punk band. Which is exactly what she did. "In March 1978, a local fledgling punk band called Red Alert, placed an advert in the *Redditch Advertiser* freebie newspaper, 'Drummer and guitarist wanted. Influences, Clash, Sex Pistols. No hippies!' I turned up for the audition with my kit and my beat. The singer and bass player loved the fact that I played loud and hard, so did the newly recruited guitarist, my soon-to-be lifelong friend David Ditchfield. David was the best musician in the band with a cool Purple Burns guitar which he would use to thrash out his three-chord punk riffs. But this was punk—the songs fast and raw and I felt equal to any of the musicianship of my male bandmates. We were an odd bunch, but it was a great energy while it lasted. Red Alert fizzed in and out of existence in a matter of months. We only did a handful of gigs, but the energy of being a part of a radical new subculture in 1978 felt exciting. Punk felt like a seismic social change in our city backwater and we felt like a gang, a shared punk identity, and our new gang regularly went out to gigs to see other bands."

It was while seeing one of these other bands that the gang received creative inspiration for a new group. Jenny says, "One night, we all went to see the Clash at the Birmingham Top Rank venue. They were amazing. But the support band were something else—a Midlands band who called themselves the Coventry Automatics. Terry Hall, the lead vocalist, had floppy hair. The other musicians wore a rag bag mixture of clothing and their sound wasn't unique in any stand-out way. They'd do a punk influenced song, then a song that seemed inspired by the Clash. But the Coventry Automatics seemed different. They had something distinct from all the punk bands around them and it wasn't just to do with the fact that they were the first truly multi-racial band I'd ever seen at a gig. It was because in their embryonic sound, their confidence, self-belief, you could tell they had potential, a sense of possibility, the hint of becoming something bigger than the sum of their parts. And it was a restless energy that said change was coming, punk was evolving into something else. Red Alert was over."

She continues, "The Coventry Automatics really inspired something in me and David, but it wasn't yet fully formed. We stayed in touch after Red Alert and even jammed together, but we still hadn't consolidated our sense of change into anything meaningful. It felt like a waiting period, a time when you knew what you didn't want to sound like but you couldn't quite put your finger on how you did want to sound. It was as though we were waiting for some genuine inspiration to take hold. That

215

inspiration came on one warm spring evening in April 1979, when we saw the same band playing another gig in a Students Union Hall in Aston University—only by now, they'd changed their name to the Special AKA and that night, we knew we were seeing something really special. When I think back to that event, it seemed like the venue was almost empty—a big hall with only around 30 to 40 people milling around on the dark dancefloor in front of the stage. But now, Terry Hall's hair was as charismatic as his deadpan delivery, the band had the sneering attitude of punk and the Special AKA had a sound that seemed entirely new. That night was our first experience of hearing ska and rocksteady rhythms driving memorable songs about social issues and it was unlike anything we'd heard before. It was electric. A couple of months later, David heard their single 'Gangsters' played on BBC Radio One. You knew it was going to happen."

"Inspired by what we'd seen and heard, David started putting together some songs, urgent, pacey, edgy songs which suited my fast, frenetic self-taught drumming style and we recruited a childhood friend of David's to play bass [Noel Green]. We rehearsed in my parents' shop at night, and we named ourselves the Mood Elevators," Jenny says. According to David Ditchfield, they then recorded a demo with the aid of a friend who funded it for them. "We met this guy called Mike Horseman, who called himself a friend of the stars. He knew everybody around Birmingham and he kind of took us under his wing. And he said, 'I want to put you guys in the studio and record a demo tape' and he offered to pay for it. It was a ridiculously small amount of money because it was a tiny studio and it was owned by this guy called Bob Lamb who also lived in Birmingham. Now Bob Lamb recorded UB40's first album in this studio, which is unbelievable. When we arrived, this guy Mike, we met him and he took us to the doorway and we went in and Bob Lamb was still in bed. His bed was literally above the mixing desk, so it was what we call a bedsit in the UK—you live in one room. So we did this demo and it was great. It was like a four-track machine, so it was very, very small, but the sound that Bob Lamb got was really cool. And that was that."[471] The demo tape was recorded February 13th and 14th, 1980 at Highbury Studio where just five months early Lamb had also recorded Duran Duran's demo tracks.[472]

Shortly after that, the Mood Elevators were ready to perform live. "Our first gig in April 1980 was a support slot, opening for a popular reggae band called Reality," says Jenny. "The venue was the infamous and cool Barrel Organ pub venue in Digbeth, Birmingham. And instead of doing a conventional 'gig' poster to advertise our slot, we fly-posted a flyer around town—an image of the three of us sat in Noel's mum's open-top Triumph Herald car, a huge full moon behind us as we appeared to float in space. No words, no gig listing, nothing other than our name as a small logo by the car. It didn't advertise the gig, it advertised us as a creative force and we fly-posted it everywhere. And that's how the Beat became aware of us."

[471] Ditchfield, David. All quotations, unless otherwise noted, from interview with the author, 6 Feb. 2021.
[472] "Duran Duran 1979 Demos." soundcloud.com/duranduranitalia/sets/duran-duran-1979-demos. Accessed 15 Dec. 2022.

The Mood Elevators became protégé to the Beat, though they certainly held their own. But the Beat had already established themselves, whereas the Mood Elevators had not, as Jenny explains. "At that time, the Beat were huge. They'd already had a hit single with 'Tears of a Clown' on the 2 Tone label and were just entering the UK charts with 'Mirror in the Bathroom' on their own Go Feet label. So, when we got a phone call on the morning of our debut support gig from the Beat's co-manager Jane, asking if 'the boys' could be put on our guest list as they'd like to see us play, we were blown away. She explained that the band had seen our homemade flyers and were intrigued. The gig was crowded that night. Even though we were the support band, in those days, most people turned up right from the start. I can still remember seeing the Beat walk in through the pub door and all the heads in the crowd turning round in shock. These guys were on *Top of the Pops* the week before, and now they were making their way through the packed small crowd towards the front as we thrashed out one of David's edgy, 100mph songs. They watched as we played. We went down well, blasted through a quick encore, then loaned the Beat our gear so they performed a couple of songs to the huge delight of the packed crowd. Then they disappeared."

"The following day, we had another phone call. It was Jane again. More surprises. She said, 'The boys really liked your set,' and asked if we'd like to open for the Beat at Aylesbury Friars in a couple of weeks' time. We'd barely started gigging and there we were, being offered a support slot on the opening night of a UK sell-out tour. It felt insane, wonderful, exciting. I borrowed £200 to buy a better drum kit—a Yamaha, five-shell, white, shiny, almost new, and some spare drumsticks. A friend with an old transit van drove us to the Aylesbury gig. I don't remember much of it. I think I was frozen with fear and completely blown away by the surreal experience of playing to a sell-out crowd of nearly two thousand very excited people. I'd had no experience of sound engineers, technicians, guitar roadies, drum roadies, miles of on-stage cabling, leads, songlists taped to huge monitors, and most startling of all, huge lighting rigs with blinding spotlights that illuminated the three of us on stage, like rabbits in headlights. I remember counting in each song, my drumsticks clicking the tempo, but far too fast as I was so nervous. But I also remember a sense of awe at being in that place at that time, being able to do what I was doing. I'd never imagined anything like this was possible for someone like me," Jenny says.

"After our gig, I remember standing at the side of the stage watching the Beat play. They were amazing to see live at this stage of their career, Everett Morton's persistent, driving rhythms; David Steele's relentless, looping basslines; Andy Cox's urgent choppy rhythm guitar; Dave Wakeling's edgy singing; Ranking Roger's toasting; and the self-possessed charisma of Saxa. And we had the best view of all, stood at the side of the stage. Apparently, we went down well that first night, so the Beat and their management offered us more and more support gigs on the rest of the UK tour—huge venues, everywhere sold out—Birmingham Top Rank, Bristol Locarno. They kept coming in. Then we were offered the London show at the Rainbow along with the Belle Stars, which was amazing. And from the first night onwards, the Beat generously invited us to travel in their minibus and kindly put us up in their hotel each night, paying all our accommodation and touring expenses."

David Ditchfield says that Jenny was an incredible drummer and everyone noticed. "There was a lot of percussion in there as well, in her style. She wasn't just using the bass drum, hi-hat, and snare. She was putting in all sorts of syncopated rhythms in. She was great. I remember we did one gig in London and there was a band called the Belle Stars and they tried to poach Jenny. They turned to the Beat and said, 'Oh, we want her in the band.' They were really courteous. They came up and told us that, you know, 'we want to tell you first.' And so I was going, 'Jenny, you should take it!' Because the Belle Stars were taking off at that point. 'Go for it!' Yeah, she was approached by a few different bands because her of her style and at that point there weren't many female drummers around."

But Jenny wasn't interested in leaving. She was devoted to the Mood Elevators who were her friends, and familiar in an unfamiliar environment. "It was an intensely exciting time and my old world, with its limited opportunities, was being replaced by new possibilities and new challenges," says Jenny. "As I watched Everett Morton play night after night on tour, my drumming definitely improved. But on a personal level, the touring experience brought the limitations of my old world more sharply into focus. Most of the people involved in the tour had a way of speaking, a vocabulary, tastes, clothing, mannerisms, a type of cultural knowledge that signalled they were part of a particular social class that was very distinct from mine. Their heads may have been shaved but underneath, they had nice middle-class backgrounds. And even though we all shared the excitement about being a part of a sell-out tour, it was the first time I'd really got to know such people and it was the first time I first noticed feeling a sense of 'lack' in my own education and cultural awareness. Take the food for example. I quickly learned that when successful bands go on tour, they have professional caterers, trained chefs who cook and prepare fresh food for all the musicians and crew. And on this tour, the chefs served us a kind of food I'd never seen before. In my working-class upbringing, I'd become used to being 'the problem vegetarian,' typically offered a frozen cheese pizza as the only non-meat choice. But these vegetarian options were incredible, with exotic, delicious, complex ingredients I'd never seen before. This was a whole new social environment where vegetarianism was accepted without problem or judgement—I just had to learn what all these new exotic ingredients were."

Jenny was certainly gaining an education on many levels and was undeterred by the differences. The heavy gigging had proven that the band was ready to record and the Beat took notice once again. "After the tour finished, the Beat were confident we could produce a hit single of our own, so offered to sign us up to their Go Feet record label. We recorded two of David's songs, 'Annapurna' for the A side, and 'Driving by Night' for the B side. Bob Sargeant, the producer of the Beat's debut album *I Just Can't Stop It* produced 'Annapurna' and David Steele and Andy Cox produced the B Side, calling themselves 'The Punjab Brothers.' 'Annapurna' was released in the spring of 1981 and although it didn't make the UK chart, the feeling of hearing your record played by the likes of John Peel and Richard Skinner on BBC Radio One was incredible. We were then offered a session with Richard Skinner, which we recorded the following month."

Dave Wakeling says that establishing their own label, Go Feet as a subsidiary of Arista, gave them the ability to maintain their creativity, and provide opportunities to other bands—like the Mood Elevators. "We suddenly, by January [1980], had every major record label desperate to sign us up," Wakeling says, "and so instead of going for what was just the biggest offer, we went toward a label that would give us our own version of 2 Tone, the ability to have some artistic control over our own music and also to be able to invite people to bring their singles on our own label. So we started the Go Feet label."[473] The Beat used this label to release a number of their own singles as well as others, as Ranking Roger recalled. "We just carried on having hits on that label. We also put out a couple of other bands on that label. The Mood Elevators who were a band from Birmingham, and we put out a tune of theirs called 'Annapurna' which didn't do anything in the charts but we wanted that record label, not necessarily as a hit machine, but really we put them on there because we loved them and we liked their kind of music. It was pop music, but kind of sounding slightly Arabian or Eastern or something like that. Very interesting and weird."[474]

Despite the song not charting well, the Beat still continued to support the Mood Elevators. Jenny says, "A few months later, the Beat offered us the opening slot for the whole of their second UK tour, and once again, we supported them every night, along with the brilliant Au Pairs. I remember it was even better on the second tour as we'd found our feet, we'd grown up a bit, we were more confident." The Mood Elevators released one other single just a few months later on Red Records. "It was a reworking of a song called 'Georgie Girl,' and even though we were no longer signed to the Beat's Go Feet label, it was recorded with the help of the Beat's production and featured the guest vocals of Ranking Roger on the B-side," Jenny says.

It was shortly after the end of the second tour with the Beat that the Mood Elevators broke up. Jenny, for all of her talent, left music behind. She explains, "One night, at the Portland Hotel after the Beat's Hammersmith Palais gig, we were all sat round the bar, celebrating yet another tour night when John Mostyn, the Beat's co-manager said, 'bands only last a couple of years.' We were really shocked. How could that be the case? The Beat were incredible, surely they'd go on forever? Surely, we would too? But we soon realised he was absolutely right. The UK music scene in the 1980s was powerfully fuelled by movements, ideas, energies. Things moved fast. By the time the Mood Elevators had released our second single, we'd lost our direction in sound and our bassist. Creativity is a fragile, mysterious process. There was a time when everything felt like it worked. Then it didn't. And you don't know why. You just know that the energy suddenly feels wrong, and you can't make it right, and as much as we hated to admit it to ourselves, we'd lost our way, it was over."

---

[473] Wakeling, Dave. All quotations, unless otherwise noted, from interview with the author, 29 Jan. 2008.
[474] Charlery, Roger. All quotations, unless otherwise noted, from interview with the author, 27 June 1997.

Jenny Jones continued with the Beat members Andy Cox and David Steele in their next venture. "She did stuff with the Fine Young Cannibals," says Ditchfield. "They asked her to come and play drums with them and stuff, because we stayed friends with them after the Mood Elevators split and also after the Beat had split. We were all living in the same town. And so she played on both albums on a couple tracks, and did some backup vocals. She also did some stuff herself. She's a very talented songwriter. And yeah, she got married. So she kind of stopped thinking about music. I mean, it's, it's just one of those things." Noel Green moved to France in 1993 and at that time was working for the European Space Agency.[475] David Ditchfield spent a few more years in music but then in 2006 was nearly killed when he was trapped in the automatic doors of a commuter train. He was dragged along on the platform, pulled between the space of platforms, and then under the train. He had a near death experience and miraculously survived. Today he has written a book, paints, and composes music for orchestras.

Reflecting on her life with the Mood Elevators, Jenny says this time of her life was transformative. "My time in the Mood Elevators, being a part of that incredibly exciting movement was life-changing for me. Before that, I'd had little exposure to anything that offered possibility beyond limited working-class horizons. But after touring, releasing singles, meeting so many amazing people, I imbibed the realisation that anything is possible if you have the courage to try it out. I was part of a restless, oppressed working class youth who could relate to punk and 2 Tone, and through these movements, connect with musicians who shared a similar passion. Ska didn't feel elitist. It didn't seem exclusive. For the first time, with punk and ska, I could recognise myself in the musicians and the worlds the musicians sang about. For the first time, I felt I could see my world and I could also see opportunities far beyond it. And that gave me freedom. When I reflect on these memories, I hold that time with great affection and some pride. At the tender age of 18, we formed a band, wrote songs, designed our own posters, dressed ourselves from jumble sales and this DIY ethic, this self-possessed naïve confidence is the biggest take-away I have from the whole experience. To have faith in your own judgement, do your own thing and if you really believe in what you are doing, things will happen. For that I give thanks."

---

[475] Email correspondence between Kevin Feinberg and Noel Green, 20 Feb. 2007.

The Mood Elevators flier that drew the attention of the Beat (above) and group photo with Jenny Jones on drums (below)

The Mood Elevators flier (above) and at a gig in Manchester, 1981 (below)

Splashdown

Sara Raybould: vocals, keyboard
Debbie Shields: vocals
Kim Shields: vocals
The Swinging Laurels: horns

Trevor Elroy Evans: vocals, percussion
Lynval Golding: guitar
Johnnie St. John: vocals, percussion

The rather cheesy plug on the back of their record sleeve heralded, "Catch the drops while you can!" And for the five-piece "band" Splashdown, that warning of evaporating fame, what little of it there was, certainly was a portent. Although Splashdown may have been a flash in the pan, the experience made waves whose ripples (oh the puns could go on and on!) would impact countless future musicians.

Comprised of five members who mostly sang or provided limited percussion—sisters Kim and Debbie Shields, Sara Raybould (who only went by her first name), Trevor Elroy Evans, and Johnnie St. John— Splashdown's music was supplied by Lynval Golding on guitar and horns from the Swinging Laurels. Neville Staple and Golding produced Splashdown's recordings which were part of Staple's and Golding's label, Shack Records. The label was founded by Staple and his then-girlfriend Stella Barker of the Bodysnatchers and Belle Stars. "Neville and I did start the label together, but I can't remember any details like where we got the funding from or how we actually put it together," says Stella of the venture.[476] "Splashdown was Neville's long-term-friend Trevor's band. Trevor was at one time a roadie for the Specials," she says.

Staple provides a little commentary on Splashdown in his book *Original Rude Boy*. He says that the duo 21 Guns, comprised of roadies Trevor Evans and Johnny Rex, was "enjoying some success on the college circuit" with their single release. Rex then left to pursue his education, leaving Evans looking for his next venture. Staple writes, "Trevor teamed up with an ex-girlfriend of his, Kim Shields, and her sister Debbie—Franklyn had been seeing Debbie at some point." Franklyn was Neville's brother. "A girl called Sarah [sic] came into this new band on keyboards and I'd been seeing her for a while. Then a guy called Johnny [sic] St. John was recruited as a vocalist and together they became Splashdown."[477]

Sara Raybould says that joining Splashdown was a result of her experience in performing which she began at a young age in Marson Green outside of Coventry. "I grew up in a complete music household, you know, proper working-class family, and my dad always used to put himself out to make sure I had music lessons, so I always had piano lessons. That's where my background was, and then as I got a bit older, I had singing lessons so I started performing, you know, playing piano and singing from quite an early age. And I used to fund my lessons from the money I earned

[476] Barker, Stella. All quotations, unless otherwise noted, from interview with the author, 19, Jan. 2021.
[477] Staple, Neville. *Original Rude Boy*. Aurum Press, 9 July 2010, p. 243-244.

performing. So that was from age 12 onwards. As I got into my teens, I sort of wandered around the world, singing in various places and doing sort of cabaret type things."[478]

She says she doesn't remember how she met Neville Staple but they likely crossed paths in venues around the Coventry area. "I met Neville Staple and that's where it really got started. Because I sang, they were putting a band together at the time. So, it was all part of Fun Boy Three, which I think was a big band at the time, and so Neville was the person that really drove it with Terry [Hall] writing a lot of the music for the band. And literally, I suppose it was one of the first bands that had been put together in a manufactured way. 'Oh, look, we've got these two guys who sing, we've got these sisters who sing and look, actually, we've got somebody who is a singer who plays keyboards as well.' So the band was sort of put together that way around, really. Terry used to write the music. I think Neville worked some of the lyrics or Lynval did. I used to just turn up and then record the music and occasionally play keys on it, and it didn't really last for very long," Sara says.

Still, the experience was significant in making a large impression on a young girl. "I was very young at the time, I think I was only 17 or 18. In fact, I just started doing a summer season at Warner's holiday camp when I got the call from Neville saying, look, the band's gonna get signed, can you get out of it? So a few weeks into me starting my first summer season as a singer in this holiday camp, I left to go and do that instead. We were signed to Red Bus which was that sort of Waterman factory at the time, and all sorts of people were walking past—Hall and Oates, Fun Boy Three were always there, and Bananarama were wandering in and out. It was a really good opportunity to try and pursue it and see where it went. We toured with Kelly Marie for a while. It was a time when all that high energy stuff was going on in gay clubs. So we did a tour of gay clubs with the kind of music that we did, as a promo tour," she says.

Staple references this tour in his book and states, "The gritty urban look of 21 Guns was exchanged for white shirts and trousers, with red bow ties. Like us, they also had to surrender to the inevitable beach shorts. Wham! had a lot to answer for. Produced by me, they signed to Red Bus Records and released a single with the songs 'To Your Heart' and 'Actions Speak Louder Than Words.' … Trevor pretty quickly found that it was a very different kind of venue that wanted to book his new bubblegum act. Splashdown went on tour and found themselves playing gay bars and clubs from Blackpool to Brighton. As Trevor says: 'We had girls in the Splashdown for the girls to fancy. And boys for the boys to fancy.' … Standing there in his white beach sorts, the former Specials roadie got his fair share of unwanted attention …"[479]

The tour promoted their three songs released on two singles—"Actions Speak Louder Than Words," "It's a Brand New Day," and "To Your Heart" which featured "The Boys from Brazil," though it is not known who this was. Recording

[478] Raybould, Sara. All quotations, unless otherwise noted, from interview with the author, 18 Aug. 2022.
[479] Staple, Neville. Original Rude Boy. Aurum Press, 9 July 2010, p. 243-244.

involved additional session musicians including the Swinging Laurels. John Barrow, saxophonist and co-founder of the Swinging Laurels, says they were brought into the studio after the vocals were already recorded and as such, they never met the members of the group. "Our involvement with Splashdown was fleeting. We didn't actually meet the band although we caught up with Trevor in later years. When we recorded the brass parts for 'It's a Brand New Day' and 'Actions Speak Louder Than Words,' the tracks were already down. We just met up with Lynval and Neville at Bridge Studios in London. We just added the brass lines over the existing recordings. That happened a number of times during our session careers," says Barrow[480] who details more of his experiences in his very funny book, *How NOT to make it in the Pop world (diary of an almost has-been)*.

Sara says that Splashdown disappeared as quickly as it began. She says that deciding to leave was a result of the way the band was naturally dissolving. "I could see that the band wasn't going where I particularly wanted it to go. And because I was a solo singer anyway, I just carried on, you know, singing without the band. And I think the band sort of finished at that point anyway. You have those points where you try and when it doesn't go anywhere you stop. I think we only ever recorded about two or three tracks. To be honest, it was a really small project. It was one of those flash-in-the-pan moments, really great fun. I learned a lot about the Coventry music scene, because I virtually lived over there while the whole thing was happening. I spent a lot of time with Debbie and her sister." When asked why she decided to pursue this opportunity, rather than continuing with the cabaret circuit or similar performances, Sara states, "In those days, of course, you could make money through recording music, which you can't do now. But I think it was just this opportunity to do something completely different. Because I'd always sung covers, I'd always done that sort of more cabaret type thing. And this was doing something new."

But then, Sara's career entered a new realm, into academia where she would touch the lives of countless young people who looked to performance and music as a career. "My path from crazy singer!" she says, looking back. "Today my actual title at the university is Senior Pro Chancellor, Student Experience and Education, which means I'm one of the three people that run a 172 million pounds university. That's my job. But every time I meet a new student, I say that might be my title, but actually, I'm a girl singer. That's how I started." This beginning dramatically shaped her path. She explains, "I was meeting a lot of people that had great musical talents, but had no concept of music language, or theory, or structure. They could be naturally talented, but had no way to harness it as much as they probably could do, to better advantage themselves, and it stayed with me. So randomly, one of my friends asked me to teach one day, teach singing, and I started by teaching three hours a week at a popular music school in 1999. My passion was that everybody had an opportunity in popular music, to understand the real theory and underpinnings of popular music—not classical music but popular music. Thinking all the way back to those times in Coventry, what

---

[480] Barrow, John. All quotations, unless otherwise noted, from interview with the author, 30 Jun. 2021.

was very apparent to me was even if some of those people I was working with had wanted to have that kind of education background, because of who they were and where they came from, they one—weren't given opportunity to learn music because lessons cost money, and two—were not in the environment where music study was encouraged and in fact, actively discouraged, and three—had no idea that there might be opportunities out there."

This is what drove Sara to create what didn't exist in the sphere of academia. "At the time, there weren't that many popular music opportunities in higher education. So I wrote one of the first popular music degrees in higher education with colleagues at the time. And so from that, teaching, I then became head of voice at that private institution. I then became head of the degree course in popular music, and the validating university at the time, Thames Valley, they asked me if I could work part time at the University, part time at the private provider, which I did. And then I became Director of Studies at the London College of Music. I then became deputy head, and then director of London College of Music. And London College of Music sits inside the university I now work in, the University of West London. And my chancellor spotted me and said he wanted me to apply to be an Associate Pro Chancellor, which I did, and then I became a Pro Chancellor, and then I became a Senior Pro Chancellor. It's been quite a journey."

Sara says that she is driven by the passion to provide access to everyone. "I do a lot of work here in widening participation in equality, diversity, and inclusion. I remind myself, some people aren't even given the opportunity to enter that, because there's a lot of lead up before you come into higher education. And if you've not come from a background where it's supported financially, or even philosophically, you don't stand a chance of getting on the right rung to get you entry into higher education. So, my work is about how do we get people to come into universities that feel it's not for them, and there is no place, and how do we legitimize the arts as a legitimate qualification that gives you a good career prospect."

Before she came into academia though, between Splashdown and the university, she worked as a product specialist for a number of music instrument manufacturers, which also showed her the dearth of women in this industry as well. "I worked for Yamaha, Technics, and Roland as a product specialist. And I was one of only two female product specialists in the country—myself and a girl called Wendy who eventually moved to America. Nobody ever imagined that you could have a brain in music, music tech particularly, and be a woman. And I've seen that change, but you still struggle to find female music producers. We actively push it now. But in particular, female black music producers—almost unheard of. So, there's had to be a very positive push, and a lot of lived-experience exponents so that people can actually see themselves recognized."

Sara explains what she means by "lived-experience exponents." She states, "If you did not see one of my dear friends Marcia Worrell as an incredible black, Afro-Caribbean woman who was a professor and only one of eight in the entire country, if you can't see that, how can you aspire to it? So, I think that whole industry had a lot of work it needed to undertake. I mean, how many female black drummers have you ever seen? How many female black bass players have you ever seen? I say female and black because that is the demographic that is least seen in the UK. Go to other parts of the world and you will see a slightly different demographic, but certainly, that demographic struggles to come through and women struggle to come through in some of those instrument types, let alone technology types. We're getting better now, but it's still not there. It's because of access. It's because of opportunity. I think it's also because of expectation if you don't see that representation, how do you aspire to it? Until there was a female prime minister, who thought they could have a female prime minister? It's a slightly different route, obviously, but once you've witnessed it you see it's possible."

As a female in a male-dominated music industry during the days of Splashdown, Sara reflects on her experience. "At that time, I used to think it was great if they treated me as one of the boys. Now, I would go nuts if anybody said that. At the time, I realized I was in a male environment. And I was one of very, very, very few women in that male environment. It was a bit unusual that I played keys. That's changed. Keys is a bit more female based. You do see the guitarists and occasionally bass players, but there's a rarity of drummers. If you actually look at the demographic of popular music education, you will still see nearly all the singers are women. The guitarist, the bass player, the drummers tend to be more males, many more males, and the keys players are kind of even balanced, which is different than the classical world. The classical world has always been a little bit more equal across. But my first point of frustration came when I sat down at a piano and they said, 'Can you play a solo?' and I said, 'Can I have the chord chart?' And they went, 'What? We haven't got a chord chart, just use your ears.' So I was a fish out of water. Because I'd grown up only reading music. And that's how I suddenly was forced into a situation where, oh my God, what do I do if I've got no music in front of me? So that was a learning curve in the opposite way for me as well."

She also says that as a whole, this era in music history, centered around the city of Coventry, was important to making the shift to more access for all. "I think the period of time was really exciting, because musically, there was a pop factory coming through. And there was nothing wrong with that particular approach. And I think Splashdown particularly was coming out of the approach of pop factory, but trying to at least keep the essence of that sort of whole ska—that Coventry factor— I'm going to call it the Coventry factor. And the Coventry factor was built on always seizing the moment, to create something new, to try and be different, but without losing that underpinning of the Coventry factor, which was about the people about the place, and about the struggle, quite honestly. So, I think that's what I felt musically about the period."

Sara continues, "Also for me, it gave me an insight into a world that I had really not appreciated before. So, I had a traditional kind of music background, but it just threw at me the importance of being creative by the ear, having things thrown at you, musically, that you would just immerse yourself in and get involved in. It opened my eyes to a different way of looking at music. And I suppose, as I've gone back, and I reflect upon it now, I think it flavored me. I looked at music in a very different way from then on out. I never ever looked down upon people who don't have the education and can't read music and don't have the theory and understand the structure, because they understand it in a different way, from a different perspective, and quite often just with a slightly different language. And I hope I have brought that through my entire career in music education and into higher education where equality, diversity, and inclusion are my key columns that I follow on a daily basis. Somewhere in there, there's a bit of that Splashdown experience that never left me."

Splashdown with Sara Raybould center (above) and Sara Raybould today (below)

The Mo-Dettes

Ramona Carlier: vocals
Kate Corris: guitar
June Miles-Kingston: drums

Jane Perry Crockford: bass
Melissa Ritter: guitar
Sue Slack: vocals

On Saturday, October 13, 1979, the Electric Ballroom in London was pumping with the sound and energy of ska. The Selecter and the Beat performed their new singles just released on the 2 Tone label—"On My Radio" and "Tears of a Clown," respectively. One week later the first official 2 Tone Tour would kick off with the Selecter joining the Specials and Madness for 25 performances in just shy of a month's time. But for now, both the Selecter and the Beat were joined by another band on stage. The Mo-Dettes were a four-piece all-female line up that ran in the same circles and the same scene as the 2 Tone bands. And their sound mixed the same influences of West Indian music and culture with punk, like the 2 Tone bands. But the Mo-Dettes output was definitely not ska. It was a bit punk, a bit dub, and all energy.

The Mo-Dettes was comprised of Kate Corris on guitar, Jane Perry Crockford on bass, June Miles-Kingston on drums, and Ramona Carlier on vocals. The group of women met while living at ground zero during the late 1970s— London's West End. Kate Corris was friends with Joe Strummer who was dating her friend and bandmate Palmolive in the Slits; June Miles-Kingston and Kate Corris worked together on the Sex Pistols' film, *the Great Rock 'n' Roll Swindle*; Jane Perry Crockford lived in a squat with Johnny Rotten and Sid Vicious; and Ramona Carlier lived in a squat above Joe Strummer's room. It cannot be understated how intertwined these musicians were, and those who weren't musicians were soon empowered to take up an instrument or microphone as the punk era ushered in the era of anyone can do it.

Katherine Corris, who says that she avoided correcting misspellings of her last name (Korus, Korris, Chorus) to remain undetected by immigration and to take on a stage name, was born and raised in New York. Kate moved to London to begin working in the music industry, which is exactly what she did. "I arrived in England in '74," says Kate, "and I had one name of one person who *might* give me a job if I needed one, from a friend. He gave me Richard Ogden's name, and I arrived in England basically broke, so I had to go to work. I called this guy and he was working in Hawkwind's office as their PR guy. So I got a job there and that's how I ended up meeting people in the music business—Lemmy, Nik Turner, and then the 101ers [Strummer's pre-Clash band] café was three doors down the street. The London music scene is actually quite small and incestuous for such a big city. You soon got to know everybody. It was impossible not to be involved in the punk scene. You kind of got sucked in! I kind of fell into the Slits thing, Paloma was a friend."[481]

Paloma Romero, better known as Palmolive, lived in the same squat as Kate Corris, along with Joe Strummer who was Palmolive's boyfriend. And Kate was dating the 101ers roadie, John "Boogie" Tiberi.[482] It can be very confusing to map the connections and relationships of all players during this era and soon the Venn diagrams begin to just resemble completely overlapping circles. Palmolive had recently taken up the drums, and Kate had done the same with the guitar. Both planned to start up a band and were on the lookout for members. According to music historian Vivien Goldman in her book, *Revenge of the She-Punks*, Joe Strummer taught Kate to play. "The Clash's singer-songwriter Joe Strummer showed the novice Korris [sic] a couple of guitar chords, and advised, "You can do anything with those two pieces of info; go for it.' 'And he was right!' laughs Korris [sic]."[483] Kate had a natural ear for music, though, having played piano as a child. "I started playing piano when I was three years old on my Daddy's knee, and somewhere along the line I've always done something to do with music," she said.[484]

The remaining members of the Slits joined after Kate and Palmolive saw Patti Smith perform at the Roundhouse in London in May 1976. There they witnessed 14-year-old Ariane Forster, who later took the stage name Ari Up, arguing with her mother, Nora (who later went on to marry John Lydon), and causing quite a ruckus. "She was being funny with her mum, throwing her hair around, and I thought, that's great! I asked her if she wanted to be in a band," said Palmolive.[485] The next day they rehearsed at Palmolive and Strummer's squat, practicing for their first gig as the Slits. The name was conceived by Kate Corris as a way to convey a number of concepts in one. "It was sharp, cutting, memorable and rather biological, but like everything they were to go on and achieve, open to interpretation. Was it a reference to female genitalia? Was it a reference to slashed-up punk fashion or aggression? The group didn't really mind which way it was translated … The Slits' 'offensive' name was the concave mirror to the convex phallic innuendo of Sex Pistols," wrote one historian.[486]

Kate also claimed naming rights for the Mo-Dettes, but before she'd get that chance, she would first play her first gig with fellow members Palmolive, Ari Up, and Tessa Pollitt as the Slits. Kate helped to write some of the Slits more well-known songs. "I helped to write 'New Town,' 'Shoplifting,' 'Let's Do the Split (Vindictive),' 'Number One Enemy.' I was the person who could figure out chords, Palmolive or Ari would come in with a lyric, they were both really creative."[487] Bass player Tessa Pollitt recalls, "The first Slits gig we played, we played with the Clash. It was in Harlesden. I had only picked up the bass two weeks before. I wasn't a musician. I was

[481] Ogg, Alex. *The Mo-dettes: The Story So Far*. Cherry Red. Liner notes.
[482] Howe, Zoe. *Typical Girls? The Story of The Slits*. Omnibus Press, 2009, p.14.
[483] Goldman, Vivien. *Revenge of the She-Punks*. University of Texas Press, 2019, p. 132.
[484] Laye, Mike. "Swanky Mo-Dettes." *Sounds*, 28 June 1980, p. 33.
[485] Howe, Zoe. *Typical Girls? The Story of The Slits*. Omnibus Press, 2009, p.14.
[486] Ibid. p. 15.
[487] Ibid.

terrified, but you know I was just 17, and at that age you have so much energy and excitement in you, it carries you. I remember at one point onstage, me and Palmolive (The Slits' drummer, now a member of a reclusive Christian sect) looked at each other in amazement as if to say, 'What the fuck are you doing?' We were all playing a different song from each other! But we got away with so much, and the audience didn't care. The energy was what mattered. We were playing from our heart. Literally. With spirit. Our spirit was there."[488] Kate agrees the performance was rough. "Palmolive couldn't really carry a tune, and she couldn't keep a beat really, but I thought she was great, primal, great fun, but not reliable, and she didn't have a broad scope."[489]

What Palmolive did have, however, was Joe Strummer's ear, and so after that first gig opening for the Clash, it may have very well been Strummer, or perhaps other musicians in the tightknit scene, that suggested to Palmolive to give Kate the boot. Whomever the influential critic was claimed that Kate wasn't "cool" enough on stage.[490] Kate explains, "'Paloma said: "You're out," or words to that effect,' Kate explains. 'She made it sound like a band decision, although the others tell me now that it was presented to them as a done deal. 'Someone' had told Paloma I was crap on stage, and that 'someone' has never been named. We all have our theories. ... Strummer was good. Any of his female friends who had bands he would try and get them a gig, because he was keen to be seen to be behind women in music. But it could have been him who said, "She's crap, get rid of her," because he did the same thing to me with Ramona in the Mo-Dettes. But there are any number of people it could have been, and I doubt he would have wanted to take the blame. ... But it may just have been that she [Palmolive] saw Viv as the more viable person and she thought she should get rid of me to get Viv in, I really don't know."[491]

So Kate Corris was replaced by Viv Albertine in the Slits. She performed other short stints with the Castrators and the Raincoats, the latter of which was cited by Kurt Cobain as an influence on his music. Even John Lydon in 1980 proclaimed that "Rock' n 'Roll is shit ... music has reached an all-time low—except for The Raincoats."[492] But Kate's long-time band was the Mo-Dettes, although she had originally thought the lineup would not be all-female. Forming a group full of femmes, however, was just a matter of functionality. "After the Slits, I moved away from the all-girl idea. It seemed to place us in a kind of 'freak' status that felt unnatural to me. But in trying out players to form a band with the drummer June Miles-Kingston, we couldn't find guys who weren't either scared or trying to dominate us. We weren't all girls because of a premeditated stance, but because we found no suitable males

[488] "The Slits - Tessa Pollitt 1." punk77.co.uk/groups/slitstessapollittinterview.htm. Accessed 30 Sept. 2022.
[489] Howe, Zoe. *Typical Girls? The Story of The Slits*. Omnibus Press, 2009, p.26.
[490] Ibid.
[491] Ibid. p. 29-30.
[492] "The Raincoats biography." theraincoats.net. Accessed 30 Sept. 2022.

available. The bass player, Jane Perry Crockford, was having a similar experience, and we gravitated toward each other."[493]

Jane had also performed in a band prior to forming the Mo-Dettes as a bass player and vocalist for the punk band, Bank of Dresden—a band that played only about a dozen gigs before imploding. Jane was a self-proclaimed wild child who had a hard life prior to moving to Soho. She explains, "I was born in 1956 and in 1956, if you were an unmarried mother, oh, tsk tsk tsk, you were a slut. You were a pariah of society. And at that time, there was no help from the state. My mother tried her hardest. She tried to keep me and after one and a half years, literally, I was starving. She was working and I was in a day nursery, but she couldn't keep me safe and she couldn't keep me healthy. So I was put up for adoption. My adoptive parents were good people, working class. My dad was a plasterer and my mom was a cleaner and they rented a beautiful little house in Chiswick. But I wasn't a happy adoptee. Suddenly my mother was gone and I cried and I made hell for my parents. I really did. Growing up, I was a pain in the ass. They didn't deserve it, they were good people," she says.[494]

To console herself, Jane turned to music. "I sang all the time. I used to walk to my junior school and I would sing all the pop songs of the day—Beatles, Rolling Stones, Cilla Black, Dusty Springfield—all of this, I would sing. And people would tell me, 'Shut up! You can't sing! Shut up!' And I didn't listen. I wouldn't. I wasn't having it. That was my comfort. That's what really made me happy." In school, Jane played the recorder, which she enjoyed, and she also played a piano that her Auntie Marge had, though visits to her home were infrequent enough to satisfy her need to learn to play an instrument. After a teacher at school identified musical ability in Jane and suggested she take lessons, she asked her parents if she could. "They laughed and said, 'We can't afford that.' And then I asked about dance lessons. Got laughed at again. And I was 13 when I remember I said to my mom that when I leave school, I want to go to art school. And again, it was, 'Ha ha. Look, when you leave school, you're going to work at Woolworth and earn your keep.' Each time, batted down. I ran away when I was 13 and when I was 14, so I was put in foster care, children's homes. Even though I loved my parents very much, I was quite wild and I was very broken."

While at home, Jane listened to music she played on her dad's record player. She says, "My first single that I actually bought was 'Honky Tonk Women' by the Rolling Stones. That's 1970. Then I discovered, because at that time, this is in '68, '69, we had the Windrush generation, thank god, because British people are fucking boring and oh, this stupid class divide is crap. We had these people West Indians immigrating, bringing life, color, and their music. So I was quite mad. I mean, I was a skinhead during the week, and I was a hippie at the weekend. I would take my mom's fur coat.

[493] Goldman, Vivien. *Revenge of the She-Punks*. University of Texas Press, 2019, p. 131-132.
[494] Crockford, Jane Perry. All quotations, unless otherwise noted, from interview with the author, 13 Feb. 2021.

I would tell my parents I was going off to Ladbroke Grove to stay with friends and they'd give me 50p for pocket money and I'd go into Soho, go into an all-night club and take acid. And basically, I was a big liar too. I was a terrible liar. But then I discovered *Tighten Up Volume 2,* which is really naughty! I thought, oh wow!" She sings, 'I need a man to wreck a buddy!' And my best friend and I would play it and sing it, and I started buying singles—'Elizabethan Reggae,' 'Skinhead Moonstomp'— and I went to clubs. There was a local club down by the river and we would dance and oh! But I loved Alice Cooper! He's jolly good. One of my first concerts was the Who at the Hammersmith Palais and I remember seeing Tyrannosaurus Rex before he went electric, and Pink Floyd, and all manner of things. And don't forget David Bowie! I went to one of his first ever London concerts at the Queens Festival Hall there on the South Bank where he performed *Ziggy Stardust.* I mean, that saved my life," she says, singing, 'Star Man.' I mean, I remember, I'd first heard David Bowie when he released 'Major Tom' and I had a little transistor radio and I'd be under my pillow at night as a child listening to Radio Luxembourg, which was a pirate station. And it would come in and out, waiting for them to play it, 'this is ground control to Major Tom' and I totally fell in love with that! I loved music. Music was heaven to me."

After Jane had run away from home for the final time, she continued to pursue her passion for music and became part of the life in Soho. "There was a basement around Paddington, top of Westbourne Grove, there was a squat and I was only visiting. I was visiting. And down in their basement they had like drums and stuff and there was a piano. And before that, I had heard a reggae song. I forget who performed it, but it was like 'Swan Lake,' and it was wonderful and I taught myself to play that, playing two hands. And that's my little party piece, I could play that. And Joe Strummer came by and he said, 'Oh! You can play, you can play!' And it's like, 'Oh yes, I can play!' I can't tell him that's the only thing I could play! But Joe Strummer was a person who always saw and spoke out about the positive in someone. He would look and see the positive. So he was an angel. John Lydon would find your weakest and darkest secrets, and he would dive in. He was a bitch. Yeah, he was a devil. People were terrified of his tongue because he was extremely witty, he was, and so he was the dark side. But at the same time, we did become really good friends. For a time, we would live together in a squat in Hampstead. We each had our own room—myself, John Lydon, and Sid Vicious. It had been Sid's squat and he'd invited me to join him," Jane says.

Living with Sid Vicious certainly didn't help to provide Jane with the stability her life needed at that point, but it did provide her with a friendship, loyalty, and family of a different kind. "Sid was a right speed freak and we would get drunk and do very very foolish things. And his heroin hadn't kicked in—that came with Spungen, but he did have that background. His mother [Anne] Beverley was a total heroin addict and he was very broken. He was far more broken than I was, and I know I always feel a great deal of guilt because I sort of took him to the next level of, well, we were talking one night, all night, just talk talk talk, and he was saying in fights he'd run away, run a mile. And I said, no I've never run away from a fight because I'm scrappy. I'm quite scrappy. I don't know why, but I just couldn't bear if somebody offered me out [challenged to a fight]. I would be like, okay, come on! And whatever would happen would happen. And I taught Sid that and we actually put it into action one day, and well, twice. And then he really went over the top."

She tells that story: "We'd been drinking at William IV in Hampstead. John [Lydon] was generally rehearsing and out because Sid wasn't in the Pistols then. It was the summer of '76 and it was very hot and beautiful and wonderful. And there was always a hamburger stall at night for the people coming out of the pub and we were there getting a hamburger. A lot of time we went without food. We had no money. We did starve. And this great big, what we would call a chuffy Northerner, big fat lug, nylon shirt open, and he looks at us, and you know, punk hadn't been advertised yet. It was growing. It was there, there was a buzz, but the music press hadn't discovered us yet. But we did look pretty wild, pretty whatever. Sid looked like a praying mantis. And he comes over, this big fella and is like (growls), and all this but we just walk away because we want to eat our burger. Also, two weeks before, I'd come off a Harley Davidson trails bike and fractured my collar bone, so I'm all strapped up. Sid would brush my teeth and wash my face for me. He was so sweet. So we're walking away, but this guy, he's a bit drunk, and he's like (growls), and comes after us. But instead of grabbing Sid, he grabs my shoulder—and the pain! And just ahead of us is a corner shop and then an alley that leads to where our squat was. And outside this little corner shop, they always had crates of milk bottles where people would buy milk in the morning and have them delivered. So I saw these long pint glass empty milk bottles. Now I don't know if you've seen *A Clockwork Orange*, when he comes out of the lady's flat who he's just killed, and the police are coming and he gets the milk bottle across the face? That was my intention. And this guy's really tall and I'm tiny. I got the milk bottle, put it behind my back and I just walked towards this big fat fucking chuffy Northern, and you know what Sid did? And this proves him to be a hero, actually. He came up behind me, took the milk bottle, and he did it for me. Smashed it right across this guy's head. And this was somebody who like a couple of weeks before had said, no, run away from fights. And I'm just like, whoa! I mean, it was perfect. But this guy was not knocked out. He just picked Sid up and he threw him through a plate glass window. A shop front. And all this glass is falling down, and Sid just grabs a shard and he gouges the guy. All the time there's these little rockabilly kids who deliver the papers, they're like ten years, eleven years old. They're all rockabillies and they're really cute, and they're all watching this. And so after the guy collapses in a puddle of blood, we actually do a runner. We run away back to our squat, and they [rockabilly kids] told us the next day that the guy had about 47 stitches and the whole incident had been watched by the local police in their police car, but they decided not to do anything. And there were other times that Sid stepped up to the mob for me, looked out for me in the physical sense. He stood by me, because, as I said, I was pretty mad. John [Lydon] used to—my name used to be Mad Jane."

Another incident involving broken glass and "Mad Jane," has become somewhat of an urban legend, and Jane sets the record straight. The event occurred at one of the Clash's early gigs on October 23, 1976 at the Institute of Contemporary Arts in London. In the audience that night was Patti Smith who came to hear the Clash after her own performance at the Hammersmith Odeon. Also in the audience was a young Shane MacGowan before he founded the Nipple Erectors and subsequently the Pogues. Additionally, Jane Perry Crockford was in the audience and in the company of MacGowan. Both were engaged in some heavy drinking, though not anything further, despite proclamations of newspaper headlines. "Cannibalism at Clash Gig," read the *NME* article on November 6, 1976 written by Barry Miles. The review, a positive one for the Clash, contained the observation, "A young couple, somewhat out of it, had been nibbling and fondling each other amid the broken glass when she suddenly lunged forward and *bit his ear lobe off*. As the blood spatted she reached out to paw it with a hand tastefully clad in a rubber glove, and after smashing a Guinness bottle on the front of the stage, she was about to add to the gore by slashing her wrists when the security men finally reached her, pushing her through the trance-like crowd who watched with cold, calculated hiptitude."[495] The caption of the photo, an action shot, stated, "Ten Seconds Later, My God, they're eating each other. These people are cannibals! The young man howls with pain as his blood-spattered young lady is dragged away, all the while trying to slash her own wrists. But for the dudes in the audience, it's just a regular Saturday gig. Maybe they eat earlobes themselves! Edgar Froese [Tangerine Dream] (left) wonders if they'll be turning out for T. Dream. 'Can't these Englishers afford sausages?'"

The sensationalism of that account hardly died down in the years since. The myth has perpetuated, to MacGowan's advantage. The event landed him in music newspaper headlines, his photo featured instead of the Clash themselves. Since then, writers have claimed it was his "pre-fame fame"[496] or the moment when "the legend was born."[497] Julien Temple, who was also at the gig, and has since released a documentary on MacGowan recalls, "The ICA thing was obviously a big deal that brought him into focus. He became the focal point down the front absorbing every atom of the energy that was coming off the stage at a Clash gig or a Pistols gig. He was very charismatic in the crowd as a London punk."[498] But Jane says it was certainly not as the papers had portrayed, then nor since. "Shane MacGowan and I were at a Clash gig at The Mall and were enjoying the evening rather intensely under the

[495] Miles, Barry. "Cannibalism at Clash Gig." *NME*, 6 Nov. 1976, p. 43.

[496] Hattonstone, Simon. "'Of course I like life!' Shane MacGowan on the Pogues, his 'death wish' and his sideline in erotic art." *The Guardian*. 4 Apr. 2022. theguardian.com/music/2022/apr/04/of-course-i-like-life-shane-macgowan-on-the-pogues-his-death-wish-and-his-sideline-in-erotic-art?fr=operanews. Accessed 10 Oct. 2022.

[497] Smith, Kyle. "The Pleasure and the Pain of Shane MacGowan." *National Review*, 5 Dec. 2022. nationalreview.com/2020/12/movie-review-crock-of-gold-a-few-rounds-with-shane-macgowwan-profiles-pogues-singer-songwriter. Accessed 10 Oct. 2022.

[498] Kevin, Perry EG. "Cartoons, cannibalism and The Clash: inside Julien Temple's new Shane MacGowan doc." *NME*, 2 Dec. 2020. nme.com/features/shane-macgowan-inside-julien-temples-new-documentary-2830129. Accessed 10 Oct. 2022.

influence of a few drinks. I had dropped my bottle and it had broken and we were making faux thrusting movements in fun, but it caught his ear, which then bled copiously. And I tried to kiss it better. Shane was lovely about it. There was no biting whatsoever. You know the press! It was a playful moment of silly ferocity."[499]

That gig and most gigs featured a who's who of musicians who are today legendary. And Jane, definitely in the center of it all, didn't realize that she wanted to be in a band just yet, though she enjoyed being around the energy. She admits that she was confused about her life, given her unstable home environment and living conditions. She thought she might become a writer since she loved reading the works of Jean Genet, William Burroughs, and Jean Cocteau. Jane wrote poetry and planned to one day write a book, but in the summer of 1977, she met Ari Up of the Slits, and the two became fast friends, which further bonded Jane to the world of music. "Ari Up kind of presented herself to me and said, 'I'm going to be your friend,' and I said, 'No you're not, you hippie slag, fuck off!' I was horrible! I hated everybody. But she wouldn't have it and she did become my best friend. We used to go to all the blues clubs which were like town halls, the main hall taken over by dub. There were whole walls of speakers. And this is in Fulham, all in southwest London, Wandsworth, Fulham, all over the place. And we would go in and literally there's just a group of us white kids, and we used to go and skank and dance and we used to get bottles thrown at us but we carried on," she says.

Jane says that though she became familiar with the bass guitar through her relationship with Ari Up, as she explains, it was deepened when she had the chance to fiddle with one a short time later. "While I was around Ari Up, Tessa [Pollitt] had shown me how to, you know, pull off on her bass guitar. And then I actually looked after somebody's house for him while he was on tour with Olivia Newton John. He had played for Cat Stevens and he was a lovely, lovely man, beautiful man, Jean [Roussel], a pianist. So Ari's mom had said, 'Well look, have Jane look after your house while you're all away,' and he had 1950s Fender bass guitars, and he had a Tannoy sound system, and that's when I started to learn. Because I would go and buy dub records. I would spend all my money on dub. And by playing it really loud, I could hear the dub and I could play it. I mean, I had been dancing with the bass literally shaking my whole body. You couldn't really hear bass guitar on a lot of things, but you could on dub. Now I could play it nice, teaching myself. So I spent one-and-a-half years teaching myself. And Jeanette [Lee], who played with John Lydon and PiL, she leant me a bass guitar."

Jane then started playing with the Bank of Dresden and the Tesco Bombers. She explains how she joined, though band membership, so to speak, was loose and free, given the environment in which these musicians lived was more of an incubator than a rigid arrangement. She says, "Neal [Brown] had a group called the Tesco Bombers. He had two bands—the Vincent Units, which was his serious band, and the Tesco Bombers, and we'd play in the local pubs, Chippenham pubs. And in the

---

[499] Crockford, Jane Perry. Email correspondence with the author, 27 July 2021.

Tesco Bombers, you would have guest drummers, guest bass players. Gina from the Raincoats, she lived in the same place but she lived upstairs and you had the lower two floors, the basement and ground floor. Gina Birch, she would play bass, I would play bass, but usually you had me singing. I did a couple of songs, which were ridiculous, but they were wonderful. And then they said they were going to do a big gig at Acklam Hall under the expressway. And I thought it would be a very good idea if we had a group called the Tesco Bomberettes that was lined up with women, and Neal couldn't be in it unless he wore a dress and lipstick. Richard Dudanski and his first band, it was called Bank of Dresden. They needed a bass player, and so I'd already sort of joined this band. They had me over to rehearsal in Islington and they had a bass that I could play. And they said, 'Well, listen to this and see what you can do with it.' And it was like this progression guitar, 'dum dum dum dum dum' [ascending]. So I went, okay, 'bup bup bup bup bup' [ascending]. And they said, 'Well, you can play.' I said, 'Oh, that's good!' But they wanted a stupid blonde bint who would just do what they wanted. I wrote songs and I did this and the other, but anyway, I thought I need to get some girls together for the Tesco Bomberettes, to have a little surprise show. We'd just run on stage, we'd pick up everybody else's instruments, and just plug in."

This is precisely when the planets aligned or the fates conspired or the mélange of Soho organized to put these four women, who just happened to all be looking to form a band, together in their life paths. Jane says, "So I saw Kate Corris in a dole queue [unemployment line] in Lisson Grove and I said, 'I'm looking for, you know, you play guitar and do you know anyone? Because I've got this girl, this beautiful French girl.' She was a French ballet dancer—she's actually Swiss French, and she was in love with Neal but Neal, no, didn't want to see her, and I asked her, can you sing? And she said, 'Ah, je ne sais pas. I don't know.' But she could. She could. And that's Ramona."

Ramona Carlier grew up in Geneva, Switzerland but moved to London in her teenage years to escape her difficult homelife. "I had a tough childhood," she says, "not in terms of money, but my father was an alcoholic after terrible experiences in the war, and my mother was depressive. Don't get me wrong, I was loved, but it was often quite scary. I wanted to escape Geneva and the memories."[500] She had a background in the arts, though not necessarily in music. She states, "I started doing ballet at the age of 8 and was on stage a lot. I was dancing as an extra in musicals and in operas, when they needed children, and other theatre productions. I loved being on stage. As a child around 9 to 10, I used to write little books that I distributed to my classmates. I also wrote little plays that I used to put together with kids from the neighbourhood and invite parents to watch us or in summer camps. I did ballet until I was 18 when I became really anemic and skinny and stopped dancing."

Shortly thereafter, Ramona moved right into the heart of the music scene in the late 1970s, as she explains. "I came over to London because I met Robin Wills

---

[500] Wilkins Carlier, Ramona. All quotations, unless otherwise noted, from interview with the author, 30 Apr. 2021.

from the Barracudas in Geneva. Then he went back to the UK and one day rang me and said, 'Come over here! I know the Slits and lots of other punk bands,' and another friend of mine, Anne, was an au pair in Kensington. So I had to find an excuse to leave Switzerland. I booked an English course for three months in September 1978 and came to London. I stayed in Paddington in a run down B&B where the Barracudas were staying as well. Some of them were Americans living a very rock 'n' roll lifestyle. So obviously I went to their gigs and started hanging around with music people from West London, particularly around Westbourne Grove near Notting Hill. It was very much a squatting thing at the time—rundown housing and post-Rachman flat, big West Indian community where the Windrush generation had settled in the 1950s. It was a fantastic melting pot for creativity and individuality."

The powerful lure of the punk "anyone can do it" ethos, combined with the positioning at ground zero of this movement, created opportunity, space, and possibility for all who moved in this sphere. Ramona's orbit revolved around those at its center. "I went to lots of gigs—the Slits at the Acklam Hall (underneath the Westway), Tesco Bombers, Bank of Dresden, Vincent Units with Richard Dudanski, drummer of the 101ers and later Public Image Ltd. I used to hang around the Music Machine, Marquee, and the World's End King's Road with other punks. It was a very exciting period to be in the centre of the whole punk movement," she says.

Which is how Ramona came to the attention of Jane who was putting together her Tesco Bomberettes band for a bit of a giggle. Ramona says, "Being friends with Neal Brown of the Vincent Units introduced me to Jane Crockford who was playing bass with the Tesco Bombers. Jane came one day to Neal's squat and asked me if I wanted to join a band. I said that I couldn't play anything, so she said, 'Do you want to be the singer?' I replied okay. In those days, everybody was in a band, and it was quite loose and it didn't matter if you were any good, as long as you had the right attitude."

Incidentally, Rhoda Dakar says she had once thought about joining the Mo-Dettes. "I'd wanted to be in a band for a long time but it was all about boys that had been playing in their garages for about 100 years. Punk made it seem possible. And then I heard about the Mo-Dettes being put together and they were looking for a singer. I thought, 'Should I? Nah, I won't.' Then I went to see them at Acklam Hall and thought, 'Oh, I really wish I had now.' The Mo-Dettes made more sense. I liked the punk-pop kitsch Sixties influence. It was more like who I was."[501]

Jane Perry Crockford, on bass, had assembled Ramona Carlier as vocalist, Kate Corris on guitar, and Kate brought with her June Miles-Kingston on drums. Both Kate and June worked together on Julien Temple's film, *The Great Rock and Roll Swindle* about the Sex Pistols (see also Fun Boy Three chapter). "Kate had June," says Jane, "and so we got together and the Sex Pistols had the rehearsal room on Denmark Street, Tin Pan Alley, and we went to rehearse there. And it just, you know, we got just a few numbers together for this show. I already had my one song that I'd written

---

[501] Rachel, Daniel. *Walls Come Tumbling Down*. Picador, London, 2016, p. 90.

for Bank of Dresden, that's 'The Kray Twins,' that was a jazz number, and we did a cover of 'Paint It Black' and we just sort of fooled about. And I'd prefer to rehearse with the girls than go to a Bank of Dresden rehearsal and I went back to Monmouth Road, to my little room and I remember Richard Dudanski coming into the room and saying, 'Where were you?' and I'm sort of, 'Oh, well, I didn't come.' It was our first rehearsal as the Mo-Dettes. And they also told me, 'We don't want you to write songs anymore. We just want you to play bass.' And they said, 'You're sacked. You're fired.' Good. I've got a new band anyway. So the idea of the Tesco Bomberettes became the Mo-Dettes."

So what's in a name, anyway? The same woman who had named the Slits, Kate Corris, is responsible for naming the Mo-Dettes, which many people then, and still now, confuse with the mods. Kate explains, "Mods? I don't think so! I did love 'My Generation' though! And the Small Faces! We put the hyphen in there to emphasize the pronunciation—Moe dettes—which was supposed to hark back to the 60s girl groups, not Mod."[502] Think Motown. The hyphen was added to prevent mispronunciation. "We have our hyphen in the right place," says Jane.[503]

When asked how the Mo-Dettes formed, June recalls, "Kate and I started playing together and then we met up with Jane and Ramona and we'd literally, within about a month or so, we got a short set, very short set of covers and one of our own songs. Joe [Strummer] gave us our first support in Notre Dame Hall. Then we were supporting Madness, we supported Siouxsie, and we were a hit! It was shit! But for some reason, it just worked. It just worked."[504] Things did move that quickly for the Mo-Dettes, largely because of the space they worked in. Their sound was also both a product of their environment, as well as creative, never derivative. This was largely due to their talent and rawness. June says, "Jane was an amazing bass player, Kate was fantastic—she had this energy. It was a real New York kind of energy and she played those kind of licks, and put that to a very strange bass—Jane played this kind of very melodic bass. It was insistent. It never stopped. I found that quite difficult, so that's when I thought, I've got to really pare this down. I've got to hold this down and keep a really low, constant beat. It was so important to me that the drums were the right tone. I would literally work on tuning them until I thought it was right. I didn't know what I was doing, but I just knew the sound that I wanted. It was a reggae sound because all those beats and those songs that I love, like Tamla, like all the ska stuff, the old reggae stuff, I mean, one of the first records I ever heard was 'Return of Django.' Oh my god! That crisp drum! And it just makes you feel alive. And I knew I wanted it like that—a really deep bass drum, a really really crisp snare, no ring and a mic on the rimshot so you could get lots of sound on the rimshot. So that's what we did, and I think it worked. It never recorded well. We never recorded anything that I liked—but live—it was full of energy."

[502] Ogg, Alex. *The Mo-dettes: The Story So Far*. Cherry Red. Liner notes.
[503] Wright, Paul. "Puis—je vous presenter la Mo-Dettes!" *Killin' Time*. 1980. flickr.com/photos/paulwrightuk/8131959413/in/photostream. Accessed 5 May 2022.
[504] Miles-Kingston, June. All quotations, unless otherwise noted, from interview with the author. 18 Dec. 2020.

Meanwhile, Ramona had stopped attending school and took odd jobs, cleaning and waitressing. Her housing situation changed too. "As I became homeless, Kate invited me to move in the top bedroom of the squat at Daventry Street, above Joe Strummer's room, which was on the first floor. The ground floor (Kate's room) had just been used for a scene in the *Great Rock'n'Roll Swindle*—the scene when Sid Vicious puts a record on the juke-box and starts singing. We started rehearsing in the basement of the Daventry Street squat which was tiny, claustrophobic and damp. However, we had some good laughs there—it was the same place that the Slits had rehearsed and also Strummer had rehearsed with the 101ers. Paul and Steve from the Sex Pistols loved the band and paid for the first demos," says Ramona. The demos became their first recording—the single, "White Mice" with the B side, "Masochistic Opposite." It was released by their own label, Mode, and distributed by Rough Trade.

The single caught the attention of radio DJ John Peel, whose endorsement almost always ensured a band's success. He said of the Mo-Dettes' debut single that it was "the musical equivalent of the Battersea Power Station made out of eggboxes."[505] To translate, it was energetic yet fragile—a winning combination in Peel's eyes. He invited the Mo-Dettes into his studio to perform for his show on January 28, 1980, and subsequently two more times, on August 26, 1980 and July 11 1981.[506] The Mo-Dettes live performances, supporting acts that are now legends, began at that first gig at Notre Dame Hall supporting the Clash on July 6, 1979. On October 13, 1979, they supported the Selecter at the Electric Ballroom and two days later supported Siouxsie & the Banshees at the Hammersmith Odeon. In February of the following year, 1980, the Mo-Dettes hit the road in support of Madness on a week-long tour of Manchester, Liverpool, Glasgow, Birmingham, and London.

Jane recalls that the gig with the Selecter didn't go over so well with audiences who expected to hear ska, which the Mo-Dettes were not, but she explains how the Madness tour then happened. "We had gone to see Madness, Selecter, the Specials. They were playing at the Nashville Room. All these bands came and they're playing all this ska music, and I'm like, wow! They're really fucking good! And I was really impressed. And then we heard from John Curd, a promoter, a couple of days later, 'Oh, they're [Selecter] playing the Electric Ballroom, we need someone to open,' and we're like, 'Yeah!' And so basically we almost got booed off by the audience. They really didn't like the idea of us, but we carried on. I think June got down off her drumkit and just went to the front and said, 'Alright, come on then,' because she's an East End girl, she wasn't going to have any muck."

In Pauline Black's memoir, *Black by Design*, she recounts the Mo-Dettes' support of the Selecter and has a completely different observation of their performance. "The Modettes [sic] came on to the stage amid a bit of heckling from some of the more uncouth sexist elements in the audience. This was my first live

505 "Four Can Play: Mo-dettes." *Experiment Perilous*, 15 May 2014.
experimentperilous.blogspot.com/2014/05/four-can-play-mo-dettes.html. Accessed 10 Sept. 2021.
506 From BBC, bbc.co.uk/radio1/johnpeel/sessions/1980s/1980/Jan28modettes. Accessed 10 Oct. 2022.

experience of an all-girl band, who competently played their instruments and wrote their own material. Vocalist Ramona fronted the band. She looked just like Jean Seberg in Jean-Luc Godard's 1960 movie A Bout de Souffle. She sang in English, but with a heavy French accent, mangling the words of the song, but nonetheless possessing that je ne sais quoi that many French girls use to maximum effect. I'd been told that their guitarist Kate Korris had formerly been a member of the Slits, an all-girl band that I admired, but the revelation for me on that night was the powerful drummer, June Miles-Kingston, who sat gorgeously stony-faced behind her equipment, holding the whole, wobbly, jelly-like sound together. They won the audience over by the end of the set. After all, London was their stomping ground and this was a London audience, notoriously fickle and expectant," said Black.[507]

After the show though, things went a little better, or at least they did for Jane, as she explains. "So afterwards in the dressing room, it's like one big green room, there was Madness there. And I had a few drinks. I was a little whe-hay! June said, 'Oh, what you think of that drummer?' I said, 'Oh, he's quite cute.' I didn't think much more about him. But he totally fell in love with me, it seems, and he pursued me after that. And it was all very beautiful and a huge, big deep romance and love," says Jane of Daniel Woodgate, better known as Woody. The two were married in 1980.

The Mo-Dettes were certainly getting attention of the press who noticed this "all-girl group" that was "set to rock the music world."[508] This press, not surprisingly, could be sexist and downright offensive. One writer, a female, wrote her review in the "Mirror Woman" section of the Daily Mirror amidst an advertisement for canned salmon ("How to feel the family something special,") and another article on hairstyles ("A Short Cut to Success" by Bill Reed). The reviewer, Sue Tranter, wrote of the Mo-Dettes that "Jane is probably the most financially secure. Last year she married Woody Bedford [sic] from the nutty group Madness." Why her financial security had to be shored up by a man, in this journalist's eyes, is questionable. She noted that Kate had left home and her mother had "come to terms with her daughter's wanderings." She furthered that they got their start in "back rooms" at pubs and noted that "after hanging around for eight hours, at the end of it [performance] they will be lucky to cover their expenses." Question whether or not journalists ever implied that all-male bands were poor, loose, and drunk, and if they were, well that was likely seen as a positive.

By June of 1980, the Mo-Dettes found themselves, thanks to the publicity of the press and tours, and the success of their single, signed to the Deram label, a subsidiary of Decca. The first Mo-Dettes release on this label was a cover of the Rolling Stones tune, "Paint It Black" with the B side "Bitta Truth." The single was produced by Roger Lomas who had previously produced for the Selecter, the Bodysnatchers, and Bad Manners, and then afterward for the Specials, Desmond

---

507 Black, Pauline. *Black by Design*. Serpent's Tail, London, 12 May 2012, p. 153.
508 Tranter, Sue. "Band of Hope." *Daily Mirror*, 4 Dec. 1980, p. 9.

Dekker, Laurel Aitken, Toots & the Maytals, and numerous others. "Paint It Black" was slickly promoted and the first 20,000 copies came with a free flexi-disk that also featured a live Mo-Dettes performance of "Twist and Shout." During a session to promote the new single, the Mo-Dettes were visited by a most unusual visitor at Capital Radio. "We did our session and Prince Charles was doing an inspection. He just came in and said, 'Are you punk?' and we said, 'No, we're doing Mo-Dette music,' and that was it. No big deal. He was quite good fun really. He's very short," said Ramona.[509]

Jane also remembers that visit, as well as another a few years later with Madness. "Basically we were recording for Richard Skinner, a radio show, and at the time when we were recording, he [Prince Charles] came in and all these flanks of photographers came with him and they were in the mixing room. We were out in the studio. And so we were recording 'Paint It Black.' And he's so short! Tiny! Little man! And he came in and he said, 'Oh hello. Oh hello. Oh, very good. Did you write that?' And it's like, 'No, that would be the Rolling Stones.' I far preferred meeting Princess Diana, which was a couple of years later. Madness had opened a royal variety show, the Prince's Trust. And so they did the show and the first band at the show at a big theater in London had to play the (sings 'dah dah dah dah dah dah') the National Anthem. And they [Madness] did it on these little yazoo sticks [kazoos] which go (sings 'verf verf verf verf verf verf'). And then we had to stand up, of course. As an award for that, they later had a party on Oxford Street. The bands were invited. Now Madness was on tour, so the ladies, the Mrs. Madness's were invited instead. And so we're all gathered in our little groups at the beginning of the party, and in comes Charles. And in comes Diana. Now they had just got back from Washington where she had danced with John Travolta or something. And I'm hoping, well we don't want Charlie, because I've met him already. We want Diana. She's gorgeous. And we did, us ladies of Madness, she came across and she stood here and, oh, the temerity, I reached out and said, 'Lovely to meet you,' and tapped her on the shoulder and said, 'How was Washington?' and she was lovely. Everybody else was horrified because I touched her. I reached out and sort of touched her shoulder. Oh, she was tall. And he was still short. I think that was the main problem, you know. She was too tall for him. Like Tom Cruise and Nicole Kidman. Oh, yes. She was lovely. How I feel about it in the political sense, it was nonsensical. I could meet anybody that would be like, okay, yeah. Some people I do feel shy about it. But yes, I mean it's like you're the same as me." As a sidenote, Jane, as a "lady of Madness," was featured on advertisements for the Madness tour and single, "My Girl." The wives and girlfriends were photographed and designed in the same style as the cover of the single which pictured the Madness men.

Roger Lomas went on to produce the Mo-Dettes next single, "Dark Park Creeping" with the B side "Two Can Play" before they toured more around the UK

[509] Wright, Paul. "Puis—je vous presenter la Mo-Dettes!" *Killin' Time*. 1980. flickr.com/photos/paulwrightuk/8131959413/in/photostream. Accessed 5 May 2022.

as well as Spain. By August 1980, the Mo-Dettes were ready to record an album comprised of their singles and other songs. That album, *The Story So Far*, was also produced by Roger Lomas, and just before the release, the Mo-Dettes went on a five-week tour of the United States in the fall of 1980. Their debut in America took place in New York at Club 57, Irving Plaza. It was reviewed by Robert Palmer (not *that* Robert Palmer) in the *New York Times*.[510] Palmer stated that early in the show, the Mo-Dettes experienced malfunctioning equipment and amplifiers, but that was quickly sorted out and they performed. He wrote that they "churn out danceable rock-and-roll that's solid but unexceptional. From time to time, the quartet fuses into a unit, and that's when the Mo-Dettes are really interesting." Palmer was most fond of "White Mice" and he noted that "the high point was a performance of 'Twist and Shout' that featured several members of the group Madness. Chas Smash, Madness' 'nutty dance specialist,' exuded a more compelling stage presence than any of the Mo-Dettes and danced wonderfully," and he called the Mo-Dettes tour of the United States "a little premature." Without early access to music education, as boys were afforded on drums and guitars, and without the cultural acceptance that men received for decades prior as members of bands, it is understandable, though not excusable, why a male reviewer would rate a male dance crasher, in a sense, more favorably than the female artists who occupied this new space they took by force.

Another reviewer of the American tour was *NME's* Richard Grabel who traveled for a day with the Mo-Dettes and wrote in clichéd sexism beneath a headline that proclaimed they were "four innocent young girls."[511] He commented on "White Mice" that it was a "puff pastry, sweet and insubstantial, yet all summer it's been in the repertoires of a lot of rock-disco and rock club DJs in America, it created an audience for them." Fairly substantial, one might argue. Other songs are deemed "bounce-and-flounce pop" and Ramona is dubbed "cute." But in the second half of the article, this male writer takes a more sensationalistic approach in telling the Mo-Dettes stories on tour, including their appeal with lesbian crowds, calling the audience "dykes" and quoting "we want your tits;" and a story about the Mo-Dettes being saved from rowdy bar patrons in California by a group of Hell's Angels.

What made its way into the interviews reveals that the Mo-Dettes were aware of the judgment, even as they toured. "Even here we get this reaction, people saying we should have waited, at least till we had a record out here," commented Kate to Grabel in *NME*.[512] To which Jane added, "We intended to come to New York the first week we started. They have to understand, we're The Mo-Dettes and we'll go anywhere, 'cause that's us." The women (not girls) of the Mo-Dettes didn't need permission or approval from anyone.

The Story So Far was released just after their return from America. Recording the album, according to every member of the Mo-Dettes, was not a good experience,

[510] Palmer, Robert. "Rock: Mo-Dettes' Debut." *New York Times*, 8 Sept. 1980, p. C15.
[511] Grabel, Richard. "Exposed! to by women Threatened! by men Leered! at by Hells Angels." *NME*, 18 Oct. 1980, p. 24-25.
[512] Ibid.

nor a good fit for their sound that was much better live. In short, heavy production was not the ethos of the Mo-Dettes. "They wanted another Bananarama basically," says June, "and I wasn't interested in that. None of us were." It all came down to money, as it usually does, for the label. While Geoff Travis at Rough Trade allowed the Mo-Dettes to maintain their creative independence since they were the distributor, Roger Lomas at Deram wasn't so keen on a hands-off approach when producing. Producing means producing, and a contract is a contract. "We would have liked to have stayed independent," says Corris, "but we were running out of money to keep it going. We talked about whether we were going to take the advance and run, but we were basically going one step at a time. But when 'Paint It Black' didn't really happen—that was our first record with them—the record company just freaked. They started to try to cheat in various ways—some obvious, and some not so obvious. And that's when it all started to go south. These people had the money, and it's very hard to fight that. We did try—they went into the studio and overdubbed something on one of our tracks—we were like, 'You can't do that!'"[513]

The women were all in agreement that Lomas's production missed the mark. "We went up to Coventry, don't ask me why," says June. "I think because of the Madness connection to 2 Tone. Bob [Black], the manager, in conjunction with the record company, thought it would be a good idea. So they sent us up to Coventry to work with Roger Lomas, who had done a lot of 2-Tone stuff. He was a bit of a bear and had no idea how to treat women. ... Roger didn't get it at all. It was a shit album. It was!"[514] Jane states, "I think the majority of it could have been better. If we'd had somebody who really liked our records, we could have swapped ideas and we would have had a better attitude. As it was, Roger Lomas doesn't really like us much anyway. I think it was twelve songs that were really wasted," said Jane.[515] Ramona adds, "We would do something and then we would say, 'What do you think?' and he would say, 'I don't like the song anyway.'" June recalls, "He wanted each of us to have a really different idea of what we were doing, go in there, fucking record it, and then him produce it as quickly as possible. I've got respect for him as a producer, but not for us. He has done some good records," to which Jane responds, "That's the shame of it."[516]

In June 1981, the last single by the Mo-Dettes in their original form was released. The song, "Tonight," was a cover by Lee Hazelwood that was given to the Mo-Dettes by the label. The recording, production, and promotion was a disaster. "The record company had the brilliant idea that we should do Eurovision," says Kate, "and they came up with this song. And we said, 'We don't want to do Eurovision, and we don't like the song.' They said, 'Well, try it.' Bob [Black, manager] was really behind the idea—'It's exposure, it doesn't have to be like ABBA.' So we rewrote it.

[513] Ogg, Alex. *The Mo-dettes: The Story So Far*. Cherry Red. Liner notes.
[514] Ibid.
[515] Pete + Pedro. "Interview at the Marquee, 9/12/80." *Shout*. Standupandspit.wordpress.com/2016/02/09/mo-dettes. Accessed 25 May 2022.
[516] Ibid.

The whole record was a joke. The photo session was a joke. The cover was a joke. It was 1981, I guess, and it was just crossing over to the New Romantic thing? They paid for us to go out to Carnaby Street and spend a fortune on clothes with a make-up artist, and we did the whole photo shoot thing. But we rewrote the song as a joke song, and I don't know if anyone ever got that."[517]

The Mo-Dettes did not, in fact, "do Eurovision," but the label suits still had their eyes set on molding the band into a profitable package. They brought in the respected Barbadian Dennis Bovell who had grown up in London and been at the heart of dub culture—a perfect fit for the group. Bovell had been a member of the band Matumbi, backing Jamaican artists when they performed in London. But his production work was just beginning in the early 1980s, and it has only flourished in the years since. In the spring of 1979, Bovell produced the Slits' album, *Cut*, which is how the connection to the Mo-Dettes occurred. "That probably came about through Dick O'Dell of the Slits. He [Bovell] took us in for a week or whatever, but it was heaven for me—as a drummer, just heaven," says June. "And vocally he was so good on the vocals. And we were good on the vocals. I never got the chance to sing much, being the drummer at the back, but I got more and more confidence as time went on, and I really enjoyed that actually."[518]

Sadly, the experience did not have the intended effect for the band, nor as quickly as they demanded, so the label brought in an additional guitarist to now make the Mo-Dettes a group of five. That guitarist was Melissa Ritter. "I was born in Manhattan," she says, "and I grew up in Washington Heights. My mother was a singer and a dancer. She had a dance company. Yeah, my mother was a hippie and I'm an only child, though I have stepsisters."[519] At a young age, Melissa moved out of her home and into the Village on the lower east side of New York City. Here she was exposed to the heart of the music scene in America. "That's when everything was happening. That was in '77. I was hanging out at Max's and CBGBs every day. You know, the reason, how I got into the scene is a neat story."

Melissa recalls, "Me and my girlfriend, Lynn, rest in peace, the way I met her was, I went to the Plaza Hotel because Led Zeppelin was playing at the Madison Square Garden. And I went to the hotel because I knew where they were staying. I was on the floor where they were all staying and I met this girl—that's Lynn, and Robert Plant had kissed her on the mouth. That was like a very big deal. So we ended up becoming really good friends, like my best friend, and we did all kinds of crazy stuff together. But one night we went to the Academy of Music, which is the Palladium now, to see the Dictators and you know who is sitting behind us? David Johansen from the New York Dolls. That's how we met them—they were sitting behind us, and Bob Gruen, the photographer [who six months later took a number of provocative photos of the two girls with Johansen while they were drunk, according

[517] Ibid.
[518] Ogg, Alex. *The Mo-dettes: The Story So Far*. Cherry Red. Liner notes.
[519] Ritter, Melissa. All quotations, unless otherwise noted, from interview with the author, 25 Jan. 2021.

to Melissa]. So I was 16 and she was 18 and we're like teenage girls giggling and everything. And the next thing you know, they're like asking us if we want to come with them. We're like, okay. We went back to Bob's apartment and that's how I kind of got in the scene because the next night, or a couple of days later, we went to Debbie Harry's birthday party at Danny Fields' house and everybody was there, you know, like Debbie and the Ramones, because Danny Fields managed the Ramones at the time."

Melissa's friend Lynn became the paramour of David Johansen, Syl Sylvain, and Johnny Thunders, the latter of whom introduced Lynn to heroin, says Melissa, from which she never recovered and died. Melissa also dated musicians, namely Joe Strummer and Marc Bell, better known as Marky Ramone. "This was before he was in the Ramones. He was in Richard Hell and the Voidoids when I started dating him. We lived together for a while, like ten months. I was 18, he was 26 I think. He was such a bad alcoholic and he had orange juice in the refrigerator that had vodka in it. So he would wake up in the morning and the first thing he would have would be vodka and orange juice. And it was really crazy. And he was kind of like, oh I can't, I can't tell you everything, but he had some weird quirks, put it that way," says Melissa.

But Melissa was most interested in becoming a musician herself. She began by playing acoustic guitar in one of the rooms at Debbie Harry's birthday party, which got the attention of "a kid whose name was X and he was in a band called the Nightcaps" who was "very big on the scene, in the CBGB's scene in the late '70s. And he said, do you want to be in a band? And I said, sure, let's do it. So I guess he started coming to my house and then we got a singer. But the singer wanted me out of the band and said they didn't want to have a girl in the band, so I got kicked out for being a girl."

Melissa was with her next band, the Tiger Beats, for over a year before she moved to London. "We were very poppy—like a poppy girl group. I don't want to say like Blondie, because we did have a keyboard player. But we did stuff like copy songs that were kind of like Beach-Boy-ish. The singer is Robin, this girl I met through our boyfriends. Our guitar player was Mitchell Ames and he was in a band called the Flesh Tones right before us. And then funny enough, the Flesh Tones opened up for the Mo-Dettes in 1981," she says. "But you know who came to see the Tiger Beats that was really fun? Hall and Oates. They came to one show and then they started coming to all our shows when they were in town. And John was shorter than me, but he hit on me. He was very nice and they were very supportive."

Through her connections in the New York music world, Melissa met her husband, Hein Hoven, who managed the Stray Cats. Though the Stray Cats were a New York band that performed regularly at CBGB and Max's, they moved to London. "Their retro '50s look and sound didn't go over well around Long Island, though, and in the summer of 1980, the group headed to England, where a rockabilly revival movement was just beginning to emerge," says one writer.[520] Melissa moved to London and she and Hoven were married in England. She now had connections with the music world in England and word of mouth got around that the Mo-Dettes needed another guitarist, as dictated by their label. "My husband was friends with everybody because he was the life of the party. He was 6'6", he always had coke, so he was friends with everyone. And he was friends with Bobby—Bobby Miles-Kingston who the guitarist in Tenpole Tudor and brother of June. So that's how I found out from him. I said, 'I'm looking for a band,' and he said, 'Well, you know, the Mo-Dettes are looking at auditioning guitarists and I guess I auditioned. I came in after they did the record, which I hated and I wish I had been on the record. I came in August 1981," Melissa says.

The Mo-Dettes with Melissa Ritter toured England as well as a second tour of the U.S. Melissa recalls, "We played New York, the east coast and the west coast. We played the Peppermint Lounge, headlining because we were a known band at the time. They had fans, just always a cult following. We stayed at the Iroquois Hotel in Manhattan and at the time Iggy Pop was living there. Iggy followed me into the elevator, so it was just me and Iggy, which is funny, because I forgot when I was in the Tiger Beats, we played at a club called Tracks in Manhattan and Iggy was there and I could see him staring at me from the stage and literally as I walked off the stage he was right in my face. Iggy really hit on me but I said to myself, I don't know if I should do this. It could be really bad. He looked so bad back then, even, like a drug addict, strung-out dude. But it was so funny because I came back with the Mo-Dettes and he bee-lines into the elevator with me, so it's just me and him in the elevator, he follows me, comes with me to my room, and I had to say sorry. I had to say no to Iggy again! But we played in L.A., we played at the Perkins Palace in Pasadena, in San Diego, in Boston we played the punk club the Rat—I mean we did a lot of shows."

Those shows were not fruitful for the band, and additionally, they soon dried up. "We had a terrible manager and suddenly we didn't have any shows," says Melissa. "The only way we made money was from shows because the record didn't sell, and so we were constantly on tour just to make that little bit of money. Ramona was pissed off at the manager because she needed money so she went back to Switzerland and we got another singer. June actually sang for a while because June has a really great voice. June was fantastic. She should have been a star in her own right. I really do believe that. But she didn't want to sing lead. She wanted to stay behind the drums, so we got this girl, Sue Slack."

Ramona Carlier says being replaced by Sue Slack was painful but came at the end of a long process, and she places blame on administration at Deram. "Things were going sour. We completed the first album which did not attain the success we thought. Our single 'Paint it Black' was high in the charts and we were scheduled to appear on *Top of the Pops* which generally guaranteed success. Unfortunately, there was

[520] Huey, Steve. "Stray Cats Biography." allmusic.com/artist/stray-cats-mn0000475431/biography. Accessed 11 Oct. 2022.

a general strike at the time in UK and television was cancelled. There were power strikes, rubbish collection strikes, etc., therefore we didn't have the impact that we hoped. The record company wanted to push us in a commercial direction like the Go-Go's and suggested another guitarist, which I didn't see the point of, as Kate was brilliant, so Melissa came on the scene—whilst she was a great person, it changed the group dynamic. Also the record company decided to use Sheena Easton's producer and did a cover of 'Tonight,' which had been done by Nancy Sinatra. I felt we did a great job of it, but was too commercial and too far removed from the original Mo-Dettes sound. I think we lost the spirit of the band."

She continues, "I had to go to Switzerland for family issues with my Mum's health and out of the blue I received a phone call from someone from the band, I can't remember who, and I was told that they had done a gig without me, with June singing, without telling me first or even discussing it. I was so upset, I felt completely betrayed, because previously when June broke her toe before a big tour, we collectively decided to cancel the tour as we felt it was necessary to retain our solidarity as a group. We were a gang, a female unit that never before were compromised or conceded control. There and then, I told them on the phone that I was leaving the band. The other band members took no time in arranging another singer, step forward Sue Slack, who was the wife of Paul Slack, bass player with the UK Subs and Flying Padovanis."

Jane Perry Crockford explains the mess made by the label and how the end was inevitable, given the misdirection. She also notes that it wasn't exactly Ramona's choice to leave the band. "They said first that we had to get rid of Ramona because she couldn't sing. She could sing. She sang from here—from her heart, from her soul. God, I loved her voice. It had everything. And it was described once by the *Melody Maker* as being slapped in the face by a wet fish. But that's good! That's brilliant! I was against it, but Kate and June said, yeah, alright, and so Ramona left. And that was painful. Then we got Sue Slack to sing—pure voice, like an angel. No heart or soul whatsoever. But a beautiful voice. And then Melissa Ritter, I took her because she could really play guitar, and Kate could come up with the most wonderful licks. But Kate had to go, so then we had myself and June and Melissa and Sue, but then they dumped Melissa and June as well and the Mo-Dettes were dead at that point."

June Miles-Kingston says she left on her own terms. "I broke the Mo-Dettes up in effect because we'd been touring extensively and not making any money. But that wasn't important to me. It was fine. But I never felt like we recorded what we were really like. And then all of a sudden we couldn't do it anymore without making money. We lost control even though we tried so hard to hang onto it. So I just split up with the Mo-Dettes because it wasn't happening and then they had replaced a couple of us and I was grieving." June continued her career with Fun Boy Three and numerous other bands.

For Ramona Carlier, she too tried to continue in music, but has since stepped away. "The record company was really interested in promoting my career—they genuinely thought that I had a great opportunity to become a solo artist. They paid for me to record some demos and I worked with Glen Matlock, Henri Padovani, Chris Musto, and Val Haller. For me though, all the pleasure had gone and I became very disillusioned with the music industry. As Hunter S. Thompson said, 'The music industry is a cruel and shallow trench, a long plastic hallway where thieves and pimps run free and good men die like dogs. There's also a negative side.' I married our roadie, Ivor Wilkins, who was then working with Lords of the New Church. This made me bounce back from the Mo-Dettes debacle and then we moved to L.A. in Laurel Canyon. I have many great stories. Then we went on to have three children. Ivor managed the House of Love and I worked in their office. Eventually, we parted ways and I went to university and became a teacher in a secondary school which was tough and situated in a deprived area of London. Ivor and I are still very good friends."

Melissa Ritter continued performing and still plays today. She met Jennie McGeown after seeing the Belle Stars perform at the Hope and Anchor and the two became fast friends. When their bands broke up, the two began making demos in Melissa's home studio. They named their group DLAM., an acronym for Dance Like a Mother. They gave a tape to Ian Flukes, owner of the Wasted Talent agency who flew them to New York to meet Gary Kurfirst who managed the Eurythmics, B-52s, the Ramones, and Joe Strummer. "The next thing I know, we're being paid to stay at the Mayflower Hotel in Manhattan and labels are picking us up. We're driving around in a limo, going to meet people at record companies with Gary. It was very exciting and very sad that we didn't have a big hit because we really thought for sure we were doing to," Melissa says. She continues to write music for artists, as well as television and movies. She and Hein Hoven are divorced and she remarried an attorney in the entertainment industry. They live in Los Angeles with their daughter.

Kate Korris left music entirely. She stopped playing guitar, she stopped doing interviews, and she denied being a Mo-Dette if she was recognized. The ruthlessness of the music industry was too brutal for a genuinely creative individual with real talent and emotions to contribute. She has empowered countless women through battles she fought during her short but meaningful career. "You've got to learn that everything they're telling you is bullshit," she told Vivien Goldman. "It's really hard because you're a girl and you're expected to think in a silly way, not know how to put lights together, or carry heavy things," she said during her short time with the Slits.[521] She continues, "If there was a message to/about girls, it was that being female is not something to apologize for or cover up. You don't have to be butch or loony to stand up for your female self. You can still like boys, wear skirts and makeup, and be your own person. 'Playing like a girl' is just as good as playing 'like a man.'"[522]

Jane Perry Crockford and Woody were divorced after 15 years of marriage. She explains, "I stopped drinking and what he had really loved was the mad woman. So you know, after one and a half years, he found another dysfunctional lady. But his father had been that wild. He had divorced their mother, Woody and Nick, like three

[521] Goldman, Vivien. *Sounds*, 11 Dec. 1976
[522] Goldman, Vivien. *Revenge of the She-Punks*. University of Texas Press, 2019, p. 131-132, p. 132-133.

years after Woody was born, and he married several other ladies. I should have seen it. Whereas my lovely adoptive parents had stuck together and were together until the end, almost 50 years, I believed in that married—that kind of friendship, companionship. I had put Woody through hell, but that's what he had wanted. Because he has gone on now after 22 years, he just left his second wife, just like that. And she was 12 years younger than him. Now he's remarried and with a lady, a wife who is 24 years younger than him. So he's gone the way of all men. Stupid idiots. My god! Midlife crisis, whatever. But he had been wonderful. Truly wonderful."

Jane says she "wasn't blessed" with children, though she did want five daughters after reading *Little Women*. Today she focuses on her sobriety and health, working with a local organic produce company in London. She found out in 2011 that her birth mom committed suicide in 1980, the same day, on September 7th, when Jane and the Mo-Dettes were featured on the front cover of *Face* magazine. She has since reconnected with her birth family, including a sister and two brothers, that she discovered through online DNA searches. Her advice to women is to stop categorizing yourself as a woman musician as an example to others. "Fuck being all girls. We just do it. It's no use having a chip on your shoulder and going round saying, 'It's so much harder because we're women.' That's just Bollocks! It's your own attitude, that you can do it."

The Mo-Dettes and Prince Charles at Capital Radio

Mo-Dettes promo photo (above) and performing at the Good Mood Club in
Halifax, Yorkshire April 26, 1980, photo by Steve Trattles (below)

The infamous Clash gig article with Shane
MacGowan and Jane Perry Crockford (left),
Jennie Matthias and Melissa Ritter in DLAM
(right), advertisement for the
Mo-Dettes supporting the Selecter in 1979,
and the My Girl advert with Jane top left.

Terry, Blair & Anouchka

Blair Booth: vocals
Anouchka Grose: vocals, guitar
Terry Hall: vocals

After Terry Hall split from the Specials and formed Fun Boy Three, and split from Fun Boy Three and formed the Colourfield, and split from the Colourfield, he formed Terry, Blair & Anouchka. It was the last days of the 1980s and Hall assembled the trio with Blair Booth, a singer from Nevada, and Anouchka Grose, a hairdresser from London. Both women had backgrounds in music and the trio was an opportunity to further their artistic abilities and create pop music with an innovative and established talent.

Anouchka Grose joined the trio after both Terry Hall and Blair Booth had already formed. Blair was the daughter of Roscoe Blair, the former chair of the music department at the University of Nevada in Reno. The family had relocated to London when Blair was a teenager and she began working as a session vocalist until she auditioned for Hall's new project. "Blair remembers that at the time another female singer songwriter Collette Meury was also being considered. During the interviewing process that went more like an interrogation, both Blair and Collette were asked who they knew in the 'business.' Collette replied she knew the cellist from the Colourfield. Blair replied she didn't know anyone. And so Blair quickly was hired," reveals Blair Booth's website.[523] Both Blair and Terry had an affinity for music from the 1960s and wanted to both cover these songs and use them as inspiration for new songs. But Hall needed a female guitarist, and Anouchka just happened to be in the right place at the right time.

"I'm Australian and I moved to London when I was quite small, like two years old," says Anouchka.[524] "So my mom and dad are both Australian and they're journalists. But my mom had been in musicals. She'd been in *My Fair Lady* and then just became a writer. And my dad, he's not a musician, but he's really into sort of blues, and Pete Seeger, kind of political music. And so that was around, and they definitely made us play instruments and all that stuff. I turned nine in 1979, and because both my mom and dad worked, we always had sort of these really young teenage girls looking after us, from Wales, and they were just obsessed with pop music. And so we would watch *Top of the Pops* every week and keep a close eye on the charts. And pop music was our favorite thing. In 1979, I think that's when I bought my first record. I bought Blondie's *Parallel Lines* with my own pocket money. But that was the year that so many records were in the charts—Selecter were in the charts with 'On My Radio,' I loved Elvis Costello and X-Ray Spex and all those kind of people.

---

[523] blairBlair.co.uk/TBA/tba.html. Accessed 4 Jun. 2021.
[524] Grose, Anouchka. All quotations, unless otherwise noted, from interview with the author, 10 Jun. 2021.

It was just this sort of explosion. And it was exactly at that age when I was crazy about pop music."

Anouchka says that her education also fostered her development in art, culture, and ultimately music. "I went to quite an experimental primary school and it had this headmistress who wanted it to be like the most multicultural school in London. And so she would collect people, like she wanted one of each type of person. And so we were Australian and we were slightly outside the area where you were allowed to go to the school, but she didn't have any Australians, so she was like, okay, you can come, so it was really lucky. And it was this amazing school where they really valued multiculturalism and all that stuff. So I guess the 2 Tone thing sort of made sense. It seemed familiar. It just resonated. It was quite a hippie school. And my favorite teacher taught us all how to play acoustic guitar, and he would teach us folk and stuff like that. And he was amazing. A brilliant, fantastic teacher. And so guitar playing started when I was 10. It was called Bousfield School and it's just like a normal state school in in West London and it was right next door to Princess Diana and we were at school at that exact time, so she was like the neighbor of the school and we would see her all the time. It was just cool and I was lucky to be there. After that I went to kind of a posh girls school and after that brilliant first school, I just hated it. I hated it. And I had scoliosis, a big curvature, so I had a big operation on my spine and had a brace and all this stuff. And because of all that I dropped out of school."

Anouchka says she was actually expelled from school, "for a mixture of having really terrible hairstyles and not doing my homework and having this spinal stuff. And so it was kind of lucky that I started doing modeling for this hairdresser called Antenna. You know these bands like Haysi Fantayzee and Boy George and all these people go there and have dreadlocks. I was modeling for that hairdresser and I would just do all their hair shows and all their photos. Because it was synthetic hair, one week it would be all pink dreadlocks and the next week it would be short hair, the next week curly, pre-Raphaelite red hair. It was really fun. And Blair came in to have her hair cut or something. She was looking for a guitarist and I was just chucked out of school, nothing to do. But I must have told the hairdresser that I can play guitar and I did a bit of singing. And so when Blair was having her hair cut, saying she needed a female guitarist, that was how I got the job."

By the time that Blair encountered Anouchka in the salon, Anouchka had already been performing at some small clubs. "I was in this psychedelic folk band with some friends and we used to play in all Londony places, like Dingwalls and small places and we had demo tapes, so I think I must have sent them a demo tape and they couldn't really tell because in our band there were brilliant guitarists and terrible guitarists, we'd all just take whatever, so they couldn't tell if I was brilliant or terrible. I was in the middle. Very in the middle. So then I had to go for an audition at Blair's house and that was good. That was really nice and fun. And then I had to go to meet Terry and I was just terrified to meet him. I was such a fan and had been such a fan since I was nine. It was scary!"

She describes that audition and the sessions that followed. "I took the train to Manchester. I think I was 18 by then, I was really young and they were both kind of nearly 30, so they seemed really old to me. It was kind of weird. So, I went to meet him in Manchester, met him at the station and then we went for a walk around the shopping center in Manchester. I remember being really shy and finding it really weird because it wasn't like an audition, or it wasn't like anything, it was just a walk around the shopping center with someone who I was a huge fan of. Really really strange. It was like I sort of passed the singing and playing bit with Blair and had to get along with Terry, and that was fine. It was informal. But it was really awkward, though, because he really is an awkward person. That's not like just for on stage. That was really real. He's a lovely person. I really got so fond of him."

Because of Hall's previous success and connections in the music industry, the band immediately had secured a label. Anouchka says, "Our band was signed to Chrysalis and we started recording pretty much straight away. I think maybe they'd even been waiting for the third member or maybe they were already recording a bit. So I had to turn up at the studio and that was when I just completely freaked out. It had been totally fine doing all the auditions at Blair's house or singing. But when I was suddenly in this really massive expensive recording studio, I was just really, really nervous. I think it was partly that they sort of wanted the band to look a certain way and they had such difficulty finding someone that I think they just thought, okay, we'll deal with her and her nerves. But I did start having guitar lessons and doing a lot of work suddenly to catch up because I just obviously wasn't anything like a session musician. So it was really weird and I was terrified of him. She was really sweet and made it quite easy for me to be there. But it was weird time for quite a long time."

Adding to the awkwardness of Terry Hall's presence was the fact that Anouchka found herself in a very professional and serious musical environment, which was completely new to her. "We were on a retainer, being paid by Chrysalis to do this recording and it was like 10,000 pounds a week for the studio. They spend so much money on the staff. I think we were at the Roundhouse for a while and then the Tears for Fears one [The Wool Hall in Bath, Somerset]. And that was the best experience. That was residential. Terry just had his baby Felix then so his wife was around a lot. And it was nice. It was kind of relaxed. I think I was very patchy, like, sometimes I just couldn't do things. And other times I would really be able to do things. But they never gave up on me, because some days it was just good. But not every day was good. And so I think they probably were being incredibly patient."

According to Blair's website, "Blair recalls Anoucka [sic] reading a lot, Terry making tea and Blair getting frustrated with the various session musos who came and went sanitizing the arrangements."[525] But the recording continued despite the awkwardness and the change in producers from Jeremy Green, who had worked with Fun Boy Three, to Bob Sargeant who had produced "Mirror in the Bathroom" for

---

[525] blairBlair.co.uk/TBA/tba.html. Accessed 4 Jun. 2021.

the Beat and was a BBC recording engineer.[526] Anouchka recalls the process: "Basically, she [Blair] and Terry were involved in the songwriting. And it was sort of difficult, tense between the two of them about writing credits and stuff, because basically the publishing bit is the bit that you want for financial reasons. Because it was sort of a business arrangement, it was just always a little fraught."

The recordings comprised an album of ten songs and was titled *Ultra Modern Nursery Rhymes*, which was released in February 1990. A single from that album, the song "Missing," was released in November of 1989 but it only charted at 75 on UK charts, and the second single, the title song, received a chilly response as well, charting at 77.[527] There was little coverage in music press. "When the album came out, we'd get sort of good responses, bad responses, and I think it was quite an odd record. Some people say that it was like an early Britpop record, and some funny people say that they really like that. I think it apparently sounded a bit odd at the time, or it didn't quite make sense to people, and maybe it was because Terry was older and there would be songs about divorce and sad stuff about growing up and all that kind of thing. So it was sort of odd sounding and it was a bit of a new thing for him. It wasn't this kind instant hit and I think everyone got a bit demoralized," Anouchka says.

After that, the trio dissolved. Anouchka recalls the way it ended. "Actually a really weird thing happened. Terry asked if I would like to just be a solo person, and he was going to kind of be Svengali-like and sort of be my producer. And that was really fun. And so we started to work on some stuff like that. We were going to do Melanie Safka or 'Animal Crackers,' this really ridiculous Sixties song. And it was all happening, working and making demos and stuff. And then one day he was going to come around for tea. I had moved to Manchester actually to be nearer, to make it easier to do work, and he was going to come to tea, we were going to get on with the work. And he didn't turn up for tea. And I've never spoken to him since." When asked if she has ever discovered what happened, she replies, "No, no, no, no, it's funny. It was always a mystery. I always wondered. I wondered all sorts of things. I wondered if his wife didn't like it, even though she is lovely and I thought that she and I got on very well. I just really don't know what happened. Very weird, but it's quite in keeping with the whole thing. Like the whole experience was weird."

Anouchka says that the trio never toured, never did any shows, though they "did really weird, miming on TV and stuff like that. There was talk of doing a light tour, but maybe when the album wasn't this sort of big hit, I think they got nervous about doing a tour. There are a couple of singles with videos, and those are beautiful. Those were beautifully done. I remember them being really fun to do and high production."

After her strange experience with the world of Terry Hall, Anouchka completely changed direction. "I got into writing nonfiction for teenagers. So I've done this book about hair and one about vegetarianism. And so then I went to this

---

[526] Ibid.
[527] officialcharts.com/artist/25773/terry-blair-and-anouchka. Accessed 28 Nov. 2022.

funny art school in Manchester, a community art school and I managed to get into Goldsmith's art school in London. I live here now and am totally settled in this part of London. So after art school I did master's in modern literature and theory. We did lots of post-colonial theory, and psychoanalysis, and feminism and all this stuff. From that I went to teach in the university in central London, and it was only then that I realized how bad the kind of racial tension was in institutions. So this whole thing of decolonizing the curriculum, for the last few years, I've had to really put in a lot of work to understand what that was. It did feel it was like quite revolutionary, in a way. My primary school sort of lulled me into this false sense of security that completely fell apart. And it was pretty big wake up."

Anouchka has taught at a variety of universities and has also published, since she has a background in writing, but she realizes that so much of one's path in life is both serendipity and opportunity, as well as making one's own way. "I sort of learned how the publishing system worked, and that's been really a great, helpful thing. My mom worked for the *Sun* newspaper, this terrible British newspaper, for a really long time. All the time I was growing up she was working there. And my dad is a writer now. I suppose all that stuff did make me think, well, you know, things are possible. It did make everything seem quite connected. I mean, especially after I got kicked out of school, I didn't really know what to do. I was doing rubbish jobs by working in a lamp shade factory, a call center, and rubbish things. And so it was hopeful and it made me think, no, you can go and try things. You can meet your heroes and mentors, so I think it made a massive impact on my life." Anouchka had a partner for 10 years, Martin Creed, and performed with him in his band, traveling. Today she has one child who is musical but attends Cambridge to study linguistics. "I'm very very proud," she says.

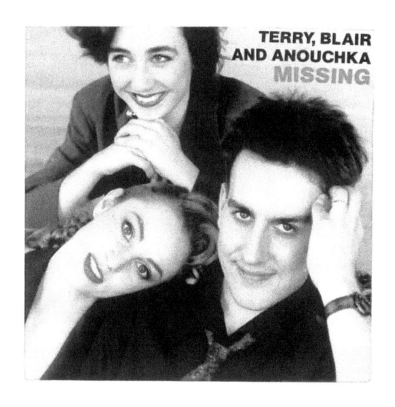

Terry, Blair and Anouchka's recordings. Anouchka pictured on bottom left on each.

Machine/Hot Snacks

Julian Bell: keyboard
Jackie Betterton: vocals
Mike Collins: vocals, guitar
Simon Finch: guitar

Silverton Hutchinson: drums
Nigel Mulvey: bass
Roland Oliver: bass

Coventry was a generator of ska in the years surrounding 2 Tone. Many bands tried to form in the mold of those they admired, including one called Machine, later changing to the name Hot Snacks. Their one recording, a song called "Character Change," was featured on the compilation *Sent From Coventry*, though this version does not include their one female member, Jackie Betterton, who had by then left the band. She explains her childhood, her involvement with this Coventry collective, and her life subsequent to the days with Machine.

"My family were totally *not* musical. But my dad was. He used to sing in the car, very tunelessly, but I used to love it when he sang because I knew he was happy. And I could hear the neighbors through the wall. They had a piano, and I told my mom I'd like to play. And eventually, she did buy me a piano for six pounds, which I learned on. After that my brother wanted to play as well—I've got two brothers—so he went to the same music teacher as me. I asked my mom and dad for a tape recorder and had a reel-to-reel tape recorder and I used to record myself and sing along. I taught myself to find out what harmonies were and how voices could blend together, and I used to get my younger brother—I taught him to do the harmonies. It was a lot of fun. So, we three kids all became very musical. My brother went on to learn the guitar and we still play together sometimes. And my other brother, he learned proper music and he's worked in choirs and gone around the world. He's got a beautiful tenor voice. He runs his own choir," Jackie says.[528]

After her childhood, dabbling rather seriously with music, Jackie pursued a formal education, though not in music. "I was encouraged to study proper stuff, so I went to study French but when I got there I managed to change it to French and film studies. So that was cool. And that's how I originally met the band members my first year. They were putting together a band and I auditioned for it, but I didn't get the part, as such. Later on, it must have been three years after that, I was on the Isle of Wight. I was working as a teacher of foreign language. I worked in the Savoy tutorial college, which was in a building right on the seafront. I was teaching English and taking them on trips and things around the Isle of Wight. You could just walk out of the college, in your bathing costume, and walk into the sea. And anyway, I had a keyboard which I bought in Birmingham, just before I moved to the Isle of Wight, and it was a bit faulty. So, a couple of months later, I decided I was going to take it back to the shop. And it was a very heavy keyboard, an Elka Rhapsody. And so I had

---

[528] Betterton, Jackie. All quotations, unless otherwise noted, from interview with the author, 27 May 2021.

to wheel it up the pier on a sort of British Rail trolley and take it on the train to London, and then a friend of mine helped me to carry it over and then on a bus, and then the bus broke down. I had some friends in Coventry and phoned them, the same friend, Julian [Bell, keyboardist], and they said oh, we need a singer for our band. They were called Machine. The people in it were Mike Collins, Julian Bell, and then there was Tony [Clarke] and Silverton [Hutchinson] and he used to be in the Selecter right before that. Oh he was such an amazing drummer, and there was another guy called Simon [Finch] as well. He was excellent."

Jackie backs up in her story to add that there was another reason that the members of Machine asked her to join the band. She explains, "When I was in school, I think I was about 12 or something. Maybe 14? Not sure. And I used to listen to radio a lot, all the time. I just always listened to radio, to music, and I was listening to a woman's hour and they had Joni Mitchell playing on it. She was being interviewed and she played that song, 'Yellow Taxi.' I was very aware of the environment, and you know, that worry, even at that age and I just thought she was just amazing to be singing about that and writing her own songs as well. And that was when I first thought—well, I mean, I had already written songs by then. I started writing when I was six or seven. I used to mess around on the piano and my mom was always saying, 'Just practice Jacqueline, practice!' Whenever I could I'd be messing about, trying different things. But I couldn't *not* play properly because she was the one that was funding my lessons!" she says with a laugh. "I did learn to play music and read music and all that sort of thing. And one of the songs I wrote when I was about 14, 15, we actually did that in the band. It's called 'Ride Higher.' I'd only just joined the band and I really loved that song. They wanted to record it and I'd only been in the band about 10 days. That's partly why they wanted me to join was because of that song. 'Ride Higher' was a reggae song."

So Jackie joined Machine, the band that had already formed in 1978, and her first gig with them was a battle of the bands. She says, "I went to see them playing because I'd only just joined the band at that point. And so they asked me if I wanted to sing but I just, I wasn't that confident. I'd only just joined and then to be suddenly in a competition? So they did their song 'Character Change,' but it was the Swinging Cats that won the competition that was held at the Lanch, at the Polytechnic in Coventry. There were all sorts of bands and they just had to play one song each and Jerry Dammers, he was one of the judges and other people, and it was great. One of the best evenings of my life, I think. It really was—just all these bands, like the Urge and I can't remember all the names of the bands, but there were all these handsome young musicians around. Eye candy. I was very shy. I already had my eye on somebody by then. It was Mike [Collins], because I'd known him at uni and we'd met up a few times and gone out as friends, to the theater and ballet. He was in the band, so there was no way I wasn't going to say yes to being in this band! We were just friends, nothing really romantic. We were both a bit shy. Occasionally we'd just go out and do silly things."

260

Though Jackie and Mike Collins struck up a friendship rather than a romantic relationship, some three years later she did find love, with John Shipley, member of the Swinging Cats—the band that beat them in the battle at the Lanch. The two married and had a child. But before then, Jackie began her musical experience with Machine and they quickly changed names, as well as their lineup. "They were called Machine, and I said, 'Well, why don't we have a name that's a bit more lively, because that's what we are. Machine sounds a bit automatic and kind of a little bit emotionless. So, then I think Ollie [Roland Oliver, AKA Doc Mustard, who replaced Nigel Mulvey on bass] came up with Hot Snacks. And we just we agreed we're going to be called Hot Snacks. I said yeah, because you can see signs everywhere for Hot Snacks, because there's this idea that you'd see hot snacks all around the place, and we'd get free advertising," she says, laughing.

The band was largely a live band, though they nearly secured a publishing deal with Carlin Music.[529] Their gigs were reviewed, some favorably, some not, by Coventry publications like *Alternative Sounds*. But the song "Character Change" was always well received. "We were energetic. Happy go lucky. But a bit edgy as well. We did 'Baby Elephant Walk,' and that's the only cover we did. And Julian [Bell] was an amazing keyboard player. I think he built his own keyboard, which is probably why they were called Machine, which I hadn't really sussed that out at the time, but certainly I realize that a bit later. I'd say it was about 80% reggae ska music, or more. It was all that pattern on the keyboard—just the up and down pattern. And amazing drums from Silverton. We had lots of weird sounds that Julian used to make on the keyboard. He sort of had a Hammond-y sound. I think he had a couple of keyboards and one of them was more of a sort of synthesizer. And I had an amazing piece of equipment. I think it was Simon Finch that gave it to me. It was like an echo machine and it was just like a little tape, like a reel to reel, but it just went around. And I think it was a figure eight or on two reels, but it was small though. And it gave you some sort of reverb and an echo-y voice. And that really helped my voice. And I felt quite professional in a band, carrying that. I suppose with the guys, I was a little bit in awe of them at first. You know, it was my first band. Then they were quite eager to do the songs that I'd written. So we did about half a dozen of those. And then it's just like, you know, somebody had written this song and somebody had written that song."

But Jackie says she then suffered from a mental breakdown, unrelated to the band, and took some time away. "It was quite and emotional time for me, and I went home to recuperate because I couldn't ... and when I came back, suddenly they didn't need me anymore. I was gone a couple of months. And I was having a breakdown. It's, it's even hard to talk about it now," she says, crying, "because it meant such a lot to me. The band and my relationship with Mike. He was doing the band thing. But I did go around to see him and he came to see me as well a couple of times and then when the band split up, we did kind of like meet up a few times as well. I don't know

529 "Hot Snacks/Machine." Hobo—A to Z of Coventry Bands.
sites.google.com/site/bandsfromcoventrypart2/home/hot-snacks-machine?pli=1. Accessed 29 Mar. 2021.

if you know, he got in an accident." Mike Collins who performed on guitar and vocals died suddenly in 1987. "It's really sad because he was knocked off his bike. A push bike. He cycled out to the organic gardens and he was knocked off by a juggernaut. I didn't get a chance to say goodbye to him. He was in a coma. It was only a few days, I think. Tragic."

When Jackie returned to Coventry after her convalescence, she looked to join another band. "And that's how I met John Shipley again. I went to Horizon Studio, and we met and played some music, and I think I was playing keyboards and singing. Or I think I was just playing keyboards at that time. I met him and then we did a bit of music together and then he used to come around to my house and we did more music together and then eventually we decided we're going to move in together. We got married. I already had a child by then. I have Frankie. I think that's definitely got me out of any depression or breakdown. It was the best thing that I could have done really. He was a miracle of life for me. Saved my life. When I was married to John. We had a lovely fairytale wedding in a country church by my mom and dad who had by then moved to the countryside in the County Durham. And then we had Ethan. He's also the light of our lives as well. Both my sons are amazing. They're in their thirties! And both of my sons have set me up with my own studio with some keyboards, a MIDI keyboard that used to be Paul Haskett's, actually. We've known Paul and his family—he's been a friend for ages."

Though Jackie and John are now divorced, they are still friends and musical collaborators. "John and I play together in various bands. We revamped the Swinging Cats a few years ago. But he had a terrible drink problem. He fell down stairs. But then he gave up drink after that. He was alright, thank God. We did get divorced, but then we still were friends, though it did take a few years of going back to friends again. In between times, I've been in an all-female band. Well, my husband wasn't that keen on me being in a band. But at that time, he was playing with some other group. And so I thought, oh, well, I'll see if I can play with women then. We played for years in a band called PassionGround. We all moved to Leamington so I could be in this band. So there were six of us to start with and it became three singers. It was very lively. And we all wrote our songs together, we wrote them as a group. And then two persons left for different reasons but they continued to support us. So it ended with the four of us anyway. So there was another Jackie, Shannon, Jane, and me. We were together about five or six years. It was so amazing, honestly, because I was brought up with two brothers and I'd never really had close relationships with many women. But we [the band] knew everything about each other—our strengths and weaknesses and of course we were very supportive of each other. We used to practice at Shannon's place which is out in the country, but it wasn't ska music. It wasn't rock, exactly. I was doing the keyboard and I was doing the Julian thing of doing all the sounds. The keyboards are quite ethereal really. I used to have an amazing keyboard. It had analog sounds on it, but you can actually use the knobs on the top to alter the sound during playing. We had a little tour. We toured Cornwall, we did festivals and local places. It wasn't a huge band. We got really good because we were dedicated. But unfortunately, the lead singer, Shannon Smy, met the man of her dreams. He lived in Glastonbury. She had to make a decision—is she going to go off with him, or is she going to be in the band. She married him." Smy has returned to music, performing at women's festivals and recording a solo album.

After PassionGround, Jackie left music, though not for good. "I decided to earn some money for my kids, whose lives were poor with poverty stricken musicians in their lives. So I decided to change to teacher and make money. I'm part-time now. I work with special needs children," she says. She never remarried and her name is now Jackie James. She explains, "My dad was James Betterton and I just wanted to have a memory of him in my name. I haven't changed it properly, so I still get called Jackie Shipley sometimes, like at work and places like that. It's sort of an unofficial name. He was the best dad. In his gruff tuneless way!" she says, laughing.

Her memories of performing with her Coventry band, Machine and then Hot Snacks, is certainly a fond one for her. "I can remember being at gigs with Pauline Black. She was one of my heroines. And everyone would just be bopping up and down. It's happy music, isn't it?" When asked if she still sings she replies, "Yes, I do. Up until the lockdown, I was in a duo with a brilliant musician on the bass, and I started playing the guitar about 20 years ago. I just thought it's so much easier to carry around. At one point I had three keyboards. And I could take the guitar into work as well. The kids used to love music so it's my main instrument now."

Jackie's children are also musical and she still has connections to many of the musicians with whom she has performed over the years. "My kids have been in bands as well. Frank does painting and decorating and dabbles in music in his spare time. He's also a daddy. And Ethan decided he was going to, at last, get his band together. I was so thrilled. So then John [Shipley] started playing in his band. There were nine of them in the band—three brass, three singers, bass, drum, guitar. Ethan plays the trumpet and my other son Frank is playing the drums. So they were in the same band called Electrik Custard. Anything that John is a part of is good. He is amazing. He is a genius. Genius on guitar. So I've been concentrating on learning to publish my own songs and also to sing, so music production. Maybe one day I'll do another version of 'Ride Higher!'"

Promo photos for Machine/Hot Snacks

Red Roll On

Angela Duignan: vocals, bass
Germaine Dolan: vocals, drums
Barbara Gaskin: vocals, keyboard

Bunny Newth: vocals, guitar
Jane Wilks: vocals

Angela Duignan's tale of how her band came to cover one of the most iconic songs in Jamaican music history, which itself was a cover, is enough to make any music lover cringe. "It was the late 1960s and a friend of mine from university was working at Island Records. And his job was to smash up all the old vinyl, reggae, and ska records that hadn't sold," Angela says, with a twinge of lamentation in her voice. "But he brought home this *Club Ska '67* album which I played nonstop and so that's the song that we did, 'Pied Piper' by Rita Marley."[530] This song, covered by the all-female band, Red Roll On, would appear on three compilations of music by Canterbury groups, or ska rarities, or "independent women," but it was never released as a single. Nor were any other songs by Red Roll On ever released, yet the group was important for being one, if not the first, band of this era to feature all women playing all of their own instruments, and for their contributions to the music and art world before, during, and after their short-lived existence.

The story begins with Red Roll On's founder, Germaine Dolan, who had been a student at art school in Canterbury during a time when some pretty important musicians were getting their start as creators and visionaries. "Well, I've always been obsessed with reggae, and it was my band, really. I started it, finished it, hired and fired, wrote most of the songs. I grew up all over the place because my dad was in the RAF, the Royal Air Force. We lived in various parts of England, Aden [in Yemen], and Cyprus for five years, so I had a traveling childhood really. We weren't a particularly musical family, but I was always obsessed. I had Elvis Presley, 'Heartbreak Hotel' when I was about 11 and that was the start of rock and roll, really."[531]

Germaine had seven siblings, though many of them stayed in Ireland, the original home of her parents. Germaine though, was born in Cambridge in England and attended school in Cyprus. "There were four different schools but they were run by the forces, English schools, one of which was a boarding school and coeducational, which was really fun. And Cyprus is beautiful, compared to England. I mean I love England in many ways, but it's cold. So then I worked in West Indian clubs when I was 18 or 19, and that's where I fell in love with it, because I just love the music and to dance. I went to college late really. I paid for it myself so I worked for about five years in between leaving school and going to college, in all sorts of jobs. And that was my favorite, hanging out in West Indian clubs in North London—little local dives with paraffin heaters and a sound man who played all the latest records from Jamaica

---

[530] Duignan, Angela. All quotations, unless otherwise noted, from interview with the author, 18 May 2021.
[531] Dolan, Germaine. All quotations, unless otherwise noted, from interview with the author, 30 Apr. 2021.

which you wouldn't have heard otherwise. These records weren't in the shops, they weren't on the radio. It was this new, amazing music to me, which I still adore it. So much good stuff, they kind of became benchmarks of my life, your favorite tunes—anytime you hear it, then I'm back," she says.

Germaine's love for West Indian music led to her involvement in music herself. "It's why I got into bands really. Ian Dury, of Ian Dury and the Blockheads, was my tutor at art college and he got me dancing with his band, which was then Kilburn and the High Roads. It was my first year at art college and I was having the time of my life, which is what I'd always wanted to do—paint. And meeting him, he was very inspirational. But I never ever thought I could have a band, particularly, but he was like, 'you can do anything, just do it.' And it was the era of punk, where anyone can do it, just thrash your guitar or whatever. You learn eventually. We all did. It's a great way to learn. Why sit alone in your room when you could be just doing it? It's so much fun. But it's very intense and creative and proactive. I just loved it."

Germaine became involved in a popular band in Canterbury, while at the same time founding one of her own. She explains, "I was living with a drummer, who was in the Purple Hipsters, which I was in, three years before Red Roll On began. And I was still in the Purple Hipsters playing the bass until the end of the Red Roll On and the end of the Purple Hipsters." The Purple Hipsters were one of many jazz-fusion/progressive rock bands that were part of the Canterbury scene during the 1960s. Others included Caravan, Camel, Gong, Hatfield and the North, and Soft Machine, among others. One of those bands that had considerable success was Spirogyra, not to be confused with the American band, Spyro Gyra. The former was formed in Canterbury and featured four members, one of which was Barbara Gaskin who eventually became part of Red Roll On.

I grew up in a place called Hatfield," says Barbara, "which is about 20 miles north of London. I was the youngest of three. My father was an office worker in London and we were not well off. We were quite poor, actually. My father came from a really poor background and a sort of agricultural background. And my mother was a was the daughter of a vicar. She had the option of going to college but couldn't go because they saved a university place for her brother. She said she was tone deaf but I don't think she was. She loved music actually. She could play piano fairly well. My father sang in the choir and he taught. He could read music a little bit. I used to sit on his knees and he'd teach me the piano a bit. So they loved music, but they weren't professional musicians."[532]

While Barbara was in school, she developed her passion for music. "The first school I went to which was a state primary school, they were keen on music. It was after the war and they were quite progressive really, and they recognized that music was important for young children. There was a director of music in the county who was very encouraging for music amongst young children, and because of that, I got the opportunity to learn the cello at school. I think the lessons were free actually, that

---

[532] Gaskin, Barbara. All quotations, unless otherwise noted, from interview with the author, 17 May 2021.

was when I was about 10. But before that, I had piano lessons at home. And I really had to beg for them because they were expensive. And my parents, they had to be sure that I wasn't going to give up because my sister had lessons and then got bored. And so I really, really had to plead with them. And I did start having piano lessons when I was about 10 or 11. I really liked my piano teacher, but it was all very classical. Anything to do with pop music was completely frowned on, it was considered to be not proper music. This is the cultural background of the 1950s. I mean, rock and roll music was there, but you weren't really aware of it because the radio was state radio. It wouldn't have lots of radio stations. So you weren't exposed to it. Whenever I was exposed to it, I really wanted to go in that direction. But it was considered that you shouldn't play music unless you had a piece of music in front of you because you would develop bad habits. But I loved classical piano music. My father used to bring home records from a library in London, and I would listen to that," she says.

After primary school, Barbara began to develop and pursue her own tastes in music. "In my secondary school, when puberty hit, it was a completely different story. And then I wanted the usual things that young girls are into—Beatles, pop music generally, folk music, Joan Baez, Judy Collins, that sort of thing. And then, once I got my hands on the guitar, that's the route I went down because it was simple to pick up rudimentary guitar, folk stuff. My sister went to art college and had a guitar, a Spanish acoustic, and when she came home for the holidays, she let me play it. It was very difficult to get it off me when she went back. She had a book of American folk songs, which I've still got. But then I wanted a guitar and I didn't have one, and I bought one from a very dodgy looking bloke, about 15 pounds, which is quite a lot. And it was actually terrible, but you could bash out chords and you could learn with it, a certain amount. So, at the same time as doing that, I was going through the sort of grades that you do on piano and cello in classical training. I was losing interest in it, really. I just want to do my own thing, and they wanted me to go to music college because they thought I had certain talent. But I didn't want to go because I didn't want to study classical music. You couldn't really do music in university then. It wasn't considered an academic subject. Times have changed. But if you wanted to study music you would go to music college and study classical music."

In the late 1960s, Barbara did go to university, specifically the University of Kent in Canterbury to study, not music, but literature. Here she met with a community of fellow musicians and her first band, Spirogyra, formed. "As soon as I got there, I met other people like me who actually wanted to be playing music. But they were studying other things like politics, history, and in my case, literature. I immediately joined a folk band, Spirogyra, when I got there. We had a thing called the freshers weekend where all the new students meet each other. And I met a guitar player called Steve Hillage and he was very confident, very outgoing. And he'd gone to Canterbury because he wanted to meet Canterbury musicians who were already quite well established—bands like Caravan, Soft Machine, those bands. And there was something of a noticeboard that said something like, looking for singers for concerts at the end of term. And Steve who was very confident said, 'Oh, I know this girl, she can sing,' and pushed me forward into it. I don't think I would have done it on my own, to be quite honest."

The notice for singers was put up by Martin Cockerham, a fellow student at the University of Kent, and Barbara explains that the original incarnation of Spirogyra was a much larger ensemble that was later reduced to four. "I sang with this very large group at the end of term. There were about 20 of us on stage. It was the brainchild of somebody from the north of England and it was his group, Spirogyra, and at the end of term he kind of whittled it down to four of us. And then we managed to get a record deal and we had a year off from college—we got a sabbatical from college. And we were really lucky to be able to record three albums and tour a lot—we did all the college circuit. It was great. A good opportunity. And that's the beginning of my professional music career. And I've never really done anything else. It's been a challenge, but it's kind of more like, I can't do anything else," Barbara says.

Spirogyra released four albums from 1971 to 1974 with Barbara Gaskin on vocals and keyboards. They broke up in 1974 when Cockerham moved to Ireland and Barbara eventually returned to Canterbury. "We'd had some success for about five years, gigging a lot. But then eventually, somebody went back to university, somebody left, and then the lead writer wanted out. And then it was at that point that I went off traveling, because I knew that I didn't want to do anything conventional. But when I came back after three years, that's when I met Germaine. Well actually, I had a house with Germaine before I went away, and she used to drive me nuts. My bedroom was over hers, she had a room on the ground floor, it was a shared student house, and she used to go out, and I'd go to sleep about like, 12 or one o'clock and I'd be in bed and Germaine would come back in at about two or three in the morning and put her records on. It really drove me nuts. And in the morning, I'd say, 'Germaine, you put your records on and it was four in the morning.' She said 'Oh, I thought you're asleep!' As if you could sort of sleep through it! She's amazing. She's an amazing person, actually. So I didn't really know what I was going to do when I got back to England, and punk had happened. And punk was quite liberating, because it meant that people that weren't really musicians could form a band. It was a really good thing, opened things up. And Germaine simply asked me if I would like to join the band. And I just simply said, yeah."

So Barbara Gaskin reconnected with Germaine Dolan who had started to assemble the band Red Roll On with two other women, one of which was Angela Duignan. She was one of three children in her family and was born in the north of England, but moved to the south when she was younger. "We moved a lot. I mean, I went to eight schools, but music was always a part of my family—from Ella Fitzgerald to Louie Armstrong, big bands, Glen Miller, you know, all that great music of my father's generation. Lots and lots of music. I left home at 18 as most of us did then to go to university. So I headed straight for London, of course in the late 1960s, which was great—culture, lots of music. And I lived in Ladbroke Grove off Portobello Road, which is sort of a great West Indian community. I met lots of musicians and had a musician boyfriend. I mean, I didn't like his music much because he was in a prog rock band, but lots of reggae, and lots of multiculturalism, so that was great. And then I didn't last a year at university doing physics. I wasn't very successful, so then I had to work. I worked in Woolworths on Portobello Road. And then I got a job writing software as a computer programmer. Well, I mean, I'd never seen a computer, who had? But anyway I did that for a few years, which was interesting. The computer took up an enormous room, which as a software writer, you didn't really see in those days, you just did your stuff and passed it down, and two hours later you got your program back. I was told, here is the manual, this is the computer program with unraveling sheets and sheets of paper, get to it and learn it. I was the only woman. It was an engineering company, so as usual, just like at university doing physics, it was all men."

Angela worked for some time in computer programming before moving to Canterbury where she returned to the classroom. "I had a boyfriend who was moving to Canterbury to do a PhD, so I moved with him. And then I went back to college to do English literature, because I'd always wanted to do science and English and you couldn't here, you know, you had to choose. I did my three years of English, which was lovely, lots of women. And I had maths as a second subject. I'd split up from the boyfriend, seems to be what happens, and met up with a group of quite political people. And then I met Germaine. She was part of the art school crowd so I was good friends with them. And then I was in a relationship with Paddy who was a friend of Germaine's. He and I were together for the next 28 years, and he played marimba in the Purple Hipsters," Angela says.

The community of musicians and students was incredibly active. "Canterbury was quite a strong music scene then. There were bands like Caravan and, not my sort of music, but very nice people. We were more into Little Feat and Ry Cooder, and blues and reggae, I suppose in the late 1960s." This is when Angela's friend from Island Records, the vinyl smasher, brought her a copy of *Club Ska '67* and introduced her to the song that became part of Red Roll On's repertoire. She also began to develop her own musical abilities. "I'd sort of been playing guitar when I was a teenager but didn't really play guitar much until the late '70s so when I met Germaine, I just bought myself an electric guitar. But she'd already got money to play guitar and she wanted to play drums, so I said, 'Okay, I'll learn to play the bass then.' It's incredible. It was that post-punk, get-up-and-do-it time."

The final member of Red Roll On was Bunny Newth, who was then named Bunny James. "I grew up in the south of UK, in a rural suburb of London. And my father was a doctor and my mother was sort of cultured. Her father had been an art dealer and she was very interested in the arts and we had a lot of art from his gallery when he died. So art was there. I mean, I was the most artistic in the family. My sister became an actress. My brother did something creative too, but we're all creative in our different ways. I was probably the most artistic but I also was into music but not academically, more just sort of messing around and playing by ear and that's how I got into music really. I did play publicly a lot and I had a choir actually. So I did a lot of formal singing. And I had already decided I was going to art school" says Bunny.[533]

"So I went to Canterbury art college, in Kent. It was the late 70s, early 80s, and everybody was interested in creating a band. Everyone just was messing around playing music. And I think, even if you couldn't play an instrument, you just got up there and played it anyway, even if it was pretty bad. I met Germaine and Angela, locally, socially, and Germaine was an artist and she was in a band at the time called the Purple Hipsters and her partner was in a band called Kilburn and the High Roads which was the band that in Ian Dury was in too, so they were all friends of Ian Dury. Ian Dury was a lecturer at the art college. He was also an artist, so I knew him as well, so we were all sort of part of that sort of social scene. Chris, her partner at the time, was the drummer of Kilburn and the High Roads, so there were lots of inter links. And the singer for her band was a good friend of mine at the time, and we were all in the same year at art college, some of us. Germaine was about 12, or maybe more older than me. So she and Angela were more mature, really, and they had sort of, quite clear ideas of what they were wanting to do. I think they decided to create a band and I think Germaine just asked me if I wanted to be part of it. I was a sort of friend and I saw quite a lot of her socially."

So Red Roll On was assembled, and the name was selected to represent a number of concepts. Germaine says, "I think of it like a deodorant, and only it's red. So you can draw with it. I'm a painter. I liked the name Red Roll On, because I saw it as a painting device. I still wish there were such things, actually. I'd like to invent them. Color which just rolled on, no brush. I should have patented it." Bunny offers her perspective on the name, "It was a sort of feminist name for sure. And it had to be something that had a feel of punk and edginess. We came up with some various others like the Belladonnas and things like that but we decided against that and I think Red Roll On felt feisty and edgy and on the sort of pulse of what was going on at the time. I think it was a pun on a roll on deodorant, but at the same time, rock and roll and the color red being slightly you know, aggressive and at the same time being sort of feminist, it was, it was an analogy really. It wasn't literal, if that made sense."

The band featured all women on their instruments, but also, all women sang with no front person, as such. They did have a lead vocalist for a short time who also played the saxophone. Bunny explains, "There was also close girlfriend of mine who was in my year, and she became a saxophonist, but she didn't last very long because she went to the Royal College of Art. So she was more into her art at the time. Jane Wilks, she'd sung in various bands, I think, and Jane became the front singer. Jane lasted a period of time, perhaps a year to a year and a half, and then she left. And then instead of just a front person singing, we all wrote our own songs and all sang, which was great. It was it was much freer and I think our style became a lot more interesting as a result."

---

[533] Newth, Bunny. All quotations, unless otherwise noted, from interview with the author, 22 Apr. 2021.

The music that Red Roll On performed was pop music, but it was influenced by the reggae music that Angela and Germaine listened to. Barbara says of Germaine, "She was very into Toots and the Maytals. It was her idea to do 'Pied Piper.' That was the version [Rita Marley] that we copied and it has a ska beat to it. We span quite a big age group in Red Roll On. Germaine I think is five years older than me. Bunny was probably five years younger. So there was quite a big age range. So Germaine was already kind of a very confident mature person and she had had a life. She'd been to Australia and back, she'd been to art college, she told me that she used to go to West Indian clubs in London and dance. Something that I never did. She'd been kind of exposed to Jamaican music. It wasn't my musical area but what I was intrigued by was being in a band with other women actually. It was so different, honestly."

Bunny explains the influences and sound of Red Roll On, "I don't think we played reggae so much. We were much more influenced by bands like the Specials, the Beat. I, at the time, was running the student union and I would get access to all these bands to play at the art college. So they would come down and play and we had all of them actually, the Selecter, all of them were sort of fast and furious. We were probably more influenced by ska and that sort of style. I was playing rhythm guitar. I will say that Germaine's drumming was brilliant. It was a bit like Maureen Tucker from the Velvet Underground. Unique, but actually really brilliant. Angela was bass. Barbara was on keyboard and Barbara was definitely classically trained. She was very good. I think we all became pretty good actually, in our own areas. We had quite a good tight sound towards the end. I don't think we were political. I wouldn't say that. On the other hand, perhaps we were feminist. Some of the initial stuff, it was sort of reggae, ska, but we sort of gradually developed our own style, which was a collective, I would say, not specifically tied to any one genre. It was a mix."

Red Roll On didn't just cover songs, like "Pied Piper," they definitely wrote their own music. Bunny says, "We stopped doing cover versions and we started doing quite interesting, quite quirky music. It was perhaps sort of inspired by people like Patti Smith, Chrissie Hynde. Maybe sort of bands like the Doors perhaps, and Velvet Underground, that sort of feel. And we lasted about three, four years, I think. And we were very close to being signed up by Virgin interestingly. There was a bloke who approached us, two people approached us, but I think we were sort of not mainstream, really. In fact, I think what we were doing was quite interesting. I was a bit impatient because I was younger, and I think I probably wanted to do more mainstream, or more of what was going on at the time, like Siouxsie and the Banshees, and that sort of stuff. But the others were, perhaps more with maturity, I think they had a rounder idea of what we were, which was, perhaps, quite interesting, really."

Angela says that the way the band created was a very collaborative effort with a variety of musical influences. "I think everyone had their place really. To me it was Germaine's band. Barbara was a musician but we all just worked on our own little bit. I mean, we didn't play very much reggae or ska, you know, but it's what we loved and probably if we'd been capable we would have done it. But certainly in Ladbroke Grove, in the late 60s, Aswad were always playing. There was the Mangrove restaurant, there was lots of reggae going on. And I think it's just sort of you know, by osmosis. Of course, we were huge fans of Toots and the Maytals, I mean, whenever I could see them, I would."

Being in a group of all women, in a creative space, creating music was an experience that all of the members of Red Roll On speak of with great fondness. They were strong and supportive of one another and good friends. For Barbara, who had spent years touring as the only female in the band with Spirogyra, being in a group of all women was a refreshing change of pace. "So it was quite difficult, actually, I think being the only woman in that band [Spirogyra]. But in Red Roll On it was really good fun, because we were very supportive of each other. We used to dress up—we'd say, hey, try these earrings. It was fun. And we were like a little sort of solid unit that supported each other. There weren't very many all women groups then. I sort of think we were one of the first. I think there was a band in England called the Raincoats. There were the Slits, but they came a bit later actually. Yeah, I think we were one of the first. It was rare. I got back to England in September, 1978. So sometime after I got back, Germaine invited me. I wasn't living in Canterbury though, I was living in London, and I had to hitchhike down for rehearsals. Having a band of all women is just not what women did. You had women in front of bands, you know, singers, but you didn't have any female instrumentalists. Not in rock anyway. I mean, obviously, in classical music you did, but it was just a bit unusual, and it was really the force of Germaine's personality which drove it along. I used to hitchhike down there and I used to stay with Bunny. She's youngest in the band. In fact, she was pregnant in the later days of Red Roll On and she could hardly get her guitar on I remember. I used to sleep on Bunny's floor and she had a cat, and she used to sleep on top of me, the cat, but we'd stay up until four in the morning talking. It was very nice. I miss it."

Red Roll On didn't have much success outside of Canterbury, though they do have their friendships, memories, and some recordings to show for their efforts, as well as the experiences that led to other endeavors. Bunny says, "We did a few recordings. We recorded an album as part of a whole load of bands in Canterbury which was produced by a guy called Rupert Heinz, and it didn't really come off, but he selected a whole variation of bands from the area and we all played one or two pieces on that album. Then we went and did some recordings ourselves. And we took some of our tapes to Johnny Walker, who was then on Radio One and he was interested in them, as was a guy called Rob Gould, who was at the time working for Virgin music. And we had a meeting with Rob Gould, and he was watching what we were doing, seeing how we would develop. I don't think we would have been hugely popular. We were a little bit too complex, perhaps, and we didn't appeal necessarily just to young people, because Germaine and Angela were in their mid-30s. So there was a real range of age in the group, which made it a great deal more interesting in many respects, but we weren't like a teenage band. So I think it was difficult to identify the sort of demographic that would be specifically interested in us."

The band was strong as a unit, so as a result, any outside influences that went against their goal as a group were simply dismissed. "It was fun and collaborative. I mean obviously like in any group you know, there were small tensions but mostly no, we really enjoyed it. I can remember one time we were doing a remix and we were recording in London and a friend of mine who was a record producer said 'oh, you need a manager,' and so we though, oh alright, you know, and they were all male. And one guy came in and said, after he'd listened to us, he said, 'Could you just play with more balls please?' And we just sort of looked at each other and thought, 'Okay, we don't need a manager.' There are lots of bands that have women in them, but there still are not that many bands where women are playing. They're mostly standing at the front and singing. I know when we did some recording, the suggestion was that we put down our instruments and just wiggle about at the front and sing and get Ian Dury's band the Blockheads to actually play the music. So that went down really well, as you can imagine," says Angela.

Bunny says that their relationship as friends and musicians helped to keep the band strong. "I think there were a lot of women bands, sort of female bands, forming at that time and quite a lot of women manipulated by producers, you know, they were interested that everyone was good looking, and you felt that perhaps they were interested in us sometimes for the wrong reasons, so on and so forth. I mean, everybody was good looking for sure. And, you know, we all had a slightly different style, which is quite nice too. We didn't adhere to anything that was necessarily derogatory of what women would be like. I think we like to be clear about the fact that we didn't want a front person actually. I think that was quite different because every other band, particularly the band that Germaine was in, an awful lot of blokes are vying for the centerpiece. She got fed up with it and what she liked about our band was that we just go on, we didn't argue, we just agreed on things, and we gave each other space and support. And it was so interesting that the parallel band, the Purple Hipsters, kept throwing people out of the band all the time. And it was so narcissistic by comparison. And I think that was really demonstrated, the way we operated really showed them up and demonstrated how women do work so well together. It was a feminist statement without being in your face. We weren't, any of us really, aggressive at all in our delivery. We were, in some respects, restrained, but I think we were, at the same time, assertive."

Ultimately, Red Roll On broke up, not because of discontent or lack of success, the latter of which wasn't a goal—it was simply to create and express. The band broke up when the events prevented the band from continuing. It was a culmination of things that occurred in the women's lives. The event that occurred first involved Barbara Gaskin who had a professional career in London where she lived while traveling to Canterbury for rehearsals and performances with the band. Barbara explains, "One really horrible thing happened and one really exciting thing happened. The horrible thing that happened first was when I hitchhiked down to Canterbury, I was attacked on the way. It was really horrible. I was actually attacked on a trip down there. I had to go to hospital. That kind of put a kind of hiatus in the rehearsals. Then at the same time, a record that I'd done with Dave, just for fun, suddenly started roaring up singles charts." The Dave that Barbara refers to is Dave

Stewart, the music producer, songwriter, and musician best known for his work in Eurythmics with Annie Lennox. Barbara Gaskin and Dave Stewart have been life partners since 1981. "Steve Hillage had been in school band with Dave. He introduced me to Dave in about 1969 and I was pretty impressed then. But we didn't get together until much much later. We were sort of friends for a long time," Barbara says. Dave Stewart and Barbara Gaskin recorded a cover of "It's My Party," which reached number one on UK music charts. "I suddenly got very busy with that. We came to America, we did a sort of radio tour of America, where we flew around the place talking to radio stations. I just got caught up in that, and then we recorded an album. And I think I paid for some recording for Red Roll On and they went into studio somewhere. But basically, I sort of stopped doing that for those two reasons. But they carried on for a bit." Since then, Barbara Gaskin and Dave Stewart have performed together as a duo, releasing a number of albums, and they have produced and performed on countless other albums for musicians, including Jane Wiedlin of the Go-Go's (see also the Specials and the Special AKA chapter).

For Angela Duignan, the breakup came because she was working as a teacher at the same time as rehearsing, recording, and performing, which took a toll on her personally. "It was very intense because we were all working. And that thing about working and then Friday night after a week of teaching, loading up the van and driving up the motorway to do gigs. But we did it. We did it. It was a great time to just get up, do it. So I ended up teaching maths for the next 30 years. I taught for eight years at quite a challenging high school. And then I stopped and went away on holiday with Germaine to Greece for a bit. And then I came back and went to teach a grammar school, which is a sort of selective school, and then eventually, I was head of maths and I taught maths and computer studies. And played lots of music." Angela lived with her partner, Paddy, for 28 years until he passed away. She says they never married and explains, "I think my generation, I think that whole feminist thing, the reaction against the sort of 50s housewives, getting married was seen as a bit of a cop out or, I don't know, not wanting to forge your own path." She retired from teaching in 2007 after 32 years. She still resides in Canterbury and plays a ukulele in a local group for fun.

For Germaine Dolan, the end of Red Roll On came as a result of wanting to focus on her art. "I was playing live and rehearsing twice a week with Red Roll On, and I was rehearsing three nights a week with the Purple Hipsters. The building where we did all these things, was an old school I hired originally as a studio. We had left college by then, so I was working and still painting, so I had a studio. There was a rehearsal room in this old school, Holy Cross. So we ended up having a recording studio, but I always had a painting studio going. And we all, the Purple Hipsters and Red Roll On, rehearsed in the same space. I painted Victorian reproduction furniture which was destined for America, and I worked in a pizza parlor and any old thing to keep painting and playing music. After Red Roll On, I had another band that didn't last very long, and then I went traveling. I'd been working in kitchens and black rehearsal rooms and I needed to get out, really. And everything fell apart that year. I split up with the drummer from the Purple Hipsters. We'd been together for ages. It just seemed like the time of big change. Today I play the ukulele occasionally, I do percussion at parties very willingly and successfully. I think people like it, usually. I know what I'm doing."

Germaine has exhibited her art in galleries all over the world, and she has also owned her own galleries. She lived and worked in London for 18 years but today she lives and works in Canterbury. "I think my painting is very similar to my drumming," she says. "Little patterns and little, or big, motif. I love African painting. I'm quite knowledgeable about world art. I love it, as I do world music, African, Latin American, anything that's really good." She has one son who is a music journalist and was a DJ on Red Light Radio in Amsterdam in addition to making music himself. "We spent half our life in the Sinai desert, me and my son. A fantastic place. In my opinion, it's the most beautiful place ever. The people are amazing. The Bedouin are all amazing. I'm still painting and I want to travel."

Bunny Newth says of the end of the band, "I became pregnant, so things became diverted. And I carried on playing for quite a while, but it became difficult. I think we lost the sense of just keeping it together. I was busy doing the student union job, because I was doing it as a job after I finished my degree, and I thought, this is great and I'll carry on doing this. And then this very unplanned incident of pregnancy happened, and so I was very much taken off in another direction by it. It was quite frustrating to be honest. But of course now I have no regrets. It was one of the best decisions I made. But at the time, I was not sure whether it was a good decision, so I was very conflicted. But I got into my art really, and it also gave me a living. I did art for corporate spaces for quite a long time, and I did printmaking, textile printing, and ran a business with that for about 10 years."

When there was a recession in the late 1980s and the art business was stifled, Bunny changed course. "I got into teaching, which I really enjoyed for about 10 years. I was teaching fine arts, and so was my partner, and then we decided to have our own school. So we formed our own school in France, which we did for 10 to 12 years. We teamed up with a few colleges, whereby their students could get part of a degree, a sort of module with us. So it was a great experience. I came back to England when my mother was very ill and I cared for her along with my sister, and at the same time my daughter, who is a psychologist and a teacher, started having babies, so I was a grandmother and a care giver. I did teach in between that, and I was trying to get my own career back as an artist. And that's really what I'm doing now. I'm an artist," Bunny says, adding that her granddaughter is musical and the two of them "rock together."

Bunny reflects back on her time with Red Roll On and says she misses those days. "I would love to get back to it in a way. I would just love to play some music with them again, actually. It would be really fun to reconvene. I've still got my guitar and I do sing a lot. And I regret that we didn't stay together. I think that was one of my biggest regrets. Just circumstances change. But it was a really interesting and exciting collaboration."

Angela Duignan, Germaine Dolan, Barbara Gaskin, Bunny Newth (L to R)

Ded Byrds/Walkie Talkies

Denyze D'Arcy: vocals, saxophone
Wayne Hussey: vocals, guitar
David Knopov: vocals

Jon Moss: drums
Ambrose Reynolds: bass
Dave Wibberley: guitar

There is the misconception that Jerry Dammers started it all. And surely, such a statement will rile the ire in a few folks, because The General is certainly worthy of all credit for the ska revival and all that entails. But there were musicians who conceived of mixing Jamaican music and punk before Dammers and it was not the sole creation of a sole individual—it was more organic than that. The sound of revival ska came from the communities where West Indian immigrants lived among the working class and the musical output that came from these cities, towns, and neighborhoods was a mixture of all influences. Coventry was one center of this musical communion, as was Birmingham and London. Add to this list Liverpool, which in June of 1978 produced the band Ded Byrds who offered their take on the West Indian reggae and punk blend of ska.

The one female member of Ded Byrds, Denyze D'Arcy, today Denyze Alleyne-Johnson, says that the band formed after a group of young musicians got together after they put the proverbial cart before the horse. They assembled as a result of securing a gig. "This is a very funny story. I was at an all-girl church school, and it was boring as hell. I had a good friend and she was a bit mad like me. We went to town drinking when we shouldn't have, and this singer who ended up in the band, David Knopov, he was gorgeous. Gorgeous. He was as young as us or a year older, and he was in town and he took a shine to me and came run over and sat with me and said he was in a band and he was the singer. He was in some school band, I think. I tried to impress him and I went, 'Well, I'm a sax player.' And I wasn't, I just had one but I'd never played a note. Anyway, I told him I was at university doing geography. I wasn't. I was at school. Anyway, he bought us a Coke and we left. And I was in love, totally in love. Anyway, I forgot about it. A couple of weeks later, I was in town again having a sneaky drink behind my mom's back and he came running over shouting oh my god, I've been looking for you everywhere. We've got a gig. And I went, 'Oh, I was joking. You know, I can't play,' and he said, 'Well you better had because we've got a gig, and I've told everybody I've got a school girl on sax.' He knew darn well I wasn't in uni."[534]

Denyze certainly wasn't in uni. She was just 15 years old and had just acquired her saxophone, though she had long been interested in music. "Yeah, I grew up in Liverpool. And I was actually born in Penny Lane in the 1960s. So, it was very musical. I went to a school called Dovedale. And Dovedale was where John Lennon went and

---

[534] Alleyne-Johnson, Denyze. All quotations, unless otherwise noted, from interview with the author, 8 Apr. 2021.

the Beatles actually, that was the junior school they went to. So I went to the same school as them and it was so musical. I don't think we learnt any actual knowledge, we just did music and the arts. It was great. It was lovely. And my older cousin, who was a lot older than me, worked in the Cavern Club, and she used to have to babysit me when my mum and dad were out, but she used to take me down there when she wasn't working to watch the bands playing. I'm sure there was some subconscious influence in there some time," she says.

"I got into David Bowie when I was about 10 or 11. I just saw him on TV and I thought, 'What a weird man, I've got to play that instrument.' And he was standing there playing saxophone to Lulu doing 'Man Who Sold the World,' Lulu's version, and David Bowie was standing behind her. He was so thin with this Gatsby hat on and this suit. And I just fell in love with him and what he was doing. He was so weird. It was escapism. At that age, you think, I'm not going to work in an office. My mom worked in an office and I thought, no way, I'm doing what that man does. My mom was a secretary and my dad was a manager at British Rail. So they worked very hard. And I thought, there's got to be an easier way of doing things, as you do. My sister's a lawyer. You know, she was doing law, she's older than me, so seeing David Bowie doing this, I thought, I want to do that. So I asked for a saxophone as a present for Christmas, and it took a couple of years for them to take me seriously, but I got one in me early teens. And they were Philistines—really, I'm not calling them as such, they were very academic, but they didn't want me to have music lessons. So I'm self-taught. They wouldn't pay, but they'd pay for things like maths lessons, but music lessons, no, it's a waste. So it was very good that I did join a punk band because I was self-taught."

After meeting with David Knopov, who told Denyze about their gig, she immediately began to learn her instrument. "I went home to my sister who was doing law at university and I'd gone, 'Oh what have I done?' and she paid for 10 lessons, crash course lessons for one week. And it was this old jazz player I went to, this old man, he was in his 70s and he was great. And I told him what happened and he was laughing his head off. He told me about the embouchure, how to literally press me lips on the back reeds and what reed I'd need and he taught me basic keys, and so I could hold it right, put it together, put the mouthpiece on and all this. Because I couldn't do it and had no lessons and he actually taught me how to go toot toot."

"So I turned up for the rehearsal. And he [Knopov] said his guitarist had let him down. And he said, 'I'm really sorry, but we won't be able to rehearse today.' Nicola, my friend had another friend named Dave who was at school. He was a Mormon. I mean, you really could not make this up. So she rang him and he said, 'Well, I'll come down. I'll be there within half an hour, but can I bring me mate? He's visiting from Bristol, and his name's Wayne—he's staying at the Mormon church and I'm putting him up." So we said yeah, come down, so Wayne Hussey walked in with Dave Wibberley, who incidentally is the head of LIPA, which is the performing arts school in Liverpool now. He walked in with Wayne Hussey, and we're all young, we were all, I mean, I was 15, they must have been about 17 or 18, Wayne's a bit older than me. And they walked in and Wayne had a beret and a pair a little round glasses, and he couldn't look more divvy, to be honest with you. At the time he had this cropped hair and he was a Mormon. They were both Mormons. And we were more intrigued. And the singer, David Knopov, was a little Jewish lad, and the drummer was Jewish and we all laughed, and we thought we were like, great, you know, because we're all mixed, and me at a church school. We were laughing about it," Denyze said.

Wayne Hussey recalls joining the band in his book, *Salad Daze*. "I was invited down to join them on Monday morning. As well as Wibbs [David Wibberley] the band comprised David Knopov, a well-known character around town who was, aptly, the singer. Ambrose Reynolds, whose father, Stanley, was a very well-respected *Guardian* journalist, played bass. Jon Moss, who fancied himself as a photographer and worked in the City Centre Virgin Records store, and not to be confused with his namesake who later kept rhythm and more for Boy George, battered the drums. And Jon's girlfriend's little sister, Denyze D'Arcy, played saxophone. They already had maybe three or four tunes kind of worked out so as I was setting up my amp and guitar they ran through the songs for my benefit. Pretty ramshackle they were it has to be said, although they definitely had a spark and an originality."[535]

Denyze says that Wayne Hussey also came with a few songs he had written. She says, "Wayne sat down with his guitar and just said, 'Here, I'll play this for you,' because we were all seeing who had tunes for this gig. And he said, here, I've written one called "I Want to Be A Monk," which we found highly amusing. So David Knopov, who was Jewish, he added to it, 'shabbat shalom' in the lyrics. And then we suddenly became this punk band. We all hit it off. I was going toot toot. It all just gelled so well that we did this gig. And we were signed very, very quickly because everyone thought we were so funny. I sat with Wayne Hussey, me and him, and he literally wrote my parts with me. He would tinkle around on the guitar, while I tinkled around to get the right notes. And between us, we worked well together. You know, for somebody who was 15, and between the two of us, we knocked the tunes together. The good thing about the band we were in, it was riffs, it was riff playing. Which is the type of playing in that they do in ska and they do in 2 Tone and in reggae, it's riff playing. It's a lot of repetitive riff playing, and it's very rhythmic. So that's quite easy to do when I first started, and I learned as I went along and got more complicated and better and better. So that was kind of my musical background."

"Our first stage was at the Everyman Bistro on Hope Street," says Hussey.[536] "I'm guessing that must've been June 1978. The room was packed with other curious local musicians as well as thespian types popping down from the theatre upstairs after they had finished work for the night, but mostly with friends of Knopov and Ambrose as they were both already well-known faces around town. We went down fantastically well. I guess you could describe Ded Byrds as being satirical art-school punk if you're into classification and feeling pretentious enough. With songs such as 'Lily's Off To

[535] Hussey, Wayne. *Salad Daze*. Omnibus Press, 2019, p. 112.
[536] Ibid. p. 115.

Paris,' 'Plastic Love,' 'AWOL,' and a rousing version of the Beatles' 'Why Don't We Do It In The Road,' it was all very chic, trendy and artsy."

Ded Byrds began playing in other local clubs and supported Ultravox as well as the Pretenders. Denyze says, "And that's how we ended up doing a kind of 2 Tone single just before it took off, really, we brought one out. And that's because we were a more new wave punk band and we got signed very quickly to Sire Records, which was Warner Brothers. So we toured with reggae bands and we loved it. So we were the support for Matumbi and Black Slate, which are British reggae bands from London way. And it was great. We played all the Jamaican clubs. We played in Brixton, proper grassroots Jamaican clubs, which welcomed punks. So we were an ideal opener because in all of the punk and new wave clubs like Eric's in Liverpool. We were signed in Eric's, supporting the Pretenders. We would support them on a regular basis. We toured with the Pretenders for quite a few gigs. We were signed by Seymour Stein who signed Madonna."

"I have a fond memory of opening for, I think it was Black Slate in a Jamaican club in Liverpool. It was packed and it was a predominantly black club. And I remember as a young girl going into the toilets to get changed because it was all male in the dressing room. I was the only female. So I went up to get changed in the toilets and a load of girls walked in. I thought, I hope they don't pick on me because I'm the only white face around you know. They were lovely. Lovely. Because I went to an all-girl church school, so it was a bit of an eye opener for me. They said to me, in a big Jamaican accent, 'de punks and de reggae, we all stick together.' And I felt so at home. So we toured and had a great time. So it was bound to come out in our music because what had been bash, bash, bash, bash, kind of punk new wave band, we just took a very fast reggae rhythm, and we were really bass orientated. And it just came out like that in a lot of our tunes. It's fascinating because people think that really that sound started with Jerry Dammers and the Specials. But it didn't. We were before that, really. They got together during that time, but their hits were kind of towards late 70s. And I'm talking probably 78 for us."

That 2 Tone-sounding song that the band recorded on the Sire label is a tune called "Rich and Nasty" with the B-side, "Summer in Russia," both penned by Wayne Hussey. By then, though, Ded Byrds was known as Walkie Talkies, as Denyze explains. "You know the Liver Birds in Liverpool. It's our landmark. Liver Birds are on our main building called the Liver Building in Liverpool City Centre. And you'll have seen it, even on Beatles videos, and 'Ferry Across the Mersey,' and all that. You see the Liver Birds are the big, huge, iconic birds on the Liver Building as the ferry comes in. So if you watch Gerry and the Pacemakers, and he sings, (sings) 'ferry across the Mersey' and then you see you see the Liver Birds on top, and it's Liverpool. Even LFC Liverpool Football Club has got the emblem of the Liver Birds. So we called ourselves the Ded Byrds. And DED BYRDS, because we were punks. We were going to be called the Liver Birds, but we thought sod that, we're the Ded Byrds. We had a huge following, believe it or not. And when we got signed to Sire Records, and we had the tour booked with the Ramones, they didn't like the name Ded Byrds. They

[Sire] said they wouldn't play us on American radio at the time, with the Byrds, Ded Byrds was seen as derogatory and a negative name, so think of a new name for airplay. So we thought of Walkie Talkies. And that's why it changed. But we were actually known as the Ded Byrds. Walkie Talkies was our signed name."

But the band didn't last long enough to have their song associated with the ska revival, or make any significant mark at all. "It was a shame that we split up because we're just about to go on tour with the Ramones and we just got signed, but we were so young. Wayne Hussey, I love him to bits, he is a good friend, but he was such an egotist. And we had our singer, David Knopov, was an egotist, and they argued all the time, so it was bound to happen," she says. Hussey acknowledges this in his book, writing, "I wasn't there to be liked and didn't care if they did or they didn't. I just wanted us to be as good as I knew we could be. And we were good."[537] Denyze concurs, "Such a shame, because we just had that single hit the charts and we became good, and I'm not just saying it. We became very good. But it was a learning curve. But because we all gelled and everyone was a real character and we had all this chemistry between us. It was great. You know, it was only when the record companies got involved that everyone started pitching against each other, well I didn't, but trying to outdo each other, that it fell apart. But it was great. We had two years of great fun."

Denyze says that she is still close with the members of the band, even after all of these years. "They were absolutely like brothers. We still keep in touch and we're all friends. My drummer at the time, Jon Moss, he ended up marrying my sister so he's still my brother-in-law. And me and Wayne are very close, we always were, so I go stay with him from time to time. Wayne Hussey went to the Pauline Murray Band and Dead or Alive with Pete Burns, and then I think he went in Sisters of Mercy pretty much after that," she says. Hussey was also in the Mission. Ambrose Reynolds formed Frankie Goes To Hollywood with Holly Johnson, BF Tin, and Steve Lovell in 1980.

As for Denyze Alleyne-Johnson, she continued her life in music, as she explains. "I was in local bands quite a lot. I gigged about five nights a week. And then I married a guy called Ed Alleyne-Johnson who was in New Model Army. So Ed and I brought out three albums together. He wrote the violin on 'Vagabonds,' which was New Model Army's biggest hit and they were on *Top of the Pops*. I met Ed when he was in New Model Army and he was sick of touring and he wanted to go solo. So he brought an album out called *Purple Electric Violin Concerto*. And it was during that time we met up again. On and off, we'd met over the years because we knew each other from Liverpool. And he asked me to do an album with him. So I left the band I was with. I worked with Ed and did three albums. So I did one called *2020 Vision*. I did another one called *Fly Before Dawn* and I'm very proud of the lyrics on them and I think I became a singer on those, not a sax player. I played saxophone, doing a lot of session work with Liverpool bands over the years and I wrote the music for a TV show on BBC, I wrote and then sang and performed on telly. I became a front person, a singer in a rock band and played sax, so I did all that. But with Ed I sang and I did

---

537 Ibid., p. 113.

the choir. I've done all the choirs in his choral stuff on his solo violin albums as well. So Ed and I, we're divorced now but he'll come here tonight, he's always here, because we've got two sons together. So we're still very, very close."

She says that music came full circle for her a few years ago when she performed for a cancer charity gig. "So I still play sax. I've picked it up again and I bought a new saxophone a couple of years ago. And I've never done covers, I've always done original stuff, but I was asked to do a cancer charity gig and I put a band together and did about 10 gigs last year. I did a version of Lulu's 'Man Who Sold the World.' So I played David Bowie's bit and I felt great doing it. I got out and played the piece that made me start playing saxophone, and I sang Lulu's bit as well," she says. Denyze also owns her own beauty salons and explains, "It was something I did to earn a living in the background. Well, it's also something I'm passionate about. So I used to have a tanning and beauty salon for seven years and then sold that and I bought a hair dresser two years ago."

Throughout her career, Denyze Alleyne-Johnson says she has always felt comfortable performing with men. "Many bands that I've have been in, they've been like brothers. I was protected. And not just the band, but like when we did play all the Jamaican clubs and stuff, so respectful to the little school girl in the corner, 'look after her,' 'do you want to sit here.' The only time I've been chatted up was when I was in an all-girl band called the Escorts. The two of the girls were good friends and they were lesbians—they used to touch me up on stage for a laugh because they knew when I started laughing I couldn't play saxophone. They used to pinch me bum and I was just about to go into a saxophone solo and it used to crack me up laughing."

As for the Ded Byrds, she says that the members have been talking about a reunion. "The club, Eric's, was 40 years last year. So they were asking all the bands that did get signed to come back for a reunion gig, so we were talking to Wayne about that. David Knopov rang me and said, 'Would you do it?' And I said I'd do it. So we were going to go do a few songs. Yeah, then COVID happened and put blocks on that." Perhaps the future will allow the band to perform once again.

Ded Byrds/Walkie Talkies and their single "Rich and Nasty"

SIRE RECORDS threw a party recently to announce their latest UK signing, The Walkie Talkies. A Liverpool five-piece group, their first single Rich And Nasty is set for August release when the band will also be touring the UK. Pictured left to right: Seymour Stein (head of Sire), Wayne Hussey of the group, Beth Reinstein (Sire receptionist), Andy Ferguson (Sire independent promotion manager), David Knopof, John Moss and Denise D'Arcy (all of the Walkie Talkies) and Jonathan Clyde (artist development manager WEA).

Press from the Walkie Talkies' signing (above) and a performance with an enthusiastic David Knopov on vocals with Denyze D'Arcy on sax (below)

The Deltones

Jeremy Brill: drums
Jacqui Callis: vocals
Verona Davis: vocals
Amanda Fen: vocals
Nicky Ford: saxophone
Dill Hammond: vocals
Gilly Johns: saxophone

Anna Keegan: saxophone
Penny Leyton: trumpet
Julie Liggett: keyboard
Sara McGuinness: keyboards
Serena Parsons: guitar
Angela Risner: bass

For ska fans in the United States, their first exposure to the Deltones likely came via Unicorn Records' *Skankin' 'Round the World* compilations. The Deltones tune "Stay Where You Are," was featured on volume one, "Scream Jean" was on volume two, and "Running Around" appeared on volume three. But in the UK and all over Europe, fans had a more lengthy and deep relationship with the Deltones since the band had been performing as a group of eleven women and one man for half a decade by the time Unicorn made its releases available in the U.S. Even though they formed after 2 Tone, one listen revealed, the Deltones weren't 2 Tone. They were clearly inspired by Jamaican ska and Jamaican rocksteady. They were Motown and harmonies and a chorus of horns, lively, talented, and very danceable. They were undeniably more than just another song on just another compilation. The Deltones were, in many ways, both pre- and post-2 Tone ska.

The Deltones began around 1985 when Julie Liggett and Serena Parsons decided to put together a band of all women as a sister band to the Potato 5. They had both been friends with members of the Potato 5, the post-2 Tone ska band promoted by Gaz Mayall, and thought they'd form a group of their own. "The Potato 5 were doing pretty well. We thought, if the guys can do it, then surely it can't be that difficult. We should be able to do it ourselves," said Julie.[538] And so, a band was born.

Julie Liggett grew up in the musical mecca Liverpool, though she says her own family wasn't very musical at all. "I've learned more recently that my mother was quite an accomplished pianist and violinist when she was young, but she encouraged us to do dance. I'm the second of four daughters and the story that she told me once was, she had not really got along with her piano teacher and she really had not enjoyed piano lessons, so she steered us towards dancing more than music. And we just sort of went along with that. We were sort of quite young. So we weren't really brought up with much music in the house other than just pop music records and radio. But when we got to about seven or eight years old, each of us were starting to do music at school. So for me, I learned the recorder, which just about every child in the UK does. And my oldest sister had a guitar and she had guitar lessons. But my parents always said we need to share the guitar, that they couldn't afford to buy one for each,

---

[538] Liggett, Julie. All quotations, unless otherwise noted, from interview with the author, 11 Jan. 2021.

but my older sister wasn't particularly keen to share it. I think she thought I was probably going to break it or something. So the consequence was that although I attended the lessons, I never ever had a guitar to play. So I didn't really pursue anything in the way of music at all. I was quite creative, so I wrote poetry and that sort of thing," she says.

When the family moved from Liverpool to the south coast, Julie continued playing the recorder in school, as well as taking ballet and dance lessons and she says she gained "a good grounding for music and rhythm." But Julie she wanted to learn an instrument of her own. "I remember sort of pestering my mom that I really wanted to learn, but it all came down to two things. One is not being able to afford the lessons, and the other was just space in the house for a piano or anything like that. I had a friend who was very musical at that time and she taught me to just play tunes on the piano from beginning to end—not the theory of the notes and how the chords are made up or anything, but just how to play, so I kind of got an interest in it from then and wasn't afraid of the keyboard."

During her later years in school, Julie listened to Motown and soul. But in her small town, she didn't have the opportunity to see much live music outside of the few local bands that she says were predominantly male. "To be honest, I was trying to think if I ever saw a single woman in a band at the rock club and I actually don't think I did. It was terrible, really. It was surprising. There were women that were creative and artistic, women who were singing, dancing, taking piano, recorder, violin lessons or whatever, and I think it was just sort of the background at the time, but performing music seemed to be very much more encouraged with young boys and men, and not so much with young girls. So I think girls were kind of pretty much leaving music by the wayside and just listening to it, amongst my friends, anyway," she says.

Julie attended the University of East Anglia and says it was here that she experienced music and made musical connections that would bear fruit in later years. "The university had a very good entertainment manager who seemed to be able to book the absolute latest biggest bands, so people like Madness, the Specials, the Selecter, the Beat, the Pretenders, the Jam—you know, all the bands of the time, which was just amazing. I was doing English and American studies, so predominantly literature, and I went to see a lot of live gigs, but was not at all remotely interested in playing and had long since left anything creative behind. And there was a bit of a music scene in Norwich at the time, but it was predominantly men, and it was quite indie, so it wasn't the music I was listening to. Then after graduating, I moved to London. I had two friends at university, twin brothers, Simon and David Driscoll who were in the Potato 5, so they were a year above me so when I came to London, they were already there and had started their band. And from meeting back up with Simon and David, that's how I met Serena and Martin [Aberdeen]," Julie says.

Serena Parsons grew up in Sutton and says she was always into music, even at a young age. "I always wanted to play in a band, but I didn't really think that I would. I'd been in a couple of bands before, but just kind of when I was younger," she says.[539] Serena and Julie both lived in Brixton, met through the members of the Potato 5, and became fast friends. "We used to go to a pub together called the George Canning and so we'd go every weekend and as much as possible. So we all met in the pub. Amanda [Fen] used to go out with my brother, so that's how I met her, and then she was one of the people in Brixton we'd meet up with to go to the pub regularly. There was a bit of a dilemma because I'd played a little bit so I could play a little guitar and a little bass, and so the idea was that I wasn't going to play the guitar, but I was going to do something different. I think I was going to be the trumpet player. I can't remember, but Julie ended up on bass and then went to keyboards, but she was really quick about picking it up. She's really good at that kind of stuff." Ultimately, the bass player for the band was Angela Risner.

Serena did end up performing guitar for the Deltones, and she was a big fan of original Jamaican music. Jamaican ska, rocksteady, and reggae was a definite influence on their style. "I would buy loads of records and stuff and I had quite a big collection of old ska records, you know, blue beat and stuff like that. And the way the band started is that me and Julie Liggett decided that, just for something to do, we would start a band and what we would do is, our friends who had recently started the Potato 5, we thought we would play all their songs, and that would be our band, you know, we'd just copy them," says Serena. But this was hardly a model for a new band—copying another band's music, especially when that other band was too difficult to copy for new musicians. "Yeah, we didn't really go with the plan in that we realized that we couldn't play any of their songs."

Instead, the Deltones drew upon Jamaican originals for covers. There were certain tracks that I really liked and I thought we could probably play them. Badly. But I thought no one would know because no one's ever heard them. So that was the idea and I picked 10 songs that I thought no one is really going to know, and the funny thing was, the song we were most known for, which is 'Stay Where You Are' is from Gloria and the Dreamlets. No one at that time knew who that was, and up until recently, Simon from the Potato 5 said to me, 'I thought you wrote that.' So I got these obscure songs, or what seemed obscure at the time. We started off doing a few Owen Grey songs and we did 'Cool School' by Chuck and Dobby. So a mixture of blue beat stuff and early Island tracks. But the idea being that we could play them, they've got nice vocals."

Taking up the position of vocals for the Deltones would be multiple women in order to give that full harmonious sound characteristic of rocksteady and soul. One of those vocalists was Dill Hammond who had been singing since she was a very young girl. "I'd done quite a lot of theater and music," Dill says.[540] "I'd done musicals and that sort of thing. I grew up in a little village in Oxfordshire, and then when I was 21 I moved to London. So when I was 17 or 18 I went to live in Oxford and worked with a youth theater. We studied with some really amazing people like Theatre de

---

[539] Parsons, Serena. All quotations, unless otherwise noted, from interview with the author, 16 Dec. 2020.
[540] Hammond, Dill. All quotations, unless otherwise noted, from interview with the author, 17 Dec. 2020.

Complicite. They play at the National Theatre but back then they were just a sort of theater troupe. Anyways, then I got really into singing. I did a Brecht show that featured singing and I realized that I really liked it. I did *Mahogany Songspiel*, which is a Brecht play that features a lot of music. I just got really into the music side and I just thought I'd really fancy joining a band. Then decided to move to London. I went to live with these other girls in a squat in Hackney. I answered an ad taken in *City Limits* and *Time Out* saying 'singer wanted in ska band.'"

Verona Davis also joined as a vocalist and came to the band through a friend as well. "I come from a big family," says Verona.[541] "There are six brothers and me and my sister, so there are eight children. I'm the oldest. My mother was busy! I grew up in the East End of London, Newham, and I was born in London in 1962. My mother came from St. Lucia and my father from South America, Guyana. When I got to about, I'd say I was about seven, I realized I wanted to be a singer because I used to sit in the house, and I'd be singing my lungs out. And my mother used to say, 'shut up with all that noise!' She never stopped me from singing—she used to like singing too and I grew up listening to all kinds of music like reggae, jazz, she was an Ella Fitzgerald fan, a lot of country music too because she liked Hank Williams, and so, you know it kind of stayed with me. And one day I watched *Westside Story*, and from that moment on, I thought, I want to sing. It was the first time I saw interracial couples and that inspired me because I thought, you know, how can you communicate with different cultures but through music?"

Verona says that when she left home at the age of 18, she took singing lessons with a teacher named Tona de Brett. "She was great. She really helped me discover my voice. And then from there on, I just thought, okay, I'll try to get my voice to a place where I know I could maybe go on stage. And I started singing in some cover bands. There was a band called the Nomadic and they were based in Camden where I moved to, Kentish Town, and I met a lot of different musicians. I met the Deltones because of people looking for singers. Penny [Leyton] said to me, 'Come along to an audition,' which I did. I met her from one of the musicians in my band. So from then on, it was just like, 'okay, you're in!'"

The other singer was Amanda Fen who had been friends with Serena Parsons at the onset of the band. Amanda says she grew up with music around her, though they didn't play any instruments as such. "In my household my both my parents really liked music, but I was pretty much raised on older music. They had the radio on all the time more than the TV so it was definitely a musical family. And then when I was 12 or 13 I got completely obsessed with music, like a lot of kids do. I was very obsessed with Kate Bush. She was my heroine. I loved her, and I still do. And I listened to quite a lot of punk, really, the Clash, things like that. I was born in Wimbledon in London, so I grew up in Wimbledon. And then my mother moved to Hastings when I was 10. I didn't like very much so I went back to London on my own when I was 17 and went to Brixton, and then it was black culture. And we started

---

[541] Davis, Verona. All quotations, unless otherwise noted, from iInterview with the author, 27 Nov. 2020.

listening to loads of early Jamaican music. And a lot of the pubs had that kind of music and a lot of friendship groups that we made were into reggae, ska. That's how I kind of got into it," says Fen.[542]

She became involved in the Deltones through meeting Serena. She explains, "I had a boyfriend who said, 'my sister is starting this band and she wants someone to sing.' And it was Serena, who started the band, really. Serena was Julian's sister and I was dating Julian, and I came along and we started listening to the early Jamaican stuff, that was her influence. And that's how the music thing started."

Joining the horn section was Penny Leyton from the Bodysnatchers and the Belle Stars—not on keyboard, as she had been in her previous bands, but on trumpet. "I loved playing in the Deltones. That was my favorite band of them all because we were kind of on the brink of having success many times. We never quite achieved it but I just loved it. It was just much more fun. I think people were more down to earth," says Penny.[543] It's not a surprise that Penny picked up a different instrument for the Deltones, as she was always a multi-instrumentalist. She played piano, guitar, bass guitar, and the trumpet, which she bought before she joined the Bodysnatchers." I had actually bought a trumpet in a market, almost like fate, about three months before. I'd been in Camden Market and I'd seen this trumpet, and I just thought, 'Oh, I'd like to learn the trumpet.' So I bought it and I started learning. So I mean, I wouldn't say I could play very well, but I could certainly sort of play the basics."

Gilly Johns joined on saxophone and like many other female musicians of this era, she came to the Deltones as the result of being part of a creative community in art school. She grew up in a lower middle class family and attended Catholic school where she says she was taught by nuns and her brother attended a monastery. She gained a solid education, but even at an early age knew there was abuse in the Catholic church so she chose not to become a Catholic. "To be honest, now I'm quite grateful for it because it helped me understand what I don't want. The education was really good, but if you wanted to go into the arts, they didn't give you any help at all. They wanted us all to be scientists. So when I said I wanted to do a fine art degree, they didn't give me any career help at all because it wasn't something they were proud of. I had to do all the research myself, which is fine," Gilly says.[544]

She was sent to Lourdes by the nuns as part of the mission of the school, which furthered her push away from the church and into the arts. Gilly states, "I was sent to Lourdes and I worked in the hospital, looking after sick people and then I was drinking vodka with the priests in the evening. I personally didn't have any trouble, and I wasn't abused, because I was watching them. But it made me very aware of what's out there in the world from a young age. And it politicized me. So I became pretty left wing when I left school. I became feminist, left wing, and I went on loads of demonstrations and anti-racist, anti-sexist movements. So really, it helped me get

[542] Fen, Amanda. All quotations, unless otherwise noted, from interview with the author, 22 Nov. 2022.
[543] Leyton, Penny. All quotations, unless otherwise noted, from interview with the author, 20 Dec. 2020.
[544] Johns, Gilly. All quotations, unless otherwise noted, from interview with the author, 13 Dec. 2020.

to that stage and also it taught me what I want to focus on, which was community, politics, values. And art is expression."

After graduation, Gilly attended art school at Leeds which was an incubator of creativity and music. "It was the heady days, so '76 to'79. There's been a lot written about it. There was a lot of performance art, there was lots of music. It was very, very radical and it produced a lot of bands. I think the Sex Pistols did their first gig at Leeds Poly, and so punk was just happening. My best friend at art college was Marc Almond [Soft Cell], and he's just had this amazing career. He was my year and as soon as he finished his degree he released 'Tainted Love,' and then he just went poof! That was him. But there are loads of bands—Gang of Four, the Mekons, and the band I particularly liked was Scritti Politti. Green Gartside was in third year when I was first year and for his final arts degree show it was just sheets of paper about Marxism. And instead of lectures, we all used to go to the pub and talk about socialism and art. It was a real hotbed, and a political hotbed," she says.

Gilly didn't perform music in school and instead studied the medium of photo montage and silkscreen, among other fine art media. "So when I left there, I thought, what do I do next? And then I was asked to join an all-male band and learn the bass guitar. And I thought, why not? So I learnt the bass guitar, just some basic things, and we had our first gig a week later. It was called Household Name, and we didn't become a household name! We gigged and we ended up doing a John Peel session at Abbey Road. I was the only girl in the band and I learned to play the bass guitar sitting down, so I'd be on stage sitting down and John Peel wrote a review, like this cool girl plays sitting down," she says, laughing. "We were kind of a post-punk funk band, quite raw. And that was with all my fellow art students, afterwards. I mean, we all had day jobs, but you know, you're young, you don't have kids, and it's incredibly exciting. You get to play all these big venues without having to pay to get in."

At the same time Gilly began working in the world of art. "And I became a community artist," she continues, "so this fits in with my politics. So I became a mural artist for about three or four years. I painted murals in hospitals, daycare centers, outdoors, big community centers. I was a paid mural artist. I loved it because it was people who were stuck in care homes, or whatever, and it was participatory so I would do it with them. I would meet them and ask them what they wanted, and we would facilitate it and paint it together and I'd make sure it was a good finished product. And then we'd have an opening and then they were left with this painting that they helped produce. I was really lucky to do that. We were in Yorkshire and the organization was called Shape Up North. So that was my very first job. So some evenings we'd rehearse and then some weekends we'd have gigs. But I didn't want to become famous, so the closer we got, the less I liked it."

Gilly was the only artist in her family. Her two sisters and one brother are "all scientists and I was the black sheep, which I quite like," she says. When asked if her parents supported her life in the arts, she replies, "they kind of had to put up with it," and they did attend her gigs, even with the Deltones. She explains how she came to be a part of the all-female-but-one-male group. "I was still in Household Name and then I applied to do a post-graduate at Goldsmiths College in London, so I got sucked into London and ended up staying for 15 years. And then my friends were saying they were looking to form a girl ska band, do you want to join? And I thought, and this sounds really cocky, but I'm not being cocky at all—I'd never played the saxophone or played the clarinet and they were looking for a saxophonist, and I just thought, well, I'll buy a saxophone and start playing. So this was it. I finished my post grad and joined the Deltones, and we just learned. Everybody learned all the instruments together, and that's the beauty of it."

Other saxophonists joined the Deltones during the five or six years that the band was together, including Anna Keegan and Nicky Ford. And the Deltones recruited a drummer as well—the sole male in the group. "The Deltones originally were all women but then we just couldn't find a woman drummer that was reliable enough, so we ended up having a male drummer. We let a man into the band, and that was Jeremy [Brill]," says Penny. It was always a loose lineup due to the size and the multi-faceted lives of the members of the Deltones, which at first, according to Serena, was not called the Deltones. "We were called the Fat Boys. Everyone in Brixton knew us as that. But unfortunately then the other imposters came along and stole it from us and became famous, so we didn't have a choice," Serena says with a laugh. She continues, "Our band was going to be called A Bunch of Stupid Girls, at one point. So there was a long time trying to find a name and no one really liked the Deltones, actually, but it was just kind of the best of a bad lot—something we could all sort of agree on. But yeah, we were the Fat Boys for a long time!" Serena says.

The Deltones didn't gig right away, even as the Fat Boys. It took some time for them to practice and get comfortable with the idea that they were a proper band. "It took quite a long time, but eventually we did do one gig at some club," says Serena, "because Penny had joined by then and so she knew someone that ran a club in central London, so we went and played that. We'd been talking about it for so long and it actually went really well and we sold it out. They were quite keen to get us back because we brought quite a lot of people, so that's how the live stuff started out. We weren't really planning on doing that, but then once it started then it all kind of snowballed." In addition to gigging on their own, the Deltones frequently performed with their brother band, the Potato 5.

Serena says that they soon came to the attention of John Peel and were invited to do a session, which further increased their visibility as a band. "He saw us with the Potato 5 and I just remember him saying that someone should record you now before you learn how to play. I think those were his words. And I mean, we had a lot of reviews, like in the *Observer* and all the music papers, but every single one, when you look at the word that they all use, was 'shambolic,' which is insulting really. But I don't want to harp on about how terrible we were. But if you have a bunch of women on stage and it's already bouncy, fun, and uplifting, and you can dance and everyone always used to get up pretty much straight away, then you're having a good time. You don't notice how bad the band are."

John Peel certainly felt differently. "From the moment they struck up, I was a fan," Peel wrote of that performance on July 3, 1986 for a six-year anniversary celebration of Gaz's Rockin' Blues.[545] "Since a typically untidy adolescence, I have suspected that women know something we men do not, that they can have an understanding and co-operative spirit that combative men can rarely, if ever, match. I'm limping through minefields here, I know, but I cannot imagine 11 men playing together on stage with the sense of community radiated by the Deltones. As far as their music goes, the Deltones perform a mixture of their own songs and little-known Jamaican numbers from the 1960s with considerable verve, the occasional wrong note adding to the authenticity of the sound. What counts here is spirit and the Electric Ballroom crowd, more diverse and in a better humour than any encountered in London for a long time, clearly felt that the Deltones had spirit by the vanload." Peel called the show with the Potato 5 supported by the Deltones "the best night out I have had this year," which certainly is quite an endorsement, given Peel's copious serving of music.

Peel hit on something that members of the Deltones are sure to point out, when asked to position themselves in the musical timeline and dissection of ska. They were more akin to Jamaican ska rather than 2 Tone. Jacqui Callis, who joined the Deltones as vocalist from time to time says, "The Deltones were nothing to do with 2 Tone. Everybody likes to make it all nice and neat, you know, history redefines itself and likes to put it into a certain way, but I don't remember it being a rudie kind of 2 Tone sort of audience that would be there. Because 2 Tone kind of came from punk, 2 Tone was fast. It was very fast and they were playing the same circuits as Stiff Records would play, the circuits with Elvis Costello and people, and then 2 Tone would then do their circuit, gigs around the country. We were ska and rocksteady but the people that formed the Deltones were not 2 Tone and were not listening to 2 Tone. They were listening to original ska music. I wouldn't be the one to class it, and to be honest, I think the people that started it wouldn't be able to class it either. They were all just thinking, hey, look why don't we get a women's band together."

Jacqui filled in on vocals for Amanda Fen who had health issues which required periodic hospital stays. She had grown up in Scotland before attending art college in Leeds where she was friends with the members of the Potato 5 and the Deltones. "It was more like the women just knew each other and that's kind of how it came to be," says Jacqui. "It was just synergy, energy. And I didn't join properly, the Deltones. I just stood in when Amanda would have to go to the hospital a few times, so I just sang at local gigs, local festivals round London really. And then what happened was that Amanda came back and they said, why don't you stay with us, we want to have three singers, but by then I got another band together and I said I was going to leave and then I think they got Verona in and I did that Electric Ballroom gig that John Peel did and they were always really well attended. People would come

---

[545] Peel, John. "Stepping on the Gaz." *Observer*, 4 May 1986.

in and just start dancing because it's infectious and you didn't get that in London outside of ska music."

Jacqui estimates she performed about 20 gigs with the Deltones, but she also performed with the Mekons and Delta 5. She then moved on to a completely different kind of music—cowpunk, which she describes as being influenced by skiffle, punk, and alt-country. She wasn't on any of the Deltones recordings, though she was on the John Peel recording. Though she left music for a number of years and worked in multimedia while raising her children, she has begun singing again. "I've got two kids and I'm an artist and my partner is also an artist. We both kind of earn money through doing art projects and then we do the music as well and it all fits together. I started a CIC, a community interest company, working with people with autism and learning disabilities doing songwriting and so they'd be like a band, we'd write songs, and it was using creativity as advocacy. My son is autistic but he's such a fantastic musician. We still play with him—my partner, Tony, he plays double bass and we've just played in bands, playing every weekend, gigs around Cornwall," she says. Music extends to more of her family, as Jacqui's brother, Joe Callis, was in the Rezillos and the Human League. "He helped them to get some hits, so he wrote a lot of *Dare* and 'Don't You Want Me Baby?' He wrote the music for that."

Sara McGuinness also joined on keyboard when Julie Liggett needed a temporary fill-in. That temporary status turned permanent, as Julie explains, "The Potato 5 were doing gigs in pubs and community centers, maybe outdoor festivals, and their keyboard player left. And so Martin [Aberdeen] said to me, did I fancy joining the Potato 5 to replace the keyboard player, and I said that I would, but you know, I literally can't play. Someone taught me a few notes and said, 'Just don't worry, come on and I'll teach you some more notes, more chords, and then you just take it from there.' He basically just came around with a small Casio keyboard and taught me chords. I used to play with just one hand! He taught me sort of twiddly bits and how to structure the chords, enough to play the songs that were on that setlist, so I did that," said Julie.

Sara had a more formal education in music and other fields, but says she also had a love of the music that the Deltones played. "My parents are both academics and today I run the master's course in performance at the London College of Music at the University of West London. I'm also a musician as well. My mom is American, from Connecticut, and my dad was Irish, but we lived in the UK. So I was born in Oxford, but then, when my parents divorced when I was about eight, I moved because my mum went to work at Royal Holloway College. I was at a girls school so the only options for playing music was just classical. So I played classical music and I stopped when I was about 12 because I grew up on reggae and soul music. So I stopped playing classical music and then I went off to university and did an electronics degree. I got interested in it and I was very good at math and physics and things. I started playing in small bands and a friend called me, because I'd done engineering, and he said to come and do the sound for his soul band. But I didn't know anything about sound engineering at the time, but I went along and they knew I used to play piano. They

293

said, look, the keyboard player has gone on holiday, can you just learn the keyboard parts? And they taught me and I did one gig and they said, right, you're our keyboard player now. It was call Soul Assistance and it was never famous. But I got involved with a whole reggae community and everything because I prefer reggae. I love ska, but I *love* reggae. So I was doing that and then the Deltones asked me to play keyboards for them."[546]

So Sara McGuinness performed with the Potato 5 as needed since Julie Liggett had recently given birth to a son, and Sara was also performing with the Deltones. She met the musicians through sax player Andy Minnion. They all hung out together and performed together. It was a community. "When I was playing with the Deltones," she says, "we were gigging all the time. On a Friday we might be in Liverpool and then Saturday down south, and so there was this really thriving live music scene in the 80s. And also in London, because there was support for the arts, because the whole ska and 2 Tone thing was quite big. There were a couple of clubs like the Fridge in Brixton which was a big venue, there was the Town & Country Club—Wendy May the DJ, she had a night there. And there was the Estoria which has now closed, right in the center of town and they're all quite big venues. And they'd all have weekly nights where they'd have a whole range of bands on that whole circuit. Usually one night a weekend, we'd be playing at one of those big venues. They'd have regular gigs and we'd also be all over the country playing all the time. I mean, we didn't have very much money, wages were small. But that was playing music."

For years, the Deltones performed in clubs all over the country. They were supported by Gaz Mayall who also helped to support the Potato 5 and numerous other bands. Mayall started with a record player on a table and two speakers during the Notting Hill Carnival, but he then grew his set into a proper soundsystem which became a fixture and then an enterprise. Each Thursday since July 2, 1980, Gaz's Rockin' Blues spins ska, rocksteady, and reggae in Soho. His band, the Trojans, has recorded with the likes of Prince Buster, Megumi Mesaku, and Vin Gordon and Gaz has connected with and supported numerous artists throughout the years as a promoter. "Gaz was sort of trying to promote both of the bands," says Julie of the Deltones and the Potato 5. "He was very helpful in trying to get us gigs and so on. I had a young baby so I was finding it was just too much to do, and sometimes there were clashes with the gigs, so I left the Deltones and I was their manager for a while. We were still obviously very close friends, so there was no animosity about me leaving or anything, and I did a lot more with the Potato 5 then, and went to Japan with them. It was just a really exciting amazing time. So we'd hooked up with Laurel [Aitken] and I think that was Gaz because he was very much in touch with all sorts of people from the old Jamaican days, because of his club. Gaz paired us up with Laurel Aitken and also with Floyd Lloyd Seivright. So Floyd became a key part of the Potato 5. Laurel was more of a guest vocalist so he wasn't necessarily with us all the time, but can you imagine, to play with him? He was such a personality on stage as well. He used to

---

[546] McGuinness, Sara. All quotations, unless otherwise noted, from interview with the author, 15 Dec. 2020.

wear these really shiny wigs that were all multicolored like tinsel, wave his head around, for fun."

It was at this time, though, that Julie began having doubts about herself and so she decided to leave the Potato 5 and return to the Deltones. She explains, "I was starting to feel very much a kind of imposter syndrome in that band because I really felt like, I'm not really that good. They're really going places, they're getting a lot of interest. When we went to Japan, women would come up to me at the end of the gig, all ages, being kind, giving me gifts and telling me how great it was, and I was so flattered but I just kind of felt I was a bit of a cheat because I'm not really that good. So I really thought also with having Sam [her son], I can't really be away from home for long periods of time and the band was getting offers, to tour the U.S. and I just thought, I'm not going to be able to do any of that. So I sat down with the band at that time an I just said, I'm going to leave, give it all up. I was quite sorry because obviously I'd loved doing it. I really loved playing the music. I really felt I had accomplished something."

"So after Serena knew that I'd left the Potato 5," Julie continues, "she just said to me, would you consider at all coming back to the Deltones, because she said, we're not playing anywhere near as much as they are, you know, we're not gigging as much, mostly it's in London. It's just much smaller. So I said, remember, I'm not particularly good. She said, no, you'll be fine for us. So then I went back to the Deltones. So that was probably spring in 1988, I think. So they were still playing some of the songs that I'd written when I'd been with them, so that was quite nice, and then by then Dill had joined, who is just an amazing singer, amazing woman. Amanda was still there, Verona had joined, also amazing, so the three singers were just such a force on the stage. Before I rejoined, I went to see them and I was just absolutely blown away by how brilliant they were and how good they had become since I played with them."

Only a few months later, in the summer of 1988, the group as they now existed, traveled to France to record their one and only album, *Nana Choc Choc in Paris*. Julie recalls the ways the women bonded while recording in another country. "We recorded in Paris, which was exciting in itself. And what was good for me was it was lovely being in a band of all women and also several of the women in the band had children, so Verona had a child—he was about a year older than my son, so it was nice to be in a band with another mom. Angela, the bass player, she had a little baby and she took her daughter Lillie with her—I think she was only about three or four months old at the time that we did that recording, and we had Amanda who was pregnant. Verona and I had left our sons at home because they were a bit older, but it was just lovely to be in a band of women and other parents who kind of understood more of the pressures that might be understood as a woman. The intensity of the friendship was strong." The album is dedicated to the children of these mothers.

The recording was produced by Didier Le Marchand and released in France on the Boucherie Productions label. It was released the following year, in 1989, in the UK on the Unicorn label. "Ska music was boiling over in Europe and the label that was leading the way was UK-based Unicorn Records," wrote Steve Shafer in *The People's Ska Annual* in the summer of 1998.[547] "At the demise of 2 Tone era ska, around '83 or '84, the last records weren't really even close to ska. Before the rise of the US ska scene in the early-to-mid nineties, the only ska scenes that were thriving were the UK and German ska scenes. While at the time there were several labels releasing amazing ska records … the one label that unified the European and worldwide ska scene was Unicorn—and in its heyday (approximately 1988-1991), it released a stunning amount of quality ska music," Shafer stated.

As Shafer continues, Unicorn was founded in 1986 by Mark Johnson. In his review of the Deltones release on Unicorn, *Nana Choc Choc in Paris*, Shafer writes, "The Deltones were probably deserving of the attention they received solely on the basis that they were just about the only girl ska group in a scene filled with rude boys. Having said that, the Deltones were very talented songwriters (writing lots of semi-melancholy ska tunes about boys, girls and relationships) and not bad musicians to boot. Their sound was more Jamaica via the girl groups of Motown than 2-Tone-y Bodysnatchers descendants and their re-invention of the genre made all the difference." In 1990, the album was reissued as a cassette in the U.S. on the ROIR label (Reachout International Records), not as *Nana Choc Choc in Paris*, but instead as *Oddball Boy*, the title of one of the songs and a reference to their lineup.

Julie recalls recording in the studio. "We did it overnight. We were sleeping all day and we were very kindly accommodated just by friends of the guys that were running the studio and doing the sound engineering and the production. They arranged with some of their friends to put us all up so we weren't all together, obviously, with 11 of us in the band, so we were scattered about among different households. So we just slept all day and then we would be going in on the Metro when everyone else was coming home. There was something so lovely about that—doing it through the night. I never thought I would sort of take to it, but I really loved it. It was just an exciting feeling—six, seven o'clock in the evening, getting on the Metro to go to do a night of recording. And it was a big, sort of famous Paris studio, and we were told Dire Straits had recorded there. The time was cheaper because it was at night and obviously condensed into this really short period, so we had to bash through everything. I remember that the recording of it was on digital tape. When I recorded with the Potato 5, we had done a lot of analog stuff, so it was quite exciting, the technology that they had in that studio."

She explains the origin of the odd-named title for the album. "Amanda told us a story about when she was little and her Nana was coming to see her—her grandmother who she called Nana. She would always have chocolate and so she just got into referring to her grandmother as Nana Choc Choc. So when we were in the Deltones and we would be thinking, oh gosh, you know, has anyone got any chocolate? It became a thing that Amanda would say, oh god, I wish Nana Choc Choc

---

[547] Shafer, Steve. "Unicorn Records and 'The New Ska Classics.'" The People's Ska Annual #5, Summer 1998, p. 48.

would turn up with her bag of chocolates, so we just started having this thing that anytime we wanted to buy sweets, we'd say we were just going off to see Nana Choc Choc. And then when we came to think of a title for the album, it started off as a sort of joke, because it sounded vaguely French—choc choc, and we recorded it in Paris, so why not? So it's nothing particularly clever," says Julie. This is contrary to the liner notes of the cassette release where Elena Oumano claims the title was what they were called by their fans and that it means "tasty birds."[548]

Verona Davis remembers recording the album fondly and explains a bit about how that happened. "We ended up going off to tour in Belgium and we went to France. We were playing at a festival in Rennes, on the coast, and there was a guy called Phillippe, he was based in Paris. And he organized us playing the concert in Paris, and so at the same time, while we were there, we decided we were going to make a quick album. And in 10 days we managed to do this album, *Nana Choc Choc in Paris*. So there were like five days of recording and then five days of mixing, and then we could take the stuff back to England. I've never done something like that in all my life."

Recording the album was a special experience for Amanda Fen who remembers the support she received from her friends in the band. She says, "When we recorded the album, I was about six months pregnant and it wasn't a good situation in terms of not being with the father. And I remember thinking, gosh, you know, like, this is crazy. I've got these two lives going on—this one, that I'm trying to be a grown up in, and my fun life is still being in a ska band. But somehow, it all worked out. The band was amazing." After the album, a number of other women became mothers, and Amanda says this only brought them closer together. "Julie [Liggett] had a baby, and then Nicky [Ford], and then we would go on tour, but we were all mothers, so we really got it. You could sort of say, 'oh, I'm really missing her, or him,' so the moms would talk about the mum's stuff, and all the rest carried on being how you are before you have kids, carefree basically."

Amanda says she has one memory of recording a television show shortly after they recorded the album, and shortly after she gave birth to her first daughter. It exemplifies the challenges that women have to face that men simply do not. "Suddenly, I found myself pregnant. And I was trying to sort of get through that and it was very difficult because it was a time in my life where I didn't expect to become pregnant and have the house and have partner and all of that stuff, that wasn't in play, so it was just me trying to navigate. And really, it's quite funny because we now had this sort of mascot, this little baby in the game. But it was challenging, because I remember we had a TV show, I can't remember what TV show, and it was the first time I'd left her. I think she was maybe three or four weeks old. And we're doing a TV show and I looked down and the whole of my front was just covered in milk. So I felt kind of funny and I looked down and my T-shirt was stuck to my stomach, because I hadn't been able to—because she was feeding all the time when she was

[548] Oumano, Elena. *Oddball Boy*, cassette, liner notes, 1990.

with me. And I remember dancing and then they came and spoke to us and we had to speak on the TV and I remember just being absolutely completely weirded out from being in this kind of environment, and yet I had this little baby and milk was pouring from my boobs, and I was really quite young and it was really really strange. I was still with the band and we did make it work—I left her with my auntie when we toured, but it was it was difficult because I wasn't with her dad and I really wanted to carry on with the band, but we sort of made it work."

The following year, the Deltones performed in Germany during the time that the Berlin Wall came down. Amanda says, "We were in Berlin, the tour was kicking off, and it just so happened that we went to the wall and got on the wall and partied all night. We just happened to be there. None of us brought any wall home, which was really stupid, but it was just an incredible, incredible part of history to be involved in. None of us were German, but we really felt so honored to be able to be there and have that experience. And I think about that a lot. It was just a fantastic night, in the right place at the right time. And that's the thing, I mean, we knew what was going on, but we didn't know the gravity of it at the time," says Amanda.

Verona explains how the tour in Germany came about and how she fell in love with the country and its people, enough to now call Germany home. "We ended up doing a concert in Brixton with the Busters and Thomas Shooks, the organizer for Germany, he got us to play in Germany. We played one of the gigs in Heidelberg [Schwimmbad Music Club, November 16, 1989]. That was quite amazing because I mean, the stage was not very big but it got us all on there. For some reason, because it was so packed, people were jumping around, dancing dancing dancing, and at one point, as I was singing in the microphone, somebody hit the microphone and it hit me on my tooth. And I have a crown on one of my teeth and I broke the crown. We had a gig the next day and I was like, there's no way I'm going on stage! You know, I'm not the guy from the Pogues! So a guy from Die Toten Hosen, which is a kind of punk band, his sister organized me going to a dentist in Heidelberg and I got a crown to cover the tooth and saved the day! So I had my son with me, Darien, and that was like, you know, it really opened my eyes the way the Germans were. I don't seem to come across any kind of racism. But my decision to come here was because my guy was German."

Verona left the Deltones and married Jan Brahms of the Busters whom she met during the Brixton and Germany gigs. Together they had two children. Brahms had performed trombone with the Busters and he went on to perform with Bad Manners, which produced another opportunity for Verona. "Bad Manners was looking to do a track, and it was 'Going to Get Along Without You Now, and so we did it, and for the video they got me to dress up in an old Edwardian kind of dress with Chucks, Converse All-Stars, and we went to the Cambridge River on a little boat with an umbrella and singing. At one point, the boat tips over and I get dragged under the water with this dress. And Dougie, the singer of Bad Manners, he was like a fish! He dived into the water. All I remember is seeing this big kind of whale coming towards me, and this guy grabbed me and pulled me up out of the water because this dress was dragging me down. I was quite a good swimmer, but I couldn't handle it. He came out of nowhere, he pulled me and, and, and then I managed to hang onto the edge of the boat. His girlfriend Angie, she was there, and she was like, 'Oh my god! I thought she was a goner!'"

Perhaps Verona Davis is most well known, not for her work with the Deltones or Bad Manners, but with another group, the Stereo MCs whose song "Connected" made her voice recognizable all over the world. Through work with a band called Giant, Verona met Owen Rossiter. "He said to me that he was working on another band, which was kind of a hip hop rap band. They were looking for singers. I went to check out a concert and I was pregnant with my second son at the time, and my friend Karen who came with me, she said to me, oh, you can do that! I met them backstage and they seemed like nice people, and then the rep, he rang me and left me a message to come down to Brixton. I went to do an audition with them, walked into his house, and in his room he had this record player with lots of records all over the place. Anyway, he just put some tracks on and so I started jamming around and next thing I know, they asked me to come down to the studio. And I sang on their album, *Connected.* That was great. On the *Connected* album, I'm singing on a few tracks and I'm also in the video. They got me to come down again and do the track, to do the vocal again. And when I heard the final mix, I was like, what?! All my friends were like, that's Verona! And then we came to America in '92 and did a tour all over the place. And that was also an experience. We supported U2 and when we came back to England, they took us on their tour, so we were the ones to support them."

The pinnacle moment for Verona came during a performance on August 21, 1993. Verona explains, "We were at Wembley and before us on the tour was Bjork and I was able to get my brother, my mother, my sister, and my other brother to come backstage. But my mother was on the podium where the mixing desk was. And when I came up to do the beginning of the Stereo set, I came out on the stage and all I could see was my mother with a white hankie, waving at me!" she says, laughing. "And I started waving back and everybody started waving back at me! At that moment, she realized that I'm a singer. Because she used to say, 'why don't you get a proper job, you know, like become a doctor or a lawyer.' But my dream was always to be a singer. My brother was talking about it recently and he said, 'Verona, if you didn't do anything else, you made it then!' They realized that's their sister doing her thing." She has been awarded a gold record for her work with the Stereo MCs.

Verona had to balance being a mother with being a performer, but she makes no apologies and has no regrets about doing so. "I had my son in 1990 and did the first tour in 1992, so the time it took for the recordings and then the mixing and then to organize the tour, that gave me enough time to recover. And I can remember taking both of my sons, Darien and Joshua, on tour with me. At one point we were all on the tour bus and I had the kids sleeping in the bunk and I slept on the seat. I can remember when Darien was like three or four, taking him on tour with me, and I can remember when he was at the concert, sometimes the organizers would be like, 'Can you keep him backstage?' And I was like, 'Well, he's not a little puppy, you know.' I think it was a good experience because they were really taken care of and I always thought it was important that my children at the time would understand that this was part of my life. But they came first. If they had the flu, I had to cancel. It was like, sorry, but my kids come first. I'm determined to show people that it's possible. My sons are not a commodity, they're actually a part of my life. Instead of me adjusting to everybody else, they have to learn to adjust to a child being around. They couldn't do things like smoke in the same room. It's a child. You can't do that. I even turned down a tour to Japan because it would have meant me missing my first day at my son's school. I was thinking to myself, and it was good money going to Japan, but I just couldn't do it. There'll always be more money to make, but never be another first day of school."

Today, Verona is divorced from Brahms. Her oldest son Darien lives in Liverpool and also has a son, her son Joshua is a rapper in Germany, and her youngest son Fabienne is studying to be a physiotherapist. Verona still lives in Germany and she and her partner, Thomas Hinkel, have a band, Pop the Moon. She has struggled with her health, including having two kidney transplants, but she reflects on her time with countless musicians and the Deltones fondly. "What I liked about ska music is that it was for everybody. It was a black, white, Asian, everything. Every mixture was there. And that's what music does. It should bring you together and not pull you apart." She plans to continue performing and is always collaborating and writing. "My time is not up yet!" Verona says.

Julie says that her reasons for leaving the Deltones were similar to the reason many women cite for exiting music—she had to make money. "So I'd only been back with them for a year and we recorded the album and done quite a lot of gigs but then I was pregnant with my second child, and I just thought that I needed to get a proper job and earn some money. I've got a family to support. So after I had my second son, I went back to work full time and I was just not able to socialize and be in touch with the band, let alone go see a gig." Julie then worked in human resources and administration in several non-governmental organizations before moving to the south coast. She is not only a mother, but also a grandmother now.

Since the Deltones and the Potato 5, Sara McGuinness has continued to perform as a musician, playing with Maroon Town and now a number of bands that are not ska. Today she performs salsa, Cuban, and Latin American music in London. She has also earned a master's of performance from The School of Oriental and African Studies, a practice-based PhD, and she has a Cuban spouse. She explains, "For many years now I've been running a Cuban music holiday—people come and they stay there and then we go to the top studio in Cuba and people learn Cuban music with a lot of Cuban musicians and me," says McGuinness. "But as a woman in music, still today, it's very difficult to be a musician and a parent. As a single parent, it's tough. When I came to this college [London College of Music], I was teaching popular music and out of 60 students there were no female instrumentalists at all. Because the money you can make for music had decreased, so musicians have to have another job. And so what it means is when times get tougher, the people who are less established get pushed out. And women will be the ones who get pushed out. So it's a tough one."

Jacqui Callis recognizes that the opportunity the Deltones and that musical space afforded her were life changing and life shaping. She reflects, "Before punk, women were just girlfriends, sitting, watching men play instruments, or jamming. But punk enabled women to get up and play as well, to get them to form their own bands. And you learned while you were playing in the band. And that is what the Deltones did. They were all learning their instruments while they were gigging, almost. They had a basic knowledge, but they kind of got better as they played. They were good at performing. And they were young and beautiful and it had an energy to it. Punk certainly gave the space to me, which is why it was difficult when you suddenly saw women not playing again. But then actually now there's lots more women playing. Lots more women's bands around, it seems, so that's good."

Dill Hammond says she too enjoyed her years with the Deltones but when she had children, she found it difficult to continue performing. "We toured with Bad Manners and the Hotknives, Fishbone, Desmond Dekker, Laurel Aitken—but then the band members started having more long-term relationships and they started having children. You know, people's lives did move on or did change. After that, I joined a lot of other bands, actually. I got into dance music and house music and sort of worked with programmers and stuff. I got into writing music, I got really into rap music, doing club appearances and that sort of thing. And that went on really until my children were born. And then it just got quite difficult. I mean, not impossible. I miss it to this day, actually. The one love of my life really is music and performing," Dill says. She has two sons, one in college and one in high school. Neither, she says, are musical.

Gilly Johns says that performing with Desmond Dekker was a highlight of her time with the Deltones. "He was really respectful. Because he totally got it. Out of all the famous people that we met, he was the best. He was just about music and not about a lot of cheesiness in the music business. It was about the integrity of making music," Gilly says. She left the Deltones because, she says, "I felt it had run its course for me. By that time I'd met somebody, a male that I was having a relationship with and we were going to write songs together. So I left to write songs with him. And we did. But I did miss the Deltones for about six months. My heart really hurt. It was my decision to leave, but things don't last forever and it was kind of a real wrench." Gilly ended up leaving the relationship and moved to her family home in Cornwall to raise her two sons. She has spent her life focused on art, painting for community centers as well as art galleries. "When you're a mum, you're looking after tiny children, your whole mentality changes. I have to make a living and raise a family," she says.

Amanda Fen also left to focus on her family. "Guys go out and tour and don't have to worry about leaking boobs and feeling incredibly guilty. I remember feeling really, really awful about leaving her [first daughter] and going out on tour. She was fine and she loved staying with my auntie, because my mom was working full time. My mom's only 20 years older than me, so she was very young, but I thought, what am I doing, trying to be a pop star when I've got a baby hanging off my boob. It was a challenge. But it was a challenge that we definitely got through and somehow it made me more resilient, trying to have babies as a single mom and be in a band, as well. You know, you have to step up. So I feel proud of that. And my daughter actually loves all the stories of when she was a baby, and she's seen the pictures of me when I was on stage, and she loves the story of her unusual start. She's going to be 34 next week. Crazy! But then I met my husband and we were having our second daughter. It was around about that time that other people were having children and the Deltones had been together for long enough. I think it might have been, you know, altogether something like seven years from the start, from when I first started doing that, and I think it was time for people. It tends to be a bit natural, from my point of view. I'd had my second child, I was getting married, and it was trying to do something else. There was no falling out or anything like that. It was just time to move on really. And after that, I moved to Hastings. My mom was here. I didn't carry on doing music. I started making things and selling things. I did market stalls, festivals, making jewelry and selling it and I still do that. Now I've got a jewelry shop. I sell silver jewelry and I sell online. It's called Stargazy. My husband is a scientist and I have three daughters—one is a medic, one does law, and one works in housing with homeless people.

Serena Parsons did continue her life in music, though not in a band, nor playing an instrument. Around the same time as the Deltones were recording *Nana Choc Choc in Paris*, Serena had started up her own music agency. "Well, someone had started the company, and then it turns out there was going to be a booking agency because everyone was in a band and everyone we knew was in a band, so surely we can book them. So that's how that started. Originally it was called RPM Promotions. And then, at the moment, I'm working at Primary Talent, so I'm part of the ICM Partners, one of the major agencies. Over the years I've worked with reggae and ska acts—well, mainly reggae. Loads of people. I mean, most of them are dead now. At the moment, the only one that's left is Lee Perry [died on Aug. 21, 2021]. I represent him exclusively for the UK and I've done that for years. I've worked with Horace Andy and I also do left field hip hop, is what I specialize in—not quite straightforward hip hop. I do struggle to find much that I like these days. I think reggae in the '90s was amazing. There's loads of stuff. But now, I mean, everything's kind of turning into the same things. I mean, autotune, it's not really for me. It doesn't have to be old school, but then I find it difficult to find any really quality acts that I like." Serena doesn't have any children and is not married.

At the beginning of November 2022, Serena Parsons reported, "Potato 5 got back together recently with several of the original line-up. They played their first London gig a couple of weeks ago and most of the Deltones went. Several of us hadn't seen each other for over 30 years!"[549]

---

[549] Parsons, Serena. Email correspondence with the author. 5 Nov. 2022.

The Deltones, as photographed on album sleeves

The Potato 5 and The Gymslips

The Gymslips:
Paula Richards: vocals, guitar
Suzanne Scott: vocals, bass
Karen Yarnell: drums

The Potato 5:
Martin Aberdeen: guitar
Malcolm Buck: tenor saxophone
Simon Driscoll: trombone
Andy Minnion: tenor & baritone
    saxophone
Paula Richards: bass
Rick Walker: alto saxophone
And others

    Ska music is notorious for silly names, particularly during the 1990s when ska puns jumped the shark. While the Potato 5 moniker may be tame in comparison to some of the goofier names that would appear in later years, it still was a rather strange and nonsensical name. There weren't five members of the London-based late '80s ska band—there were six, seven, eight, sometimes nine. And potato? Who can speculate the meaning. But they were important despite their name, and as writer Marc Wasserman observed, "In hindsight, the band did help to pave the way for the 3rd wave of ska that began to emerge towards the mid 1990s in both the U.S. and around the world."[550]

    Members of the Deltones have described their group as the sister band to the Potato 5, so then it could be argued that the Potato 5 were the brother band to the Deltones (see also the Deltones chapter). Though the members of the Potato 5 were largely men, there were a number of women who stepped into roles for the Potato 5 from time to time as needed, including Julie Liggett and Sara McGuinness who performed keyboards for both bands. But the Potato 5 had a regular female member, Paula Richards, who played bass after leaving her former band, the Gymslips—an all-female punk band.

    As a kid, Paula Richards taught herself to play guitar since her family wasn't particularly musical. "I was adopted in 1963 and became part of the Richards family," says Paula.[551] "I had a brother and a sister and we lived in the suburbs of London in a middle class affluent area. My family were completely unmusical although loved listening to it. I adored music from a very early age and would annoy my family by taking up any instrument possible and constantly playing. They tolerated my recorder, violin, harmonica and finally guitar playing. My parents bought me a guitar when I was around 13 and I remember announcing one day I had written my first song. I then proceeded to perform a punky song I had written called, 'I'm a drug pusher and

[550] Wasserman, Marc. "The Potato 5 -Rare and Unreleased Tracks From Late 80's UK Trad Ska Band." 18 Oct. 2008. marcoonthebass.blogspot.com/2008/10/potato-5-rare-and-unreleased-tracks.html. Accessed 3 Jan. 2023.
[551] Richards, Paula. All quotations, unless otherwise noted, from interview with the author, 17 Feb. 2021.

you're my hooker.' I had absolutely no idea what a hooker even was at the time, so my parents were rather shocked."

Paula says she hated school while growing up and found all of her education irrelevant. "In those days in the UK, if you were female you were being trained in school for shop work, secretarial work, or marriage and all seemed ridiculous to me. At around 14, myself and a few local lads formed a band. I was the guitarist but as soon as they got a gig at the local college, they told me I couldn't be on stage with them as it would look really bad because I was a girl. That was the point when I knew I needed to be in a female band. So I started to answer adverts in the music magazines and eventually met a few different women, did a few auditions and rehearsals and finally met the girls I formed my first band with, the Gymslips," she says. The band, which formed in 1979, featured seven women at the start.[552] One year later there were four members, and then by 1981 they were three—Paula Richards on guitar and vocals, Suzanne Scott on bass and vocals, and Karen Yarnell on drums.[553] That same year they released their first single, a cover of the Suzi Quatro song, "48 Crash" on the Abstract label.

"We were quite lucky at the time as quite quickly we got spotted by a small record label and the Radio 1 DJ John Peel. We were invited into the radio station to do a session which went really well. This led to another five sessions and an album deal. When working for John Peel, you didn't really get to see much of him. We spent a lot of time in the BBC canteen to be honest but he did pay us a visit when we were making our first single '48 Crash' and came down the studio with his producer John Walters to sing the backing vocals. In total we released one album and four singles and weirdly only just this week [February 2021] we were offered a new record deal to re-release our earlier stuff, sessions and demos, so it seems this band lives on for some," says Paula. The one album that the Gymslips released was called *Rocking with the Renees*, also on the Abstract label. A "Renee," as the back of the album stated, had an appearance that was "slightly round, double chin, in most cases short hair" with a diet of "excessive alcohol, pie and mash," clothing featured "jeans, monkey books, denim jacket (leather in winter), T-shirt," and habits were "most disgusting things." They also noted that "the male counterparts are known as Ronees."[554] Paula explained, "It started off just a nickname from these blokes we knew. They would call us Renees cause it was a name that girls were called in the mod times, and so we started calling ourselves Renees and called all girls Renees. But since then we've given a Renee a proper definition."[555] In one article, Paula Richards explained to Garry Bushell, who called the Gymslips "bosomy boozers," that "Renees are working class girls who drink a lot, smoke, fart, and wear smelly socks."[556] Their music, though, critics really liked. Bushell said their songs were "high on hummability, frisky," and

[552] Smith, Winston. "Girls Talk." *Sounds*, 1 Jan. 1983, p. 15.
[553] Ibid.
[554] *Rocking with the Renees* album cover.
[555] Snow, Mat. "The Gymslips: Smelly Socks And Belches." *NME*. 24 Sept. 1983.
[556] Bushell, Garry. "Reneegades." *Sounds*, 18 Jun. 1983.

"foot-tapping fun."[557] Another reviewer said the Gymslips produced "some of the most authentically catchy, funny and boisterous knees-up music in London town since Madness emerged over four years ago. … The Gymslips are staunch believers in the merits of '60s pop-song writing and class of '76 rude energy."[558]

For as fierce as the Gymslips were, they still faced their fair share of sexism. They were careful not to label themselves as a "feminist" band, but they acknowledged that being all female was "an advantage when you're doing gigs, but when it comes to getting a recording contract it's so much more difficult than if you was blokes, because they feel they've got to market you in some sort of way," said Suzanne Scott.[559] Paula adds, "They don't know how to put us across, they don't know what we are. A couple of record companies said 'What's their image? What sort of music do they want to play?' We said we want to play what we play. They said, 'That's neither one thing nor the other.' Unless you're really ultra-feminine or reggae or something they can't do anything with you, whereas with bloke bands they just fit into a category. We don't want to be remembered as a girl band when we split up. We want to be remembered as a band."[560]

The Gymslips did, in fact, split up in the mid-1980s and Paula Richards continued her career in music. "Myself and a couple of friends decided to start our own entertainment agency. We knew so many people in bands and thought this would be a great way of making a living by booking them gigs. This was how I ended up in the Deltones and Potato 5. The Deltones were one of the bands we booked and their bass player was having a baby so I covered for a year or so whilst she had the baby and eventually she came back. With the Potato 5, they kept being offered gigs that they couldn't do because they didn't have a bass player. In the end I agreed to play the bass as well as being their agent so they could at least gig again. I really enjoyed being in the Potato 5. We did lots of great gigs and the guys were really good fun. We toured Europe and even America with No Doubt and a couple of other bands. Eventually it just kind of fizzled out as everyone seemed to be getting married and having babies. My last band the Renees was put together by myself and the Gymslips drummer. We were missing gigging and had been offered a record deal by a French label. We put out one album, *Have You Got It*, and one single, 'He Called Me a Fat Pig and Walked Out On Me.' Neither did very well but it was fun," she says.

"Another side project around this time was a little record label I started called Paradise Records. We only put out one album called *Postcard from Paradise* which was a compilation album of 12 female UK bands. One of the bands was the Rude Girls, which was actually myself and a couple of the Deltones. We did a kind of skacid version of the Bodysnatchers Rocksteady," says Paula. Skacid, or acid ska, is explained by Marc Wasserman: "For the uninitiated, acid ska features the signature characteristics of house and techno, namely a Roland TR-909 drum machine, a

---

[557] Ibid.

[558] Snow, Mat. "The Gymslips: Smelly Socks And Belches." *NME*. 24 Sept. 1983.

[559] Ibid.

[560] Ibid.

Roland TB-303 bassline synth and an MC vocalist/toaster. Where acid ska was different than straight techno and house music was that it replaced the classic breakbeat sample with a ska or pitched-up reggae rhythm guitar sample. The most sophisticated of acid ska tracks had melodic horn sections in the same arrangement that a typical ska song would include them. Historically, acid ska is the predecessor to jungle, dub step and other reggae hybrids that have proliferated in the U.K. in the last 20 years."[561]

Paula also worked with singer Samantha Fox as her agent, bass player, and co-writer. But she decided to leave the music industry after growing tired of the lifestyle and challenges. "We often worked with sleazy men who made us feel very uncomfortable. In fact, I have been chased around by them on some occasions and felt at risk but luckily nothing happened. I remember record companies trying to redesign the Gymslips image and offering us deals if we agreed to change how we looked. However, the women's music scene was very supportive to each other and eventually a great network of women friendly companies and contacts was established. With the Gymslips I felt quite uncomfortable with our audience. We attracted quite a large skinhead following who seemed quite aggressive. Occasionally we would attract bikers as well as skinheads and that would cause a bit of a clash. We also attracted the female gay crowd, so it was a slightly uncomfortable situation sometimes."

"In my personal life, I realised from a young age that I was gay so despite a few failed relationships with boys/men I settled into gay life. I have been with my partner Kate for 14 years and she has a 17-year-old son who I have helped raise. He is incredibly musical and often plays along to my old bands. In 2003 I moved to Cornwall, wanting to do something different with my life. After a while, hanging out with musicians and industry people, you begin to need something a little more normal. I had been a vegetarian most of my life and had experienced awful vegetarian food whilst touring. Once in Denmark I was given a bowl of grated carrot for my dinner and once in Belgium served a rabbit as my vegetarian meal. I decided you didn't need to be that brilliant to run a great vegetarian restaurant, so I set up the Bean Inn which is now in its 18th year (despite the pandemic) and we hope it continues for many more," says Paula.

---

[561] Wasserman, Marc. "Acid Ska - A Look Back At A Late 80's U.K. Ska Phenomenon." Marco on the Bass, 15 Jan. 2010. marcoonthebass.blogspot.com/2010/01/acid-ska-look-back-at-late-80s-uk-ska.html. Accessed 23 Nov. 2022.

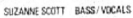

SUZANNE SCOTT   BASS / VOCALS   KAREN YARNELL   DRUMS / VOCALS   PAULA RICHARDS   GUITAR / VOCALS

The Gymslips

The Renees with Paula Richards on left

The Potato 5 with Floyd Lloyd

The Loafers

Nasser Bouzida: drums
Denise Butler: saxophone
Jon Downer: guitar
Tony Finn: vocals

Sean Flowerdew: keyboards
Trevor Harding: bass
Jim Robinson: vocals

Although 2 Tone had waned and ceased many years before, the late 1980s still presented a few ska bands in the UK who performed in the same style as their predecessors. The Hotknives, the Deltones, Maroon Town, Potato 5 and the Loafers, among others, continued to carry the ska torch, performing on bills together, and with pioneers like Laurel Aitken and Prince Buster. One of these bands, the Loafers, strengthened their 2 Tone ties by working with John Bradbury of the Specials who produced their debut album. They didn't stay together for long, but members of this band have maintained their dedication to ska to this day.

The one female member of the Loafers, Denise Butler, began playing saxophone at an early age. Though her family wasn't very musical, she was recruited to play in the band since the members all grew up together in a small town about an hour outside of London. "Well, my parents, they run their own business," she explains.[562] "They ran horse drawn boats on the canal, which sounds very odd if you've never seen it. My brother still has that company. But when we were kids, they kind of bought that when I was about eight years old. And so basically, there was no kind of musicality of such. I mean, my parents love music, but they were in their 60s and they had a very free attitude when they were younger. I wouldn't say that they were hippies. I think they would have liked to have been, if they could have broken any rules, but they weren't rule breakers by any stretch. They were hardworking people. And when I was young, my cousins always played instruments, Kate and Caroline, so I kind of took the lead from them. And my parents were always really encouraging. As soon as I found a recorder, like lots of people, I went on to a treble recorder, and then I kind of moved on to clarinet, which I really loved. When I was in primary ed, I loved playing the clarinet and I just had a real love of performing. And then, when I was a couple years into secondary education, I decided that I wanted to move on to the sax, which was kind of a natural progression."

Denise grew up in Newbury in Berkshire, and through her brother she became friends with the members of the Loafers. "I met Sean [Flowerdew] from when I was about six. He came over from Zimbabwe when his parents settled over here. And he was good friends with my brother. And this is how the story starts, I guess. All the boys were good friends with my older brother Steve. And then Nas [Nasser Bouzida], he moved up from London when we were about eight years old. And then we kind of just fell into the band, really. The guys were doing music and they'd said

---

562 Butler, Denise. All quotations, unless otherwise noted, from interview with the author, 21 Dec. 2020.

to Steve, 'Do you think your sister might be interested in playing?' And so I just went along with my friends, and we just, you know, had a bit of a play in a jam, and they were kind of, 'wow, this person really knows music!' And we were all friends. I mean, we'd known each other for a very long time. So, it was quite an organic process. The first band that we were in had the most ridiculous name. So it was the Man from Tneopoo. I don't think they'd done a demo at that point, but they'd done like this little tape on a cassette and I think I was the only one that bought one. It was my price to join the band. My brother sold it to me an inflated rate, I might add. He charged me a quid, and they were going for a 50p, and I was probably the only one who bought one, and they were really good but there were probably about three tracks on it and they recorded it up in his bedroom! And so that was the start," she says.

The first gig that the Loafers played was covered in the local newspaper, the *Newbury Weekly News*. The reviewer was Nasser Bouzida's mother. With the headline, "New teenage band makes debut," she wrote, "Greenham Court Community Centre rocked to the sounds of talented teenage group the Man From Tneopoo on Saturday, when they made their debut performance. Formed just a few months ago, the line-up consists of Nasser Bouzida (drums), Sean Flowerdew (keyboards), Johnny Downer (guitar), Declan Kyle (bass player) and Denise Butler (saxophone). Vocalists are Marie Bateman and Tracey Huxter. All the band members are 15, save Denise who is 14, and all are St. Bartholomew's pupils. The Man from Tneopoo presented eight songs they had written themselves, and covers of 'Stepping Stone' and 'Wipe Out,' which won them an encore."[563]

Denise recalls that debut gig, "It was so well supported. It was phenomenal. The turnout was crazy. And it was all of our friends really, but you have to imagine that there was nothing going on. There was nothing to do. We'd just kind of hang around each other's houses. But as soon as we started doing gigs, everybody turned up, everybody. All of our friends turned up and that kind of carried on a little bit when we when we got into doing the Loafers. We were supported phenomenally by our friends. We did some local gigs and they were just epic, great fun. Lots of energy, lots of energy." The Loafers performed throughout the late 1980s with gigs at the Majestic in Reading, King's Hall in Herne Bay, and The Fridge in Brixton. They were performing in the tradition of 2 Tone, as Denise explains. "All the guys were really big fans of the 2 Tone era. We'd all grown up listening to the Specials and Madness—in particular Madness I think were quite key because I kind of think we could always identify with these kinds of bands, people like the Bodysnatchers and the *Dance Craze* kind of era. I remember when they released the *Dance Craze* video, and we were all really excited about it so that we could actually see the gig. I was born in '72 so we hadn't had that experience, so it was great to see that when it came out, and the boys were really into the origins of the music," says Denise of the Jamaican era as well.

---

[563] The Loafers Facebook page, 22 Jan. 2022. facebook.com/theloafersska/photos/4919830518074051. Accessed 21 Nov. 2022.

312

The lineup of the Loafers changed from that first gig as the Man from Tneopoo and a bit later as the Loafers. In the early days they had a vocalist, Jim Robinson, who appeared on their first album, *City Skanking* on the Skank Records label. He was then replaced by Tony Finn, or Finny, as he was known. Trevor Harding, or Trev, joined on bass and appeared on the first and subsequent albums. The Loafers were, first and foremost, friends. Their relationship was strong and so the group connected on a level deeper than the music. "We were still really quite young. Most of the band, at some point or another, had lived in our house. Allie, who was my dear friend and Trev's girlfriend at the time, she was kind of like, the other Loafer. She was pivotal in the band. She was our driver and she was kind of like the big sister of the band. She was pivotal to actually just getting us to gigs, and being the sensible one, and she was an awesome influence on me at the time. She was really, really sound and really solid. So Allie moved into our place and I got to know Trevor really well. And then, when Allie moved out, Nasser moved in, so Nasser was living in our house at some point. And then Nasser moved out, Finny moved in. So at some point or another, they all lived in my parents' house. And Sean quite literally lived around the corner, so we were all really close. We were a family—a family without a doubt."

Because they were all friends, and were all young, they had a different approach to playing than those bands who had put label demands before music, and music before friendship. "We just didn't take ourselves too seriously," says Denise. "Over half the time, I think I was terrified of looking like a complete idiot. You're so self-conscious. I think we did my first London gig, I was about 15, and we all looked pretty ghastly—we're all going through puberty at the time. You're trying to fit in with all of these people that are cool and they're in London and I think half the time I didn't talk to anybody because I was terrified all the time. You just don't want to be making a fool of yourself. We just loved doing the music and we loved being together. Whereas other kids did sports, we played gigs. It was quite an organic process. Sean was pivotal in getting gigs so he would branch out to people that were in pivotal places. I don't know how we managed to get these first gigs. I'm guessing that we threw demos out to people, I don't know. But we did the Dublin Castle, which is obviously a key venue in the scene. And then we did Gaz's Rocking Blues. They kind of grew from that because it was very very quick."

The Loafers released their first album, *City Skanking*, on the prolific Skank Records label in 1988. That following year they switched to Staccato Records and released two albums—*Contagious*, and *Skankin' the Place Down*, as well as the EPs, *Living in A Suitcase*, *The Undertaker*, and *Mad About Ska*, the latter of which featured Jamaican legend Laurel Aitken. This EP contained four songs including "Rudy Got Married," "Skin Head," "Mad About You," and the song from which the publishing company of this book is named, "Sally Brown." Denise describes their writing process for their songs. "The guys would come up with the music and then I would put a solo riff over the top. And I was constantly saying to Sean, 'what key is that? What note is that?' It was very rough and ready and I think that when you listen to some of it now, it's like, oh my goodness, we were definitely a live band. That was how we played and that's how we sounded at the time, so definitely authenticity."

But then the Loafers broke up, despite their success in producing a great number of recordings in a short amount of time and frequent touring. "I think it was just a case of the guys going different directions. Sean and Finny went off and did Special Beat, so they hit the big time, really. They were playing with big names and touring across the country. And then Nas and Trev took a break and then we came up with different bands and kind of different projects, but now they're really successful with Big Boss Man. We did Skooby [a jazz funk band] which was really successful. That was kind of an offshoot from the first guys. Skooby was started and then they asked me to come and do some guest stuff and we did some gigs. But there were several bands leading up to that so the guys kind of came up with new bands and Sean and Finny were off gigging doing their kind of uber famous thing and then we kind of carried on doing gigs and built it up again. So it was just a natural time to finish. I think at the time I felt quite devastated because I thought oh my god, what am I going to do now? I've been doing this for the last three years from 15 to 18. So I thought, don't worry about it. Let's do something else. We had TV work and we were kind of a house band on Men & Motors which was like a really dodgy program on a satellite channel. We met some really exciting people when we were doing that. The show was called *Hot*. It was really good fun."

"But then what did I do? I kind of just went to work. A little bit of music, nothing too serious. I worked in a bank for, gosh, about 10 years, and then I decided that I really don't like working at a bank. I just shouldn't be working at a bank. And then I worked for a friend of mine in a shop and that was the best fun. And then I met my husband-to-be and had my gorgeous girl Lily, and I kind of drifted in and out of things. Lily now is 18. And I did little music projects, like I was in a covers band with some guys that live in Redding, just up the road from where I am, but I just couldn't commit. I just wanted to be with my kids. And doing lots of pub gigs and pub venues, you kind of think, 'Well, actually, I've been there and I've done traveling around in the back of a van now. I've scratched that itch. I'm not sure that I want to do that again,'" says Denise.

When asked what her kids think of her mom's previous life as a performer, she explains, "My son, he has Asperger's. So things like my previous life, I think, just skim over him. But Lily, I took her to one of Sean's International Ska Festivals when she was 15. And I said, 'Well, this was what mum was doing when I was 15,' just to give her a bit of insight. She probably doesn't think I'm cool. I don't think I've ever been cool, ever! We [Denise and Lily] had a great time. And the band that we watched was a mash of Maroon Town and Potato 5 and so I was in such heaven, because these two bands were so pivotal. They were absolutely fabulous and it was a great evening."

For women, Denise says that having a group of supportive friends was crucial, but it's certainly a life that has its challenges. "I think there's always going to be a choice that has to be made. And even though I mean, my husband is amazing, I love him dearly, but there's no way that I could feel comfortable with going off to gigs and saying, 'okay, it's now my weekend, I'll see you later.' With small kids, I just don't think it's fair. So there's always that element of having to make that choice."

Since the late 1980s with the Loafers, Denise Butler has accomplished quite a bit. "I got my university degree and now I work in a school. My degree is in child development and I work in a really lovely little primary school in the middle of nowhere and I just basically have the kids that maybe struggle a little bit and maybe the ones that don't kind of fit in. But I'm not officially a teacher, because that's not that's not really me. I don't think I could be serious enough for a teacher, but I'm definitely a support person. You know, I think I really fit the job. And I don't have to have the responsibility of the class but I get all the love of the kids. I'm very grateful. I'm very grateful for everything that I've had and experienced. It's been a blast. Definitely."

Denise Butler with Laurel Aitken after a performance with the Loafers

Denise Butler with the Loafers (above) and today (below)

Amazulu

Nardo Bailey: drums
Sharon Bailey: manager and
    percussion
Lesley Beach: saxophone
Debbie Evans: drums

Clare Hirst: saxophone
Clare Kenny: bass
Rose Miner: vocals
Annie Ruddock: vocals
Margo Sagov: guitar

The video is cheap looking, to be frank. That, however, was by design, says Jerry Dammers who directed the "Moonlight Romance" production for Amazulu— a band of mostly women that had just signed to Island Records after a number of somewhat successful singles. Dammers had started dabbling in video production as one of his many creative endeavors, and it took him out of the studio for a short period during his lengthy undertaking of the *In the Studio* album. "You get a better video because the cheaper it is the better it looks anyway. That's the theory anyway. I like all those old B-movies. I'm gonna start doing some B-records now," Dammers said of his approach.[564] It was an attempt at camp, with a faux jungle and steaming volcano, plenty of spears and loincloths, and tribal masks and skeletons. The clueless Thomas Dolby-looking explorer is seduced by Amazulu's lead singer, Annie Ruddock, who feeds him potion-like drinks and sails with him in a Cleopatra-like boat before the scene ends in her hut. Too much to unpack here, but during the onset of the music video era, this was just enough to help distinguish Amazulu from other bands. They were fun, they were talented, and they were commercial. Unfortunately, they were also just about ready to implode.

Amazulu began as a group of friends who simply enjoyed ska, rocksteady, reggae, and dub and wanted to perform in order to participate. Three of the members had grown up together and one of those women, Lesley Beach, said the music she loved inspired her to pick up the saxophone, but that wasn't her first instrument of choice. "Me and Rose Miner [the original singer] grew up in Liverpool together. It's where the Beatles come from, but it has like the oldest African community in England and Europe, and it has a big, what we call West Indian community, what you probably call Caribbean. Lots of my friends' dads were from Jamaica or Trinidad or Africa, and we were all reggae fanatics growing up. My friend's cousin went to Jamaica for the summer one year and came back with some records for me, and that was it. So things like the Pioneers' "Long Shot Kick De Bucket," Shorty's "President Mash Up the Resident" with the whistles, Max Romeo's stuff. I mean, we were in high school and we loved singing "Wreck a Buddy," the Soul Sisters, all that lot. I wanted to be a drummer. Debbie Dread [Evans] who was our original drummer, her boyfriend was a drummer and he gave her a drum kit. And my boyfriend, his brother was in jail and he was selling everything and I bought his saxophone for 50 pounds. So it was

---

564 Irwin, Colin. "The Special AKA: Memoirs of a Survivor." *Melody Maker*, 19 Jan. 1985.

complete accident. I wanted to be the drummer but Debbie had the drum kit, so she was the drummer," Lesley says.[565]

Amazulu first formed just for fun at first, but it quickly grew more serious. "We never planned to do any gigs or anything, we just wanted to play reggae with all girls. None of the boys would give us a turn. They just wanted sweet singers. Back then, women in reggae, they got to sing. That was it. I taught myself too quickly to play sax. I do that a lot in life. If I want to learn something, I just have to go learn it right now—usually the wrong way, and then when I was forced to go to lessons and stuff, it was hard to try and do it properly. I taught myself the saxophone by listening to UB40 records. It was like that then. Punk made everything possible," says Lesley.

Punk music was a driving force for women, and anyone, for that matter. So living in London during this time, ready to receive what the universe sent their way, the young members of Amazulu began to organize into more of a formal band. "Rose and I ran away to London when I was 17, and because we were reggae fanatics, we went to the blues dances in Ladbroke Grove all night long. And then as years went by, we just decided that was what we wanted to do. And so Rose and I moved to London and then Sharon Bailey was Rose's neighbor and the three of us moved into a flat together and we started meeting women and decided to work together and play. Somebody knew Clare [Kenny] and we got Margo [Sagov] from the musicians' union book, and we knew Annie because of the whole scene in Ladbroke Grove," Lesley says.

Sharon Bailey had grown up in Milton Keynes. After moving to London she says she was eager to be a part of the band and also had planned to start a group. "I wanted to start an all-women's band and we formed Amazulu. At first, I was managing them, but I used to go to the rehearsals and jam on the congas and pick up things and play, so when they went on stage, they would drag me on and make me do it there too. I've never been to a class, I just play along to records on percussion—and recently I've started mucking around on the drums—we swap about."[566]

But Debbie Dread, or Debbie Evans, was the primary drummer at the start. She recalls how she was drawn into the band, primarily by her love for reggae. " I was born in South London to an unmusical white couple. I linked up with two Jamaican brothers in secondary school as we were in the basketball club I and used to go raving with them to Jah Shaka at the Co-op Hall in Catford when I was a skinhead," she says.[567] She furthered her interest in Jamaican music, as well as being a drummer, when she was inspired by seeing a live performance. "I saw my first live reggae band, One Style, which had a one-handed drummer in Peckham's Mr. Bees in the '60s. I then left home at 19 and moved to Brixton and shared a flat with three black guys and another white girl and raved at blues parties which cost 50p to get in. These were sound systems such as Frontline International (my fave), I-Spy, Moa Ambassa,

[565] Beach, Lesley. All quotations, unless otherwise noted, from interview with the author, 20 Feb. 2021.
[566] Steward, Sue and Sheryl Garratt. *Signed Sealed and Delivered: True Life Stories of Women in Pop*. South End Press, 1984, p. 108.
[567] Evans, Debbie. All quotations, unless otherwise noted, from interview with the author, 10 Nov. 2022.

Soferno B, Stereograph, Sir Coxsone, etc. I then moved to North London at 25 and went to drama school during the week, then raved at Phebes, Entebbe Sounds, and Chicken on weekends and other clubs and gigs." It was at this point that Debbie Dread became part of Amazulu. She explains, "I auditioned for Amazulu as a friend of mine was their singer [Rose] and she wanted to put together an all-women reggae band. Abacush and African Woman were all black female bands already gigging, whereas Amazulu were mixed. I didn't know much about drumming and had no desire to be a drummer but did it anyway."

Amazulu's bass player, Clare Kenny, also had a love of reggae and came to Amazulu through her work at the Hope and Anchor pub—ground zero for ska and punk during the early 1980s. Clare had grown up in a family with a musical background and by the time she was approached by members of Amazulu to join, she knew her way around many musical instruments. "I grew up in South Wales. I was there until I was 19 when I flew the nest. My family were musical—both my mom and dad. Not professionally, but they both sang in choirs. They had a real love of music. They were classical music, opera, because they were the slightly older generation of parents, possibly on the cusp of the introduction and arrival of pop music. They were already in their 30s, I guess. But they loved music. There was always music on in the house, even though their particular love was opera. My dad played guitar, Spanish guitar, because they lived all over. They lived in Brazil and I was actually born in Brazil. In fact, he was working in the Amazon. After they met and were engaged, he got a job, and then he came back, they got married, and they went out. And that was in the mid-50s. It wasn't common at all. He was in the shipping industry. They both spoke Spanish and Portuguese because they were in Peru to start with and then they went to Brazil," says Clare.[568]

Her parents encouraged her musical education and the same for her three sisters. She says, "My mom and dad were very keen that we had a bit of a musical education, and it was on offer in school, but in an orchestral way. So I wanted to play the cello, but I got handed a violin and that was because there weren't any cellos. So I didn't fall in love with the violin, let's put it that way. But that was my kind of schooling. I did some classical guitar lessons for a while outside of school, which I really enjoyed. All my sisters play piano. I was a little bit older when the piano lessons came in, and I sort of regret not having the patience to stick with it. I basically just jettisoned the piano playing and just went partying instead. Obviously it would be lovely to play the piano, but I didn't ever really think at a young age that I'd be involved in music professionally."

Clare says after graduation she decided to take a year off before going to university, though that year stretched into a longer amount of time. "I was going to study marine biology, but I ended up at my university town, Plymouth, and ended up joining a band and playing electric guitar whilst working in bars and picking up work and stuff, and I ended up getting another year off—you know, the universities were

---

[568] Kenny, Clare. All quotations, unless otherwise noted, from interview with the author, 5 May 2021.

really very flexible in those days, and they actually quite liked you to have a bit of life before you sort of set your nose to the grindstone and got on with further study. Needless to say, I call it running away to the circus. I never went back. And I ended up in London and I had the good fortune to work at the Hope and Anchor which is quite a seminal venue in the early '80s. I ended up in London in '79 and that's where I met Amazulu."

She explains the chance encounter that led her to become part of the band: "What happened was, they had formed in a sort of a fledgling band and they were rehearsing. But that night they had a massive bust up and two of their members, Rose, the original singer, and Sharon, who was the manager at the time and who had become the percussionist—it was all very flexible in those days—they actually had a big fight with the rest of the band. There were obviously severe musical difficulties going on within the band, so they ended up in a taxi and they decided to stop at the Hope and Anchor for a drink to talk it over. And I was off work that night, but my friend who I'd shared a flat with, she was on and she knew Rose, the original singer. And they were sort of chatting and they hadn't seen each other for years, and they mentioned that they decided to split up with the rest of the band and they were looking for a bass player and a guitarist, and they were looking for the rest of their new band. And she said, "Well, I live with a bass player," and I walked in, because I was just popping by on the way out—it was my night off, but I was popping in for a drink on my way somewhere else. And there they all were. And so I got introduced to them. And they set up an audition moment for me, and that was it."

Clare had learned to play bass guitar while living in Plymouth, though she first learned how to play guitar, "literally until my fingers bled." She had been in a punk band called the Filthy Beasts and when another band needed a bass player on short notice for a gig, Clare taught herself quickly to fill in for the show. "I thought, well, it's got to be easier than six strings. And I loved reggae and I love the sound of the bass. I've always loved reggae, so I gave it a go and did a few gigs with them on bass. And once I played the bass, that was my instrument from then on. In Wales growing up, there was a lot of reggae on the radio and particularly ska. I used to hitch with friends to London to go to massive festivals—Steel Pulse, Misty In Roots. I listened to people like Susan Cadogan and Janet Cay, Althea and Donna, and obviously Bob Marley was transitioning over into the rest of the world," she says.

With Clare on bass, a guitar player was still needed. So members turned to the musicians' union book to find Margo Sagov who had established herself as both a creative musician, and a professional one. She had an unusual upbringing compared to most of the women in this era, as she explains. "I grew up in Cape Town, South Africa. I came to the UK to study when I was 20 years old. For obvious reasons, I wanted to leave. South Africa was in the deep, dark days of Apartheid and I always knew that I wasn't going to stay there. My brother was a jazz musician and we were very unusual for a white South African suburban family in that he played jazz and he had a lot of black musicians come to the house and play. He had jam sessions from when I was like four years old. He was quite a bit older than me, so I grew up with a lot of South African jazz as well as the standard things that teenagers growing up in the Sixties would have been exposed to. I mean, people that you might not even have heard of—Abdullah Ibrahim, who was in those days called Dollar Brand, was a very good family friend and he used to come and practice at our house all the time, because he didn't have a piano. So I was exposed to some incredible music."[569]

"At the same time, I was following my own musical path with friends at school and I played in groups from when I was 13. I learned the guitar when I was about 10, and so it was really very unusual for white South Africans to have connections and be friends with black people. I can remember being taken to—it was really paranoid kind of times, and I remember going with my brother and sister one day to a concert in a black township. We all had to hide down in the well of the seats to get into the place, and I must have been about eight or nine, and it was in one of those hostels where men were segregated from women and were working in industries and so on. But it was an all-male audience. My brother was playing with this black band. At one point, a fight erupted in the place and it was very scary. They were throwing chairs around and getting really drunk and crazy because there was a lot of frustration. We were all huddled. The musicians then huddled around us and protected us because we were the only white people there and might have been a target. I remember hiding behind the piano and the double bass. It was crazy. So basically, it was a Nazi country and I lived through what I consider a Nazi era. I had a little bit of a career going as a musician, where the band that I was in got on the radio and I had gigs. I was 15 years old. We called ourselves the Little Folk. We were like a folk band, like the Mamas and the Papas, with those kinds of harmonies, and anything we fancied—Bob Dylan songs, to Muddy Waters, pop songs from the time. I was just sucking it all up. But my parents were quite middle class and they felt I need to go to university and do something," Margo says.

She says that her parents wanted her to continue her education because they thought she was going astray, leading the life of a musician. "I got kind of fed up with being in education continually, so I dropped out for about a year and moved to Johannesburg where my boyfriend came from and I worked as a musician. My parents started to worry about me, that I was drifting, living in the hippie commune. My father had a friend in the secret police, and he told me they were watching my house. It was really like that. He [father] said, if you kind of get it together, and you apply to universities overseas, we'll help you and we'll pay for your education. So, I did and took it seriously. And in 1973 I came over to Britain. I knew I was never going back. I got a place at a very good architecture school, which is what I was studying in South Africa. But I was always playing music on the side and studying. My architecture tutors used to think I was a bit of a dilettante, and my musician friends also never knew if they could rely on me because I couldn't really go on the road with them and do that stuff. It was an internal dichotomy for me, my whole life."

---

[569] Sagov, Margo. All quotations, unless otherwise noted, from interview with the author, 21 Feb. 2021.

After studying and gaining her degree, Margo began working as an architect. But during the Winter of Discontent and the Thatcher era, Margo found herself out of work. "Architecture as a profession is very subject to fluctuations in the economy," she explains. She took up work at a theatre company where she had been doing side work as musical director. She also trained as a sound engineer and started working in a recording studio. "And so, for 11 years, I didn't do any architecture at all after that. I was totally in music," she says. It was here, at the recording studio in London, that Margo developed her love for reggae. "I became studio manager for an eight-track studio. There were a lot of reggae artists. They were bringing over two-inch tapes from Jamaica and this was one of the few places in London where they had a two-inch eight-track machine. And because I liked reggae, and other people in the studio were more rock orientated, I got given those sessions to be the engineer of. It was Fashion Records who put out a lot of quite obscure authentic stuff, but I don't remember the names, but they were the real deal—people coming from Jamaica with tracks and trying to make some mixes. Then during that time, I was also playing in various bands and trying to write my own stuff and using the opportunity of having the studio in downtime. That's when I got phoned up by a person called Sharon who was the manager, quote unquote, of Amazulu. She asked me to come audition." Needless to say, that audition went well and Margo Sagov was in the band. "I knew an A chord from a G chord and that kind of thing, and I knew how to do the reggae chop, so they seemed satisfied and within about an hour of my playing with them for a bit, a journalist turned up from a magazine and started to do an interview and we all went outside and had to pose for a photo and I said, 'Well does that mean I'm in the band?' That's how I started," Margo says.

The chance meeting at the Hope and Anchor with Clare, Rose, and Sharon resulted in a gig for the newly formed Amazulu. They gained invaluable exposure to audiences, press, and the music industry. "That was our first gig," says Margo. "There was huge excitement and we were all dressed up. The gig was a stunning success and record company people were there. We got written up in *Melody Maker* or *NME* or something and that coverage was amazing for us. And it just seemed we were riding a wave, because 2 Tone and all of that had already happened at that point, or was happening. We were part of that culture. And the philosophy of the band was, as I understood it, was trying to play roots reggae, but with an English accent. So I'd play the guitar parts in that twangy guitar from like Duane Eddy or the Shadows or something like that, on top of what we were doing. We didn't have a keyboard player at that point so it was kind of thin, but the drums and bass and guitar and voices carried it. Lesley, god love her, she was never much of a sax player, but she had a lot of spirit, and she did deeply understand the vibe of the music, so I respected that. She and Rose were in that culture, much more than I was. I appreciated it musically, but I wasn't like, trying to be Rasta or anything like that. I liked the beat."

The sound of "live dub," as Margo explains their live performance was popular with audiences, as was the appeal of an all-female band. They seemed to do a fair job of securing their own gigs and managing themselves, but they had plans to grow, and in order to do that they needed someone who knew the business. "Halfway through that year we got picked up by Chas Chandler," says Margo, "and he was a famous rock and roll manager. He managed Jimi Hendrix and others and had been the bass player of the Animals. He is a famous guy in his own right. Actually he was very good, very professional. And he encouraged us. We were going places kind of with him. But towards the end of the year, he told us all these stories about how the Animals all hated each other. They had broken it up years ago but suddenly the original hit, 'the House of the Rising Sun' got in the charts in 1983. He said, 'I can't do this. I've got to go on the road with the Animals.' He stopped being our manager just before the end of the year. We were about to sign a record deal at that point with an independent label called Towerbell."

Amazulu then found themselves touring in a van, up and down the country. They gained plenty of interest from numerous record companies and were just about ready to sign with a label when they encountered a major lineup change. "There was a sort of crisis point that happened," said Margo. "I knew that something was up. We did a gig in Nottingham and then we went out to a rave afterwards. That was our custom after we did a gig—we'd find a blues dance, which is what illegal night reggae clubs were called, and get really wrecked and dance all night and then go home. Lesley got immensely drunk at this dance and was clearly upset about something. The others traveled back separately. So Lesley was with Sharon, Clare, and me traveling with the roadie, back with the equipment. It finally came out. Lesley said, 'They wanted to chuck you guys out of the band. I don't agree.' We were just on the point of signing this deal. So I said, 'Well, we should chuck them out,' and that's exactly what happened. Before they knew it, we secured all the equipment, which was our equipment anyway. We recruited Annie and another singer. We had a big gig coming up at the Rock Garden in London and we found a different drummer, who was Jah Bunny from the Cimarons, so I mean, you couldn't get more fucking roots than that. We had two gorgeous black singers in front who could sing more in tune than Rose could, so we were like, showing them. That's Annie, and there was another singer called Dee C. Lee who I knew from session work that I'd done, who had a career in her own right and eventually married Paul Weller. As Dee C. Lee had her own career beginning, she couldn't commit, it was just a one off. But Annie agreed to join and that's the band that signed and Jah Bunny put Nardo in touch with us as the new drummer—Nardo, whose surname is also Bailey, but no relation to Sharon. And at some point, Sharon decided it was more fun being in the band than being a manager just prior to this, so she had been teaching herself percussion. So the lineup then was Nardo on drums, Sharon on percussion, Lesley on saxophone, Clare on bass, me on guitar, and Annie as the lead singer."

Clare Kenny says of the split, "Well Rose and Debbie wanted to go in a much more kind of 12 Tribes, totally Rasta direction. The rest of us kind of wanted to keep it a bit more sort of neutral. There were definitely sort of political interests, but we didn't want to go down more of a religious sort of area. The first was called Amazulu Mach One," she says, laughing. "They never released anything, so Amazulu, who actually went on to release records was Amazulu Mach Two, which is just how we called it." So the original lineup had not made any recordings, though they did perform the song "Cairo" (whose instrumental melody sounds suspiciously like the one in the Specials' "Ghost Town") for a television show called the David Essex Showcase. Rose Miner, or "Rosie Posey," as she calls herself, sings lead vocals and Debbie Dread performs on drums. "Yeah, a lot of people came to see us because they have seen that programme, but we'd rather forget all about it," said Sharon Bailey. "We weren't ready to do it when it happened. We had no experience of doing TV shows so we just did as we were told and it didn't come off very well," she says.[570]

But after the band went through that first lineup change, to become Amazulu Mach Two, as Clare puts it, Annie Ruddock and Nardo changed the dynamic of the group, for both good and bad. Anne-Marie Teresa Antoinette Ruddock was born on June 22, 1963. "She had a Jamaican mother and American G.I. father, both of whom abandoned her and left her and her siblings to be brought up by their grandmother in London, and they [parents] went to America," says Margo. "She didn't have a connection to them. And both her brother and sister died—her brother of an overdose and her sister was murdered. The grandmother was a really old fashioned Jamaican granny who was like an obeah woman. She was into witchcraft, cultish sort of stuff, so it was a very strange environment to grow up in. And she was very young when she joined us and she'd been an item with a guy who was a well known reggae DJ called Papa Weasel. He also passed away. His real name was Rudy [Roodal Douglas] and he ran a club on All Saints Road in Notting Hill where we used to go to the blues dance. And he was a great DJ and they were both very stylish, very good looking people. And one day, early on in the time when she came on the road with us, she came down to the car and he'd beaten her up because he found her doing smack. And he was furious. But still. So then she got together with Sharon, not long after that, maybe on the same tour. So it was all twisted up. Sharon, on the other hand, came from a very middle class family from Belize. I think her father was an engineer and he traveled all over the world and she'd been sent to private school and had a whole different upbringing. She wasn't street like Annie was. Annie had been friends with lots of celebrities also, because she was this beautiful girl, had a lot of charisma. She was good friends with Boy George, had been in some of the Culture Club videos, and she was part of a scene—West London, Notting Hill kind of scene. And so she brought that to the party in a way. I give her credit for being a great performer and she'd never been in a band before. She'd never thought about it. It was the first time and she really rose to the occasion."

Their first single on the independent Towerbell label was "Cairo" which they promoted on a 28-date tour. Though the song didn't chart well, only up to #72, it did gain the attention of John Peel.[571] "John Peel helped us a lot," said Sharon Bailey.

[570] Joyce, Stephen. "Amazulu." eccentricsleevenotes.com/esn-5-1983. Accessed 15 Oct. 2022.
[571] Sullivan, Caroline. "Amazulu: The Exciters." *Melody Maker*. 24 Aug. 1985.

"We've done two sessions for his programme and he really likes us."[572] The B side, "Greenham Time," celebrated the women of Greenham Common who protested nuclear weapons at the Royal Airforce base. The events began in September 1981 and lasted until the year 2000, becoming one of the longest and most famous models of feminist and peace protest. Clare recalls their musical decisions and creative process: "To start with we did some really obscure covers, one of which was a song called 'Cairo' which ended up being our first single," said Clare. "And you know, it was a very obscure record that virtually nobody had heard of. And I think Rose and Sharon came up with that one. And because there was so much going on politically, we did a song called 'Greenham Common,' which was politically important at the time. We did write together, but it was quite haphazard. We didn't really know what we were doing, so we would just be in some basement rehearsal room or we'd pick up a rhythm and just start adding some color to it. And the vocalist would start playing around with melody and then Margo and I were singing backing vocals and so we were sort of quite organic. There wasn't really much organization."

The next single, "Smilee Stylee" was also released on the Towerbell label, and the band started to get exposure, which meant many outsiders came jumping to ride their coattails. Lesley says, "We had several people try to manage us, but we wouldn't do what we were told. We *couldn't* do what we were told. I mean, we had Lulu—she sang in that movie, *To Sir With Love* with Sidney Poitier, she was a big star and a great singer, so we had her brother try to manage us. I mean, they all came out of the woodwork. One guy wanted us to be called Pussy Galore. I might have gone for that," she laughs, "but not in his way, do you know what I mean? So we really wanted to be with Island, of course, who doesn't? Chris Blackwell came to see us and we did all these gigs and invited people and he said we weren't developed enough yet for Island, but a few years later we managed to get in there. But what really did it for us was we got this great tour of the universities in England. They have university balls, and we had Prince Andrew on stage—we should have beat him up when we had the chance!"

Amazulu continued to perform gigs in the UK as well as other countries. Audiences loved them. "There was lots of dancing and lots of cavorting on stage, and improvisations where we'd strip it down and it would just be bass and drums and our sound engineer really going mad with the echoes and loops and style. That never got captured on record. We played in Amsterdam lots of times, we went to Switzerland, and there were lots of really good gigs," says Margo. One of these tours, however, proved disastrous for the band. In fact, it made newspaper headlines. "Reggae group to be charged,"[573] "Punch-up tour is off,"[574] and "Amazulu Wars,"[575] read the ink. "Four girls and a man from the British reggae group Amazulu are to appear in court in Finland on charges arising out of a fight with Finnish sailors," read one article. "They were arrested last week after a brawl aboard the ferry from Stockholm, Sweden

[572] Joyce, Stephen. "Amazulu." eccentricsleevenotes.com/esn-5-1983. Accessed 15 Oct. 2022.
[573] *Belfast Telegraph*, 2 Jun. 1983.
[574] *Daily Mirror*, 27 May 1983.
[575] *NME*, 10 Dec. 1983

to Naan Taghli in Finland. The group were on a Scandinavian tour which has now been abandoned. All five are in prison at Turku, Finland."[576]

Margo Sagov, who was not among those arrested, tells the story. "It was 1983 and it was in the early days. We played in Stockholm and we went up to a festival on the coast from Stockholm. Bizarrely it was an anti-drink and drug festival and all the English bands were furious about it because they couldn't get the drink. And then we were meant to go on a ferry to do a gig in Helsinki, which was a big deal. It was going to be a radio broadcast and so we got on the ferry and it was our roadie's birthday. And we bought all this duty-free vodka, tequila, and other stuff and did a bunch of slammers and got really drunk. I was having a wild affair with the sound engineer at the time, so at a certain point during the evening, we disappeared and left them to it. And then after a while, we went back to the bar where we'd been, and it was absolute pandemonium. The whole place was trashed. There was broken glass everywhere. The band members were being dragged around the floor by their dreadlocks. Clearly things got really out of control and there were also hundreds of snarling Alsatian dogs, German Shepherds, which god knows where they came from. They were all being arrested, and I was like, what? So I kind of realized quite quickly that it had gone beyond anything I could kind of intervene in. And so I managed to slither past a snarling dog and get down the stairs and get back to the cabin. My boyfriend then reappeared about half an hour later, having been kicked down a flight of stairs and broken a couple of ribs, and he said they'd all been put down in the brig at the bottom of the boat. And the roadie had passed out, he'd gone to bed and hadn't been in the fight, and Drac, the sound engineer, and me were left thinking, what shall we do? So we made a plan."

Margo continues, "We said I'd go across as a foot passenger, Drac would present himself to the authorities and say he was the representative and try and negotiate and explain that we had this gig to do and that we really were a band. The roadie would try and drive the equipment through in the van that was in the hold of the ship. Anyway, I got through, but I was the only one who did. The other two got arrested as soon as they presented themselves. So I sat there on the dock of the bay, in this place I'd never heard of with a few pounds in my pocket, thinking, what do I do now? So I managed to make a couple of phone calls. I phoned the record company and I phoned the honorary British consul in the town, I managed to get hold of his number. That was good that I'd done that because a few minutes later, I went back to sit down in the dark, wondering where I should go or what I should do, when a door opened at one end and I saw the others being led out in handcuffs into a van. And they clocked me and I went, 'Shhhh! Don't let on!' But the guard saw and he came to me and he said, 'Are you also in the orchestra?' And I had to say yes, and so I was nicked as well."

"So then I found out what happened," she says. "We were all taken to be strip searched and internally examined. Yeah. And put in cells. And I was in a cell

---

576 *Belfast Telegraph*, 2 Jun. 1983.

with Lesley, so she told me what happened, which was that they'd been in this bar drinking from their own bottles. And at some point, the steward of the bar came and remonstrated with them and said, 'You can't drink from your own bottle. You have to drink drinks from the bar,' which is fair enough. And the Norwegian [tour manager] refused and carried on drinking from his bottle of whiskey and so the steward came and grabbed it very unceremoniously off him, and Clare, who is the sweetest nicest person, went to the back of the bar and said, 'Look, he's sorry, he won't do it again, give him back his bottle, we're sorry.' They were crazy, these Swedish and Finnish staff on the boat, who were also drunk themselves, and they started slapping her around. At which point, Lesley came in and saw this happening and went berserk. And apparently she broke a bottle and did some damage to some of them. Then it kicked off and it was the whole crew of the boat against us. And it so happened that the Finnish and Swedish dog handlers association was on board, hence the 300 snarling German Shepherds. That was the point at which I reemerged with my amour to see utter pandemonium and the whole place trashed and everyone about to be arrested and bitten by dogs and so on."

"Because I'd made the phone calls just before I got nicked," Margo continues, "somebody from the record company then turned up at the prison. So then there was real embarrassment because we were really who we said we were, did really have this contract to do this broadcast, and there were more powerful people than them in their provincial Finnish port that could put some leverage on the situation. So me and the roadie and the sound engineer got released because they had nothing on us. We weren't in the fight. But the others were held because they were trying to decide what to charge them with and which district to even charge them in. And the boys, who was Nardo and the Norwegian, we didn't know where they were—they were kept somewhere else, in some cell by the port. And it took four days before I was able to locate them. I had to get money wired over from my dad to give them and try to find local lawyers to represent them. It was a nightmare, actually. Eventually the honorary consul told us, 'You've got to get out of town,' because we were causing too much trouble, and stories were coming out in the press. And there was interest in Britain in the stories. It was the Iron Curtain kind of years and so they had these pictures of the guards with the van, showing the contraband. It was just our equipment. But we had to leave, and we had to leave them in prison. It was pretty bad that we had to go back to Britain and leave them, not knowing what was going to happen. So when I got back to Britain, I had to do various interviews. I was on John Peel and I was on the news at six and all that, trying to raise the profile of the thing. In the end, they were held for 12 days. It didn't go down well with the record company in the same way as if it had been a male band. But we weren't pliant simpering females. I can't put it any other way."

Clare Kenny, one of the members imprisoned for those 12 days states, "Finland was the most depressing time of my life. We were in these concrete cells with no food or blankets. I remember lying with one shoe under my back and another one beneath my head so the warmth wouldn't drain out of my body. It was like a fuckin' fridge, y'know. You can watch something like *Midnight Express* and be deeply affected, but that really taught me a lot about irresponsible men with the power to lock you up and throw away the key. The ridiculous thing about it was that we were accused and tried for committing GBH [Grievous Bodily Harm] on 15 Swedish sailors. Five girls and a bloke against them with tear gas and Alsatians! What actually happened was that they were picking on us because of the way we looked, and because some of us are black and the whole thing got just totally out of order. Before the trial they even tried to make us pay for ripped uniforms and loss of earnings! And then the nightmare began all over again as soon as we got back. First, I was arrested at Heathrow by Scotland Yard on some trumped up charge just so they could check out these thugs. And then we heard that we'd got a record out, which just about finished us off."[577] While the members of Amazulu were managing their legal situation, the record company, explains Sharon Bailey, decided to capitalize on the material they had without waiting for the dust to settle. "Towerbell made the record almost without us," Sharon said. "It was like you used to hear all these stories about bands not playing on their records, y'know, like The Bay City Rollers or something. 'Smilee Stylee' was just some backing tracks we'd been playing around with."[578]

Just after release, though, Amazulu gained a platform to reclaim their status as star performers. On June 30, 1983, they joined David Bowie just before he continued his tour to North America, Australia, and Asia. "We played support for his gig at the Hammersmith Odeon, which was one of his last gigs on the 'Serious Moonlight' tour," says Margo. "And apparently he specifically requested us to be on the gig. It was a charity sort of thing that had been tacked on because mostly he was playing huge stadia but this was Hammersmith Odeon, which is more of a theater, maybe about 2000 people, 3000 people capacity. He was really great. Really friendly. He made sure we got a proper soundcheck, there was all kinds of nice food laid up for us backstage, and he invited us on stage with him for the last couple of numbers of his show. It's really a pretty memorable experience. That was a nice memory."

But the band seriously need to find a proper manager who could help to commandeer them to more substantial recording opportunities and a better record label was what Amazulu needed, though that was difficult. Margo says they tried out a few managers over the years which never produced the desired results. "I think they didn't quite know what to do with us. They didn't know how to manage us properly. It may have been, in hindsight, better to have stayed with the smaller label and had more control over the music because they did, to their credit, give us a lot of control and allowed us to record our own songs more and work with producers in that way. Subsequent to that, we now were established as a name. We started to do TV shows and promos for the record and touring abroad. During the course of the next year, we then found ourselves being managed by a guy called Derrick Unwin who presented himself to us as somebody who'd had a lot of experience in the business. I later found

[577] Rai, Amrik. "Amazulu Wars." *NME*, 10 Dec. 1983.
[578] Ibid.

out that he'd been like a roadie for the Police. Formerly he'd been a paratrooper in the British Army in Northern Ireland. When he'd come off the road from the Police, he'd been in a terrible car accident and it left him with a lot of injuries so he couldn't be a roadie anymore. But he told us he had been a tour manager and that wasn't true. And he was a coke addict and on a lot of pain-killing drugs for his injuries. And he sweet talked Island Records into signing us. Island Records was, at that point, in a state of flux, because Chris Blackwell had stepped back from the music side and Dave Robinson of Stiff Records was director of both Island and Stiff Records. The deal that we had was with Island, but Dave Robinson was our point of contact. And Derrick had apparently promised Dave Robinson that he would give them our publishing, as well as the record deal. And we as a band had felt very strongly that we wanted to have our publishing somewhere else and not have all our eggs in one basket. At the same time, he got a deal with us with Desert Songs, and they had been taken over several times. Eventually it's ended up with EMI but at that point they were a small outfit. When it became known in the music press that this is what happened, it very much soured things with Island because they were furious that this sleight of hand had happened and we didn't know anything about this. But what it meant was that they didn't want to let us record our own music, or really nurture us as a band. So it was extremely disruptive, career wise. They gave us only one chance to record one of our own songs, and that was the one that Jerry Dammers produced, 'Moonlight Romance.'"

This song, in addition to being featured in a music video, was also performed during *the Young Ones*, the popular comedy sitcom on BBC2 in the early '80s which also aired on MTV in the mid-1980s in the United States. The program frequently featured a band that performed rather obtrusively in the plot and such bands included Dexys Midnight Runners, Motörhead, the Damned, and Madness. On the June 5, 1984 episode, Amazulu performed "Moonlight Romance," and the opportunity did not come through the record label or manager, as Lesley Beach explains. "A few years earlier we did a London pub tour and Jennifer Saunders and Dawn French opened for us, from *Absolutely Fabulous*, and then Jennifer married the guy in *the Young Ones* [Ade Edmondson, Vyvyan]. And that's how we got on *the Young Ones*." Still, the song failed to chart. Margo says, "It never became a bit hit because, well, they spent some money on it but they didn't really give it a proper push. It was featured on *the Young Ones* and I still get royalties from that, because it still gets repeated somewhere in the world a few times a year. They made a really terrible video of it that Jerry directed. God love him, he's not a video director. We asked for him. We thought he'd be suitable." There was even talk of Dammers producing an entire album for Amazulu, though that never came to fruition.[579] "He's very good on his own material," said Clare, "but we felt he wasn't quite right for us."[580]

[579] Sullivan, Caroline. "Amazulu: The Exciters." *Melody Maker*. 24 Aug. 1985.
[580] Ibid.

When the song didn't chart, the record label executives ramped up their control. "Because it wasn't a big hit, we were dragged into Dave Robinson's office thereafter. He said to us, 'I'm going to put you together with another producer and you're going to have to do what he says. And if you don't agree with it, we'll hold you to contract and you won't be able to do anything.' And actually, what we should have done is gone, 'Fuck you,' and just carried on touring and got out of the contract. Because we ended up then being on a train we couldn't get off. The producer that he put us together with was a guy called Chris Neil who had no fealty to the band, or fealty to the style of music that we were trying to do. And he was a guy who produced a lot of hits. He was very professional. I don't criticize him and his musical ear. I learned some things from his techniques, how he worked in the studio, but he had his own team of people. And we were a real band who played real gigs, but we didn't get to play on our records. It was all programmed. By this time, it was 1984, he had people who programmed drums, people who played all the keyboard parts, there wasn't guitar on most of the records, and it fed a lot of division and bad vibes within the band. Claire and I and Annie, we all sang on the records and he had this technique of making a very dense pop sound with lots and lots of layered harmonies so you had to kind of repeat your harmonies like 20 times. And they had spent a lot of money on him, and they spent a lot of money on videos and the art director of Island Records got involved, Bruno, and one video I think cost 60,000 pounds, which absolutely appalled us. It was a pile of shit, actually, but then we became identified with this very poppy sound that had actually nothing to do with what we really sounded like live or played live, and for my part, I wasn't interested in," says Margo.

But still, the band played on. And they finally began to experience some success on the music charts with their next single, "Excitable." It was a produced by Chris Neil who had previously worked with Sheena Easton, and though he manufactured the sound of Amazulu, as Margo explained, it seemed to resonate with mainstream listeners. "The song: 'Excitable.' A hit," proclaimed *Melody Maker* in August of 1985.[581] "We needed a bit of commercial success to be able to carry on. … in the end, you have to get into the charts. It costs a lot of money to release a single. What gets released, in the end, is the one most acceptable to everybody, with the catchiest chorus," said Clare.[582]

Amazulu continued to tour, performing for a two-week residency in Tel Aviv, and a festival in the far north of Israel. They played the Glastonbury Festival on the mainstage twice, both in 1984 and 1986. And notably they performed with the legendary Jamaican trumpeter, Edward "Tan Tan" Thornton, an alumnus of Alpha Boys School. All of the women of Amazulu speak of Tan Tan with warmth and fondness and agree it was a highlight of their experience. Margo says, "Tan Tan was, at that time, playing mostly with Aswad. I think we met when we played a festival at Notting Hill Carnival with Aswad and it actually became a live album of theirs, and

[581] Ibid.
[582] Ibid.

we were support before their set. They still had a concert stage in a part of the festival called Meanwhile Gardens, and it was a great gig. And somehow we conveyed to him that if we were touring, and he wasn't busy, we'd love him to come and play with us. He was happy to do so. And somehow it happened, then, it was quite a regular thing, during probably late 1984 through '85, whenever he could fit us in and amongst his other commitments. He and I got on really well. He is a real old school Jamaican guy. He always talked about how he loved the nuns at Alpha and how they kind of saved his life. And he was a practicing Catholic who'd go to mass on Sunday, whenever he could, in between all these other shenanigans. He was married and had a family and had a very kind of normal suburban life with his family. We'd pick him up at his house and then he'd come on the road with us and be all naughty with us, because we were naughty, and go home to his kind of regular life."

Margo continues, "One of my favorite memories of him is that he's a great cook. So we would put in orders for Ital food that he'd make, typically chicken and pimento and things like that. He had recipes and he'd do the chicken and rice thing. And we'd order them in advance and he'd supply them in plastic containers, and we'd eat it before we got out of London. Delicious food. He's a very funny guy, a lot older than us. He was really into jazz. That was his primary thing. His great hero was Clifford Brown. When he was warming up or playing in soundchecks, he'd play Clifford Brown riffs. He had a very wide musical appreciation. And I think he mentored Lesley a lot, so he'd teach her how to adjust the tuning of the mouthpiece and all of that, and phrasing and everything, because he totally knew what was what. So it was an absolute joy to play with him. And I think he really liked being on the road with us because we were crazy. We got on really well. He used to call everyone in the band princess. Except me. I was duchess. Which in his estimation, was kind of a higher comment!"

Lesley Beach also had a special bond with Tan Tan. "It was the greatest honor of my life, to have played with Tan Tan. We did *Top of the Pops* with him a few times ["Excitable," 1985] and he was so good to me. He used to cook for us—fish, rice and peas—and we'd eat it all before we got to the freeway. You know what Tan Tan has in his trumpet case? He has a picture of the Pope, a picture of President Kennedy, and a picture of Don Drummond. Biggest honor of my life," says Lesley.

As a note, Amazulu was also joined by another musician who filled in for Lesley at times while she was unable to play. Clare Hirst, who had performed saxophone with the Bodysnatchers and Belle Stars, joined the band just after leaving the latter. "I was covering in Amazulu for their sax player because she was quite ill at one point. So I did that for a bit," she says.[583] She went on to perform with the Communards, David Bowie, Hazel O'Connor, salsa bands, and others.

Even though Amazulu had impressive success, the band had issues that were too crucial for them to continue without intervention. A number of the band members had developed serious drug addictions. "There was a lot of drugs around at

---

[583] Hirst, Clare. All quotations, unless otherwise noted, from interview with the author, 8 Feb. 2021.

that time," Clare Kenny says. "I mean, obviously we'd all be smoking like chimneys, but in those days in London, there was a lot of heroin around, and that was a real weird and interesting, inverted commas, time because there was a time when in the early '80s where all of a sudden, it wasn't incredibly shameful to be doing that drug. It had sort of a little renaissance, somehow. It became very available and there was a lot of that going on. And that was what basically killed the band, because of the lack of trust and paranoia and all that. So I just wanted to get away because it was very very heavy at the end—trying to stop it from spinning away but it spinning away anyway. You know, the record company offered the three people who were the most affected by addiction a deal on their own, because they were more easy to control, I suppose, and involved the singer obviously. So it was a bit of betrayal there."

For Margo, the end of the band was inevitable. The managers who took Amazulu in a direction so far astray from their creative ideals were certainly to blame, and these managers exploited the members of the band who they knew they could control. "It was such a nightmare. We'd have to drive around London, end up waiting outside these crummy places while they went to score and we just didn't want to do that. I didn't want to be five hours late for the gig." As a result, Margo left the band. "We never got to do an album at all. The album that came out after I left was just a compilation of singles. It wasn't a proper album," Margo says. This, however, was the fault of label executives, she says. "The perception was that we weren't serious. And if any of them had bothered to come and see our gigs—I remember Chris Neil, quite late on after we'd done a few records with him, came to see one of our gigs and he was completely gob smacked. He had no idea. And he told me that. So they just had this really sexist idea. Women were not nurtured as serious musicians in the same way. A male band might have been allowed to put out two albums that might have failed before they were dropped. We never got to do an album at all. I got quite upset, actually, because I didn't feel like we were being given the space to really develop our own music and because we were so distracted with having to promote these records, it became a thing where they weren't real gigs. They were just personal appearances and mime to your record in a record store or in a club. It was just at the point where the business was really changing—from a business that was run by music enthusiasts to being run by suits."

These suits, Amazulu's managers the Captain (Nick Stewart), Guy Holmes, and Falcon Stewart, all tried to control the direction of the band, according to Margo, the latter of which split the already fragile union. "He set up a very divisive scenario in the band where he took Annie aside and said that he only really wanted her and wanted it to be a black act and suggested to her that she should have Sharon and Nardo, the other two black members of the band, as kind of the look of the band—dreadlocks. And because they were all in a little bit of a clique, taking hard drugs together—she, Lesley, and Sharon became the face of Amazulu then going forward. And so the band ended up splitting halfway through 1986 where they carried on with the name. We had a fight about it, there were lawyers involved. There was a lot of bad blood which still endures. So I played out the last few months of the gigs that we had until the middle of that year and we hammered out a kind of rather unjust sort of payment for the ones that were leaving, and that was Nardo, Clare, and me. And they had Simon Napier Bell managing them and they made a couple of records with Dennis Bovell producing, but they weren't original songs, they were just covers, and it eventually fizzled out because they were too strung out."

The breakup was hard for everyone, especially those who have come clean and come to terms with the impact on their friends. "I don't want to talk about it," Lesley says of this painful time. "I will say, we got influenced by the record company. We went down to just three of us, which, you know, I wish we hadn't done. Anyway, we did and so then, yeah, it wasn't the same anymore. I went to live in Ibiza on a hill. I had been going there on vacation and I had a boyfriend there. He's actually just died. He was a very well-known DJ, Jose Padilla. So I just had it with London and I had it with everything, so I went to Ibiza and got myself together. It was lovely. I was spending a lot of time there anyway with Jose. We did a gig in Ibiza, a festival, and I stayed there until I came to Arizona in 1992." Lesley has continued to perform music including a West African drum ensemble, Dambe, and two samba bands, Catucaxe and Solaxe.

For Clare Kenny, she continued her career as a musician and performed bass with many different musicians. "I got involved in a country band called Hang Wangford and I met one of my closest friends in that band, Kathy [O'Donoghue], who was a singer and also a mean tambourine player. I was in that band for about a year and a half. It was a very theatrical band, and it was country, and it was very funny. We used to tour in Ireland and in the UK. And then I got an opportunity that I couldn't turn down. So I went and joined Aztec Camera, which was a really big step up for me in terms of production. Scarily big gigs. There were a couple of world tours to Australia and Japan and America for the first time. And although all the guys were great, and I was sort of one of the guys in a way, after a few months on the road in a tour bus, god, I don't even know how to describe it. It's just sort of not being with your own kind," she says, laughing. Clare spent two years touring with Aztec Camera. She also recorded an album with them, in addition to a number of singles.

Clare then worked with Shakespeares Sister and says, "We had so much fun, but that was another crash and burn because, you know, Marcy [Marcella Detroit] and Siobhan [Fahey, of Bananarama] started to spiral out of love just when we were about to take over the world, and 'Stay' was at number two in the American charts or something. And it had been number one in the UK for two months. We were on *Top of the Pops* every week. It was absolutely phenomenal. But of course, Marcy was singing it and that kind of skewed what Shakespeares Sister was really about, which was much more punky. I mean, that was our sort of one ballad, and so it sort of slightly set people's teeth on edge in the upper echelons of the band. There were two lead singers in Shakespeares Sister and then there were musical differences. In the end, it couldn't really carry on. It was a bit unfortunate. But we did do a reunion tour in 2019 which was fabulous. They made up and I was playing bass and we did a lovely reunion tour of about a month in the UK just before Covid."

"And then there was Sinead [O'Connor]. I had known John Reynolds who was the producer of Sinead for many years, and he and Sinead had been married and had a son. And he got me to play on one song. He's a great reggae fan as well. He really liked my approach which was totally dubby. We've played together since then, like a bass and drum section. I did quite a bit of recording with Sinead and quite a lot of touring over the years. We were on tour with Sinead with the Lilith Fair tour. And that's where I met the Indigo Girls and I toured with them for years. We've just done a record together called 'Live Long.'"

Clare says that she never decided to have children and recognizes the challenges that many of her friends have had to make. "I didn't really have a kind of longing that you hear women talk about, to have children and be a mother. I was just having too much fun. I mean, maybe if I'd been with the right guy or person or whatever, who knows, that might have changed my mind. A lot of women managed to do both. Sinead has tried to bring the youngest of her kids on tour because of the guilt. Women who have had children, they try and bring one or two of them, or the youngest ones, and it's hell for both parties. It's a very adult world. You have to do a show, and then be mom again. Mom all day and then do a show where you kind of leave everything on the stage. With Shakespeares Sister, their first record was called *Hormonally Yours* because they had literally given birth within a couple of months of each other. And we were on tour, and Marcy was still expressing milk in the dressing room. She didn't complain, you know, but she must have been so uncomfortable. They were both pining and feeling desperately attached and yet wanting to—it's like split personalities—wanting to be there on stage because that was their life, but also having left the baby with the dad. A very difficult balancing act. The women I've worked with leave everything on the stage. I'm sure men do too, but it's an absolute privilege to work with them."

After Debbie Dread left Amazulu early on because she says she "didn't want to do poppy reggae," she toured as a stage manager for Derek Nimmo's dinner theatre to Greece, Bermuda, Singapore, Kuala Lumpur, Cairo, Jordan, Dubai, and Muscat. "I then got pregnant from a Jamaican musician living in the States who was in London doing some studio work. I joined Sister Netifa for a while then went to India when my son was seven. On return I started my own band for a couple of years. Although we all got on amazingly well, the music never really gelled. I worked in Portobello market for 12 years selling block printed throw covers and when my son was old enough, I started raving again, to Abashanti who I knew, Channel One, Jah Youth, etc. I then became a dogwalker 20 years ago, taking them out to the woods and forests outside London, five days a week. I am now working on my own reggae tracks which I shall be releasing soon. I'm not in a relationship, as that's too stressful. Although I love Studio One/Lovers. I prefer the heavy dub and roots. I was heavily influenced by Rastafari but really I'm more of a rebel, so militant style. Over the years the reggae scene has changed inasmuch as whereas I was only one of a few white faces inna the blues and clubs, now it's mostly white people. Reggae has certainly gone global and it's great to witness, but still mainly male dominated, especially with sound systems and producing tracks."

Annie Ruddock and Sharon Bailey continued to perform with Lesley Beach in Amazulu for a short time as a group of three. They also had minor roles in the Alex Cox movie *Straight to Hell* with a star-studded cast including Dennis Hopper, Joe Strummer, Grace Jones, Elvis Costello, and Edward Tudor-Pole. But at the same time as this success, their drug problem finally ended their run. "The heroin superstore," stated the headline in the *Pinner Observer* on July 30, 1987. "A gang of three who ran a lucrative drugs racket from a Harrow 'heroin superstore' were jailed for a total of 18 years yesterday," stated the article. "The network of death dealt in enough heroin to feed the habits of many local junkies and top pop stars … Harrow's Crime Squad traced [Ernest] Chuckwuka to the Kilburn home of Amazulu's Sharon Bailey … Chuckwuka had boasted that he was the main dealer in London and had supplied members of the group Amazulu."[584]

Annie Ruddock also encountered trouble during the summer of 1987. "Amazulu star slugs it out," read the headline.[585] "Wild singer Ann [sic] Marie Ruddock was recovering last night after police were called to break up a violent brawl between her and another girl. A chair was hurled through a window during the punch-up and both girls were left bloody and bruised. … 'From all the screaming we could hear the fight seemed to be about the Amazulu breaking up.' … her manager Falcon Stewart said: 'We do not wish to comment on this. The future of the band is unresolved.'" One year later, Annie again was in legal trouble. "Pop star Annie Ruddock yesterday wanted her fans not to dabble in heroin. 'It's a one-way road to death,' the former Amazulu singer said after appearing at West London court on a drugs charge. Ruddock (26), who recently managed to kick a £600-a-week heroin habit, added: 'It's been a nightmare for me, absolute hell. But it's all behind me now. I have learned my lesson. I am now involved in the anti-drugs campaign and I say to anybody thinking about using drugs to forget it.' Despite five top-ten hits with Amazulu since 1985, she says she has less than £4000 in the bank. She went solo three months ago and in April recorded her first album, 'Spellbound,' with Kool and the Gang backing her."[586] Another article said she had battled heroin addiction for three years, "treatment in clinics had failed to cure her, but, said her solicitor, she 'had finally found the strength within herself' and she had 'beaten heroin.'"[587] Margo says that Annie did eventually get clean, but after spending time in prison. "I understand she inherited her grandmother's flat, so she's living in London, married or in a stable relationship with someone, has been to college or has got some qualifications for herself. And she's not in the music business."

[584] Taberer, Donna. "The heroin superstore." *Pinner Observer*, 30 Jul. 1987.
[585] "Amazulu star slugs it out." *Daily Mirror.* 27 May 1983.
[586] "Pop star warns of heroin nightmare." *Aberdeen Press and Journal*, 3 June 1988.
[587] "I've beaten heroin." *Daily Mirror*, 6 May 1988.

Original singer Rose Miner, now Rose Reichman, has been involved in dance and was a floral headdress designer selling her crafts at the Portobello market. She declined to be interviewed saying these were "vile, dark times."[588]

As for Margo Sagov, she continued to work as an architect, and she still performs music personally and publicly. She has remained in contact with Clare Kenny, Lesley Beach, and Nardo Bailey. In fact, she plays occasionally with Nardo in her band called the Rock Candy Girlz. But the other members of the band remain estranged. She explains, "What happened subsequent was that I got chased by the Inland Revenue for the tax unpaid of my former bandmates. It took about seven years of these letters coming from the Inland Revenue to me. The others just blanked them or their management didn't help and the lawyers that used to represent us didn't help. And that's why there's bad blood. I had my career fucked and I had to pay their tax. It was for a few years worth and it wasn't a small amount. I was dragged to these horrible offices in North London where spotty individuals interrogated me about my life and I got letters from the bankruptcy division, so I went to my own accountant, not the band's accountant, and I said, can you help me with this, because the band accountant was actually useless. He negotiated it down from about 30,000 pounds to 18,000 pounds. This was like 1991 and I was already back working as an architect. Had a totally different life. I owned a property—they could come after me because I'm an honest legitimate person now that operates in a normal business world. So I had to find that money and pay it and everything that I ever made financially just went up in smoke. Lesley, to her credit, because she'd been through lots of therapy and stuff, she paid her share of tax. Clare paid me a portion of the debt as well. But I've never had a penny from the others." She says that they also never paid her back for the fees her father fronted for the Finland fracas. "There's no likelihood that the band will ever get back together. I've certainly moved on with my life."

Today, Margo Sagov lives with her long-time partner who is a jazz musician. "I've never had children with him, but he has a son from a previous relationship and I am also involved to some degree. We've been together for quite a long time now so I'm not going anywhere!" Of her time with Amazulu she says, "I don't' regret the experience that I had. We had some brilliant gigs. I think it's a great shame that our records don't really represent us very well. I think we were very ahead of our time in terms of our style and the attitude that we had, of presenting ourselves as feisty women, out there, performing and singing. There was a lot of love and in the early years we used to just cackle in the van, going to and from gigs and having a lot of fun. There was a lot of humor in the band. It just got sour the last year and a half and it was largely drug induced. Drug induced and sexism in the business and not being clear sighted enough, and not having the right management to stand up to it. If we'd actually got free of those deals and had just gone ahead as independent and been able to carry on writing and producing our own music, I think we would have endured and would have had great success."

---

[588] Reichman, Rose. Via Facebook messenger, 11 Nov. 2022.

Amazulu and David Bowie at the Odeon in 1985 with Margo Sagov front center

Margo Sagov, photo by Keith Baugh (left) and Annie Ruddock on tour in Israel (right). Photos courtesy of Margo Sagov.

Amazulu featuring (L to R) Annie Ruddock, Margo Sagov, Nardo Bailey, Clare Kenny, Sharon Bailey, and Lesley Beach in front.

Maroon Town

Kay Charlton: trumpet
Rajan Datar: bass
Mike Firn: tenor saxophone
Deuan German: guitar
Glynis German: vocals

Jan Hewison: drums
Caroline McCookweir: alto saxophone
Sara McGuinness: keyboards

Ask any fan of ska in the 1980s to name a song that deals with being followed on the street, male violence, and rape, and chances are they will cite "The Boiler" by the Bodysnatchers, recorded by the Special AKA with Rhoda Dakar—rightly so. However, at the end of that decade, another song addressed the same subject and empowered women to speak out and good men to stand up. "Women Say No" was one of hundreds of songs by Maroon Town that spoke to the social and political ills of the world which plagued men, women, and even children. The band took its name to reflect respect for the Maroons in Jamaica—the enslaved who had escaped to freedom in the mountains, established their own communities, and fought enslavers and oppressors with ferocity. Maroon Town's first album, *High and Dry,* the one that featured the song "Women Say No," was dedicated to one woman—the national hero who led the Maroons in the 18th century. "To Nanny Maroon and the spirit of her people. Forward," stated the inscription. This consciousness informed the members of the band in their writing and performance from the late 1980s through to today.

For over three decades, Maroon Town has consistently toured and recorded, but as might be expected, their lineup has changed frequently. When the band first began as a small group of friends in London, the decision was made to focus on ska—not 2 Tone, but the ska that came before it—original ska from Jamaica. "It was Deuan German," says Maroon Town saxophonist Caroline McCookweir of the decision to play Jamaican ska, "mostly because his mother was Jamaican, and his sister Glynis who was a singer. And there were other people who came to the band who were from the Caribbean. A lot of people have been through the band, but it was Deuan and Rajan [Datar] together who wanted to bring the music of bluebeat, the early ska, not the 2 Tone so much, but it was the early ska stuff. That was their vision for the band, that the band would be multiracial, multigender, and also playing this old bluebeat ska, like Prince Buster type stuff."[589]

Caroline was one of three women who were in the first lineup of Maroon Town as part of that diverse vision. She had grown up in many different locations due to her father's work, which exposed her to a variety of cultures and further enhanced her knowledge of art and music and she had a desire to one day become a musician. "We were all over the place," says Caroline of her upbringing. "We were in England, Ireland, Wales, and then we went to Hong Kong. My dad was a pilot. He

---

[589] McCookweir, Caroline. All quotations, unless otherwise noted, from interview with the author, 6 Dec. 2022.

flew. He kept changing airlines, so we were all over the place. My father was tone deaf, but my mum used to sing me to sleep, which was really lovely. And I just, I don't know, I was just drawn towards music. I really wanted to do it, even though it was kind of going in the opposite direction of everything I was supposed to be doing. So I took up the clarinet at the age of 12. I was very academically gifted, so I felt like I was supposed to go to university and all that sort of business. And I had a huge, huge rebellion against that, really, and music seemed like some kind of way out—that kind of life. I mean, nobody was pushing me to do anything, but I could just see it going that way."

"Clarinet quite often leads on to saxophone," she continues. "Many sax players have started on clarinet. We call it a hard taskmaster. Because it's actually much harder than the saxophone. I had gone to music college for a year to do a bit of classical music, and then I tried to get into a further course and didn't get in and I kind of dropped out and loafed about for a bit. And then somebody heard me singing in the toilets of a pub. She came in and started talking to me and she had a band, and they wanted a sax player and a singer. So that's how I joined. That was my very first band, an African band. ChisZa! The drummer, she was actually trans, but she'd learned to drum in South Africa."

ChisZa! was billed as a "six piece dance band, four women, two men, guitars, saxophone, and voices, driven by lush, unusual percussion and drumming."[590] They formed in 1983 and featured Helen Rautenbach (sometimes mentioned as Helen Grier) on drums, Sandra Michael on percussion, Charlie White on bass, Paul Brewer on guitar, Janet Whisker on vocals, and Caroline McCookweir on saxophone and clarinet. They performed at locations around England including in London at the Notting Hill Carnival. Though they had no recordings, they did have a demo tape for a song called "Triggered By Body Heat," and a few live recordings of songs like "Whisper," "Screaming," and "Wake Up!" exist on Soundcloud. The songs feature a distinctive hi-life Afro-pop flavor with a heavy bass and bubbling guitar. Caroline's saxophone is lively and punctuates the eerie vocals which are akin to the Cocteau Twins. A promotional flier for the band described their sound by inquiring, "Afro-punk? Passion Pop? However you describe the band, ChisZa! means warmth. Exotic rythmns [sic] enrich good punchy tunes. ... Good time dance music with a biting edge. A curious sound indeed."

"And then Deuan, from Maroon Town, headhunted me from Chisza!" says Caroline. "He'd seen us live. We met, and then asked me if I'd like to join Maroon Town. He started it with his childhood mate, Rajan, and so it was people they knew basically. They met Jan, the drummer on a train." Jan Hewison performed drums for Maroon Town for a short time, and is the songwriter of "Women Say No." She was soon replaced by Tony St. Helen on drums who joined Caroline McCookweir on alto saxophone and vocals, Deuan German on guitar, Deuan's sister Glynis on vocals, Rajan Datar on bass, Mike Firn on tenor saxophone, Sara McGuinness on keyboards,

---

590 From a flier for a show at the Old White Horse on Brixton Road, early 1980s.

and Kay Charlton on trumpet for their debut album released in 1990, *High and Dry*. But before that album was recorded, the band gigged regularly with Jan Hewison, whose name today is Jan Hobbs, as part of their lineup.

Jan's parents were both fine artists and her father earned a living from selling his art commercially. When she was ten years old, her mother bought a piano and Jan began playing on her own, teaching herself to play and writing music. When she graduated from school, Jan and her boyfriend formed a duo—her boyfriend on guitar, and Jan on keyboards. "We quickly learned, you can't play the songs you like. You can't play Bob Dylan, Bruce Springsteen—you've got to play what the audience wants. So it's covers, anything in the charts, and standards. And guess who had to work all of that out on the keyboard? Me. So it's actually very good training musically," she says.[591]

The duo went to the United States to visit a friend for a few months and later returned for a longer period of time. While there, they both joined with other musicians to form a group called the Neasden Knights. They performed in clubs around California for about 18 months. During this time, she switched instruments which was unexpected, as she explains. "Two people I knew were supposed to be going to a week-long music camp in California. And one person didn't. He didn't want to go. So he more or less said, 'Will you go?' So, yeah, sure, I'll go! So when you were there, you could take different classes or try new things. So I thought, Oh, I'll have a go at drums. I had a lesson in drums and I just thought, well, I can do this maybe. So I got into the drum thing. And I kind of learned by copying rhythms and learning what might loosely be called 'by ear.' I played for a couple of years and was able to borrow someone's kit. And then I got into an amateur band. And we were going to do our first demo, which of course in those days, was on tape. So we went into the studio and I realized, with horror, what a disaster I was. I had no training. I had no technique. The engineer was probably pulling his hair out. I just wasn't consistent. I didn't have the proper training or technique. And it was just an awful experience. But it was educational and I realized I needed a drum tutor." Jan secured a tutor named Bonnie Johnson and says she was strict but wonderful. She helped Jan to unlearn bad habits and acquire the technique she needed to pursue playing properly.

Jan left California after spending six years away from home and almost immediately became a member of Maroon Town upon her return. "I had missed England. So that's kind of when I went back and my best friend in the entire universe, Sasha, who was in California came back with me. She was going to do a uni course over here. That's when I accidentally got into Maroon Town. So I was on the train with my friend Sasha and Deuan was on the train and my friend is quite a bit of a joker. I don't remember how the conversation started up, but she pretended to be my manager. 'Oh, yes, I'm her manager. She's a drummer.' She was always doing that for me," says Jan. After such an introduction, Jan's place was secured in the band. Deuan's method of finding musicians for the band, such as poaching them from the

---

[591] Hewison, Jan. All quotations, unless otherwise noted, from nterview with the author. 12 Jan. 2023.

train, wasn't as unusual, as it might seem, says Caroline McCookweir. "Deuan is just a great communicator and has a great ability to talk to people and influence people. He would have just persuaded everyone to come into the band."

Another one of those musicians persuaded to join Maroon Town by Deuan German was trumpeter Kay Charlton. She had just finished her music education at university and was looking for work, and for a different kind of education that came only through experience. "Interestingly, I'm not really from a musical family," says Kay, "although my parents liked music, and my grandmother used to sing but I think everybody did in those days."[592] So Kay was exposed to a more formal music education through an organization called the Girls Brigade, a program akin to the Girl Scouts in America, but with a Christian component. "Not to kind of make too much of this, but it's quite creative," says Kay of her experience in the program. "We did arts and but we also did marching and that kind of thing. I enjoyed being in that when I was little. And then as I was probably 12 or 13, maybe the opportunity came to join the marching band. And I went along and someone just gave me a trumpet, like a cavalry trumpet, no valves, and just said, 'Oh, you blow it like this.' I made a good sound. That just happened to be the thing that I could do really well. And I think it happened to be the time I was just going to secondary school, so I must have been 13, I think, and the music teacher said, 'Does anybody want to learn the trumpet?' So I put my hand up and said, 'Well, I've been playing the trumpet at Girls Brigade,' so he sent me along to the trumpet teacher and that's how I started playing the trumpet."

Kay continued playing the trumpet in school and in the Girls Brigade, becoming a solo trumpeter and winning marching band competitions. She then joined an orchestra in Northampton in the Midlands on Saturdays, learning classical music, while at the same time listening to pop music she enjoyed with her friends. "I listened to pop music at home. It was the late '70s, early '80s, so Kate Bush was a big influence. I was 16 in 1979, so things like the Pretenders, Siouxsie and the Banshees, female musicians like Debbie Harry. I am gay, as well, and it was a great time for women in pop. But then I loved playing in the orchestra at the weekends. And then I went to university to study music. The only option then really was classical music. I went to the University of East Anglia, which is based in Northridge, which is in the East of England. So it's a three year music degree and they sent me to London once a month or something and I had lessons with a tutor who played with the Philharmonia Orchestra and taught at the Royal College of Music. And so I had a music education," she says.

After Kay came out of university, she says she "hung around in Norwich for a year to still do music," but then, like many musicians of this era, in 1985 she moved to London for more opportunity. She shared a flat with some other girls, but having gained her music education outside of London, Kay found that musicians who had graduated from London colleges already had established connections. She had none. "Because I'd gone to a regional university, we didn't know anybody. So I wanted to

---

592 Charlton, Kay. All quotations, unless otherwise noted, from interview with the author, 8 July 2021.

play in an orchestra and applied to do an orchestra training course, but I didn't get in. I hadn't been hot housed in that way," she says. Kay also discovered that being a female trumpet player put her at a disadvantage to male trumpet players. "My old trumpet tutor favored the boys and took the boys along to gigs, and I'm not saying that's why I didn't succeed. But generally, most women will probably say whatever career you're in, you know, it's a bit of a boys club."

She joined a number of amateur orchestras while teaching for a couple of years to sustain herself, making connections with other musicians to further her opportunities, which led to a chance encounter. "I went to a party at somebody's house in London, who I'd gone to university with. And that's where I met Deuan because he'd been at the same university. So we both went to UEA, but we didn't know each other then. Because I was at a music person's house from university and he was there as well and he said, 'oh, we're starting a band. We need a trumpet player.' And I was like, 'Yeah, great.' So that's how I started my music career in London," says Kay. The education that Maroon Town provided to her was markedly different than the education she had received prior, and she says this benefitted her tremendously. "I was really only involved in one album, *High and Dry*. I think I was probably with them for three or four years. This was my first real experience of being in a band and it was my first experience of playing music that wasn't written down and given to me, because that's how I'd always learned, because I was a classical trumpet player. I'd never done any improvisation before because it was classical music. So I remember Deuan or Rajan saying to me, 'Well, why don't you do a trumpet solo?' 'What do you mean—make it up on my own? Am I supposed to do that?' Maroon Town actually was the missing link in my education because I learned a lot about being in a band."

Kay explains the way that music creation worked in the earliest days of the band. "We'd have to rehearse on Saturday mornings in Brixton, to begin with, and Brixton in those days was pretty dodgy. We rehearsed in a really old broken up kind of rehearsal studio and the guy on the door looked like he was off his head on drugs and so we were just kind of jammed together with the others, the other guys in the horn section. So Caroline and Mike on the saxophones, and Deuan and Raj and Jan, they'd get a groove going, and then we just try and come up with some horn lines. And that I think that's how we made up all those songs. It's a good thing, actually, about it being a ska band because mostly it was all on one chord. You can improvise on one scale and not have to worry about changing scales. Like if I joined a jazz band, it would have been impossible because I wouldn't have understood the jazz theory, even though I had a good ear and my ear got better and better. The thing is just hearing one chord or maybe two chords, you could just improvise using the same notes and actually that's probably how I learned to improvise. So ska music was very good to me in that respect," she says.

Jamaican ska was new to Kay when she joined Maroon Town, though she had knowledge of 2 Tone. She says, "I knew all about 2 Tone because 'Ghost Town' by the Specials came out when I was 18. That was a really big song at that time, and Madness and 'One Step Beyond,' the Selecter, Pauline Black. It didn't feel like we were anywhere close to that, and also I knew nothing about the history of ska. I'd never really heard of ska. I didn't even know that 2 Tone was ska, really. And I learned a lot from Deuan and Rajan. They were more aware of the Skatalites and Prince Buster, and for me, because I probably played like a classical trumpet player, I remember Rajan saying to me, 'oh, listen to some James Brown, listen to some horn players.' I mean, I'd been listening to pop music, but I'd never really listened to jazz. And so for me personally, it just widened my musical tastes."

Deuan German says that the concept behind Maroon Town's music was to definitely incorporate the sounds of original Jamaican ska, but also, over the years, to bring in other influences as well. "The purpose behind the whole idea of Maroon Town was to create a group that represented as much of the world we could gather and that could only happen organically."[593] That first album, *High and Dry*, brought more than just the sounds of original Jamaican ska or other world music to audiences—it also brought the political and social commentary that was at the very foundation of ska music. The aforementioned "Women Say No" addressed male violence, while "Thatcher's Children" tackled poverty in the face of tremendous wealth, "Pound to the Dollar" also looked at poverty in the Third World and global responsibility, and others dealt with war, drugs, race, and the futility of working like an "Average Man." They covered Prince Buster's "Prince of Peace" and "City Riot," and also included a couple of instrumentals. The album was produced by John Bradbury of the Specials. "Maroon Town knew what they liked but to learn how to really play it, they gigged endlessly—on the Barcelona underground, at the legendary Gaz's Rockin' Blues in Soho and in tiny pubs and clubs all round Europe," wrote Silas Briggs in the liner notes to the album.

Jan Hewison says she wrote that song, "Women Say No," which they performed live many times. "Because I was always fiddling about on either a piano or a keyboard, I'd come up with it and the actual title, 'women say no to male violence,' was painted in white gloss paint on a railway bridge in an area of London called Clapham Junction. And because rehearsals with Maroon Town usually started with people sort of jamming a bit, Raj, the bass player, he started up with bass line, and I thought, yeah, that actually sounds a bit like my song, so I just grabbed the mic and started singing it. And he went, what have we got there, and that's how it came about. At rehearsals there would often be somebody doing something, maybe someone's got a saxophone line or a guitar piece or whatever, because the trouble with being a drummer is you're always busy setting up while other people are kind of having a bit of pre-rehearsal. So I just sort of jumped up and belted out a couple of verses, and they were interested. I finished it off, made a bridge and whatnot. I would sing it when we were playing it live," Jan says.

But Jan left the band before they had a chance to record that song together, as a group, or any other song. She grew frustrated over one of the band members

---

[593] Pete. "Back In Action, Ready To Fight the Power!" Reggae Steady Ska. 11 Apr. 2013. reggae-steady-ska.com/maroon-town. Accessed 13 Dec. 2022.

constantly turning up late—hours late—for soundchecks and even performances. She felt it was especially inconsiderate for her, as a drummer, since she was required to turn up early to set up her drumkit, only to be made to wait, time after time after time. "At that point, I thought, I don't think I can do this anymore. I really can't. It went on for months and I personally don't know how anyone else put up with it," Jan says. "And after I left they wanted to use that song ["Women Say No"] for an album, which was fine by me. Except that I said, 'If you use it, that's fine. I want to sing it. Not because I'm a great singer, but I want to portray it. I want it to sound how I want to sound, even though I'm no bloody Mariah Carey or Celine Dion! So they agreed to that and this was quite a while since I'd seen them all, and I went to this recording studio in North London somewhere and generally you just do a sort of warming up vocal and then you go for your proper take. So I did what I thought was the warming up vocal, and it was John Bradbury from the Specials producing it and he's like, 'Well, thanks. Thanks very much. Bye!' And before I knew it, I was out on the fucking street, excuse me. I wanted to do it again. I wanted to do better. So that's annoying. A little bit annoying, but it's not the end of the world."

Jan notes that some of lyrics she wrote for "Women Say No" are "out of date." This is a very good thing, as she explains. "It's talking about abuse to women and women saying no to male violence. One of one of the lines is 'husband's drunk so it's legal rape.' Well the law has changed since then. It is no longer legal for a husband to rape his wife. So that's changed, though that's a minor detail." After Jan left Maroon Town, she continued to perform, including a band called Paper Fish for three years. She doesn't play today, due to her age and the physicality of drumming, but she has a 28-year-old son and a 6-year-old grandson and still keeps in touch with many of the members of Maroon Town.

Kay Charlton recalls the early touring and recording that first album. "I remember doing some gigs in London—we played up at the Dublin Castle, which is a pub in Camden. But also we went to Spain quite a lot, which was amazing, to travel and be paid to travel. We went to Barcelona. I think it was 1990 that we did the album and the single, 'City Riot.' We did that as a single and we recorded that with Brad from the Specials. He produced it. There was lots of gigs and I remember Deuan or Rajan saying, 'Oh, someone's coming from a record label,' and nothing happened. So that happened a few times. I wasn't really doing much else. So I didn't have many responsibilities. I could come and go as I liked, and didn't scare in getting taxis home at two in the morning and things like that. It was fun and we got paid cash in hand back in those days. I was on the dole, but it was good."

For Caroline McCookweir, touring in those early days, as well as throughout her long career with the band, was the best part of playing. "I was with them about 12 years, with a gap in the middle when I kind of left the band for various reasons. I wanted to do more singing actually, and then I got kind of pulled back in again. I mean, it was such a good band to be in. It was just excellent. There were about nine of us. You know, if you're in a smaller band, you've got to work really hard just to get the right notes out. It's much more hard work. But if there's nine of you and you're playing ska mostly, which is fairly simple music, so you can relax. I used to dance on stage and play sax and sing. And it was just huge fun. And also, the other thing, we were playing for people to dance. So once people are up and moving, you can really relax. You've got your audience enjoying themselves and you can just have fun yourself. It was a very good fun band to be in."

"We were best as a band when we were touring and playing," she says, "and then it was just a great feeling of camaraderie, and the after-gig parties were legendary. They nearly took over sometimes to be honest. But it was really good to be in a band and traveling, to be on tour, seeing different places. And then having this sort of lovely live experience night after night, was really, really good. The creative side of it was slightly more problematic. We had a short-lived management company for a while, which kind of wasn't helpful, somehow. I'm not particularly blaming them. And then we had some people who kind of took on the role of producer, and I don't know, for me, being in the studio wasn't as nice, shall we say."

Spain became a regular tour destination for Maroon Town, which continues to today. "We went to Spain right from the early days, going over and staying in a flat from a mate of Deuan in Barcelona. We played some very basic songs and eventually from that, this whole relationship with Barcelona built up and we played at a festival there for several years running. So we went to Barcelona loads of times and we also toured around Spain, which was really lovely," Caroline says. This experience, playing in Spain, was so profound for Kay Charlton that she eventually made the music of Spain the center of her next creative work. "I seem to remember spending a few weeks there. That got me interested in learning Spanish. I went to Spanish classes after that. And then after Maroon Town I ended up playing in a salsa band with Sara McGuinness. So I stopped playing in Maroon Town because in this salsa band with Sara, things started to get a lot busier," Kay says. Sara McGuinness had performed keyboards with the Potato 5 and the Deltones prior to joining Maroon Town on their first album (see Deltones chapter).

Kay left Maroon Town, right after their first album was recorded in order to pursue her salsa band. "This was better for me. I enjoyed it a lot more," Kay says. "There were more women in the band, so it was maybe eight or nine of us. It was called Salsa y Ache which means power, apparently. So Sara McGuinness was in that as well, and it was an all-female horn section, and two female singers as well, and I made really strong friendships in that band. The other trumpet player is still my best friend now, 13 years later. It was quite intense. It was different from Maroon Town, more women, more ups and downs, more arguments. So in Maroon Town, I co-wrote one of the songs, which is on *High and Dry*—I co-wrote 'People,' but the rest of it was mostly just making riffs and stuff. In Salsa y Ache, I did more writing, so that was developmental. We did a lot of gigging in that band, a lot of gigging around London," she says.

Kay was with the salsa band until 1996 when she then moved into another style of world music. Through her work with a London street and carnival arts band called Crocodile Style, she met a member of her next band which had come to perform in London from India. "I was more confident at improvising, picking up stuff by ear, learning stuff, remembering stuff without music. So, in a way, Maroon Town was the training ground for this next phase. I was asked, along with a couple of other women, if we would transcribe this Indian brass band. I was given a cassette, and basically told to listen to it and write it out for the new Bollywood Brass Band. So we [members of Crocodile Style] played along with this Indian wedding band, and I'd never heard of Indian wedding bands at that point. This was in 1992, at the beginning of the Bollywood Brass Band. And initially, we just played for a few Indian weddings, and that market is absolutely huge now. There are loads of Indian wedding bands. But we were the first people to actually do that, to bring in the dhol drum, and so we've got our own individual feel. And I was one of the key arrangers for the band and we eventually got more and more busy. We did our first CD in 1999, and then started playing international festivals and really, it's just carried on. It will be 30 years next year."

Kay has played all over the world with the Bollywood Brass Band and recorded six CDs. She has developed her composition skills and has also been tutoring and teaching throughout her years since the very beginning. In 2016 she earned her master's degree in music education and has developed a curriculum and pedagogy for teaching music to kids which was published. "And I'm still playing with Bollywood Brass Band, still writing, still doing as much as we can, but also trying to do more music writing for kids and extend my composing and writing about music education as well," she says. She and her partner of 25 years live today in Kent.

Though Kay Charlton and Jan Hewison left after a short time with Maroon Town, Caroline McCookweir continued to perform and tour with the band, including a tour of Kingston, Jamaica. She explains, "We managed to get in with the the British Council, and it's a bit colonial, to be honest, but they put bands on in far flung places, and so we went with them to Jamaica and went to Canada. They went to India but I left by that stage. But the tour in Jamaica, it was quite hilarious. First, we went to Barbados, which was just beautiful, a tiny little island, and we played quite a small gig there, which was lovely. And then we went to Jamaica. I had a cold and felt absolutely dreadful. We were frightened half out of our lives by the people who were minding us and told not to go into downtown Kingston. Most of us took that advice. But the British Council had arranged for us to play in the National Stadium, and it was hilarious. There was nobody there. There were about 30 or 40 British Council employees and their mates in a bank of chairs and then this vast arena, empty. But I loved it. A performance is a performance. It didn't matter how many people were there, I had a great time. But it was very funny."

She continues, "But we did go to the Alpha Boys School, which was one of the highlights of the whole thing to me. Each of us in the band did a little kind of mini talk and playing to demonstrate. And they were so sweet, these lads and their clarinets and whatever. And then we each divided into the instruments to do a sort of workshop. One other thing we did, we went into Gun Court. We went into the prison in Kingston and played a couple of things. It was part of what the British Council

347

organized and we did get a good response. It was kind of slightly alarming because most of the prisoners were behind wire mesh, not bars, but we were not in the same space as them. But one of them still managed to sell me a painting of Nanny of the Maroons. I've still got it. And then he got really told off by one of the prison guards. I think he was just making some money and needed a bit of money."

Eventually though, Caroline did leave Maroon Town which she says was really for her own good. "It was quite complicated. As I said, the band had a really good after party culture. My alcohol consumption was just beginning to get out of hand. And then, at the same time, in the last five years I was in Maroon Town, I'd converted to Buddhism, and I was getting further and further into that. And eventually it came to a point where I actually had a kind of breakdown. I thought, I'll go to live in the country at the Buddhist center, and I'll give up music. And as a result of actually making that decision, I did have a full-blown breakdown. And then, once that had happened, I kind of had to leave the band. I'd already left but then I did kind of try to get back in. They were going to India and going to somewhere else really lovely, and I really wanted to go, but Deuan said he had to protect me and the band as a whole. And actually, I needed to make the change and the move. So it was fine in the end."

Caroline moved out of London to begin her new life. "I moved down to South Wales to be near my Tibetan teacher. And that's where I still am. It's been 20 or 25 years or so. I still play music, but not to the same degree as Maroon Town. I have no children but I have a husband who I met at the Buddhist center. He's a musician and we play together. We've just been playing our saxophones. We're playing Eastern European stuff at the moment, which is rather beautiful. I will say my main musical outlet now is Extinction Rebellion. We go out, and I do some whistling which is unique to our band, and we go out and protest. I mean, I've always loved the natural world, and when Extinction Rebellion first started getting going in 2019, I just felt drawn to it—the same way I was drawn to music when I was younger."

Though Maroon Town has been largely populated by men in their three-decade existence, they have had three female vocalists in recent years. Amaziah Rose, a female reggae singer in the UK who has "toured in the UK and internationally with Max Romeo, Alton Ellis, Leonard Dillon of the Ethiopians,"[594] toured with Maroon Town in Kosovo and performed for Queen Elizabeth II's birthday party in 2014. Vocalist Jenny Stanford performed on their 2011 album, *Urban Myths*, and Sandra James provided vocals and backing vocals on their 2018 album *Freedom Call*. Maroon Town has covered a number of Jamaican original songs in their live performances and recordings, but have also infused the musical styles of their numerous members and collaborators with that vintage Jamaican ska.

---

[594] "Catch a Fire: Amaziah Rose & the 1Ness Band." rastaites.com/events-3/catch-a-fire-amaziah-rose-the-1ness-band. Accessed 13 Dec. 2022.

Members of Maroon Town (above) with Sara McGuinness (front left), Caroline McCookweir (back), and Kay Charlton (front right).

Maroon Town in Kingston, Jamaica (above) with Caroline McCookweir center, and playing saxophone in Barcelona in 1993 (below), courtesy Xavier Guillamon

The Forest Hill Billies

Bill Andrews: bass
Dave Andrews: trombone
Matt Andrews: vocals, guitar
Slim Cyder: accordion
Amanda Duncan: vocals, washboard

Jill Sull: saxophone
Marian Woods: vocals
Alan Rowland: drums
Johnny T: violin
And others

They were well known in their namesake neighborhood in Southeast London, Forest Hill, and they were always a hit at every performance outside of community, but few have heard of the Forest Hill Billies. They were raucous and undoubtedly talented and sometimes spelled their name as three words—Forest Hill Billies, and sometimes as just two—Forest Hillbillies. Fans call them by one—the Billies. They performed homemade instruments, and on instruments that were, well, a bit unusual in a ska band. In fact, they weren't really a ska band, nor a blues band, nor a country band. The Forest Hill Billies really can't be categorized, since their musical repertoire was so eclectic that it escapes classification—which is perhaps why they never appeared on the radars of ska connoisseurs. But they should.

The Forest Hill Billies the Billies, formed in the early 1980s and began as the idea of three brothers—Matt Andrews, Bill Andrews, and Dave Andrews. The Andrews Brothers were inspired to begin their band after the oldest brother Matt became obsessed with the iconic American radio station, KFAT. This Gilroy, California radio station broadcast country and Americana, zydeco, soul, and swing, along with some early Jamaican ska and calypso.[595] "Back in 1983 Matt had a cassette recording of a Californian radio station, Radio F.A.T. … We listened to it incessantly and during a cold winter on his first trip to Canada, Matt transcribed the lyrics of several of the songs on the tape … We loved them, we learnt them and rehearsed them, and they became the basis of the early 'Billies acoustic set which we first performed at Glastonbury '84."[596]

The band grew to include 13 or 15 members at times, but they began with half that—the three Andrews Brothers, a drummer (sometimes), a saxophonist, and two singers, one of which was Amanda Duncan. She also played what is maybe the most uncommon instrument in this entire era—the washboard. "I was the original female. I think there were six or seven of us originally. And then that scaled up over the years. We went for a fairly long time. And then Marian [Woods] joined as a joint singer, and I was washboard, so rhythm, really, because the drummer was so in and out at that time that I took up washboard. And then Jill [Sull] joined and she was saxophone. We had another saxophonist, but he was also in other bands, so it was

---

[595] "Radio F.A.T. – The Billies first songs." foresthillbillies.co.uk/2022/04/26/billies-favourite-songs. Accessed 17 Dec. 2022.
[596] Ibid.

temperamental, whether he would be there or not, so Jill joined alongside. So we were, on a full day, around 13 musicians. We had a fabulous big horn section—we had two trumpets, two to three saxophonists.

Amanda grew up, as she describes, "kind of what they call a Cockney, I guess," in South London and she says her childhood wasn't one that led her to a musical life at all.[597] Her involvement in the Forest Hill Billies was purely happenstance. "So my mum worked at Ford Motors, which actually was in Dagenham. As a child, my mom moved around quite a lot. It was a very unstable childhood. My father, who I actually didn't know, but I know my background—if you look through on my birth certificates—musician, musician, musician, so I felt a real affinity, but I didn't have a very stable school. I scraped through school, actually, left school quite early through an emergency—not to do with me, but my mother. But I always played guitar, and just of my own volition, and so I was very good at strumming. And so then at the age of 19, I was actually living in a kind of squat, I guess. We were renting it. I was doing quite a few different jobs just to survive. And I went to a party as a 19 year old and I met the drummer. And he took a bit of a shine to me, gave me a lift home on his motorbike. I'd never even been on a motorbike before. And the next day, he came around and dropped off some sausages, which I remember was really wonderful and asked me out on a date. And he said, 'Would you like to come and hear me in this in this band? We've got a rehearsal.' So we cooked up the sausages and we went off on his bike, and that's when I met the band. And the story goes, they all said, 'Oh, she's quite good looking. We need a singer. Maybe that will help us out.' I started on guitar, but they didn't really need guitar. And then Richard, we called him Sticks, was in and out of rhythm, which was fairly fundamental, and they said look, would you fancy a washboard. So I picked it up and I really worked hard at it."

Amanda says that performing a washboard with intent to master the instrument is more complicated than it sounds. She was dedicated and determined to augment the complexity of the band's sound. "I have to say, we did a reunion a few years back, a little festival a few miles away, the Hope Festival, and I hadn't picked up a washboard for years and I had forgotten how much skill there is in playing washboard. Because it's both hands doing different things, It's this particular kind of rhythm that you have to really kind of tune in to everybody within the band, keep that off beat going. But also, it's quite a rasping sound. So if you made it wrong, it can really cut through and ruin the sound. So actually, I've really worked hard and mastered the washboard, which I've really enjoyed."

At the same time that Amanda was performing with the band, she was also a student, which meant she was extremely busy almost every day of the week. "I managed to get into art school around the same time. It started to really build my confidence and I applied for art school, got a place, and then weekends, we'd be off gigging. And we became really quite well paid for busking, from doing live gigs, and

[597] Duncan, Amanda. All quotations, unless otherwise noted, from interview with the author. 20 Jun. 2021

I'm so grateful that as a student, I could survive on that on that money. And we worked really hard rehearsing and then getting booked up. So we were pretty much gigging every weekend. I'd come back to art school then pretty tired, but it was fantastic," she says.

Being in the band enabled Amanda to survive, as she says, but the experience was much more than that for the young adult of a broken home. "Actually, being in the band—the band found me at the age of 19—it was very timely. It was very pivotal. It brought me into my own confidence and into a friendship group. So it was very, very powerful, very strong, very respectful, even though it was predominantly all men. They were just fantastic, as musicians, and we did so many tours, and I was the only woman but I was just treated like a brother, which was fabulous. And then obviously, when Marian and Jill joined, it was just even better. And so there were so many things, great things that came out of being in the band—stability, some revenue, the camaraderie, sort of learning a new talent, seeing different parts of the world. We traveled a lot. We got booked a lot in France. It was very exciting for, I'd say, a good eight to ten years."

Part of the reason that the Forest Hill Billies found success early on was due to the support and promotion of Gaz Mayall. Amanda says, "We would go into his club on a Thursday night, Gaz's Rocking Blues, just to check out the scene, what was going on. That led to meeting Gaz and he booked us. And then I remember the night, it was like a decider night, he trialed us. And if we were good, we'd get rebooked. And if we weren't, we wouldn't. So it was a big night, and I remember it so vividly. After that we got a lot of gigs. But the three Andrews Brothers also did a lot of the booking and the arranging, so I would say Matt, who's the older brother, was very active in getting us gigs as well. We'd done quite a few gigs before, but Gaz's was a turning point for us."

The sound of the band, says Amanda, was appealing to a wide audience. "So we'd always attract a really cool crowd—men, women when we gigged, children. It's a real hybrid because some of the songs, you know there's some real hillbilly stuff, there's 'I stopped at a road house in Texas,' you know country, it was a real mix. I don't think we were hard and fast ska but it's only because we had that kind of sense of, well, a rhythm, that kind of pulled everything in, but it was a real blend. We did mainly covers to start with. Marian wrote 'Hand in Hand,' which I really loved. And then pretty much most things were covers. We had Slim [Cyder, accordion] who wrote 'Is It Love or Food Poisoning,' so it started to get more and more original and every musician in the band brought their own slant to every track, which was really lovely. It was a very easy group to play with. Quite idyllic really. There was hardly any bickering or rows. Considering that we were so close and spent so much time together on tours, very late nights then traveling back, it was really well tempered and 100% turnout every gig—there was a real dedication there."

The Forest Hill Billies were booked with a variety of other bands due to their diverse sound, including the Pogues, Lee "Scratch" Perry, Desmond Dekker, Fergal Sharkey, Billy Bragg, the Violent Femmes, and Sigue Sigue Sputnik. They also performed with the Deltones and the Potato 5 at Gaz's Rockin' Blues,[598] as well as a cruise that featured Laurel Aitken. Matt Andrews recalls, "A memorable and thoroughly enjoyable gig for the Forest Hill Billies was Gaz and Duke Vin's Rockin' Luxury Cruise to Amsterdam in 1986. The cruise was a mini floating festival of reggae, rock steady and ska music with a great mix of people and featuring some true legends of the Jamaican music scene. The event, organised by Gaz Mayall of Gaz's Rockin' Blues and DJ Duke Vin, offered 16 hours of entertainment on a luxury sea cruise from Sheerness to Holland with sightseeing and shopping in Amsterdam from Friday 17th October 1986 returning Sunday 19th. ... On the ship there were two packed dance floors, one for the DJ Duke Vin and one for the bands and club DJs. The bands, a reggae and ska line-up included Laurel Aitken and the Full Circle, the Deltones, Luddy Sam and the Deliverers and the Forest Hill Billies. There was music and dancing all night."[599]

Another notable performance included one with some very famous celebrities in attendance. Matt Andrews recalls, "It was always a big debate in the band as to whether we should go out of our way to entertain the upper classes. After all, it was the 1980s and our thing was usually to support workers through benefit gigs— the miners, the ambulance workers, Nicaragua Solidarity Campaign, CND, Anti-Apartheid, the Artificial Limb Worker's dispute and so on. We even did Marxism '87 at the Derbyshire miners holiday camp in Skegness, but that's another story. However this was a 'charity ball' taking place at a manor house in Sussex on Lord such-and-such's country estate, and as we were always up for an adventure, we sad 'yes.' ... who did we spot in the crowd? None other than Mick Jagger of the Rolling Stones and his then wife Jerry Hall. We were introduced. Jerry Hall wanted to announce the band and asked me what she should say. I explained that we were the Forest Hill Billies, bringing to you our version of ska, rockabilly and country-skiffle all the way from Forest Hill, South East London and that you could introduce us as such. I remember asking her to repeat what I had told her, just to make sure, and she seemed to have it off-pat. When the time came for us to play we asked her up on stage for the introduction. For some unknown reason she just howled out 'woooh oooh oooh!,' completely forgetting the previously rehearsed lines."[600]

Marian remembers that performance and says that there were some technical difficulties at the fete. "This was a great night—the power generator also broke down mid set and we did an acoustic version of 'Your Cheatin' Heart' while it was being fixed. Jerry Hall had a hole in her tights and Colleen and I bummed fags off her all night. She smoked menthol."[601] Amanda recalls, "I remember the run in the tights,

[598] *Marylebone Mercury*, 6 Nov. 1986, p. 25.
[599] "Gaz and Duke Vin's Rockin' Cruise to Amsterdam with legends of the Jamaican music scene. foresthillbillies.co.uk/2022/05/03/cruise-to-amsterdam. Accessed 17 Dec. 2022.
[600] Andrews, Matt. "The Night We Met Mick Jagger and Jerry Hall." foresthillbillies.co.uk/2022/05/02/the-night-we-met-mick-jagger-and-jerry-hall. Accessed 17 Dec. 2022.
[601] Ibid.

sitting on the stairs chatting with Mick Jagger and lots of champagne. Wasn't it Jerry Hall's birthday?"[602]

Performances appealed to a broad range of people—celebrities, regular folk, young, old, all races. "It was about entertaining people. And that was the thrill because we always got people dancing and I think it was very accessible for our audiences. We really knew our audiences. They were very broad in terms of age, which was lovely. We really did welcome a real mix. I mean, there were a couple of gigs, I remember at the very beginning, where there was literally about three people, but they just grew and grew. I think that was a very compelling thing as part of the journey, to start to see the numbers starting to build and in those days, it really was word of mouth. Johnny T, our violinist, was Jamaican. Interesting chap. Actually, I think he had done some composing with Jamiroquai when he was starting out. He was classically trained. I mean, my gosh, could he play that violin, it was amazing. But he'd come from very troubled background, and I think that was the other lovely thing about us, that we weren't a group of middle-class kids. Everyone had come from quite working-class backgrounds. We worked hard at the gigs, and we worked hard with the rehearsals. When I look back, I think oh, it was really quite impressive for young people."

Though the Forest Hill Billies were largely a live band, they did make a few recordings including a maxi-single, "the Munsters," produced by Gaz Mayall in 1986 with the title song as well as "Hillbilly Jump" and "Texas Ska." That same year they also released the single, "It's the Wouluff" and "Food Poisoning" as a double A side with the B side, "Forest Hill Ska" on the Wicked Records label. In 1989 they recorded the single "I Said Yeah" and "Yeah Hot Rod" on the Blue Beat label, and the following year they released a single-sided flexi-disk—"Western Ska" and "Eleven Go Mad" on the French label Skactualités.

While the band continued to perform as a collective, Amanda chose to pursue her art career. "I was really dedicated to art school," she says. "I actually started out with ceramics and glass. And you know, it's a bit like learning the washboard, I really wanted to master it. So there were a couple of gigs that I didn't do towards the end. I got a first in my degree, and then went on to the Royal College of Art, and that's when, this is in '93, I said to the band, 'I just can't really keep going now.' Because I was doing a masters and so Marian took over on the singing. And the band could go on without me."

Since leaving the Forest Hill Billies, Amanda has been immersed in art. "My world has completely gone from one end to the other. I left Royal College of Arts and did quite a lot of teaching, which I'd always done for years. I was teaching at degree level, ceramics and glass and then had a real kind of, I don't know, epiphany where I just thought I really need to change. And I decided I was going to go into advertising. I managed to get in through doing set design, and then eventually went into special effects. That happened over a few years and I ended up running a very big visual effects company, did that for about 13 years. By which time I'd been single

---

[602] Ibid.

355

for a very long time. And then I finally found someone when I was around 37, and then had my son when I was 41, which was fabulous."

She continues, "But I'm now a single mom. I'm still in touch with the father, but I've had an interesting time. I had a partner who took his life a few years ago. His name was Gordon. It was a big, a big thing and it had a really big effect on me. But it's interesting, because out of the challenges, I mean, it was a bit like with the band, when you really need something, it feels like something comes along to fill the gap. And that was exactly the right thing for me with the band. And out of adversity, somehow you put yourself out there, and then you're moving in these different circles, and then opportunities open up. But I'm very grateful for my creativity and the ability to kind of bounce back. So now I've moved into tech. I am now founder of a children's creative writing platform. It was really fueled by all my experiences and the catalyst was losing somebody who had mental health problems. And whether children write songs, or whether they write poems, it's about unlocking the words that need to come out. It's a platform called Scribe Easy. With Gordon, it was a mind that went into a loop, and the repetition. And I just feel that as an artist, that if you can be diverted, if you could give children other things to think about, if you can do that, as a preventative right before that happens—that's been very much a mission for me, to get children writing, unlocking, seeing their words on the page and being able to address or take things further."

Amanda's son plays guitar and she says he plays more for himself. He's "not so interested in being on a stage." And she still has her guitar as well and also still plays. "I mean, I'm not very good, but I just play around on that." She reflects on her years with the Forest Hill Billies fondly and says that the band brought great joy into her life at a time when she needed it the most. "We never took ourselves too seriously. And that was great."

The Forest Hill Billies with Amanda Duncan (front left) and Marian Woods (front right)

356

Bow Wow Wow

Matthew Ashman: guitar   Leigh Gorman: bass
David Barbarossa: drums   Annabella Lwin: vocals

The Me Too Movement exposed some of the most disgusting, abhorrent, and criminal behavior of sexual abusers in a variety of professional fields, especially the field of entertainment. The brave survivors who came forward to disrupt this abuse strengthened the ability of communities of men and women to change social norms, recognize the role of power in abuse, and prevent further abuse. When looking at the past, seeing through the lens of the Me Too Movement, one can begin to question the actions of certain actors. Examining the motivations, intentions, and orchestrations of Malcolm McLaren in his design and management of the band Bow Wow Wow, and in particular the exploitation of their lead singer, Annabella Lwin, made for cautionary and incendiary conversations then, and even more complicated conversations now.

Before a discussion of the above can take place, it should be noted why a chapter on this pop band appears in such a book on the era surrounding 2 Tone. Bow Wow Wow existed in the same orbit as 2 Tone and sometimes their paths crossed. But the rhythm, so crucial in defining ska and many genres of music, for that matter, is markedly different in both 2 Tone-related music and the music of Bow Wow Wow—the former is the Jamaican-derived accent on the two and the four beats, rather than the one and the three; and the latter is characterized as a "Burundi beat," or a beat originating from a village in the east African nation of Burundi and captured on an album by French anthropologists. So why then would promoters place Bow Wow Wow on the same bill as 2 Tone-era bands in the early '80s, like the English Beat and Madness? The answer is simple: marketing. Pairing Bow Wow Wow with any music that was popular during the early 1980s was a sure way to gain exposure, gain fans, and make money. This, after all, was Malcolm McLaren's driving force.

Bow Wow Wow's story begins with Malcolm McLaren who had just been sued, and lost, a lawsuit filed against him by the very band he shaped and shoved into the spotlight—the Sex Pistols. McLaren was an art school student who had become involved in music when the New York Dolls came into the clothing store owned by his roommate, Vivienne Westwood, and he talked his way into managing the band just before their demise, even moving to America to do so.[603] He involved himself with the next band that strolled in—the Sex Pistols, partnering them with John Lydon whom he dubbed "Johnny Rotten."[604] "We put the word 'anarchy' into every kid's dictionary," said McLaren.[605] But then, in the spring of 1979, Lydon won his court

---

[603] Trakin, Roy. "Malcolm McLaren: Innovation Or Exploitation?" *Musician*, Feb. 1982.
[604] Ibid.
[605] Ibid.

case to "extricate himself from the latter's [McLaren's] managerial clutches and recover the Pistols' earnings. ... McLaren lost control of the band that had made him infamous."[606] Next in his sights was Adam and the Ants, after Stuart Leslie Goddard, better known as Adam Ant, asked McLaren to manage the band. McLaren restyled their costumes, essentially pirating the idea from Westwood. Next he ousted Adam, taking the remaining Ants, Matthew Ashman on guitar, Leigh Gorman on bass, and David Barbarossa on drums, to form Bow Wow Wow.[607]

Lest one think that McLaren's motivations for such innovation and creation of appearance and performance be commendable for his foresight and ability to tap into the commerciality of the music market, there is one other element to McLaren's vision that certainly raises an eyebrow, if not both. McLaren had long been toying with the idea of commodifying sex in a way makes one wonder if it really was just about the loot. Just after the demise of his career with the Sex Pistols, McLaren "teamed up with a pair of French screenwriters to write a 'soft-core rock 'n' roll costume musical for kids' called *The Adventures of Melody, Lyric, and Tune*, which involved three fifteen-year-old girls and their sexual exploits with adults against the backdrop of various Parisian tourist landmarks. The blatantly paedophilic material scared away any potential backers, so McLaren and his collaborators penned another script, *The Mile High Club*, and this time limited the under-age nookie to kids shagging other kids. A cross between Lord of the Flies and Emmanuelle, the screenplay concerned a tribe of teenage primitives who discover an abandoned jet formerly used by the Mile High Club (those who have sex in the cramped toilets of airplanes) and transform it into 'a children's club for sex-gang babies to make love.'"[608]

This is extremely relevant in the selection of Annabella Lwin to be the face, and body, of Bow Wow Wow. Annabella had just become a teenager when McLaren captured her to front the band. "Hasn't that been told so many times?" she responds when asked to tell the story. "Simply put, a 13-year-old girl with a part time job was asked to an audition," she says, talking about herself in the third person. "It was for Malcolm's new band. His girlfriend was the clothes designer, Vivienne Westwood. We wore all her new creations/designs from the start of our band's first photo shoot, to going on tour and TV."[609] Annabella had been born in Burma (Myanmar), moving to London at a young age with her mother and three brothers after her parents divorced.[610] "When I was at school, I was treated differently because I didn't look English. But I look 'Oriental.' I guess when I was young, I looked Chinese. I never knew the difference because I'm a child of two worlds."[611] She took that part-time job at a dry cleaner since her mother, a nurse, had to support her family. So Annabella

[606] Reynolds, Simon. *Rip It Up and Start Again*. Faber and Faber: UK, 2006, p. 304.
[607] Ibid.
[608] Ibid. p. 305.
[609] Lwin, Annabella. All quotations, unless otherwise noted, from interview with the author, 23 May 2022.
[610] "Annabella Lwin Interview." *Classic Pop*. 16 Jan. 2020.
[611] Gentile, John. "Annabella Lwin." 8 Apr. 2014. punknews.org/article/54610/interviews-annabella-lwin-bow-wow-wow. Accessed 25 Nov. 2022.

"wanted to work so that I could afford make-up and scarves."[612] She was then spotted by Dave Fishel, McLaren's talent scout, while working and singing along to one of her favorite bands, ABBA. He asked her to audition and to ensure she did, "McLaren got her fired from her job. ... 'He had a chat with my mother, and asked her—well, he didn't ask. He said, "We need her for this band."'"[613] McLaren almost included one other singer to join Annabella, but that did not come to pass. That singer was then known as Lieutenant Lush—today known as Boy George. "McLaren tried George out as a second singer to accompany Annabella, but took it no further much to George's chagrin, either because McLaren saw George as too wild to take his orders or because it was a stunt to bring his band in line and say, look I am in charge. 'I got really pissed off and first of all I just wanted revenge,' George told the *NME*. Instead, he let his music do the talking and formed Culture Club."[614]

For whatever reason, McLaren planned to debauch his newest band, as indoctrination, hazing, or perhaps a maneuver of power. "McLaren threw himself into 'training' the three male members of the group, now called Bow Wow Wow, with a nocturnal regime of whoring in Soho's red-light district. McLaren stumped up the cash for the boys as part of his plan systematically to deprave them. Although reluctant (Barbarossa had a wife and baby), the hapless lads complied. Because the fourteen-year-old Annabella initially had problems fitting in with a bunch of much older lads, McLaren even persuaded the guys that the problem was her virginity. To get her out from under her mother's sway and make her commit to the group, one of them had to do the dirty and deflower the underage singer. Reluctantly, the band drew lots, and guitarist Matthew Ashman was dispatched to perform the task. He failed."[615]

One writer called Bow Wow Wow McLaren's "latest pube prodigies" since Annabella was barely a teenager and the rest were under the age of 20. "Certain nagging questions remain: is McLaren an artist or an entrepreneur; a charlatan or a seer; an innovator or merely an exploiter?" inquired the journalist, aptly.[616] Another writer said, "McLaren was casting Annabella as an underage sexpot."[617] Yet another called McLaren a "professional child and child molester."[618] Notable writer and historian Chris Salewicz wrote of McLaren in 1981 that he was "a bit of a liar, and a manipulator, of course. Sometimes he combines the two. ... Malcolm McLaren is a very seductive, amiable figure—but then, so's The Devil."[619] In interviewing McLaren, Salewicz quotes him as saying, "Annabella's a character ... And in young people that's one thing you can do by demonstrating your authority and confidence. Which I'm very good at: I'm a good salesman, a very good salesman. I can sell an idea to an artist very well. So I gain that confidence from them. Although they might think

---

[612] "Annabella Lwin Interview." *Classic Pop*. 16 Jan. 2020.
[613] Wilson, Lois. *Bow Wow Wow Your Box Set Pet: The Complete Recordings 1980-1984*. Liner notes.
[614] Ibid.
[615] Reynolds, Simon. *Rip It Up and Start Again*. Faber and Faber: UK, 2006, p. 307-308.
[616] Trakin, Roy. "Malcolm McLaren: Innovation Or Exploitation?" *Musician*, Feb. 1982.
[617] Grabel, Richard. "Here & Now It's Bow Wow Wow!" *Creem*, June 1983.
[618] Savage, Jon. "Bow Wow Wow." *The Face*, Oct. 1980.
[619] Salewicz, Chris. "Malcolm McLaren ... the True Poison!" *The Face*, May 1981.

an idea is a bit off-the-wall, they'll accept it because I sell it to them so hard. Anyway, as far as I'm concerned it's deliberately off-the wall for the purpose of making them vociferous. Maybe they won't direct the idea in the same way that I might want them to, but I know the idea will go inside them, and something will happen, and the idea should make the whole band a very uncertain force in terms of the structure of a normal rock'n'roll band."[620] So was the very young Annabella even able to see that she had been manipulated by McLaren then, and can she see it now?

Needless to say, Annabella's mother certainly saw it. When asked if her mother supported the idea of her young daughter in the band, she replied, "Not really." And the answer to whether or not her mother ever came to terms with it, Annabella responds, "Sadly, I don't think she did. But she knew it made me happy to sing, and she didn't see any harm to giving it a go at the beginning of the band. Later on of course, things did not go as planned or as it was first portrayed by Malcolm." It is doubtful that when McLaren first presented the idea of whisking her daughter off to tour the world he mentioned that he would revive his failed soft-core underage musical vision from *The Adventures of Melody, Lyric, and Tune* into a song called "Sexy Eiffel Towers." Either the young Annabella couldn't understand the lyrics she was asked to perform, or she could, and either way, the result was the same—exploitation. "A girl's standing at the top of the Eiffel Tower about to commit suicide," said Annabella, describing the lyrics to a music journalist at the Starlight Roller Disco on Shepherds Bush Road in 1980.[621] It was here they had a six-week residency each Saturday night, and Sex Pistols fans, thinking the new McLaren creation was akin, showed up, were disappointed, and spat upon the band and Annabella as she sang. The lyrics for the song revolving around the French monument were apparently open to interpretation, for young Annabella. "She hasn't got a guy, all she's got is this building; it's tall and strong," she says, to which the journalists adds, "And phallic." Annabella continues, "'In the end I jump off.' All that ooh, aah, moan, sigh! 'I was imaging falling. I know what people will think!' That it sounds orgasmic? 'Yes, but in my mind I don't know what that's about. So they can think what they like.'"[622]

Annabella explained the lyrics to Chris Salewicz when he inquired about her mother's response. "She doesn't mind because she says they're just songs. She thinks they're good songs. She was shocked at first when she heard 'Sexy Eiffel Tower,' because it went 'Uhhh … Uhhh … Uhhh.' She said, 'Annabella, what are you doing?' She was really shocked, you know. Then I explained to her that I was meant to be falling. I know everyone thinks it was Malcolm's idea to get a sexual kind of turn on because I was breathing like having orgasms or something, but the actual thing is that I was supposed to be falling off the Eiffel Tower. That's what I'm actually singing about. Truthfully."[623] There were other songs that came later, like "Aphrodisiac," and "Quiver," which was a "near-Tin Pan Alley approach to tribalism which casts

[620] Ibid.
[621] Sutcliffe, Phil. "Bow Wow Wow: Funky Chicken." *Sounds*. 22 Nov. 1980.
[622] Ibid.
[623] Salewicz, Chris. "Malcolm McLaren … the True Poison!" *The Face*, May 1981.

Annabella as a horny Indian squaw: 'Sitting alone in my teepee/Finding a way to make him happy.'"[624] If the Eiffel Tower was innuendo, as were other songs in their repertoire, one clearly was not. "Louis Quatorze," was another of McLaren's dabbles with French culture and was "quite a naughty song in which the lad points a gun at her and orders her to undress and she laughs, tells him to stop messing about and prove he's really pleased to see her."[625] No innuendo here, just sex and violence from the mouths of babes.

Less vile but more scandalous at the time was the single "C30 C60 C90 Go!" This song encouraged kids to pirate music by recording it off of the radio and it was the first cassette single ever released. But when EMI failed to promote it, discovering the meaning of the lyrics after giving it the stamp of approval, the song didn't chart well and so McLaren jumped in again. "Whipping up Bow Wow Wow into a fury, McLaren shepherded the group to EMI's headquarters, where they trashed a top executive's office, ripping gold discs from the wall and throwing a clock out of the window."[626] Another song, "W.O.R.K.," addressed the "demolition of the work ethic." Salewicz asked Annabella, "Did you think of things like breaking down the system before you joined Bow Wow Wow?" to which she responded, "Oh, I hate routine, yeah! I hate going to school everyday and coming home and doing homework. I think 'Oh Christ, I have my geography homework to do, I've got my English homework to do,' and having to sit down and miss all those television programmes. And I don't like that, no." Again, she was just a kid. "Even their biggest hit, a cover of the Strangeloves' 1965 bubblegum tune, 'I Want Candy,' was selected for its obvious sexual connotations. The music video features Annabella getting soaked at the beach and licking an ice cream cone in slow motion," said one writer.[627]

But those were the lyrics. Now for the photographs. There was the shot that drew the attention of law enforcement over the cover of their album, *See Jungle! See Jungle! Go Join Your Gang, Yeah! City All Over! Go Ape Crazy*. The concept was to recreate the famous Eduard Manet painting, *Le Dejeuner sur L'herbe*, which was also controversial in its day due to the nudity of the subject, the female in the presence of lounging men, lunching in the woods. But McLaren's version depicted Annabella as the nude among the members of the band. Annabella was not a mere nude subject in the art world. She was only 14 years old. And McLaren knew exactly what he was doing since he had an alternative cover waiting in the wings—one that was used for the release in America that recreated a Gustave Courbet painting, *The Young Ladies on the Bands of the Seine*, which featured Annabella clothed.[628] Annabella said, "When he

[624] Riegel, Richard. "Bow Wow Wow. When the Going Gets Tough the Tough Get Going (RCA). *Creem*, July 1983.

[625] Salewicz, Chris. "Malcolm McLaren ... the True Poison!" *The Face*, May 1981.

[626] Reynolds, Simon. *Rip It Up and Start Again*. Faber and Faber: UK, 2006, p. 311.

[627] Benson, Alex. "Burundi Beat: Adam+Annabella+Appropriation." Loop and Replay. 30 May 2018. medium.com/loopandreplay/burundi-beat-the-ants-annabella-and-appropriation-258a804a2176. Accessed 25 Nov. 2022.

[628] Chapman, Ian. "Luncheon on the Grass with Manet and Bow Wow Wow: Still Disturbing After All These Years." *Music in Art*. Spring-Fall 2010, Vol. 35, No. ½, pp. 95-104.

came up with the idea I said, 'No way," but that's because I was conditioned into thinking it was bad. When I look at the picture I think it's very artistic."[629]

"Furious about the image, Lwin's mother convinced Scotland Yard to investigate the picture as child pornography, but the case went nowhere and only garnered more free publicity for the band," wrote one journalist.[630] This is the moment when Annabella's mother no longer questioned the puppet masters, and instead wanted them held accountable. The way the cover was introduced to Annabella's mother was also orchestrated by McLaren. "He had instructed the three boys in Bow Wow Wow to reveal the image to Lwin's mother by taking it round to her house and 'slamming it on the kitchen table. Malcolm told us it would be a great idea,' recalls Gorman, 'and how proud Annabella's mother would be. And of course like idiots, we fell for it. And her mother reacted as you might expect. And Malcolm hid behind a wall round the back. And he goes, "I knew that would happen." And I thought, "you bastard, you set us up." 'But,' he shrugs, 'that's the kind of thing he would do. Just cause he had the devilment in him.'"[631] "Yeah, that was a shock for my mother," Annabella says.[632] Today that photograph, shot by Andy Earl, hangs in the National Portrait Gallery in London. "It was art," reflects Annabella.[633] It is also cited as inspiration for director Sofia Coppola's biopic of Marie Antoinette.[634]

Another photograph of nude Annabella was used for the cover on the French release of "I Want Candy," produced by Kenny Laguna who had also produced and managed Joan Jett. Annabella was photographed unclothed, covered in gold, spraypainted from head to toe. It was released by RCA after Bow Wow Wow was forced to change labels, being dumped by EMI, since McLaren had created so much chaos. The final straw came for EMI executives when McLaren tried to start a child pornography magazine called *Chicken* which he aimed to use in promoting Bow Wow Wow. "McLaren invited his old cohort Fred Vermorel to be editor of the EMI-funded project. 'The idea as he first broached it was something like *Schoolkids* OZ, a magazine written from the kids' point of view and a bit outrageous,' recalls Vermorel, referring to the special edition of the sixties underground paper that resulted in a high-profile obscenity case against the editors. *Playkids* was McLaren's original working title. He talked it up to the music press as 'a junior *Playboy* for kids getting used to the idea that they needn't have careers … a magazine about pleasure technology for the primitive boy and girl.' Proposed articles included a piece by celebrity ex-convict John McVicar on crime as a career option in an age of rising unemployment, and an article by Bow Wow Wow's Lee [sic] Gorman about prostitutes—where to go, prices and so forth. … Except that now the magazine wasn't going to be *Playkids*—McLaren wanted to name it *Chicken*. 'Call us naïve, but nobody, not me and not the people at EMI, knew

[629] Young, Jon. "Bow Wow Wow." *Trouser Press*, Jan. 1982.
[630] Lyon, Joshua. "Annabella Lwin and the History of Bow Wow Wow." *V Magazine*. 6 Sept. 2016. vmagazine.com/article/annabella-lwin-and-the-history-of-bow-wow-wow. Accessed 25 Nov. 2022.
[631] McLean, Craig. "Bow Wow Wow haven't lost their bite." *Guardian*. 19 Apr. 2012.
[632] Ibid.
[633] Ibid.
[634] Ibid.

what "chicken" meant,' says Vermorel. 'So we said OK. But, of course, it's paedophile slang for young kids.'"[635]

Of the magazine, McLaren did not try to hide what it was, or at least not to non-music executives. "My original idea was to print a magazine and put the cassette on the front of the magazine, and so shove it into newsagents. So you could introduce Bow Wow Wow to a much larger audience, rather than putting it in a little corner of a record shop and have it disappear because it's too small. The non-visual aspect of cassettes is a bit of a problem. I thought that all the songs were very sexy, because they'd all come out of the idea of a sex picture I'd been writing at the time in Paris, which is how you have songs like 'Sexy Eiffel Tower.' I felt they should all be put in the context of a cheesecake Playboy-type magazine. I wanted to come up with the most audacious title, so I thought of Chicken because of its paedophiliac connections."[636]

But before EMI said no, and goodbye, McLaren proceeded with his kiddie porn rag, believing he had once again duped the label into endorsing what would cause scandal and drum up publicity. "Then there were the photo sessions. At one, Annabella was asked to pose nude (she refused). Another session was an all-day affair at a series of real people's homes, hired via an agency. The photographer told me Malcolm got increasingly heavy-handed during the day, and generated a kind of hysteria,' says Vermorel. The climax came with McLaren badgering a thirteen-year-old girl into removing her clothes: he succeeded, but only after reducing her to tears."[637] When Vermorel, one of McLaren's friends since art school, finally said he'd had enough, McLaren told him, "You should be telling all this to the judge! When the shit hits the fan, I'll be in South America."[638] Instead of telling it to the judge, Vermorel told EMI and the music press and they put the end to the entire project, though some of those photos have been leaked to the public from time to time. "It got blown up out of all proportion, and EMI got worried, and *Voila*: they stopped everything. A very stupid move, because had we brought out the magazine that cassette would have been a very, very big hit," McLaren said.[639] In 1985, when questioned by *Daily Mirror* journalist Gill Pringle about his new paramour, Lauren Hutton, with whom he had "set up home in Hollywood," McLaren stated, "Yes, I do like young girls, but that doesn't stop me from loving Lauren."[640]

Even then, as a child, it seems that Annabella recognized she was being used by McLaren and his cohorts but she was too powerless and too young to have a voice. "This business is full of really cutthroat people, people who don't five a f*** what a person feels. When I did the Manet picture and the shots for 'Candy,' I wasn't sure about them. In the end I consented because they kept telling me I had to show my

[635] Reynolds, Simon. *Rip It Up and Start Again*. Faber and Faber: UK, 2006, p. 313-314.
[636] Salewicz, Chris. "Malcolm McLaren ... the True Poison!" *The Face*, May 1981.
[637] Reynolds, Simon. *Rip It Up and Start Again*. Faber and Faber: UK, 2006, p. 313-314.
[638] Ibid. p. 315.
[639] Salewicz, Chris. "Malcolm McLaren ... the True Poison!" *The Face*, May 1981.
[640] Pringle, Gill. "The Odd Couple." *Daily Mirror*, 14 Aug. 1985.

commitment to the band. If I hadn't consented, they'd have insisted and I would have been deeply hurt; they wouldn't have cared. It's business, you see."[641] She was, at the time, only 16 when she made such an astute yet painful observation. "You've got to expect to get exploited, especially in music," said Annabella in an interview in 1982.[642] "Well, in every other business you're exploited in some way or another. There are girls walking around the streets now who are being exploited but they're doing it anyway." To which bassist Leigh Gorman responded, "And Annabella does it for free," causing Annabella to giggle and reveal her naivety, a key component for exploitation.[643]

Add to this that Annabella was still a child who had not only left home to join the band, but she had also left school. According to Vermorel, while the band was on tour, Annabella was without a tutor. "What kind of manager can't find (or afford) a tutor for a tour planned months in advance," he said of McLaren.[644] Annabella herself said, "I don't think I'll end up with anything in the way of school qualifications. I'm not interested, anyway. Not now. Certainly I've learned a hell of a lot more being in the band than I would have at school—about people, as well as the music business," she said in 1982.[645] Today such "oversights" would be illegal. But when the law dictated that Annabella, as an underage performer, be accompanied by a chaperone, she was a bit unhappy. "Punk girl must have a minder," read the headline in the *Daily Mirror* on October 9, 1981. "Adventurous Annabella, pictured nude on the cover of the band's latest album, has to be accompanied by an adult whenever she is away from her Kilburn home. That is one of the Greater London Council's rules for child performers. The order led to a row between Annabella and her mother, Annabella ran out of the family's house in the middle of the night wearing only her nightie. Now the singer's record company, RCA, say they have sorted out the problem—just in time to start a tour last night. The council signed Annabella's licence to perform after being assured that a suitable chaperone had been hired. Annabella, who has also patched up the quarrel with her mother, said: 'I was furious with the council. But in three weeks' time I'll be sixteen and I won't have to bother with these silly rules.'"[646]

With or without a chaperone, Bow Wow Wow did tour constantly, throughout the UK and in other countries as well. "We did a mini-tour in Japan with the band Madness. I always like their music and they all seemed down to earth kinda guys. I didn't know there were boxes for music," she says of the ska genre, "so if I liked a song, I'd listen to it a lot." They performed with other bands like Echo & the Bunnymen, the Police, Queen, R.E.M., the Pretenders, Joan Jett, and Wall of Voodoo. On June 1, 1983, they performed at Red Rocks Amphitheatre with the English Beat and Annabella has performed numerous times with the Beat since then. But in 1983,

---

[641] Cooper, Mark. "Bow Wow Wow: Candyed Camera." *Record Mirror*, 7 Aug. 1982.
[642] Goldstein, Toby, "Bow Wow Wow Take Trip, Yeah!" *Creem*, March 1982.
[643] Ibid.
[644] Vermorel, Fred. "McLaren." *Sounds* 11 Apr. 1981.
[645] Young, Jon. "Bow Wow Wow." *Trouser Press*, Jan. 1982.
[646] Prosser, Harry. "Punk girl must have a minder." *Daily Mirror*. 9 Oct. 1981.

just after releasing their album sans McLaren titled *When the Going Gets Tough The Tough Get Going*, the band decided to oust Annabella for reasons unknown. Or certainly, the reasons were unknown to Annabella. "I was told we were having a break for a month before an Australian tour. I thought, 'Yay! I can rest my vocals!' No one talked to me about it, not one explained it, it was all a shock," she said.[647] "'I read it in the *NME*. Then I got a call from my accountant, telling me I had no money and I wasn't receiving any more.' But 'within two weeks' she'd been offered a solo record deal. 'What's a girl to do? I was 17 and had a mortgage to pay. And I was engaged. That went south very quickly afterwards,' she sniffs. 'But life throws these curveballs at you, and you have to either lie down and take it—or get up and shake it,'" she said.[648] In 1986, Annabella released the solo album *Fever*, then left the music world for a decade.[649] Matthew Ashman died in 1995 from complications due to diabetes, David Barbarossa left music for good, and Leigh Gorman and Annabella Lwin reformed Bow Wow Wow and played periodically from 1997 until 2012 when Gorman "ousted Annabella and began performing under the name Bow Wow Wow with Chloe Demetria of the band Vigilant. Annabella now goes out under the name, 'Annabella Lwin of the original Bow Wow Wow.'"[650] Malcolm McLaren died of cancer in 2010.

When asked if she had any input at all into the music, she responds, "That's a good question! I think the 'music' was a concoction of African/Latin/jazz and punk rock elements, the same as the individuals in the band. The 'sound' was a fusion of all those elements brought together by my very own vocal stylings. I had no former experience of being a 'singer in a band' so most of it was quite rough and made up as I went along, influenced by the musical vibrations. I was given some guidance by Malcolm on the early songs we recorded." As for writing credits, those are a completely different story. "There's a lot of songs they never gave me credit for. I can't do anything about it now, as we're way, way down the road from it all. But thanks a lot, guys," she says.[651]

It seems that everyone was sounding the alarm, even during the start, that Annabella Lwin was not being exploited. "Like the rest of Bow Wow Wow, she's a victim," wrote journalist Mark Cooper. "Her plight is worse than theirs because she's younger and female."[652] Today, Annabella Lwin is a Buddhist and she continues to perform all over the world. She has never married, has no children, but has "the most wonderful pets that are my loves." Reflecting on her early days in the music industry she says, "The Me Too Movement would have been a good thing to have had back then."[653]

---

[647] "Annabella Lwin Interview" *Classic Pop*. 16 Jan. 2020.
[648] McLean, Craig. "Bow Wow Wow haven't lost their bite." *Guardian*. 19 Apr. 2012.
[649] "Annabella Lwin Interview" *Classic Pop*. 16 Jan. 2020.
[650] Wilson, Lois. *Bow Wow Wow Your Box Set Pet: The Complete Recordings 1980-1984*. Liner notes.
[651] "Annabella Lwin Interview" *Classic Pop*. 16 Jan. 2020.
[652] Cooper, Mark. "Bow Wow Wow: Candyed Camera." *Record Mirror,* 7 Aug. 1982.
[653] Ibid.

A young Annabella Lwin (left) styled by the fashions of Vivienne Westwood (right)

Others

There are a number of women who intersected with 2 Tone bands and related bands during this time in a variety of ways. The following are a few of these key female musicians and the roles they played in ska of this era.

Bette Bright

Anne Martin, known by her stage name Bette Bright, is a vocalist for the theatrical band Deaf School, as well as a solo artist. She also just happens to be the wife of Suggs, front man for the band Madness. Anne was raised in the entertainment culture and has been part of this world her entire life. "My mother [Christina] was a tap dancer with her two sisters," Anne says.[654] They were called the Catherine Dunne Trio. They used to work with the Crazy Gang and all those people, she was really glamourous. They would work in the Empire theatres, going around with all the acts. And in fact she was managed by Lew Grade [Britain's most famous impresario and TV mogul of the time]. They were quite crazy, some of the stories they told. They worked in Paris quite a bit and they'd get all their food on a tab at this Russian bistro, and get all their clothes made, they'd have their eyelashes made from their hair. But they'd have no money so they'd settle up when they could. She would do Russian dancing, on roller skates, on a pitched stage. Imagine!"[655]

Anne and her sister were born in Whitstable, Kent when their mother was in her 40s, which was most unusual during this time. But their mother had a career and she continued to perform and entertain when her girls were young. Anne says that she was "possibly" inspired by her mother to become a performer herself. As a student at Liverpool Art College in the mid-1970s, Anne and some fellow students formed Deaf School, named for the venue in which they rehearsed. One of the key members of the band was guitarist Clive Langer who later went on to co-produce Dexys Midnight Runners' *Too-Rye-Ay* album, since Kevin Rowland was a fan of Deaf School. Langer also worked with Elvis Costello and produced for Madness and according to Langer, "Once you're conscious of the bands' relationship, it's easy to hear Deaf School in Madness. Their young singer, Suggs, was an avowed Deaf School fan … Deaf School were a big influence for sure."[656] Deaf School lasted two years, from 1976 to 1978, and disbanded.

Clive Langer continued to work with Madness and says of the band, "You're never taken seriously. Just because things are fun, it doesn't mean that down below there's not this content. Madness weren't political. They tried to be but they weren't. They were very different from Jerry Dammers."[657] Langer went on to audition for

---

[654] Du Noyer, Paul. *Deaf School: The Non-Stop Pop Art Punk Rock Party.* Liverpool University Press, 2013. P. 53.
[655] Ibid.
[656] Ibid., 192-193.
[657] Ibid., p. 193.

Chrissie Hynde's new band, the Pretenders, but lost the slot to James Honeyman-Scott,[658] and instead Langer produced for David Bowie, They Might Be Giants, and Morrissey, to name a few. Anne also continued after Deaf School, going solo as Bette Bright and the Illuminations. She signed to Radar and recorded a cover of "My Boyfriend's Back" and "Captain of Your Ship" in 1978.[659] "But it was really difficult," Anne told *NME* in 1981, "because Radar were limited with finances—I ended up paying for most of that tour myself."[660] The Illuminations, her backing band, included Glen Matlock who had been bassist for the Sex Pistols. Perhaps through this connection, in 1980, "she appeared fleetingly in the *Great Rock 'n' Roll Swindle*, a film of the Sex Pistols' story as re-imagined by Malcolm McLaren, written and directed by Clive's [Langer's] friend Julien Temple."[661] She then signed to the Korova label and dropped the Illuminations from her name. In 1980 she recorded the single, "Hello I Am Your Heart," with the B side "All Girls Lie." It was produced by Clive Langer and Lee "Kix" Thompson of Madness performed on saxophone. As a result, she released an album of material in 1981, *Rhythm Breaks the Ice*, which was also produced by Langer. The album included a cover of Prince's song, "When You Were Mine" and "Shoorah Shoorah" which was later also covered by Pauline Black in 1982. Anne also "played a guest role in another sprawling art rock outfit, Holland's Gruppo Sportivo."[662]

In 1978, Clive Langer, Anne Martin, and Graham McPherson, better known as Suggs, all lived in the same Camden Town flat that was upstairs from the Swanky Modes fashion shop.[663] "I was 18 when I first met my wife, Anne, who was Bette Bright and in Deaf School and all that," wrote Suggs in the book, *Before We Was We: The Making of Madness by Madness.*[664] "Then eventually I was living with her above Swanky Modes, the designer shop on the corner of Royal College Street and Camden Road," he says. Anne and Suggs were married in December 1981 and are still married today. They have two daughters, Scarlett and Viva. Anne is also a breast cancer survivor.[665] She has appeared in Madness videos, performed from time to time with reunions of Deaf School, and recorded a live album with them in 1988, as well as collaborating with Steve Allen on recordings.[666]

---

[658] Ibid., p. 189.
[659] Ibid. p. 200.
[660] Ibid., p. 200.
[661] Ibid.
[662] Ibid.
[663] Ibid., p. 188.
[664] Lee, Thompson, Chris Foreman, Graham McPherson, Mike Barson, Cathal Smyth. *Before We Was We: The Making of Madness by Madness*. Random House UK, 2020, p. 191.
[665] Ibid., p. 201.
[666] Ibid., p. 263.

Bette Bright (Anne Martin) and Suggs at their wedding in December 1981 (left), and promo shot as a solo artist (right)

Cyndi Lauper

There are a couple brushes with ska for pop '80s artist Cyndi Lauper. One event occurred during her earliest years before she had recorded a single song. When the Specials toured in the United States, during their New York performance at the Hotel Diplomat on March 1, 1980, they were supported by Cyndi,[667] three years before her debut album, *She's So Unusual* was released in 1983.

Another event, so to speak, came when Cyndi became involved with members of the Hooters. The Hooters, as Marc Wasserman details in his book, *Ska Boom! An American Ska & Reggae Oral History*, began as a ska and reggae band in 1980 in Philadelphia. They had also opened up for the Beat as well as Steel Pulse.[668] When the Hooters took a break in 1982, band members became involved in the music industry in other ways, including as producer.[669] Lauper had seen the Hooters perform and was impressed. "Cyndi liked the punk reggae thing we were doing," said Rob Hyman, keyboardist and vocalist for the Hooters.[670]

[667] concertarchives.org/concerts/cyndi-lauper-the-specials. Accessed 18 Dec. 2022.
[668] Wasserman, Marc. *Ska Boom! An American Ska & Reggae Oral History*. DiWulf Publishing, 2021, p. 54.
[669] Ibid., p. 55.
[670] Ibid.

"In 1982, Eric [Bazilian, vocals, guitar, and melodica] and his bandmate Rob Hyman [vocals and keyboards] were asked by producer Rick Chertoff to help Cyndi Lauper write and record her first album," states Wasserman.[671] "Cyndi had seen the band perform and liked their ska and reggae meets rock sound. Eric shared this story about the process of coming up with a recorded version of 'Girls Just Want To Have Fun.' 'So Cindy [sic] came to see the band, and apparently she was impressed with Rob, initially wasn't impressed with me, so I wasn't going to be the guitarist. But then she came around. But right around the time we were starting to do these arrangements, I had bought a four-track cassette recorder, a porta-studio, and the drum machine, and I had a bass, and we were able to make fully realized demos. And 'Girls Just Want to Have Fun,' that was a great moment because Rick was determined that that title with her vocal was a hit. She hated the original. And Cindy [sic] said, "I will never sing that song." And we tried doing it as a reggae, we tried ska. And then one day we came in and we were talking about "Come On Eileen," which was all over the radio at that point. So she said, "Can we make it like Come On Eileen?" So, I turned down the tempo knob on the drum machine, programmed in the same kick drum pattern as "Come On Eileen," clicked on my guitar, and played that guitar riff. And she started singing, and that was it.'"[672]

Cyndi also recalls this event in Wasserman's book. "Rick felt like it could be an anthem. And he kept saying that to me. And we couldn't figure out where it could fit right for my voice. So I edited the song to what I thought could be an anthem. Rob studied reggae. He was a devotee of reggae. I felt at that time, that reggae was happening with all the reggae and ska bands coming from England. We heard that music and it was really new for me. My voice was actually like Eek-A-Mouse's voice, kind of on the high side."[673] She reveals that the also "wanted a reggae bass line on 'Time After Time.'"[674] Though none of these influences are evident in Lauper's album, she has performed ska during her live shows, including a ska version of "Sunny Side of the Street" in 2013.

Cyndi Lauper with Rob Hyman (right) and Eric Bazilian (left) of the Hooters.

[671] Wasserman, Marc. Facebook post, 17 June 2018.
[672] Ibid.
[673] Ibid., p. 56.
[674] Ibid.

Kim Wilde

Ska was such a dominant sound in UK in 1980 that many artists couldn't help but try their hand at it, either by their own volition, or at the suggestion of label executives. Kim Wilde was one of these artists who, in her pursuit of pop stardom, took a stab at ska. The song "26580" was definitely ska and the lyrics were about a prostitute whose services could be obtained by calling that number. It was written, perhaps a little creepily, by her father and brother—Marty and Ricky Wilde, both of whom were involved in the business.[675] Another song, the second single released by Wilde as the follow up to her massive hit "Kids in America," featured ska style in name and image, though not at all in sound. The single "Chequered Love" depicted a photo of Wilde dressed in all white and a man dressed in all black.

Despite singing about "Kids in America," Wilde was not. She was born Kim Smith in London and her father, Marty Wilde, was a singer of American-style rock 'n' roll who charted with a number of hits in the UK in the late 1950s. Her mother, Joyce Baker, was a member of a 16-member singing group called the Vernon Girls who performed in the 1960s.[676] "Joyce Baker married Marty Wilde—they formed a trio with Justin Hayward called the Wilde Three—and brought up world famous singing daughter Kim."[677] Marty and his son, Kim's younger brother Ricky, are credited with writing almost all of Kim's songs.

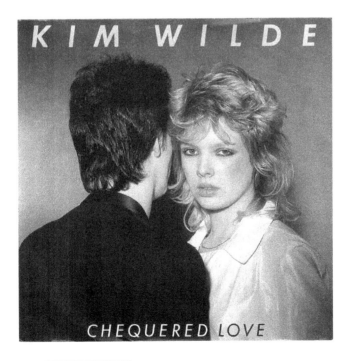

[675] From songlyrics.com/kim-wilde/26580-lyrics. Accessed 19 Dec. 2022.
[676] "The Vernon Girls." Oh Boy. ohboy.org.uk/the-vernon-girls. Accessed 19 Dec. 2022.
[677] Ibid.

The G.T.'s

Though the single recorded by the G.T.'s on the Stiff label in 1979 is not ska, there are still some ska elements to it. "Boys Have Feelings Too" with the B side "Be Careful" featured two women only known as Jackie and Bruna. Historian Kevin Feinberg was able to find some information on this one release via Steve Van-Deller (Bonnett) who "is the primary writer and performer. He played many of the parts along with the help of Kevin Wilkinson (Holly and the Italians) on drums. It's a co-production with Pat Collier (Vibrators) at his Alaska studio in London. This was meant to be the first of a series of pop/novelty releases on an imprint of Stiff that never materialized. Steve is a ska fan …"[678]

Feinberg continues, "So how did the ladies, Jackie and Bruna, enter the picture? They are a couple who he met at a pub near the studio. His [Van-Deller] guitar caught their eyes and they asked if he was working at the studio. He invited them in and offered to let them give it a shot as he was in need of some ladies to tackle the vocals for his tracks. The G.T.'s stands for 'Girls Taking' on top of the car pun. Strictly a one-off studio affair as Steve was soon busy working with another act. He's played a variety of genres." One of these genres, writes Feinberg, was reggae.

The February 19, 1980 press release from Stiff Records for the G.T.'s single called it "the Sound of Clapham." It stated, "The G.T.'s are two young ladies, BRUNA & JACKIE who work for Arding & Hobbs on Lavender Hill (this could explain the quirky, humerous [sic] sound of the single!!) Watch out—this could be a HIT!"[679]

BOYS HAVE FEELINGS TOO

---

[678] Feinberg, Kevin. Facebook post, 27 Apr. 2020.
[679] Stiff Records press release, 19 Feb. 1980. discogs.com/release/1779304-The-GTs-Boys-Have-Feelings-Too. Accessed 18 Dec. 2022.

The Mob

Later in the life of the band Machine (see also Machine chapter), by the time they had become Hot Snacks and Silverton Hutchinson left as the band's drummer, he was replaced by Jim Pryal. Pryal had previously been a member of another band from Coventry called the Mob, a nine-piece band that featured three vocalists—Kate Burns, and two others listed in a newspaper article as Mary and Julie.[680] A number of the band members were employed by Rolls-Royce. They released one single, "Send Me to Coventry," with the B side, "Mobbed."

"At the time of the 2 Tone explosion, I was drummer in a Coventry rock band Stiletto, doing mainly covers and playing bars and clubs," said Pryal to Marc Wasserman.[681] "The bass player, Arun Bhandari, had written several songs and the band was always experimenting with different beats and rhythms to try and come up with something original. Arun already had the idea of 'Send me to Coventry' so we booked studio time and drafted in other musicians— keyboard player Bob Jackson of Badfinger fame and a sax player who's name I cannot remember and some backing singers. It was a one off and a definite attempt at jumping on the bandwagon," he says, noting that only 1,000 copies were pressed.

"'Studio costs and outlay on artwork and production have cost me around a thousand pound,'" said Bhandari, "'which means I must sell a thousand discs to break even.' To try to do that Arun is sending copies of the disc to all BBC DJs and commercial radio stations to get as many 'airplays' as possible. 'Then, hopefully, a distributor will step in to control sales nationwide,' said Arun. 'Kate, Tony and the rest are already looking forward to appearing on *Top of the Pops*—and so am I!'"[682] Unfortunately, that plan never came to pass.

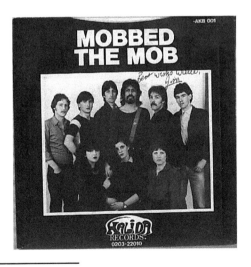

[680] Atkins, Gary. "Chart-bound ... that's the Ansty Mob." *Rolls-Royce News*, May 1980.
[681] Wasserman, Marc. "Unsung Bands of the 2-Tone Era—The Mob: 9-Piece Coventry Ska Band Record a Tribute to Their Hometown." Marco on the Bass. marcoonthebass.blogspot.com/2010/12/unsung-bands-of-2-tone-era-mob-9-piece.html. Accessed 18 Dec. 2022.
[682] Atkins, Gary. "Chart-bound ... that's the Ansty Mob." *Rolls-Royce News*, May 1980.

EMF

The ska band EMF from Coventry is certainly not to be confused with the pop band of the same name who had the hit "Unbelievable" in 1990. Coventry's EMF was formed in 1979 with sisters Donna and Sharon Elkington on vocals who formed the band by putting an advertisement in the *Coventry Telegraph* asking for interested musicians.[683] The band's name stood for Electro Motive Force and they supported the Bodysnatchers, Bad Manners, the Specials, and the Beat. Most of their songs were written by Sharon "about many of her own and her friends' experiences. ... 'I write about things that maybe people think about and won't say,' said Sharon."[684] Topics included race and eating disorders.

Other songs were written by Mojo Morgan who performed bass for the band and later performed with Roddy Radiation. "I wrote about three songs," he said, adding that the idea behind the sound of the band "wasn't to be straight or punk based ska like the Specials, but would blend blues bass lines and sax with a ska rhythm."[685] They recorded their song "Anti-Bellum" on the RCA label with the B side "One Way Girl." "Anti-Bellum" also appeared on RCA's *Battle of the Bands* album in 1981. "I can't remember how we got into Battle of the Bands in 1981 but we had to go to The Odeon in Birmingham for the first heat with all area bands, and we came in first. RCA put us up in London to go in the studio to do a single which went on to a compilation album for the best of the battle of the bands, and was given a trophy of battle of the bands. There was a lot of bickering in the band by then, and you don't need that in a band, so then I put an advert in the shop to start another band," said Morgan.[686] Donna went on to record with Belgian musician Isabelle Antena.

[683] EMF. sites.google.com/site/bandsfromcoventry/coventry-bands-a-to-z/coventry-bands-e/emf. Accessed 18 Dec. 2022.
[684] Ibid.
[685] Ibid.
[686] Ibid.

Sax Maniax

Diana Wood was a vocalist and saxophonist in a number of bands during the late 1970s and early 1980s and performed ska in a few of these collectives. She began as a member of the feminist punk band Jam Today from 1976 to 1978.[687] She then performed with the Sax Maniax with four members of the pre-2 Tone ska band, the Ska-Dows. Sax Maniax recorded a number of singles including "Never Gonna Lose Me" with the B side "Let's Twist Again" in 1981, and that same year, the single "One Hundred and Eighty" with the B side, "Somebody Help Me." The following year they released "Sara Sara Kiki" with the B side "Answerphone," and then that same year they released the album, *Oversaxed*, all from Penthouse Records.[688] Many live shows featured both the Ska-Dows and the Sax Maniax playing together.

Wood went on to record a solo album in 1997 called *Best Sax Ever* on the QED Classics label with jacket copy that said that Wood was "one of Britain's top Sax players. Diana has featured on T.V. with Courtney Pine, Bobby Womack, Grace Jones, Gary Numann [sic], Chuck Berry, has recorded with many other great names who appreciate her skill, musicianship and great sensitivity. In this, her first Solo Album, she has brought together all the great tunes the Sax is known for, plus some of her own fabulous compositions."[689]

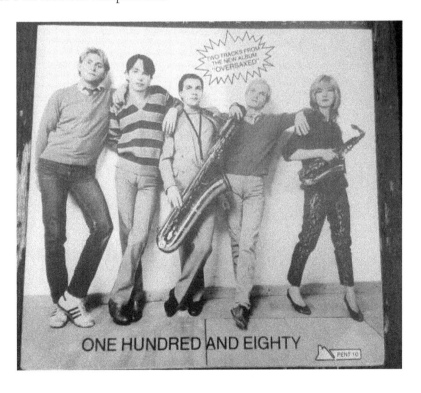

ONE HUNDRED AND EIGHTY

[687] Punk Music Catalogue. punkmusiccatalogue.wordpress.com/jam-today. Accessed 18 Dec. 2022.
[688] discogs.com/artist/1690756-Sax-Maniax. Accessed 18 Dec. 2022.
[689] discogs.com/master/1478831-Diana-Wood-Best-Sax-Ever. Accessed 18 Dec. 2022.

Tough Cookies

In 1986, a group of musicians and vocalists joined together for a cause, to campaign for the rights of residents in the London Docklands whose land was threatened by corporate development. There were two loose groups formed, the Deliverers, and Tough Cookies, who released one single and two songs on the Cultural Partnerships Ltd. label which released a number of similar songs with a cause. The songs, "Here to Stay," featured a reggae groove with horns, and "Give Us Back Our Land," was an upbeat calypso ska tune. Both featured vocals from ten women calling themselves Tough Cookies, with music supplied by seven male members of the Deliverers. The women, Paula Lewis, Joanne Martin, Lynn Kilpack, Julie Donovan, Lynn Wiltshire, Lois Acton, Christine Longbon, Jenny Stoneman, Stephanie Brice, and Gloria Richards, sang the melodies, but no harmonies.

The cause that united these musicians and vocalists to record was "part of the Democracy for Docklands Campaign, which fights for local people's needs to be taken into account in the redevelopment of docklands," stated the back copy of the single. "We are totally opposed to the policies of the London Docklands Development Corporation which puts profits for private developers before the people of Docklands. We need houses we can afford to live in, not luxury developments that block off the river front. This is why we wrote these songs, and why we will keep fighting to abolish the undemocratic LDDC, and get back the land that rightfully belongs to us."[690]

The London Docklands Development Corporation (LDDC) "worked to secure the regeneration of the London Docklands, an area of eight-and-a-half square miles stretching across parts of the East End Boroughs of Southwark, Tower Hamlets and Newham," according to their website.[691] The project was considered undemocratic in how it came to fruition, but it was completed despite opposition.

---

[690] Tough Cookies. "Here to Stay/Give Us Back Our Land," liner notes, 1986.
[691] "The London Docklands Development Corporation 1981 -1998." lddc-history.org.uk. Accessed 15 Jan. 2023.

The Beat

While there were no female members of the Beat, there are two women who were affiliated with the band in publicizing their music, performances, and recordings. In a sense, they amplified the sounds of the Beat. One of these women is Malu Halasa, the writer of *Twist and Crawl*, the book that chronicles the history of the Beat which was published in 1981. Malu's father is Jordanian, her mother is Filipina, and she was born and raised in the United States. She graduated from Barnard College and Columbia University and became a writer for *Rolling Stone* in New York City. She then moved to London and wrote about music in the UK and "was one of three music journalists to first cover rap for the UK's then burgeoning music press."[692] After writing the Beat's history, she founded her own magazine, *Tank*; wrote biographies for young readers as well as novels for adults; and she writes and speaks often about issues related to Middle East politics and culture.

The other woman, Lu Hersey, was the manager of the Beat fan club, though she went by a pseudonym, Marilyn Hebrides. She was friends with Dave Wakeling and Andy Cox before the band formed. She explains, "My father was in the forces so we moved around a lot when I was a child, but I first met Dave and Andy through a university friend from Birmingham who went to school with Dave, and ended up becoming good friends with both Dave Wakeling and Andy Cox. In fact, I went on to live in a shared house on the Isle of Wight with them for a year, working for Andy's brother in law. Dave and Andy both played guitar and would jam together all the time we weren't working or listening to music. We were all fans of reggae and punk music, and I always said they should form a band because they were so good and their sound was really unique. Anyway, they put an ad in the local Isle of Wight paper for a bassist, which is how David Steele joined, and then when the job ended and we all moved back to Birmingham, they advertised for a drummer and a sax player. Once Everett [Morton] and Saxa joined, this wonderful kid (he was only 16 back then) showed up wanting to rap with the band, and that's how Ranking Roger completed the line-up. I guess I was there in the background from the very beginning, and I helped them put up flyers for their very first gig in Birmingham. It was a very exciting time. And the Specials formed 2-tone around then, so the rest is history."[693]

Lu says she chose to go by the name Marilyn Hebrides in order to stay out of the limelight. "I chose a pen name because I wanted to stay in the background, and also my own name is actually Lucinda (which was a very uncommon name at the time) and it's the kind of name people remember (or so I'd found at school!) so I took the opportunity to change it for the purposes of running the fan club. My day job back then was teaching English as a foreign language. In the UK at that time the BBC would broadcast the shipping forecast for coastal waters several times a day, and part of the coastline always mentioned is Malin Hebrides. I always thought it would make a good pen name (slightly altered to Marilyn), although I played with using Tyne

---

[692] Halasa, Malu. Biography. pontas-agency.com/authors/malu-halasa. Accessed 7 June 2021.
[693] Hersey, Lu. All quotations, unless otherwise noted, from interview with the author, 25 June 2021.

Fisher or Dogger Bank or even German Bite, also places that crop up every day on the shipping forecast, but decided they were too male sounding," she says.

Lu says she enjoyed the opportunities that supporting the band presented which dovetailed well with her skills. "I was always interested in writing and publishing and went on to work for WOMAD when the band split up, and then worked in publishing before becoming an advertising copy writer. I hated the job but it's the only kind of writing that pays and by then I had four children! More recently I've become a children's writer (no money, but better job satisfaction). And I always loved music but while working for WOMAD I became pregnant with my eldest daughter and had to leave because music business hours and looking after children don't really mix, which is why I moved into publishing, and later as a single parent, when I needed more money, to copywriting."

"I'm still in touch with Andy and Dave," she says. "I haven't seen Dave in years as he lives in the States now, but we've been communicating through Twitter DMs throughout the pandemic. I visit Andy and Malu in London when I'm up there (I live in Glastonbury) and sometimes message Everett in Birmingham, though sadly recently it has been mostly to do with funerals."

Materials from Lu Hersey's fan club archives which she still owns today.

Index

Printed in the USA
CPSIA information can be obtained
at www.ICGtesting.com
LVHW080618240823
756069LV00006B/330